BLACK LITERATU
PS 508 N355

P9-AGP-798

1

BLACK LITERATURE IN AMERICA

A Casebook

Black Literature in America

A Casebook

edited by **Raman K. Singh** *and* **Peter Fellowes**

MARY WASHINGTON COLLEGE
OF THE UNIVERSITY OF VIRGINIA

THOMAS Y. CROWELL COMPANY / *New York · Established 1834*

To
Martin Luther King, Jr.,
Malcolm X,
and
Eldridge Cleaver

PREFACE

This casebook is designed for freshman courses in composition and reading as well as for courses in Afro-American literature. Included here are both primary and secondary sources by and about black writers, brief biographical notes on the authors represented, a selected bibliography, and suggested topics for discussion and research.

To facilitate the student's introduction to this unique literature, the primary sources are divided according to genre: poetry, fiction, essay, and drama. We have avoided classifying the material into thematic units because we feel that such an imposition of the editors' personal opinions would tend to confine or inhibit the reader's reaction. The secondary sources, of both a specific and a general nature, by white and black commentators alike, provide a wide range of comments on Afro-American thought as well as pertinent remarks about the authors of the selections.

In both the primary and secondary selections bracketed numbers indicate the page numbers of the original source. When a page in the original ends with a hyphenated word, we have indicated the original pagination after the entire word.

We wish to acknowledge the aid and advice of our colleagues, especially Professor Sidney Mitchell and Mr. Daniel Dervin. We wish also to thank the staff of the Lee Trinkle Library and the administration of Mary Washington College for their assistance.

R. K. S.
P. F.

Fredericksburg, Va.

CONTENTS

Contents

Contents

II: Selected Criticism

III: Appendices

I: BLACK LITERATURE

ARMAND LANUSSE

Epigram

"Do you not wish to renounce the Devil?"
Asked a good priest of a woman of evil
Who had so many sins that every year
They cost her endless remorse and fear.
"I wish to renounce him forever," she said,
"But that I may lose every urge to be bad,
Before pure grace takes me in hand,
Shouldn't I show my daughter how to get a
    man?" [136]

(*Translated by Langston Hughes*)

Source: Langston Hughes, *The Langston Hughes Reader* (New York: George Braziller, Inc., 1958), p. 136. Copyright © 1958 by Langston Hughes. Reprinted by permission of Harold Ober Associates Incorporated.

JAMES D. CORROTHERS

An Indignation Dinner

Dey was hard times jes 'fo' Christmas round our neighborhood
one year;
So we held a secret meetin', whah de white folks could n't hear,
To 'scuss de situation, an' to see whut could be done
Towa'd a fust-class Christmas dinneh an' a little Christmas fun.

Rufus Green, who called de meetin', ris' an' said: "In dis here
town,
An' throughout de land, de white folks is a-tryin' to keep us
down."
S' 'e: "Dey 's bought us, sold us, beat us; now dey 'buse us 'ca'se
we 's free;
But when dey tetch my *stomach,* dey's done gone too fur foh
me!

"Is I right?" "You sho is, Rufus!" roared a dozen hungry throats.
"Ef you 'd keep a mule a-wo'kin', don't you tamper wid his oats.
Dat 's sense," continued Rufus. "But dese white folks now-
adays
Has done got so close an' stingy you can't live on whut dey pays.

"Here 't is Christmas-time, an', folkses, I 's indignant 'nough to
choke.
Whah 's our Christmas dinneh comin' when we 's 'mos' completely broke?
I can't hahdly 'fo'd a toothpick an' a glass o' water. Mad?
Say, I 'm desp'ut! Dey jes better treat me nice, dese white folks
had!"

SOURCE: *The Century Magazine,* Vol. XCI; New Series, Vol. LXIX, Nov.
1915 to Apr. 1916 (December 1915), 320. Copyright by the Meredith Cor-
poration. Reprinted by permission of Appleton-Century-Crofts.

Well, dey 'bused de white folks scan'lous, till old Pappy Sim-
mons ris',
Leanin' on his cane to spote him, on account his rheumatis',
An' s' 'e: "Chilun, whut 's dat wintry wind a-sighin' th'ough de
street
'Bout yo' wasted summeh wages? But, no matteh, we mus' *eat*.

"Now, I seed a beau'ful tuhkey on a certain gemmun's fahm.
He 's a-growin' fat an' sassy, an' a-struttin' to a chahm.
Chickens, sheeps, hogs, sweet pertaters—all de craps is fine
dis year;
All we needs is a *committee* foh to tote de goodies here."

Well, we lit right in an' voted dat it was a gran' idee,
An' de dinneh we had Christmas was worth trabblin' miles to
see;
An' we eat a full an' plenty, big an' little, great an' small,
Not beca'se we was dishonest, but *indignant,* sah. Dat 's all.
[320]

JAMES WELDON JOHNSON

Lazy

Some men enjoy the constant strife
   Of days with work and worry rife,
But that is not my dream of life:
   I think such men are crazy.
For me, a life with worries few,
A job of nothing much to do,
Just pelf enough to see me through:
   I fear that I am lazy.

SOURCE: N. I. White and W. C. Jackson, eds., *Poetry by American Negroes* (Durham, N. C.: Duke University Press, 1924), pp. 177–178. Copyright held by Mrs. James Weldon Johnson. Reprinted by permission of Mrs. Johnson.

On winter mornings cold and drear,
When six o'clock alarms I hear,
'Tis then I love to shift my ear,
    And hug my downy pillows. [177]
When in the shade it's ninety-three,
No job in town looks good to me,
I'd rather loaf down by the sea,
    And watch the foaming billows.

Some people think the world's a school,
Where labor is the only rule;
But I'll not make myself a mule,
    And don't you ever doubt it.
I know that work may have its use,
But still I feel that's no excuse
For turning it into abuse;
    What do *you* think about it?

Let others fume and sweat and boil,
And scratch and dig for golden spoil,
And live the life of work and toil,
    Their lives to labor giving.
But what is gold when life is sped,
And life is short, as has been said,
And we are such a long time dead,
    I'll spend my life in living. [178]

PAUL LAURENCE DUNBAR

Sympathy

I know what the caged bird feels, alas!
When the sun is bright on the upland slopes;
When the wind stirs soft through the springing grass,

SOURCE: *The Complete Poems of Paul Laurence Dunbar* (New York: Dodd, Mead & Company, Inc., 1962), pp. 162–163. Reprinted by permission of the publisher.

And the river flows like a stream of glass;
When the first bird sings and the first bud opes, [162]
And the faint perfume from its chalice steals—
I know what the caged bird feels!

I know why the caged bird beats his wing
Till its blood is red on the cruel bars;
For he must fly back to his perch and cling
When he fain would be on the bough a-swing;
And a pain still throbs in the old, old scars
And they pulse again with a keener sting—
I know why he beats his wing!

I know why the caged bird sings, ah me,
When his wing is bruised and his bosom sore—
When he beats his bars and he would be free;
It is not a carol of joy or glee,
But a prayer that he sends from his heart's deep core,
But a plea, that upward to Heaven he flings—
I know why the caged bird sings! [163]

CLAUDE MCKAY

The Lynching

His Spirit in smoke ascended to high heaven.
His father, by the cruelest way of pain,
Had bidden him to his bosom once again;
The awful sin remained still unforgiven.
All night a bright and solitary star
(Perchance the one that ever guided him,
Yet gave him up at last to Fate's wild whim)
Hung pitifully o'er the swinging char.

Source: Claude McKay, *Selected Poems* (New York: Twayne Publishers, Inc., 1953), p. 37. Reprinted by permission of the publisher.

Day dawned, and soon the mixed crowds came to
     view
The ghastly body swaying in the sun.
The women thronged to look, but never a one
Showed sorrow in her eyes of steely blue;
And little lads, lynchers that were to be,
Danced round the dreadful thing in fiendish
     glee. [37]

LANGSTON HUGHES

I, Too, Sing America

I, too, sing America.

I am the darker brother.
They send me to eat in the kitchen
When company comes,
But I laugh,
And eat well,
And grow strong.

Tomorrow,
I'll sit at the table
When company comes.
Nobody'll dare
Say to me,
"Eat in the kitchen,"
Then.

Besides,
They'll see how beautiful I am
And be ashamed—

I, too, am America. [275]

Source: Langston Hughes, *Selected Poems* (New York: Alfred A. Knopf, Inc., 1959), p. 275. Copyright 1926, renewed 1954 by Langston Hughes. Reprinted by permission of the publisher.

Juke Box Love Song

I could take the Harlem night
and wrap around you,
Take the neon lights and make a crown,
Take the Lenox Avenue busses,
Taxis, subways,
And for your love song tone their rumble down.
Take Harlem's heartbeat,
Make a drumbeat,
Put it on a record, let it whirl,
And while we listen to it play,
Dance with you till day——
Dance with you, my sweet brown Harlem girl. [10]

Passing

On sunny summer Sunday afternoons in Harlem
when the air is one interminable ball game
and grandma cannot get her gospel hymns
from the Saints of God in Christ
on account of the Dodgers on the radio,
on sunny Sunday afternoons
when the kids look all new
and far too clean to stay that way,
and Harlem has its
washed-and-ironed-and-cleaned-best out,
the ones who've crossed the line
to live downtown
miss you,

SOURCE: Langston Hughes, *Montage of a Dream Deferred* (New York: Henry Holt, 1951), p. 10. Copyright 1951 by Langston Hughes. Reprinted by permission of Harold Ober Associates Incorporated.
SOURCE: Langston Hughes, *Montage of a Dream Deferred* (New York: Henry Holt, 1951), p. 57. Copyright 1951 by Langston Hughes. Reprinted by permission of Harold Ober Associates Incorporated.

Harlem of the bitter dream,
since their dream has
come true. [57]

Trumpet Player: 52nd Street

The Negro
With the trumpet at his lips
Has dark moons of weariness
Beneath his eyes
Where the smoldering memory
Of slave ships
Blazed to the crack of whips
About his thighs.

The Negro
With the trumpet at his lips
Has a head of vibrant hair
Tamed down,
Patent-leathered now
Until it gleams
Like jet—
Were jet a crown.

The music
From the trumpet at his lips
Is honey
Mixed with liquid fire.
The rhythm
From the trumpet at his lips
Is ecstasy
Distilled from old desire—

Desire
That is longing for the moon
Where the moonlight's but a spotlight

SOURCE: Langston Hughes, *Selected Poems* (New York: Alfred A. Knopf, Inc., 1959), pp. 114–115. Copyright 1947 by Langston Hughes. Reprinted by permission of the publisher.

In his eyes,
Desire
That is longing for the sea [114]
Where the sea's a bar-glass
Sucker size.

The Negro
With the trumpet at his lips
Whose jacket
Has a *fine* one-button roll,
Does not know
Upon what riff the music slips
Its hypodermic needle
To his soul—

But softly
As the tune comes from his throat
Trouble
Mellows to a golden note. [115]

Spirituals

Rocks and the firm roots of trees.
The rising shafts of mountains.
Something strong to put my hands on.

> Sing, O Lord Jesus!
> Song is a strong thing.
> I heard my mother singing
> When life hurt her:

Gonna ride in my chariot some day!

> The branches rise
> From the firm roots of trees.
> The mountains rise
> From the solid lap of earth. [113]

SOURCE: Langston Hughes, *Fields of Wonder* (New York: Alfred A. Knopf, 1947), pp. 113–114. Copyright 1947 by Langston Hughes. Reprinted by permission of the publisher.

The waves rise
From the dead weight of sea.

Sing, O black mother!
Song is a strong thing. [114]

COUNTEE CULLEN

For a Lady I Know

She even thinks that up in heaven
Her class lies late and snores,
While poor black cherubs rise at seven
Tó do celestial chores. [33]

Incident

Once riding in old Baltimore,
Heart-filled, head-filled with glee,
I saw a Baltimorean
Keep looking straight at me.

Now I was eight and very small,
And he was no whit bigger,
And so I smiled, but he poked out
His tongue, and called me, "Nigger."

Source: Countee Cullen, *On These I Stand* (New York: Harper & Row, Publishers, 1947), p. 33. Copyright 1925 by Harper & Brothers, renewed 1953 by Ida M. Cullen. Reprinted by permission of the publisher.

Source: Countee Cullen, *On These I Stand* (New York: Harper & Row, Publishers, 1947), p. 9. Copyright 1925 by Harper & Brothers, renewed 1953 by Ida M. Cullen. Reprinted by permission of the publisher.

I saw the whole of Baltimore
From May until December;
Of all the things that happened there
That's all that I remember. [9]

RICHARD WRIGHT

Between the World and Me

And one morning while in the woods I stumbled suddenly upon
the thing,
Stumbled upon it in a grassy clearing guarded by scaly oaks and
elms.
And the sooty details of the scene rose, thrusting themselves between the world and me. . . .

There was a design of white bones slumbering forgottenly upon a
cushion of ashes.
There was a charred stump of a sapling pointing a blunt finger ac-
cusingly at the sky.
There were torn tree limbs, tiny veins of burnt leaves, and a
scorched coil of greasy hemp;
A vacant shoe, an empty tie, a ripped shirt, a lonely hat, and a
pair of trousers stiff with black blood.
And upon the trampled grass were buttons, dead matches, butt-
ends of cigars and cigarettes, peanut shells, a drained gin-
flask, and a whore's lipstick;
Scattered traces of tar, restless arrays of feathers, and the lingering
smell of gasoline.
And through the morning air the sun poured yellow surprise into
the eye sockets of a stony skull. . . .
And while I stood my mind was frozen with a cold pity for the
life that was gone.

Source: Partisan Review, II, 8 (July-August, 1935), 18–19. Copyright
held by Richard Wright. Reprinted by permission of Paul R. Reynolds,
Inc., as agent for the author.

The ground gripped my feet and my heart was circled by icy walls
of fear—

The sun died in the sky; a night wind muttered in the grass and
fumbled the leaves in the trees; the woods poured forth the
hungry yelping of hounds; the darkness screamed with thirsty
voices; and the witnesses rose and lived:

The dry bones stirred, rattled, lifted, melting themselves into my
bones.

The grey ashes formed flesh firm and black, entering into my flesh.

The gin-flask passed from mouth to mouth; cigars and cigarettes
[18] glowed, the whore smeared the lipstick red upon her
lips,

And a thousand faces swirled around me, clamoring that my life
be burned. . . .

And then they had me, stripped me, battering my teeth into my
throat till I swallowed my own blood.

My voice was drowned in the roar of their voices, and my black
wet body slipped and rolled in their hands as they bound me
to the sapling.

And my skin clung to the bubbling hot tar, falling from me in
limp patches.

And the down and quills of the white feathers sank into my raw
flesh, and I moaned in my agony.

Then my blood was cooled mercifully, cooled by a baptism of gasoline.

And in a blaze of red I leaped to the sky as pain rose like water,
boiling my limbs.

Panting, begging I clutched childlike, clutched to the hot sides of
death.

Now I am dry bones and my face a stony skull staring in yellow
surprise at the sun. . . . [19]

MARGARET WALKER

We Have Been Believers

We have been believers believing in the black gods of an old land,
believing in the secrets of the seeress and the magic of the
charmers and the power of the devil's evil ones.

And in the white gods of a new land we have been believers believing in the mercy of our masters and the beauty of our
brothers, believing in the conjure of the humble and the
faithful and the pure.

Neither the slavers' whip nor the lynchers' rope nor the bayonet
could kill our black belief. In our hunger we beheld the welcome table and in our nakedness the glory of a long white
robe. We have been believers in the new Jerusalem.

We have been believers feeding greedy grinning gods, like a Mol-
och demanding our sons and our daughters, our strength and
our wills and our spirits of pain. We have been believers, silent and stolid and stubborn and strong.

We have been believers yielding substance for the world. With our
hands have we fed a people and out of our strength have they
wrung the necessities of a nation. Our song has filled the twilight and our hope has heralded the dawn.

Now we stand ready for the touch of one fiery iron, for the cleans-
ing breath of many molten truths, that the eyes of the blind
may see and the ears of the deaf may hear and the tongues of
the people be filled with living fire. [16]

SOURCE: Margaret Walker, *For My People* (New Haven: Yale University
Press, 1942), pp. 16–17. Copyright 1942 by the Yale University Press. Reprinted by permission of the publisher.

Where are our gods that they leave us asleep? Surely the priests and the preachers and the powers will hear. Surely now that our hands are empty and our hearts too full to pray they will understand. Surely the sires of the people will send us a sign.

We have been believers believing in our burdens and our demi-gods too long. Now the needy no longer weep and pray; the long-suffering arise, and our fists bleed against the bars with a strange insistency. [17]

GWENDOLYN BROOKS

The Birth in a Narrow Room

Weeps out of Kansas country something new.
Blurred and stupendous. Wanted and unplanned.
   Winks. Twines, and weakly winks
Upon the milk-glass fruit bowl, iron pot,
The bashful china child tipping forever
Yellow apron and spilling pretty cherries.

Now, weeks and years will go before she thinks
"How pinchy is my room! how can I breathe!
I am not anything and I have got
Not anything, or anything to do!"——
But prances nevertheless with gods and fairies
Blithely about the pump and then beneath
The elms and grapevines, then in darling endeavor
By privy foyer, where the screenings stand
And where the bugs buzz by in private cars
Across old peach cans and old jelly jars. [3]

SOURCE: Gwendolyn Brooks, *Annie Allen* (New York: Harper & Row, Publishers, 1949), p. 3. Copyright 1949 by Gwendolyn Brooks Blakely. Reprinted by permission of the publisher.

The Chicago Defender
Sends a Man to Little Rock

Fall, 1957

In Little Rock the people bear
Babes, and comb and part their hair
And watch the want ads, put repair
To roof and latch. While wheat toast burns
A woman waters multiferns.

Time upholds or overturns
The many, tight, and small concerns.

In Little Rock the people sing
Sunday hymns like anything,
Through Sunday pomp and polishing.

And after testament and tunes,
Some soften Sunday afternoons
With lemon tea and Lorna Doones.

I forecast
And I believe [87]
Come Christmas Little Rock will cleave
To Christmas tree and trifle, weave,
From laugh and tinsel, texture fast.

In Little Rock is baseball; Barcarolle.
That hotness in July . . . the uniformed figures raw and implaca-
        ble
And not intellectual,
Batting the hotness or clawing the suffering dust.
The Open Air Concert, on the special twilight green. . . .
When Beethoven is brutal or whispers to lady-like air.

SOURCE: Gwendolyn Brooks, *Selected Poems* (New York: Harper & Row, Publishers, 1963), pp. 87–89. Copyright © 1960 by Gwendolyn Brooks Blakely.
Reprinted by permission of the publisher.

Gwendolyn Brooks

Blanket-sitters are solemn, as Johann troubles to lean
To tell them what to mean. . . .

There is love, too, in Little Rock. Soft women softly
Opening themselves in kindness,
Or, pitying one's blindness,
Awaiting one's pleasure
In azure
Glory with anguished rose at the root. . . .
To wash away old semi-discomfitures.
They re-teach purple and unsullen blue.
The wispy soils go. And uncertain
Half-havings have they clarified to sures.

In Little Rock they know
Not answering the telephone is a way of rejecting life,
That it is our business to be bothered, is our business
To cherish bores or boredom, be polite
To lies and love and many-faceted fuzziness. [88]
I scratch my head, massage the hate-I-had.
I blink across my prim and pencilled pad.
The saga I was sent for is not down.
Because there is a puzzle in this town.
The biggest News I do not dare
Telegraph to the Editor's chair:
"They are like people everywhere."

The angry Editor would reply
In hundred harryings of Why.

And true, they are hurling spittle, rock,
Garbage and fruit in Little Rock.
And I saw coiling storm a-writhe
On bright madonnas. And a scythe
Of men harassing brownish girls.
(The bows and barrettes in the curls
And braids declined away from joy.)

I saw a bleeding brownish boy. . . .

The lariat lynch-wish I deplored.

The loveliest lynchee was our Lord. [89]

The Bean Eaters

They eat beans mostly, this old yellow pair.
Dinner is a casual affair.
Plain chipware on a plain and creaking wood,
Tin flatware.

Two who are Mostly Good.
Two who have lived their day,
But keep on putting on their clothes
And putting things away.

And remembering . . .
Remembering, with twinklings and twinges,
As they lean over the beans in their rented back room that is full
   of beads and receipts and dolls and cloths, tobacco crumbs,
   vases and fringes. [72]

The Vacant Lot

Mrs. Coley's three-flat brick
Isn't here any more.
All done with seeing her fat little form
Burst out of the basement door;
And with seeing her African son-in-law
(Rightful heir to the throne)
With his great white strong cold squares of teeth
And his little eyes of stone;
And with seeing the squat fat daughter
Letting in the men
When majesty has gone for the day—
And letting them out again. [11]

SOURCE: Gwendolyn Brooks, *Selected Poems* (New York: Harper & Row, Publishers, 1963), p. 72. Copyright © 1959 by Gwendolyn Brooks Blakely. Reprinted by permission of the publisher.

SOURCE: Gwendolyn Brooks, *Selected Poems* (New York: Harper & Row, Publishers, 1963), p. 11. Copyright 1945 by Gwendolyn Brooks Blakely. Reprinted by permission of the publisher.

Langston Hughes

                        is merry glory.
Is saltatory.
Yet grips his right of twisting free.

Has a long reach,
Strong speech,
Remedial fears.
Muscular tears.

Holds horticulture
In the eye of the vulture
Infirm profession.
In the Compression—
In mud and blood and sudden death—
In the breath
Of the holocaust he
Is helmsman, hatchet, headlight.
See
One restless in the exotic time! and ever,
Till the air is cured of its fever. [123]

BRUCE MC M. WRIGHT

To Be Dazzled by
the Racing of Her Blood

To be dazzled by the racing of her blood,
The competitions in our veins,

SOURCE: Gwendolyn Brooks, *Selected Poems* (New York: Harper & Row, Publishers, 1963), p. 123. Copyright © 1963 by Gwendolyn Brooks Blakely. Reprinted by permission of the publisher.

SOURCE: This poem was written especially for this volume.

The loving war
That burns and cures us both
In all our fluid riddles,
Is with gods to live the legends of their birth.
Thus are we shaped and joined, each upon a perfect wave,
All welcome in the rising,
The coming to impatient crest,
The plunging fall and spume,
Where love astride
Roars drowsing
In a boiling happiness of sweat.
And when pulsing walls in the comfort of their breach
Blaze,
And the eye-sight's palette
Dances with the innocence of original fire
In the spectrum of first flesh,
There are tender frictions sledging in the easy cave
And she who comes to me within the uses of my gloom
Redresses every cruel syntax in the word of day.

RAY DUREM

Award

> *A Gold Watch to the FBI
> Man who has followed
> me for 25 Years.*

Well, old spy
looks like I
led you down some pretty blind alleys,
took you on several trips to Mexico,

SOURCE: Langston Hughes, ed., *New Negro Poets U. S. A.,* (Bloomington: Indiana University Press, 1964), p. 33. Reprinted by permission of the publisher.

fishing in the high Sierras,
jazz at the Philharmonic.
You've watched me all your life,
I've clothed your wife,
put your two sons through college.
what good has it done?
the sun keeps rising every morning.
ever see me buy an Assistant President?
or close a school?
or lend money to Trujillo?
ever catch me rigging airplane prices?
I bought some after-hours whiskey in L.A.
but the Chief got his pay.
I ain't killed no Koreans
or fourteen-year-old boys in Mississippi.
neither did I bomb Guatemala,
or lend guns to shoot Algerians.
I admit I took a Negro child
to a white rest room in Texas,
but she was my daughter, only three,
who had to pee. [33]

CONRAD KENT RIVERS

The Still Voice of Harlem

Come to me broken dreams and all
    bring me the glory of fruitless souls,
I shall find a place for them in my gardens.

Weep not for the golden sun of California,
    think not of the fertile soil of Alabama . . .

SOURCE: Langston Hughes, ed., *New Negro Poets U. S. A.,* (Bloomington: Indiana University Press, 1964), p. 44. Reprinted by permission of the publisher.

nor your father's eyes, your mother's body twisted
     by the washing board.

I am the hope of your unborn,
     truly, when there is no more of me . . .
there shall be no more of you. . . . [44]

LE ROI JONES

Vice

Sometimes I feel I have to express myself
and then, whatever it is I have to express
falls out of my mouth like flakes of ash
from a match book that the drunken guest
at the grey haired jew lady's birthday party has
set on fire, for fun & to ease the horrible boredom.

& when these flakes amass, I make serious collages
or empty them (feinting a gratuitous act) out the window
on the heads of the uncurious puerto rican passersby.

ACT I. The celibate bandit pees in the punch bowl.

(curious image) occurring friday evening, a house
full of middle class women & a photogenic baker.
Baby bear has eaten her porridge, had her bath, shit
& gone to sleep. Smoke rises (strange for mid-summer)
out of a strange little shack in the middle of the
torn down cathedral. Everything seems to be light green.
I suppose, a color of despair or wretchedness. Anyway,
everything is light green, even the curling little hairs
on the back of my hand, and the old dog scar glinting
in the crooked (green, light green) rays of an unshaded bulb.

SOURCE: LeRoi Jones, *Preface to a Twenty Volume Suicide Note* (New York: Corinth Books/Totem Press, 1961), pp. 27–28. Copyright © 1961 by LeRoi Jones. Reprinted by permission of the publisher.

There doesn't seem to be any act 2. The process is stopped.
Functional, as a whip, a strong limb broken off in the gale
lying twisty & rotten, unnoticed in my stone back yard.
All this means nothing is happening to me (in this world).

I suppose some people are having a ball. Organized fun.
Pot Smokers Institute is going on an outing tomorrow; my
corny sister, in her fake bohemian pants, is borrowing something
else. (A prestige item). These incomprehensible dullards!

Asked to be special, & alive in the mornings, if they are green
& I am still alive, (& green) hovering above all the things I
seem to want to be a part of (curious smells, the high-noon idea
of life . . . . a crowded train station where they broadcast a slice,
just one green slice, of some glamourous person's life).
& I cant even isolate my pleasures. All the things I can talk about
mean nothing to me. [27]

This is *not* rage. (I am not that beautiful!) Only immobile coughs
& gestures towards somethings I don't understand. If I were lucky
enough to still be an adolescent, I'd just attribute these weird
singings in my intestine to sex, & slink off merrily to mastur
bate. Mosaic of disorder I own but cannot recognize. Mist in me.

There must be some great crash in the slinky world: MYSTIC
        CURE . . .
Cunning panacea of the mind. The faith of it. the singed hairs
of human trust, corrupt & physical as a disease. A glass stare.

Resolution, for the quick thrust of epee, to force your opponent
cringing against the wall, not in anger, but unfettered happiness
while your lady is watching from the vined balcony, your triumph.

& years after, you stand in subways watching your invincible hand
bring the metal to bear again & again, when you are old & the
        lady,
(o, fond memories we hide in our money belts, & will not spend)
the lady, you young bandits who have not yet stolen your first
        purse

the lady will be dead.

And if you are alone (if there is something in you so cruel)

You will wonder at the extravagance

of youth. [28]

The New Sheriff

There is something
in me so cruel, so
silent. It hesitates
to sit on the grass
with the young white
                    virgins
of my time. The blood-
letter, clothed in what
it is. Elemental essence,
animal grace, not that, but
a rude stink of color
huger, more vast, than
this city suffocating. Red
street. Waters noise
in the ear, inside
the hard bone
of the brain. Inside
the soft white meat
of the feelings. Inside
your flat white stomach
I move my tongue [42]

Notes for a Speech

African blues
does not know me. Their steps, in sands

SOURCE: LeRoi Jones, *Preface to a Twenty Volume Suicide Note* (New York: Corinth Books/Totem Press, 1961), p. 42. Copyright © 1961 by LeRoi Jones. Reprinted by permission of the publisher.
SOURCE: LeRoi Jones, *Preface to a Twenty Volume Suicide Note* (New York: Corinth Books/Totem Press, 1961), p. 47. Copyright © 1961 by LeRoi Jones. Reprinted by permission of the publisher.

of their own
land. A country
in black & white, newspapers
blown down pavements
of the world. Does
not feel
what I am.
                    Strength
in the dream, an oblique
suckling of nerve, the wind
throws up sand, eyes
are something locked in
hate, of hate, of hate, to
walk abroad, they conduct
their deaths apart
from my own. Those
heads, I call
my "people."
(And who are they. People. To concern
myself, ugly man. Who
you, to concern
the white flat stomachs
of maidens, inside houses
dying. Black. Peeled moon
light on my fingers
move under
her clothes. Where
is her husband. Black
words throw up sand
to eyes, fingers of
their private dead. Whose
soul, eyes, in sand. My color
is not theirs. Lighter, white man
talk. They shy away. My own
dead souls, my, so called
people. Africa
is a foreign place. You are
as any other sad man here
american. [47]

Ostriches & Grandmothers!

All meet here with us, finally: the
uptown, way-west, den of inconstant
moralities.
Faces up: all
my faces turned up
to the sun.

1.

Summer's mist nods against the trees
till distance grows in my head
like an antique armada
dangled motionless from the horizon.

Unbelievable changes. Restorations.
Each day like my niña's fan
tweaking the flat air
back and forth till the room
is a blur of flowers.

Intimacy takes on human form . . .
& sheds it like a hide.
                                        Lips, eyes,
tiny lace coughs
reflected on night's stealth.

2.

Tonight, one star.
eye of the dragon.
                        The Void
signaling.
Reminding someone
it's still there. [20]

SOURCE: LeRoi Jones, *Preface to a Twenty Volume Suicide Note* (New York: Corinth Books/Totem Press, 1961), pp. 20–21. Copyright © 1961 by LeRoi Jones. Reprinted by permission of the publisher.

LeRoi Jones

3.

It's these empty seconds
I fill with myself. Each
a recognition. A complete
utterance.

Here, it is color; motion;
the feeling of dazzling beauty
Flight.

As
the trapeeze rider
leans
with arms spread

wondering at the bar's
delay [21]

Look for You Yesterday, Here You Come Today

Part of my charm:
        envious blues feeling
        separation of church & state
        grim calls from drunk debutantes

Morning never aids me in my quest.
I have to trim my beard in solitude.
I try to hum lines from "The Poet In New York."

People saw metal all around the house on Saturdays. The Phone
        rings.

SOURCE: LeRoi Jones, *Preface to a Twenty Volume Suicide Note* (New York: Corinth Books/Totem Press, 1961), pp. 15–18. Copyright © 1961 by LeRoi Jones. Reprinted by permission of the publisher.

terrible poems come in the mail. Descriptions of celibate parties
                            torn trousers: Great Poets dying
                            with their strophes on. & me
                            incapable of a simple straight-
                            forward anger.

It's so diffuse
being alive. Suddenly one is aware
                that nobody really gives a damn.
                My wife is pregnant with *her* child.
                "It means nothing to me", sez Strindberg.

An avalanche of words
could cheer me up. Words from Great Sages.
                Was James Karolis a great sage??
                Why did I let Ora Matthews beat him up
                in the bathroom? Haven't I learned my lesson.

I would take up painting
if I cd think of a way to do it
better than Leonardo. Than Bosch.
Than Hogarth. Than Kline.

Frank walked off the stage, singing
"My silence is as important as Jack's incessant yatter."

I am a mean hungry sorehead.
Do I have the capacity for grace?? [15]

To arise one smoking spring
& find one's youth has taken off
for greener parts.

A sudden blankness in the day
as if there were no afternoon.
& all my piddling joys retreated
to their own dopey mythic worlds.

The hours of the atmosphere
grind their teeth like hags.

                (When will world war two be over?)

I stood up on a mailbox
waving my yellow tee-shirt
watching the grey tanks
stream up Central Ave.

                    All these thots
                    are Flowers Of Evil
                    cold & lifeless
                    as subway rails

the sun like a huge cobblestone
flaking its brown slow rays
primititi

          once, twice,. My life
          seems over & done with.
          Each morning I rise
          like a sleep walker
          & rot a little more.

All the lovely things I've known have disappeared.
I have all my pubic hair & am lonely.
There is probably no such place as BattleCreek, Michigan!

Tom Mix dead in a Boston Nightclub
before I realized what happened.

People laugh when I tell them about Dickie Dare! [16]

What is one to do in an alien planet
where the people breath New Ports?
Where is my space helmet, I sent for it
3 lives ago . . . when there were box tops.

What has happened to box tops??

O, God . . . I must have a belt that glows green
in the dark. Where is my Captain Midnight decoder??
I can't understand what Superman is saying!

          THERE *MUST* BE A LONE RANGER!!!

                    ****

but this also
is part of my charm.

A maudlin nostalgia
that comes on
like terrible thoughts about death.

How dumb to be sentimental about anything
To call it love
& cry pathetically
into the long black handkerchief
of the years.

   "Look for you yesterday
   Here you come today
   Your mouth wide open
   But what you got to say?"

     —part of my charm

      old envious blues feeling
      ticking like a big cobblestone clock.

I hear the reel running out . . .
the spectators are impatient for popcorn:
It was only a selected short subject

F. Scott Charon
will soon be glad-handing me
like a legionaire [17]

My silver bullets all gone
My black mask trampled in the dust

& Tonto way off in the hills
moaning like Bessie Smith. [18]

31

David Henderson

DON JOHNSON

O White Mistress

O White Mistress,
O tangible feeling of superiority,
Stand if you wish
But your child is sleepy
Lay him next to me and I
Will give him warmth. Poor soul,
        Wretched existence, vain life,
O egoism, pride, Southern mores,
O indoctrinated cattle of an illusion. [40]

DAVID HENDERSON

Downtown-Boy Uptown

Downtown-boy uptown
Affecting complicity of a ghetto
And a sub-renascent culture.
Uptown-boy uptown for graces loomed to love.

Source: Langston Hughes, ed., *New Negro Poets U. S. A.*, (Bloomington: Indiana University Press, 1964), p. 40. Reprinted by permission of the publisher.

Source: Langston Hughes, ed., *New Negro Poets U. S. A.*, (Bloomington: Indiana University Press, 1964), pp. 99–100. Reprinted by permission of the publisher.

Long have I walked these de-eternal streets
Seeking a suffix or a number to start my count.
Cat-Walk
Delicate pelican manner
Trampling the Trapezium to tapering hourglass
Behind the melting Sun.

I loved a girl then.
My 140th St. gait varied from my downtown one.
I changed my speed and form for lack of a better tongue.
Then was, love you, Pudgy:
Thin young woman with a fat black name.
It is the nature of our paradox that has us
Look to the wrong convex.

2

I stand in my low east window looking down.
Am I in the wrong slum?
The sky appears the same;
Birds fly, planes fly, clouds puff, days go . . .
I stand in my window.
Can I ride from a de-eternal genesis?
Does my exit defy concentric fish-womb?
Pudgy! your Mama always said Black man
Must stay in his balancing cup. [99]
Roach on kneebone I always agreed.
Was this Black man's smile enjoying guilt
Like ofay?
> *Long has it been that I've mirrored*
> *My entrances through silk-screen.*

3

Did this tragedian kiss you in anticipation
Of blood-gush separating from your black mirror?
Did I, in my complicity-grope relay the love
Of a long gone epoch?
> *Sometimes questions are not questions*
If I desire to thrust once more, if I scamper to embrace
Our tragedy in my oblique arms! . . .
> *Nevermind.*
You know.
You are not stupid, Pudgy.

You look for nothing of a sun where you live,
Hourglass is intrinsic . . . where you live.
The regeneration in your womb is not of my body.
You have started your count.
I cannot. [100]

LUCY SMITH

Face of Poverty

No one can communicate to you
The substance of poverty—
Can tell you either the shape,
    or the depth,
       or the breadth
of poverty—
Until you have lived with her intimately.

No one can guide your fingers
Over the rims of her eye sockets,
Over her hollow cheeks—
Until perhaps one day
In your wife's once pretty face
You see the lines of poverty;
Until you feel
In her now skinny body,
The protruding bones,
The barely covered ribs,
The shrunken breasts of poverty,

Poverty can be a stranger
In a far-off land:
An alien face

SOURCE: Langston Hughes, ed., *New Negro Poets U. S. A.* (Bloomington: Indiana University Press, 1964), pp. 45–46. Reprinted by permission of the publisher.

Briefly glimpsed in a newsreel,
An empty rice bowl
In a skinny brown hand,
Until one bleak day
You look out the window—
And poverty is the squatter
In your own backyard.

Poverty wails in the night for milk,
Not knowing the price of a quart. [45]
It is desperation in your teen-ager's face,
Wanting a new evening gown for the junior prom,
After going through school in rummage store
    clothes.
It is a glass of forgetfulness sold over the bar.

And poverty's voice is a jeer in the night—
        "You may bring another child
        Into the rat race that is your life;
        You may cut down on food
        To buy contraceptives;
        You may see your wife walk alone
        To a reluctant appointment
        With an unsterile knife—
        Or you may sleep alone."

And one morning shaving
You look in the mirror—
And never again will poverty be alien,
For the face of poverty is not over your shoulder,
The face of poverty is your own.
And hearing the break in your wife's voice
At the end of a bedtime story,
You realize that somewhere along the way
The stock ending in your own story went wrong.
And now you no longer ask
That you and your wife
Will live happily ever after—
But simply that you
And your wife
And your children
Will live. [46]

JULIAN BOND

Habana

Soldiers fuzz the city in khaki confusion
Pincushioned with weapons
Seedy orange venders squeeze among the pulpy
     masses
Camera pregnant tourists click down the Prado
Lotería salesmen tear along the dotted line
Guitars pluck loafers into corner bars
Uniformed schoolgirls genuflect languorously
Climactic roaming rainbow dresses cling slowly
Punctuating neon orgasms in the mambo night
and above Fidel's sandpaper voice,
"You want a girl, maybe?" [86]

SOURCE: Langston Hughes, ed., *New Negro Poets U. S. A.* (Bloomington: Indiana University Press, 1964), p. 86. Reprinted by permission of the publisher.

CHARLES WADDELL CHESNUTT

The Goophered Grapevine

We alighted from the buggy, walked about the yard for a while, and then wandered off into the adjoining vineyard. Upon Annie's complaining of weariness I led the way back to the yard, where a pine log lying under the spreading elm afforded a shady though somewhat hard seat. One end of the log was already occupied by a venerable-looking colored man. He held on his knees a hat full of grapes, over which he was smacking his lips with great gusto; and a pile of grapeskins near him indicated that the performance was no new thing. We approached him at an angle from the rear, and were close to him before he perceived us. He respectfully rose as we drew near, and was moving away, when I begged him to keep his seat.

"Don't let us disturb you," I said. "There is plenty of room for us all." [254]

He resumed his seat with some embarrassment. While he had been standing, I had observed that he was a tall man, and though slightly bowed by the weight of years, apparently quite vigorous. He was not entirely black, and this fact, together with the quality of his hair, which was about six inches long and very bushy, except on the top of his head, where he was quite bald, suggested a slight strain of other than Negro blood. There was a shrewdness in

SOURCE: *Atlantic Monthly*, LX, 358 (1887), 254–260.

his eyes, too, which was not altogether African, and which, as we afterwards learned from experience, was indicative of a corresponding shrewdness in his character. He went on eating his grapes, but did not seem to enjoy himself quite so well as he had apparently done before he became aware of our presence.

"Do you live around here?" I asked, anxious to put him at his ease.

"Yas, suh. I lives des ober yander, behine de nex' san'hill, on de Lumberton plank-road."

"Do you know anything about the time when this vineyard was cultivated?"

"Lawd bless you, suh, I knows all about it. Dey ain' na'er a man in dis settlement w'at won' tell you ole Julius McAdoo 'uz bawn en raise' on dis yer same plantation. Is you de Norv'n gemman w'at's gwine ter buy de ole vimya'd?"

"I am looking at it," I replied; "but I don't know that I shall care to buy unless I can be reasonably sure of making something out of it."

"Well, suh, you is a stranger ter me, en I is a stranger to you, en we is bofe strangers ter one anudder, but 'f I 'uz in yo' place, I wouldn't buy dis vimya'd."

"Why not?" I asked.

"Well, I dunno whe'r you b'lieves in conj'in' er not—some er de w'ite folks don't, er says dey don't—but de truf er de matter is dat dis yer ole vimya'd is goophered."

"Is what?" I asked, not grasping the meaning of this unfamiliar word.

"Is goophered—cunju'd, bewitch'."

He imparted this information with such solemn earnestness and with such an air of confidential mystery that I felt somewhat interested, while Annie was evidently much impressed, and drew closer to me.

"How do you know it is bewitched?" I asked.

"I wouldn' spec' fer you ter b'lieve me 'less you know all 'bout de fac's. But ef you en young miss dere doan' min' lis'nin' ter a ole nigger run on a minute er two w'ile you er restin', I kin 'spain to you how it all happen'."

We assured him that we would be glad to hear how it all happened and he began to tell us. At first the current of his memory —or imagination—seemed somewhat sluggish; but as his embarrassment wore off, his language flowed more freely, and the story acquired perspective and coherence. As he became more and more absorbed in the narrative, his eyes assumed a dreamy expression, and he seemed to lose sight of his auditors, and to be living over again in monologue his life on the old plantation.

"Ole Mars Dugal' McAdoo," he began, "bought dis place long many years befo' de wah, en I 'member well w'en he sot out all dis yer part er de plantation in scuppernon's. De vimes growed monst'us fas', en Mars Dugal' made a thousan' gallon er scupernon' wine eve'y year.

"Now, ef dey's an'thing a nigger lub, nex' ter 'possum, en chick'n, en watermillyums, it's scuppernon's. Dey ain' nuffin dat kin stan' up side'n de scuppernon' fer sweetness; sugar ain't a suckumstance ter scuppernon'. W'en de season is nigh 'bout ober, en de grapes begin ter swivel up des a little wid de wrinkles er ole age—w'en de skin git sof' en brown—den de scuppernon' make you smack yo' lip en roll yo' eye en wush fer mo'; so I reckon it ain' very 'stonishin' dat niggers lub scuppernon'.

"Dey wuz a sight er niggers in de naberhood er de vimya'd. Dere wuz ole Mars Henry Brayboy's niggers, en ole Mars Jeems McLean's niggers, en Mars Dugal's own niggers; den dey wuz a settlement er free niggers en po' buckrahs down by de Wim'l'ton Road, en Mars Dugal' had de only vimya'd in de naberhood. I reckon it ain' so much so nowadays, but befo' de wah, in slab'ry times, a nigger didn' mine goin' fi' er ten mile in a night w'en dey wuz sump'n good ter eat at de yuther een'.

"So atter a w'ile Mars Dugal' begin ter miss his scuppernon's. Co'se he 'cuse' de niggers er it, but dey all 'nied it ter de las'. Mars Dugal' sot spring [255] guns en steel traps, en he en de oberseah sot up nights once't or twice't, tel one night Mars Dugal'—he 'uz a monst'us keerless man—got his leg shot full er cow-peas. But somehow er nudder dey couldn' nebber ketch none er de niggers. I dunner how it happen, but it happen des like I tell you, en de grapes kep' on a-goin' des de same.

"But bimeby ole Mars Dugal' fix' up a plan ter stop it. Dey wuz a cunjuh 'oman livin' down 'mongs' de free niggers on de Wim'l'ton Road, en all de darkies fum Rockfish ter Beaver Crick wuz feared er her. She could wuk de mos' powerfulles' kin' er goopher—could make people hab fits, er rheumatiz', er mak 'em des dwinel away en die; en dey say she went out ridin' de niggers at night, fer she wuz a witch 'sides bein' a cunjuh 'oman. Mars Dugal' hearn 'bout Aun' Peggy's doin's, en begun ter 'flect whe'r er no he couldn' git her ter he'p him keep de niggers off'n de grapevimes. One day in de spring er de year, ole miss pack' up a basket er chick'n en poun'cake, en a bottle er scuppernon' wine, en Mars Dugal' tuk it in his buggy en driv over ter Aun' Peggy's cabin. He tuk de basket in, en had a long talk wid Aun' Peggy.

"De nex' day Aun' Peggy come up ter de vimya'd. De niggers seed her slippin' 'round, en dey soon foun' out what she 'uz doin' dere. Mars Dugal' had hi'ed her ter goopher de grapevimes. She sa'ntered 'roun' 'mongs' de vimes, en tuk a leaf fum dis one, en a grape-hull fum dat one, en den a little twig fum here, en a little pinch er dirt fum dere—en put it all in a big black bottle, wid a snake's toof en a speckle hen's gall en some ha'rs fum a black cat's tail, en den fill' de bottle wid scuppernon' wine. W'en she got de goopher all ready en fix', she tuk 'n went out in de woods en buried it under de root uv a red oak tree, en den come back en tole one er de niggers she done goopher de grapevimes, en a'er a nigger w'at eat dem grapes 'ud be sho ter die insid'n twel' mont's.

"Atter dat de niggers let de scuppernon's 'lone, en Mars Dugal' didn' hab no 'casion ter fine no mo' fault; en de season wuz mos' gone, w'en a strange gemman stop at de plantation one night ter see Mars Dugal' on some business; en his coachman, seein' de scuppernon's growin' so nice en sweet, slip 'roun' behine de smoke-house en et all de scuppernon's he could hole. Nobody didn' notice it at de time, but dat night, on de way home, de gemman's hoss runned away en kill' de coachman. W'en we hearn de noos, Aun' Lucy, de cook, she up'n say she seed de strange nigger eat'n' er de scuppernon's behine de smoke-house; en den we knowed de goopher had be'en er wukkin'. Den one er de nigger chilluns runned away fum de quarters one day, en got in de scuppernon's, en died de nex' week. White folks say he die' er de fevuh, but de niggers knowed it wuz de goopher. So you k'n be sho de darkies didn' hab much ter do wid dem scuppernon' vimes.

"W'en de scuppernon' season 'uz ober fer dat year, Mars Dugal' foun' he had made fifteen hund'ed gallon er wine; en one er de niggers hearn him laffin' wid de oberseah fit ter kill, en sayin' dem fifteen hund'ed gallon er wine wuz monst'us good intrus' on de ten dollars he laid out on de vimya'd. So I 'low ez he paid Aun' Peggy ten dollars fer to goopher de grapevimes.

"De goopher didn' wuk no mo' tel de nex summer, w'en 'long to'ds de middle er de season one er de fiel' han's died; en ez dat lef' Mars Dugal' sho't er han's, he went off ter town fer ter buy anudder. He fotch de noo nigger home wid 'im. He wuz er ole nigger, er de color er a gingy-cake, en ball ez a hossaple on de top er his head. He wuz a peart ole nigger, do', en could do a big day's wuk.

"Now it happen dat one er de niggers on de nex' plantation, one er ole [256] Mars Henry Brayboy's niggers, had runned away de day befo', en tuk ter de swamp, en ole Mars Dugal' en some er de yuther nabor w'ite folks had gone out wid dere guns en dere dogs fer ter he'p 'em hunt fer de nigger; en de han's on our own plantation wuz all so flusterated dat we fuhgot ter tell de noo han' 'bout de goopher on de scuppernon' vimes. Co'se he smell de grapes en see de vimes, an atter dahk de fus' thing he done wuz ter slip off ter de grapevimes 'dout sayin' nuffin ter nobody. Nex' mawnin' he tole some er de niggers 'bout de fine bait er scuppernon' he et de night befo'.

"W'en dey tole 'im 'bout de goopher on de grapevines, he 'uz dat tarrified dat he turn pale, en look des like he gwine ter die right in his tracks. De oberseah come up an axed w'at 'uz de matter; en w'en dey tole 'im Henry been eatin' er de scuppernon's, en got de goopher on 'im, he gin Henry a big drink er w'iskey, en 'low dat de nex' rainy day he take 'im ober ter Aun' Peggy's, en see ef she wouldn' take de goopher off'n him, seein' ez he didn't know nuffin' erbout it tel he done et de grapes.

"Sho nuff, it rain de nex' day, en de oberseah went ober ter Aun' Peggy's wid Henry. En Aun' Peggy say dat bein' ez Henry didn' know 'bout de goopher, en et de grapes in ign'ance er de conseq'ences, she reckon she mought be able ter take de goopher off'n him. So she fotch out er bottle wid some cunjuh medicine in it, en po'd some out in a go'd fer Henry ter drink. He manage ter git it down; he say it tas'e like w'iskey wid sump'n bitter in it. She 'lowed dat 'ud keep de goopher off'n him tel de spring; but w'en de sap begin ter rise in de grapevimes he ha' ter come en see her ag'in, en she tell him w'at he's ter do.

"Nex' spring, w'en de sap commence' ter rise in de scuppernon' vime, Henry tuk a ham one night. Whar'd he git de ham? *I* doan know; dey wa'n't no hams on de plantation 'cep'n' w'at 'uz in de smokehouse, but I never see Henry 'bout de smokehouse. But ez I wuz a-sayin', he tuk de ham ober ter Aun' Peggy's; en Aun' Peggy tole 'im dat w'en Mars Dugal' begin ter prune de grapevimes, he must go en take 'n scrape off de sap what it ooze out'n de cut een's er de vimes, en 'n'int his ball head wid it; en ef he do dat once't a year de goopher wouldn't wuk agin 'im long ez he done it. En bein' ez he fotch her de ham, she fix' it so he kin eat all de scuppernon' he want.

"So Henry 'n'int his head wid de sap out'n de big grapevime des ha'f way 'twix de quarters en de big house, en de goopher nebber wuk agin him dat summer. But the beatenes' thing you eber see happen ter Henry. Up ter dat time he wuz ez ball ez a sweeten' 'tater, but des ez soon ez de young leaves begun ter come out on de grapevimes, de ha'r begun ter grow out on Henry's head, en by de middle er de summer he had de bigges' head er ha'r on de plantation. Befo' dat, Henry had tol'able good ha'r 'roun' de aidges, but soon ez de young grapes begun ter come, Henry's ha'r begun to quirl all up in little balls, des like dis yer reg'lar grapy ha'r, en by de time de grapes got ripe his head look des like a bunch er grapes. Combin' it didn' do no good; he wuk at it ha'f de night wid er Jim Crow, en think he git it straighten' out, but in de mawnin' de grapes 'ud be dere des de same. So he gin it up, en tried ter keep de grapes down by havin' his ha'r cut sho't.

"But dat wa'n't de quares' thing 'bout de goopher. When Henry come ter de plantation, he wuz gittin' a little ole and stiff in de j'ints. But dat summer he got des ez spry en libely ez any young nigger on de plantation; fac', he got so biggity dat Mars Jackson, de oberseah, [257] ha' ter th'eaten ter whip 'im ef he didn' stop cuttin' up his didos en behave hisse'f. But de mos' cur'ouses' thing happen' in de fall, when de sap begin ter go down in de grape-vimes. Fus, when de grapes 'uz gethered, de knots begun ter straighten out'n Henry's ha'r; en w'en de leaves begin ter fall, Henry's ha'r commence' ter drap out; en when de vimes 'uz bar', Henry's head wuz baller'n it wuz in de spring, en he begin ter git ole en stiff in de j'ints ag'in, en paid no mo' 'tention ter de gals dyoin' er de whole winter. En nex' spring, w'en he rub de sap on ag'in, he got young ag'in, en so soopl en libely dat none er de young niggers on de plantation couldn' jump, ner dance, ner hoe ez much cotton ez Henry. But in de fall er de year his grapes 'mence' ter straighten out, en his j'ints ter git stiff, en his ha'r drap off, en de rheumatiz begin ter wrastle wid 'im.

"Now, ef you'd 'a' knowed ole Mars Dugal' McAdoo, you'd 'a' knowed dat it ha' ter be a mighty rainy day when he couldn' fine sump'n fer his niggers ter do, en it ha' ter be a mighty little hole he couldn' crawl thoo, en ha'ter be a monst'us cloudy night when a dollar git by him in de dahkness; en w'en he see how Henry git young in de spring en ole in de fall, he 'lowed ter hisse'f ez how he could make mo' money out'n Henry dan by wukkin' him in de cotton-fiel'. 'Long de nex' spring, atter de sap 'mence' ter rise, en Henry 'n'int 'is head en sta'ted fer ter git young en soopl, Mars Dugal' up'n tuk Henry ter town, en sole 'im fer fifteen hunder' dollars. Co'se de man w'at bought Henry didn' know nuffin 'bout de goopher, en Mars Dugal' didn't see no 'casion fer ter tell 'im. Long to'ds de fall, w'en de sap went down, Henry begin ter git ole ag'in same ez yuzhal, en his noo marster begin ter git skeered les'n he gwine ter lose his fifteen-hunder'-dollar nigger. He sent fer a mighty fine doctor, but de med'cine didn' 'pear ter do no good; de goopher had a good holt. Henry tole de doctor 'bout de goopher, but de doctor des laff at 'im.

"One day in de winter Mars Dugal' went ter town, en wuz santerin' 'long de Main Street, w'en who should he meet but Henry's noo master. Dey said 'Hoddy,' en Mars Dugal' ax 'im ter hab a seegyar; en atter dey run on awhile 'bout de craps en de weather, Mars Dugal' ax 'im, sorter keerless, like ez ef he des thought of it—

" 'How you like de nigger I sole you las' spring?'

"Henry's marster shuck his head en knock de ashes off'n his seegyar.

" 'Spec' I made a bad bahgin when I bought dat nigger. Henry done good wuk all de summer, but sence de fall set in he 'pears ter be sorter pinin' away. Dey ain' nuffin pertickler de matter wid 'im —leastways de doctor say so—'cep'n' a tech er de rheumatiz; but his ha'r is all fell out, en ef he don't pick up his strenk mighty soon, I spec' I'm gwine ter lose 'im.'

"Dey smoked on awhile, en bimeby ole mars say, 'Well, a bahgin's a bahgin, but you en me is good fren's, en I doan wan' ter see you lose all de money you paid fer dat nigger; en ef w'at you say is so, en I ain't 'sputin' it, he ain't wuf much now. I spec's you wukked him too ha'd dis summer, er e'se de swamps down here don't agree wid de san'-hill nigger. So you des lemme know, en if he gits any wusser, I'll be willin' ter gib yer five hund'ed dollars for 'im, en take my chances on his livin'.'

"Sho' nuff, when Henry begun ter draw up wid de rheumatiz en it look like he gwine ter die fer sho, his noo marster sen' fer Mars Dugal', en Mars Dugal' gin him what he promus, en brung Henry home ag'in. He tuk good keer uv 'im dyoin' er de winter—give 'im w'iskey ter rub his rheumatiz, en terbacker ter smoke, en all he want ter eat—'caze a nigger w'at he could make a thousan' dollars a year off'n didn' grow on eve'y huckleberry bush. [258]

"Nex' spring, w'en de sap rise en Henry's ha'r commence' ter sprout, Mars Dugal' sole 'im ag'in, down in Robeson County dis time; en he kep' dat sellin' business up fer five year er mo'. Henry nebber say nuffin 'bout de goopher ter his noo marsters, 'caze he know he gwine ter be tuk good keer uv de nex' winter, w'en Mars Dugal' buy him back. En Mars Dugal' made 'nuff money off'n Henry ter buy anudder plantation ober on Beaver Crick.

"But 'long 'bout de een 'er dat five year dey come a stranger ter stop at de plantation. De fus' day he 'uz dere he went out wid Mars Dugal' en spent all de mawnin' lookin' ober de vimya'd, en atter dinner dey spent all de evenin' playin' kya'ds. De niggers soon 'skivver' dat he wuz a Yankee, en dat he come down ter Norf C'lina fer ter l'arn de w'ite folks how to raise grapes en make wine. He promus Mars Dugal' he c'd make de grapevimes b'ar twice't ez many grapes, en dat de noo winepress he wuz a-sellin' would make mo' d'n twice't ez many gallons er wine. En ole Mars Dugal' des drunk it all in, des 'peared ter be bewitch' wid dat Yankee. W'en de darkies see dat Yankee runnin' 'roun' de vimya'd en diggin' under de grapevimes, dey shuk dere heads, en 'lowed dat dey feared Mars Dugal' losin' his min'. Mars Dugal' had all de dirt dug away fum under de roots er all de scuppernon' vimes, an' let 'em stan' dat away fer a week er mo'. Den dat Yankee made de niggers fix up a mixtry er lime en ashes en manyo, en po' it 'roun' de roots er de grapevimes. Den he 'vise Mars Dugal' fer ter trim de vimes close't, en Mars Dugal' tuck 'n done eve'ything de Yankee tole him ter do. Dyoin' all er dis time, mine yer, dis yer Yankee wuz libbin' off'n de fat er de lan', at de big house, en playin' kya'ds wid Mars Dugal' eve'y night; en dey say Mars Dugal' los' mo'n a thousan' dollars dyoin' er de week dat Yankee wuz a-ruinin' de grapevimes.

"W'en de sap ris nex' spring, ole Henry 'n'inted his head ez yuzhal, en his ha'r 'mence' ter grow des de same ez it done eve'y year. De scuppernon' vimes growed monst's fas', en de leaves wuz greener en thicker dan dey eber be'n dyoin' my rememb'ance; en Henry's ha'r growed out thicker dan eber, en he 'peared ter git younger 'n younger, en soopler; en seein' ez he wuz sho't er han's dat spring, havin' tuk in consid'able noo groun', Mars Dugal 'git de crap in en de cotton chop'. So he kep' Henry on de plantation.

"But 'long 'bout time fer de grapes ter come on de scuppernon' vimes, dey 'peared ter come a change ober 'em; de leaves witherd en swivel' up, en de young grapes turn' yaller, en bimeby eve'ybody on de plantation could see dat de whole vimya'd wuz dyin'. Mars Dugal' tuk'n water de vimes en done all he could, but 't wa'n no use; dat Yankee had done bus' de watermillyum. One time de vimes picked up a bit, en Mars Dugal' 'lowed dey wuz gwine ter come out ag'in; but dat Yankee done dug too close under de roots, en prune de branches too close ter de vime, en all dat lime en ashes done burn de life out'm de vimes, en dey des kep' a-with'in' en a-swivelin'.

"All dis time de goopher wuz a-wukkin'. When de vimes sta'ted ter wither, Henry 'mence' ter complain er his rheumatiz; en when de leaves begin ter dry up, his ha'r 'mence' ter drap out. When de vimes fresh' up a bit, Henry'd git peart ag'in, en when de vimes wither' ag'in, Henry'd git ole ag'in, en des kep' gittin' mo' fitten fer nuffin; he des pined away, en pined away, en fin'ly tuk ter his cabin; en when de big vime whar he got de sap ter 'n'int his head withered en turned yaller en died, Henry died too—des went out sorter like a cannel. Dey didn't 'pear ter be nuffin de matter wid 'im, 'cep'n de rheumatiz, but his strenk des dwinel' [259] away 'tel he didn' hab ernuff lef' ter draw his bref. De goopher had got de under holt, en th'owed Henry dat time fer good en all.

"Mars Dugal' tuk on might'ly 'bout losin' his vimes en his nigger in de same year; en he swo' dat ef he could git holt er dat Yankee he'd wear 'im ter a frazzle, en den chaw up de frazzle; en he'd done it, too, for Mars Dugal' 'uz a monst'us brash man w'en he once git started. He sot de vimy'd out ober ag'in, but it wuz th'ee or fo' year befo' de vimes got ter b'arin' any scuppernon's.

"W'en de wah broke out, Mars Dugal' raise' a comp'ny, en went off ter fight de Yankees. He say he wuz mighty glad wah come, en he des want ter kill a Yankee fer eve'y dollar he los' 'long er dat grape-raisin' Yankee. En I 'spec' he would 'a' done it, too, ef de Yankees hadn' s'picioned sump'en en killed him fus'. Atter de s'render, ole Miss move' ter town, de niggers all scattered 'way fum de plantation, en de vimya'd ain' be'n cultervated sence."

"Is that story true?' asked Annie doubtfully, but seriously, as the old man concluded his narrative.

"It's des ez true ez I'm a-settin' here, miss. Dey's a easy way ter prove it: I kin lead de way right ter Henry's grave ober yonder in de plantation buryin'-groun'. En I tell yer w'at, marster, I wouldn' 'vise you to buy dis yer ole vimya'd, 'caze de goopher's on it yit, en dey ain' no tellin' w'en it's gwine ter crap out."

"But I thought you said all the old vines died."

"Dey did 'pear ter die, but a few un 'em come out ag'in, en is mixed in 'mongs' de yuthers. I ain' skeered ter eat de grapes 'caze I knows de old vimes fum de noo ones, but wid strangers dey ain' no tellin' w'at mought happen. I wouldn' 'vise yer ter buy dis vimya'd."

I bought the vineyard, nevertheless, and it has been for a long time in a thriving condition, and is often referred to by the local press as a striking illustration of the opportunities open to Northern capital in the development of Southern industries. The luscious scuppernong holds first rank among our grapes, though we cultivate a great many other varieties; and our income from grapes packed and shipped to the Northern markets is quite considerable. I have not noticed any developments of the goopher in the vineyard, although I have a mild suspicion that our colored assistants do not suffer from want of grapes during the season.

I found, when I bought the vineyard, that Uncle Julius had occupied a cabin on the place for many years, and derived a respectable revenue from the product of the neglected grapevines. This, doubtless, accounted for his advice to me not to buy the vineyard, though whether it inspired the goopher story I am unable to state. I believe, however, that the wages I paid him for his services as coachman, for I gave him employment in that capacity, were more than an equivalent for anything he lost by the sale of the vineyard. [260]

barbarism

W. E. B. DU BOIS

On Being Crazy

It was one o'clock and I was hungry. I walked into a restaurant, seated myself, and reached for the bill of fare. My table companion rose. [126]

"Sir," said he, "do you wish to force your company on those who do not want you?"

No, said I, I wish to eat.

"Are you aware, sir, that this is social equality?"

Nothing of the sort, sir, it is hunger—and I ate.

The day's work done, I sought the theatre. As I sank into my seat, the lady shrank and squirmed.

I beg pardon, I said.

"Do you enjoy being where you are not wanted?" she asked coldly.

SOURCE: *An ABC of Color: Selections from Over a Half Century of the Writings of W. E. B. Du Bois* (Berlin: Seven Seas Publishers, 1963), pp. 126–128. Reprinted by permission of Mrs. Shirley Graham Du Bois.

Oh no, I said.

"Well you are not wanted here."

I was surprised. I fear you are mistaken, I said, I certainly want the music, and I like to think the music wants me to listen to it.

"Usher," said the lady, "this is social equality."

"No, madame," said the usher, "it is the second movement of Beethoven's Fifth Symphony."

After the theatre, I sought the hotel where I had sent my baggage. The clerk scowled.

"What do you want?"

Rest, I said.

"This is a white hotel," he said.

I looked around. Such a color scheme requires a great deal of cleaning, I said, but I don't know that I object.

"We object," said he.

Then why, I began, but he interrupted.

"We don't keep niggers," he said, "we don't want social equality."

Neither do I, I replied gently, I want a bed.

I walked thoughtfully to the train. I'll take a sleeper through Texas. I'm a little bit dissatisfied with this town.

"Can't sell you one."

I only want to hire it, said I, for a couple of nights.

"Can't sell you a sleeper in Texas," he maintained. "They consider that social equality."

I consider it barbarism, [127] I said, and I think I'll walk.

Walking, I met another wayfarer, who immediately walked to the other side of the road, where it was muddy. I asked his reason.

"Niggers is dirty," he said.

So is mud, said I. Moreover, I am not as dirty as you—yet.

"But you're a nigger, ain't you?" he asked.

My grandfather was so called.

"Well then!" he answered triumphantly.

Do you live in the South? I persisted, pleasantly.

"Sure," he growled, "and starve there."

I should think you and the Negroes should get together and vote out starvation.

"We don't let them vote."

We? Why not? I said in surprise.

"Niggers is too ignorant to vote."

But, I said, I am not so ignorant as you.

"But you're a nigger."

47

Yes, I'm certainly what you mean by that.

"Well then!" he returned, with that curiously inconsequential note of triumph. "Moreover," he said, "I don't want my sister to marry a nigger."

I had not seen his sister, so I merely murmured, let her say no.

"By God, you shan't marry her, even if she said yes."

But—but I don't want to marry her, I answered, a little perturbed at the personal turn.

"Why not!" he yelled, angrier than ever.

Because I'm already married and I rather like my wife.

"Is she a nigger?" he asked suspiciously.

Well, I said again, her grandmother was called that.

"Well then!" he shouted in that oddly illogical way.

I gave up.

Go on, I said, either you are crazy or I am.

"We both are," he said as he trotted along in the mud. [128]

ARNA BONTEMPS

A Summer Tragedy

Old Jeff Patton, the black share farmer, fumbled with his bow tie. His fingers trembled and the high, stiff collar pinched his throat. A fellow loses his hand for such vanities after thirty or forty years of simple life. Once a year, or maybe twice if there's a wedding among his kinfolks, he may spruce up; but generally fancy clothes do nothing but adorn the wall of the big room and feed the moths. That had been Jeff Patton's experience. He had not worn his stiff-bosomed shirt more than a dozen times in all his married life. His swallow-tailed coat lay on the bed beside him, freshly brushed and pressed, but it was as full of holes as the overalls in which he worked on weekdays. The moths had used it badly. Jeff twisted

SOURCE: S. C. Watkins, ed., *American Negro Literature* (New York: Random House, Inc., 1944), pp. 77–86. Copyright 1944 by Random House, Inc. Reprinted by permission of Harold Ober Associates Incorporated.

his mouth into a hideous toothless grimace as he contended with the obstinate bow. He stamped his good foot and decided to give up the struggle.

"Jennie," he called.

"What's that, Jeff?" His wife's shrunken voice came out of the adjoining room like an echo. It was hardly bigger than a whisper.

"I reckon you'll have to he'p me wid this heah bow tie, baby," he said meekly. "Dog if I can hitch it up."

Her answer was not strong enough to reach him, but presently the old woman came to the door, feeling her way with a stick. She had a wasted, dead-leaf appearance. Her body, as scrawny and gnarled as a string bean, seemed less than nothing in the ocean of frayed and faded petticoats that surrounded her. These hung an inch or two above the tops of her heavy unlaced shoes and showed little grotesque piles where the stockings had fallen down from her negligible legs.

"You oughta could do a heap mo' wid a thing like that'n me— beingst as you got yo' good sight."

"Looks like I oughta could," he admitted. "But my fingers is gone democrat on me. I get all mixed up in the looking glass an' can't tell wicha way to twist the devilish thing."

Jennie sat on the side of the bed, and old Jeff Patton got down on one knee while she tied the bow knot. It was a slow and painful [77] ordeal for each of them in this position. Jeff's bones cracked, his knee ached, and it was only after a half dozen attempts that Jennie worked a semblance of a bow into the tie.

"I got to dress maself now," the old woman whispered. "These is ma old shoes an' stockings, and I ain't so much as unwrapped ma dress."

"Well, don't worry 'bout me no mo', baby," Jeff said. "That 'bout finishes me. All I gotta do now is slip on that old coat 'n ves' an' I'll be fixed to leave."

Jennie disappeared again through the dim passage into the shed room. Being blind was no handicap to her in that black hole. Jeff heard the cane placed against the wall beside the door and knew that his wife was on easy ground. He put on his coat, took a battered top hat from the bed post, and hobbled to the front door. He was ready to travel. As soon as Jennie could get on her Sunday shoes and her old black silk dress, they would start.

Outside the tiny log house, the day was warm and mellow with sunshine. A host of wasps were humming with busy excitement in the trunk of a dead sycamore. Gray squirrels were searching through the grass for hickory nuts, and blue jays were in the trees, hopping from branch to branch. Pine woods stretched away to the left like a black sea. Among them were scattered scores of log houses like Jeff's, houses of black share farmers. Cows and pigs wandered freely among the trees. There was no danger of loss. Each farmer knew his own stock and knew his neighbor's as well as he knew his neighbor's children.

Down the slope to the right were the cultivated acres on which the colored folks worked. They extended to the river, more than two miles away, and they were today green with the unmade cotton crop. A tiny thread of a road, which passed directly in front of Jeff's place, ran through these green fields like a pencil mark.

Jeff, standing outside the door, with his absurd hat in his left hand, surveyed the wide scene tenderly. He had been forty-five years on these acres. He loved them with the unexplained affection that others have for the countries to which they belong.

The sun was hot on his head, his collar still pinched his throat, and the Sunday clothes were intolerably hot. Jeff transferred the hat [78] to his right hand and began fanning with it. Suddenly the whisper that was Jennie's voice came out of the shed room.

"You can bring the car round front whilst you's waitin'," it said feebly. There was a tired pause; then it added, "I'll soon be fixed to go."

"A'right, baby," Jeff answered. "I'll get it in a minute."

But he didn't move. A thought struck him that made his mouth fall open. The mention of the car brought to his mind, with new intensity, the trip he and Jennie were about to take. Fear came into his eyes; excitement took his breath. Lord, Jesus!

"Jeff. . . . O Jeff," the old woman's whisper called.

He awakened with a jolt. "Hunh, baby?"

"What you doin'?"

"Nuthin. Jes studyin'. I jes been turnin' things round 'n round in ma mind."

"You could be gettin' the car," she said.

"Oh yes, right away, baby."

He started round to the shed, limping heavily on his bad leg. There were three frizzly chickens in the yard. All his other chickens had been killed or stolen recently. But the frizzly chickens had been saved somehow. That was fortunate indeed, for these curious creatures had a way of devouring "poison" from the yard and in that way protecting against conjure and black luck and spells. But even the frizzly chickens seemed now to be in a stupor. Jeff thought they had some ailment; he expected all three of them to die shortly.

The shed in which the old T-model Ford stood was only a grass roof held up by four corner poles. It had been built by tremulous hands at a time when the little rattletrap car had been regarded as a peculiar treasure. And, miraculously, despite wind and downpour, it still stood.

Jeff adjusted the crank and put his weight upon it. The engine came to life with a sputter and bang that rattled the old car from radiator to tail light. Jeff hopped into the seat and put his foot on the accelerator. The sputtering and banging increased. The rattling became more violent. That was good. It was good banging, good sputtering and rattling, and it meant that the aged car was still in running condition. She could be depended on for this trip.

Again Jeff's thought halted as if paralyzed. The suggestion of the [79] trip fell into the machinery of his mind like a wrench. He felt dazed and weak. He swung the car out into the yard, made a half turn, and drove around to the front door. When he took his hands off the wheel, he noticed that he was trembling violently. He cut off the motor and climbed to the ground to wait for Jennie.

A few minutes later she was at the window, her voice rattling against the pane like a broken shutter.

"I'm ready, Jeff."

He did not answer, but limped into the house and took her by the arm. He led her slowly through the big room, down the step, and across the yard.

"You reckon I'd oughta lock the do'?" he asked softly.

They stopped and Jennie weighed the question. Finally she shook her head.

"Ne' mind the do'," she said. "I don't see no cause to lock up things."

"You right," Jeff agreed. "No cause to lock up."

Jeff opened the door and helped his wife into the car. A quick shudder passed over him. Jesus! Again he trembled.

"How come you shaking so?" Jennie whispered.

"I don't know," he said.

"You mus' be scairt, Jeff."

"No, baby, I ain't scairt."

He slammed the door after her and went around to crank up again. The motor started easily. Jeff wished that it had not been so responsive. He would have liked a few more minutes in which to turn things around in his head. As it was, with Jennie chiding him about being afraid, he had to keep going. He swung the car into the little pencil-mark road and started off toward the river, driving very slowly, very cautiously.

Chugging across the green countryside, the small battered Ford seemed tiny indeed. Jeff felt a familiar excitement, a thrill, as they came down the first slope to the immense levels on which the cotton was growing. He could not help reflecting that the crops were good. He knew what that meant, too; he had made forty-five of them with his own hands. It was true that he had worn out nearly a dozen mules, but that was the fault of old man Stevenson, the owner of the land. Major Stevenson had the odd notion that one mule was all a [80] share farmer needed to work a thirty-acre plot. It was an expensive notion, the way it killed the mules from overwork, but the old man held to it. Jeff thought it killed a good many share farmers as well as mules, but he had no sympathy for them. He had always been strong, and he had been taught to have no patience with weakness in men. Women or children might be tolerated if they were puny, but a weak man was a curse. Of course, his own children———

Jeff's thought halted there. He and Jennie never mentioned their dead children any more. And naturally, he did not wish to dwell upon them in his mind. Before he knew it, some remark would slip out of his mouth and that would make Jennie feel blue. Perhaps she would cry. A woman like Jennie could not easily throw off the grief that comes from losing five grown children within two years. Even Jeff was still staggered by the blow. His memory had not been much good recently. He frequently talked to himself. And, although he had kept it a secret, he knew that his courage had left him. He was terrified by the least unfamiliar sound at night. He was reluctant to venture far from home in the daytime. And that habit of trembling when he felt fearful was now far beyond his control. Sometimes he became afraid and trembled without knowing what had frightened him. The feeling would just come over him like a chill.

The car rattled slowly over the dusty road. Jennie sat erect and silent with a little absurd hat pinned to her hair. Her useless eyes seemed very large, very white in their deep sockets. Suddenly Jeff heard her voice, and he inclined his head to catch the words.

"Is we passed Delia Moore's house yet?" she asked.

"Not yet," he said.

"You must be drivin' mighty slow, Jeff."

"We just as well take our time, baby."

There was a pause. A little puff of steam was coming out of the radiator of the car. Heat wavered above the hood. Delia Moore's house was nearly half a mile away. After a moment Jennie spoke again.

"You ain't really scairt, is you, Jeff?"

"Nah, baby, I ain't scairt."

"You know how we agreed—we gotta keep on goin'."

Jewels of perspiration appeared on Jeff's forehead. His eyes rounded, blinked, became fixed on the road. [81]

"I don't know," he said with a shiver, "I reckon it's the only thing to do."

"Hm."

A flock of guinea fowls, pecking in the road, were scattered by the passing car. Some of them took to their wings; others hid under bushes. A blue jay, swaying on a leafy twig, was annoying a roadside squirrel. Jeff held an even speed till he came near Delia's place. Then he slowed down noticeably.

Delia's house was really no house at all, but an abandoned store building converted into a dwelling. It sat near a crossroads, beneath a single black cedar tree. There Delia, a cattish old creature of Jennie's age, lived alone. She had been there more years than anybody could remember, and long ago had won the disfavor of such women as Jennie. For in her young days Delia had been gayer, yellower, and saucier than seemed proper in those parts. Her ways with menfolks had been dark and suspicious. And the fact that she had had as many husbands as children did not help her reputation.

"Yonder's old Delia," Jeff said as they passed.

"What she doin'?"

"Jes sittin' in the do'," he said.

"She see us?"

"Hm," Jeff said. "Musta did."

That relieved Jennie. It strengthened her to know that her old enemy had seen her pass in her best clothes. That would give the old she-devil something to chew her gums and fret about, Jennie thought. Wouldn't she have a fit if she didn't find out? Old evil Delia! This would be just the thing for her. It would pay her back for being so evil. It would also pay her, Jennie thought, for the way she used to grin at Jeff—long ago, when her teeth were good.

The road became smooth and red, and Jeff could tell by the smell of the air that they were nearing the river. He could see the rise where the road turned and ran along parallel to the stream. The car chugged on monotonously. After a long silent spell, Jennie leaned against Jeff and spoke.

"How many bale o' cotton you think we got standin'?" she said.

Jeff wrinkled his forehead as he calculated.

" 'Bout twenty-five, I reckon."

"How many you make las' year?" [82]

"Twenty-eight," he said. "How come you ask that?"

"I's jes thinkin'," Jennie said quietly.

"It don't make a speck o' difference though," Jeff reflected. "If we get much or if we get little, we still gonna be in debt to old man Stevenson when he gets through counting up agin us. It's took us a long time to learn that."

Jennie was not listening to these words. She had fallen into a trance-like meditation. Her lips twitched. She chewed her gums and rubbed her gnarled hands nervously. Suddenly, she leaned forward, buried her face in the nervous hands, and burst into tears. She cried aloud in a dry, cracked voice that suggested the rattle of fodder on dead stalks. She cried aloud like a child, for she had never learned to suppress a genuine sob. Her slight old frame shook heavily and seemed hardly able to sustain such violent grief.

"What's the matter, baby?" Jeff asked awkwardly. "Why you cryin' like all that?"

"I's jes thinkin'," she said.

"So you the one what's scairt now, hunh?"

"I ain't scairt, Jeff. I's jes thinkin' 'bout leavin' eve'thing like this—eve'thing we been used to. It's right sad-like."

Jeff did not answer, and presently Jennie buried her face again and cried.

The sun was almost overhead. It beat down furiously on the dusty wagon-path road, on the parched roadside grass and the tiny battered car. Jeff's hands, gripping the wheel, became wet with perspiration; his forehead sparkled. Jeff's lips parted. His mouth shaped a hideous grimace. His face suggested the face of a man being burned. But the torture passed and his expression softened again.

"You mustn't cry, baby," he said to his wife. "We gotta be strong. We can't break down."

Jennie waited a few seconds, then said, "You reckon we oughta do it, Jeff? You reckon we oughta go 'head an' do it, really?"

Jeff's voice choked; his eyes blurred. He was terrified to hear Jennie say the thing that had been in his mind all morning. She had egged him on when he had wanted more than anything in the world to wait, to reconsider, to think things over a little longer. Now she was getting cold feet. Actually, there was no need of thinking the question through again. It would only end in making the same painful decision [83] once more. Jeff knew that. There was no need of fooling around longer.

"We jes as well to do like we planned," he said. "They ain't nothin' else for us now—it's the bes' thing."

Jeff thought of the handicaps, the near impossibility, of making another crop with his leg bothering him more and more each week. Then there was always the chance that he would have another stroke, like the one that had made him lame. Another one might kill him. The least it could do would be to leave him helpless. Jeff gasped—Lord, Jesus! He could not bear to think of being helpless, like a baby, on Jennie's hands. Frail, blind Jennie.

The little pounding motor of the car worked harder and harder. The puff of steam from the cracked radiator became larger. Jeff realized that they were climbing a little rise. A moment later the road turned abruptly, and he looked down upon the face of the river.

"Jeff."

"Hunh?"

"Is that the water I hear?"

"Hm. Tha's it."

"Well, which way you goin' now?"

"Down this-a way," he said. "The road runs 'long 'side o' the water a lil piece."

She waited a while calmly. Then she said, "Drive faster."

"A'right, baby," Jeff said.

The water roared in the bed of the river. It was fifty or sixty feet below the level of the road. Between the road and the water there was a long smooth slope, sharply inclined. The slope was dry, the clay hardened by prolonged summer heat. The water below, roaring in a narrow channel, was noisy and wild.

"Jeff."

"Hunh?"

"How far you goin'?"

"Jes a lil piece down the road."

"You ain't scairt, is you, Jeff?"

"Nah, baby," he said trembling. "I ain't scairt."

"Remember how we planned it, Jeff. We gotta do it like we said. Brave-like."

"Hm." [84]

Jeff's brain darkened. Things suddenly seemed unreal, like figures in a dream. Thoughts swam in his mind foolishly, hysterically, like little blind fish in a pool within a dense cave. They rushed again. Jeff soon became dizzy. He shuddered violently and turned to his wife.

"Jennie, I can't do it. I can't." His voice broke pitifully.

She did not appear to be listening. All the grief had gone from her face. She sat erect, her unseeing eyes wide open, strained and frightful. Her glossy black skin had become dull. She seemed as thin, as sharp and bony, as a starved bird. Now, having suffered and endured the sadness of tearing herself away from beloved things, she showed no anguish. She was absorbed with her own thoughts, and she didn't even hear Jeff's voice shouting in her ear.

Jeff said nothing more. For an instant there was light in his cavernous brain. The great chamber was, for less than a second, peopled by characters he knew and loved. They were simple, healthy creatures, and they behaved in a manner that he could understand. They had quality. But since he had already taken leave of them long ago, the remembrance did not break his heart again. Young Jeff Patton was among them, the Jeff Patton of fifty years ago who went down to New Orleans with a crowd of country boys to the Mardi Gras doings. The gay young crowd, boys with candy-striped shirts and rouged brown girls in noisy silks, was like a picture in his head. Yet it did not make him sad. On that very trip Slim Burns had killed Joe Beasley—the crowd had been broken up. Since then Jeff Patton's world had been the Greenbriar Plantation. If there had been other Mardi Gras carnivals, he had not heard of them. Since then there had been no time; the years had fallen on him like waves. Now he was old, worn out. Another paralytic stroke (like the one he had already suffered) would put him on his back for keeps. In that condition, with a frail blind woman to look after him, he would be worse off than if he were dead.

Suddenly Jeff's hands became steady. He actually felt brave. He slowed down the motor of the car and carefully pulled off the road. Below, the water of the stream boomed, a soft thunder in the deep channel. Jeff ran the car onto the clay slope, pointed it directly toward the stream, and put his foot heavily on the accelerator. The little car leaped furiously down the steep incline toward the water. The [85] movement was nearly as swift and direct as a fall. The two old black folks, sitting quietly side by side, showed no excitement. In another instant the car hit the water and dropped immediately out of sight.

A little later it lodged in the mud of a shallow place. One wheel of the crushed and upturned little Ford became visible above the rushing water. [86]

LANGSTON HUGHES

Thank You, M'am

She was a large woman with a large purse that had everything in it but a hammer and nails. It had a long strap, and she carried it slung across her shoulder. It was about eleven o'clock at night, dark, and she was walking alone, when a boy ran up behind her and tried to snatch her purse. The strap broke with the sudden single tug the boy gave it from behind. But the boy's weight and the weight of the purse combined caused him to lose his balance. Instead of taking off full blast as he had hoped, the boy fell on his back on the sidewalk and his legs flew up. The large woman simply turned around and kicked him right square in his blue-jeaned sitter. Then she reached down, picked the boy up by his shirt front, and shook him until his teeth rattled.

After that the woman said, "Pick up my pocketbook, boy, and give it here."

She still held him tightly. But she bent down enough to permit him to stoop and pick up her purse. Then she said, "Now ain't you ashamed of yourself?"

Firmly gripped by his shirt front, the boy said, "Yes'm."

The woman said, "What did you want to do it for?"

The boy said, "I didn't aim to."

She said, "You a lie!"

SOURCE: Langston Hughes, *The Langston Hughes Reader* (New York: George Braziller, Inc., 1958), pp. 77–80. Copyright © 1958 by Langston Hughes. Reprinted by permission of Harold Ober Associates Incorporated.

By that time two or three people passed, stopped, turned to look, and some stood watching.

"If I turn you loose, will you run?" asked the woman.

"Yes'm," said the boy.

"Then I won't turn you loose," said the woman. She did not release him.

"Lady, I'm sorry," whispered the boy.

"Um-hum! Your face is dirty. I got a great mind to wash your face for you. Ain't you got nobody home to tell you to wash your face?"

"No'm," said the boy. [77]

"Then it will get washed this evening," said the large woman, starting up the street, dragging the frightened boy behind her.

He looked as if he were fourteen or fifteen, frail and willow-wild, in tennis shoes and blue jeans.

The woman said, "You ought to be my son. I would teach you right from wrong. Least I can do right now is to wash your face. Are you hungry?"

"No'm," said the being-dragged boy. "I just want you to turn me loose."

"Was I bothering *you* when I turned that corner?" asked the woman.

"No'm."

"But you put yourself in contact with *me,*" said the woman. "If you think that that contact is not going to last awhile, you got another thought coming. When I get through with you, sir, you are going to remember Mrs. Luella Bates Washington Jones."

Sweat popped out on the boy's face and he began to struggle. Mrs. Jones stopped, jerked him around in front of her, put a half nelson about his neck, and continued to drag him up the street. When she got to her door, she dragged the boy inside, down a hall, and into a large kitchenette-furnished room at the rear of the house. She switched on the light and left the door open. The boy could hear other roomers laughing and talking in the large house. Some of their doors were open, too, so he knew he and the woman were not alone. The woman still had him by the neck in the middle of her room.

She said, "What is your name?"

"Roger," answered the boy.

"Then, Roger, you go to that sink and wash your face," said the woman, whereupon she turned him loose—at last. Roger looked at the door—looked at the woman—looked at the door—*and went to the sink.*

"Let the water run until it gets warm," she said. "Here's a clean towel."

"You gonna take me to jail?" asked the boy, bending over the sink.

"Not with that face, I would not take you nowhere," said the woman. "Here I am trying to get home to cook me a bite to eat, and you snatch my pocketbook! Maybe you ain't been to your supper either, late as it be. Have you?"

"There's nobody home at my house," said the boy.

"Then we'll eat," said the woman. "I believe you're hungry—or been hungry—to try to snatch my pocketbook!"

"I want a pair of blue suede shoes," said the boy. [78]

"Well, you didn't have to snatch *my* pocketbook to get some suede shoes," said Mrs. Luella Bates Washington Jones. "You could of asked me."

"M'am?"

The water dripping from his face, the boy looked at her. There was a long pause. A very long pause. After he had dried his face, and not knowing what else to do, dried it again, the boy turned around, wondering what next. The door was open. He could make a dash for it down the hall. He could run, run, run, *run!*

The woman was sitting on the daybed. After a while she said, "I were young once and I wanted things I could not get."

There was another long pause. The boy's mouth opened. Then he frowned, not knowing he frowned.

The woman said, "Um-hum! You thought I was going to say *but,* didn't you? You thought I was going to say, *but I didn't snatch people's pocketbooks.* Well, I wasn't going to say that." Pause. Silence. "I have done things, too, which I would not tell you, son—neither tell God, if He didn't already know. Everybody's got something in common. So you set down while I fix us something to eat. You might run that comb through your hair so you will look presentable."

In another corner of the room behind a screen was a gas plate and an icebox. Mrs. Jones got up and went behind the screen. The woman did not watch the boy to see if he was going to run now, nor did she watch her purse, which she left behind her on the daybed. But the boy took care to sit on the far side of the room, away from the purse, where he thought she could easily see him out of the corner of her eye if she wanted to. He did not trust the woman *not* to trust him. And he did not want to be mistrusted now.

"Do you need somebody to go to the store," asked the boy, "maybe to get some milk or something?"

"Don't believe I do," said the woman, "unless you just want sweet milk yourself. I was going to make cocoa out of this canned milk I got here."

"That will be fine," said the boy.

She heated some lima beans and ham she had in the icebox, made the cocoa, and set the table. The woman did not ask the boy anything about where he lived, or his folks, or anything else that would embarrass him. Instead, as they ate, she told him about her job in a hotel beauty shop that stayed open late, what the work was like, and how all kinds of women came in and out, blondes, redheads, and Spanish. Then she cut him a half of her ten-cent cake.

"Eat some more, son," she said. [79]

When they were finished eating, she got up and said, "Now here, take this ten dollars and buy yourself some blue suede shoes. And next time, do not make the mistake of latching onto *my* pocketbook *nor nobody else's*—because shoes got by devilish ways will burn your feet. I got to get my rest now. But from here on in, son, I hope you will behave yourself."

She led him down the hall to the front door and opened it. "Good night! Behave yourself, boy!" she said, looking out into the street as he went down the steps.

The boy wanted to say something other than, "Thank you, m'am," to Mrs. Luella Bates Washington Jones, but although his lips moved, he couldn't even say that as he turned at the foot of the barren stoop and looked up at the large woman in the door. Then she shut the door. [80]

RICHARD WRIGHT

Almos' a Man

Dave struck out across the fields, looking homeward through paling light. Whut's the usa talkin wid em niggers in the field? Anyhow, his mother was putting supper on the table. Them niggers can't understan nothing. One of these days he was going to get a gun and practice shooting, then they can't talk to him as though he were a little boy. He slowed, looking at the ground. Shucks, Ah ain scareda them even ef they are biggern me! Aw, Ah know whut Ahma do. . . . Ahm going by ol Joe's sto n git that Sears Roebuck catlog n look at them guns. Mabbe Ma will lemme buy one when she gets ma pay from ol man Hawkins. Ahma beg her ta gimme some money. Ahm ol ernough to hava gun. Ahm seventeen. Almos a man. He strode, feeling his long, loose-jointed limbs. Shucks, a man oughta hava little gun aftah he done worked hard all day. . . .

He came in sight of Joe's store. A yellow lantern glowed on the front porch. He mounted steps and went through the screen door, hearing it bang behind him. There was a strong smell of coal oil and mackerel fish. He felt very confident until he saw fat Joe walk in through the rear door, then his courage began to ooze.

"Howdy, Dave! Whutcha want?"

"How yuh, Mistah Joe? Aw, Ah don wanna buy nothing. Ah just wanted t see ef yuhd lemme look at tha ol catlog erwhile."

"Sure! You wanna see it here?"

"Nawsuh. Ah wans t take it home wid me. Ahll bring it back termorrow when Ah come in from the fiels."

"You plannin on buyin something?"

"Yessuh."

"Your ma letting you have your own money now?"

SOURCE: *Harper's Bazaar,* LXXIII, 2732 (January, 1940), 40–41, 105–107. Copyright 1940 by *Harper's Bazaar.* Reprinted by permission of Paul R. Reynolds, Inc., as agent for the author.

Richard Wright

"Shucks. Mistah Joe, Ahm gittin t be a man like anybody else!"

Joe laughed and wiped his greasy white face with a red bandanna.

"Whut you plannin on buyin?"

Dave looked at the floor, scratched his head, scratched his thigh, and smiled. Then he looked up shyly.

"Ahll tell yuh, Mistah Joe, ef yuh promise yuh won't tell."

"I promise."

"Waal, Ahma buy a gun."

"A gun? Whut you want with a gun?"

"Ah wanna keep it."

"You ain't nothing but a boy. You don't need a gun."

"Aw, lemme have the catalog, Mistah Joe. Ahll bring it back."
[40]

Joe walked through the rear door. Dave was elated. He looked around at barrels of sugar and flour. He heard Joe coming back. He craned his neck to see if he were bringing the book. Yeah, he's got it! Gawddog, he's got it!

"Here, but be sure you bring it back. It's the only one I got."

"Sho, Mistah Joe."

"Say, if you wanna buy a gun, why don't you buy one from me? I gotta gun to sell."

"Will it shoot?"

"Sure it'll shoot."

"Whut kind is it?"

"Oh, it's kinda old. . . . A lefthand Wheeler. A pistol. A big one."

"Is it got bullets in it?"

"It's loaded."

"Kin Ah see it?"

"Where's your money?"

"Whut yuh wan fer it?"

"I'll let you have it for two dollars."

"Just two dollahs? Shucks, Ah could buy tha when Ah git mah pay."

"I'll have it here when you want it."

"Awright, suh. Ah be in fer it."

He went through the door, hearing it slam again behind him. Ahma git some money from Ma n buy me a gun! Only two dollahs! He tucked the thick catalogue under his arm and hurried.

"Where yuh been, boy?" His mother held a steaming dish of black-eyed peas.

"Aw, Ma, Ah jus stopped down the road t talk wid th boys."

"Yuh know bettah than t keep suppah waitin."

He sat down, resting the catalogue on the edge of the table.

"Yuh git up from there and git to the well n wash yosef! Ah ain feedin no hogs in mah house!"

She grabbed his shoulder and pushed him. He stumbled out of the room, then came back to get the catalogue.

"Whut this?"

"Aw, Ma, it's jusa catlog."

"Who yuh git it from?"

"From Joe, down at the sto."

"Waal, thas good. We kin use it around the house."

"Naw, Ma." He grabbed for it. "Gimme mah catlog, Ma."

She held onto it and glared at him.

"Quit hollerin at me! Whut's wrong wid yuh? Yuh crazy?"

"But Ma, please. It ain mine! It's Joe's! He tol me t bring it back t im termorrow."

She gave up the book. He stumbled down the back steps, hugging the thick book under his arm. When he had splashed water on his face and hands, he groped back to the kitchen and fumbled in a corner for the towel. He bumped into a chair; it clattered to the floor. The catalogue sprawled at his feet. When he had dried his eyes, he snatched up the book and held it again under his arm. His mother stood watching him.

"Now, ef yuh gonna acka fool over that ol book, Ahll take it n burn it up."

"Naw, Ma, please."

"Waal, set down n be still!"

He sat down and drew the oil lamp close. He thumbed page after page, unaware of the food his mother set on the table. His father came in. Then his small brother.

"Whutcha got there, Dave?" his father asked.

"Jusa catlog," he answered, not looking up.

"Yawh, here they is!" His eyes glowed at blue and black revolvers. He glanced up, feeling sudden guilt. His father was watching him. He eased the book under the table and rested it on his knees. After the blessing was asked, he ate. He scooped up peas and swallowed fat meat without chewing. Buttermilk helped wash it down. He did not want to mention money before his father. He would do much better by cornering his mother when she was alone. He looked at his father uneasily out of the edge of his eye.

63

"Boy, how come yuh don quit foolin wid tha book n eat yo suppah."

"Yessuh."

"How yuh n old man Hawkins gittin erlong?"

"Suh?"

"Can't yuh hear. Why don yuh listen? Ah ast yuh wuz yuh n ol man Hawkins gittin erlong?"

"Oh, swell, Pa. Ah plows mo lan than anybody over there."

"Waal, yuh oughta keep yo min on whut yuh doin."

"Yessuh."

He poured his plate full of molasses and sopped at it slowly with a dunk of cornbread. When all but his mother had left the kitchen he still sat and looked again at the guns in the catalogue. Lawd, ef Ah only had the pretty one! He could almost feel the slickness of the weapon with his fingers. If he had a gun like that he would polish it and keep it shining so it would never rust. N Ahd keep it loaded, by Gawd! [41]

"Ma?"

"Hunh?"

"Ol man Hawkins give yuh mah money yit?"

"Yeah, but ain no usa yuh thinin bout throwin nona it erway. Ahm keepin tha money sos yuh kin have cloes t go to school this winter."

He rose and went to her side with the open catalogue in his palms. She was washing dishes, her head bent low over a pan. Shyly he raised the open book. When he spoke his voice was husky, faint.

"Ma, Gawd knows Ah wans one of these."

"One of whut?" she asked, not raising her eyes.

"One of these," he said again, not daring even to point. She glanced up at the page, then at him with wide eyes.

"Nigger, is yuh gone plum crazy?"

"Aw, Ma—"

"Git outta here! Don't yuh talk t me bout no gun! Yuh a fool!"

"Ma, Ah kin buy one fer two dollahs."

"Not ef Ah knows it yuh ain!"

"But yuh promised one—"

"Ah don care whut Ah promised! Yuh ain nothing but a boy yit!"

"Ma, ef yuh lemme buy one Ahll never ast yuh fer nothing no mo."

"Ah tol yuh t git outta here! Yuh ain gonna toucha penny of tha money fer no gun! Thas how come Ah has Mistah Hawkins pay yo wages t me, cause Ah knows yuh ain got no sense."

"But Ma, we needa gun. Pa ain got no gun. We needa gun in the house. Yuh kin never tell whut might happen."

"Now don yuh try to maka fool outta me, boy! Ef we did hava gun he'd hava fit."

He laid the catalogue down and slipped his arm around her waist. "Aw, Ma, Ah done worked hard alls summer n ain ast yuh fer nothing, is Ah, now?"

"Thas whut yuh spose t do!"

"But Ma. Ah wants a gun. Yuh kin lemme have two dollah outa mah money. Please Ma. I kin give it to Pa. . . . Please, Ma! Ah loves yuh, Ma."

When she spoke her voice came soft and low.

"What yuh wan wida gun, Dave? Yuh don need no gun. Yuhll git in trouble. N ef yo Pa just thought Ah letyuh have money t buy a gun he'd hava fit."

"Ahll hide it, Ma. It ain but two dollahs."

"Lawd, chil, whuts wrong wid yuh?"

"Ain nothing wrong, Ma. Ahm almos a man now. Ah wants a gun."

"Who gonna sell yuh a gun?"

"Ol Joe at the sto."

"N it don cos but two dollahs?"

"Thas all, Ma. Just two dollahs. Please, Ma."

She was stacking the plates away; her hands moved slowly, reflectively. Dave kept an anxious silence. Finally she turned to him.

"Ahll let yuh git the gun ef yuh promise me one thing."

"Whuts tha, Ma?"

"Yuh bring it straight back t me, yuh hear? It'll be fer Pa."

"Yessum! Lemme go now, Ma."

She stooped, turned slightly to one side, raised the hem of her dress, rolled down the top of her stocking, and came up with a slender wad of bills.

"Here," she said. "Lawd knows yuh don need no gun. But yer Pa does. Yuh bring it right back to me, yuh hear. Ahma put it up. Now ef yuh don, Ahma have yuh Pa lick yuh so hard yuh won ferget it."

"Yessum."

He took the money, ran down the steps, and across the yard.

"Dave! Yuuuuuuh Daaaaaave!"

He heard, but he was not going to stop now. "Naw, Lawd!"

The first movement he made the following morning was to reach under his pillow for the gun. In the gray light of dawn he held it loosely, feeling a sense of power. Could killa man wida gun like this. Kill anybody, black or white. And if he were holding this gun in his hand nobody could run over him; they would have to respect him. It was a big gun, with a long barrel and a heavy handle. He raised and lowered it in his hand, marveling at its weight.

He had not come straight home with it as his mother had asked; instead he had stayed out in the fields, holding the weapon in his hand, aiming it now and then at some imaginary foe. But he had not fired it; he had been afraid that his father might hear. Also he was not sure he knew how to fire it.

To avoid surrendering the pistol he had not come into the house until he knew that all were asleep. When his mother had tiptoed to his bedside late that night and demanded the gun, he had first played 'possum; then he had told her that the gun was hidden outdoors, that he would bring it to her in the morning. Now he lay turning it slowly in his hands. He broke it, took out the cartridges, felt them, and then put them back.

He slid out of bed, got a long strip of old flannel from a trunk, wrapped the gun in it, and tied it to his naked thigh while it was still loaded. He did not go in to breakfast. Even though it was not yet daylight, he started for Jim Hawkins's plantation. Just as the sun was rising he reached the barns where the mules and plows were kept.

"Hey! That you, Dave?"

He turned. Jim Hawkins stood eyeing him suspiciously.

"What're yuh doing here so early?"

"Ah didn't know Ah wuz gittin up so early, Mistah Hawkins. Ah wuz fixing hitch up of Jenny n take her t the fiels."

"Good. Since you're here so early, how about plowing that stretch down by the woods?"

"Suits me, Mistah Hawkins."

"O.K. Go to it!"

He hitched Jenny to a plow and started across the fields. Hot dog! This was just what he wanted. If he could get down by the woods, he could shoot his gun and nobody would hear. He walked behind the plow, hearing the traces creaking, feeling the gun tied tight to his thigh.

When he reached the woods, he plowed two whole rows before

he decided to take out the gun. Finally he stopped, looked in all directions, then untied the gun and held it in his hand. He turned to the mule and smiled.

"Know whut this is, Jenny? Naw, yuh wouldn't know! Yuhs just ol mule! Anyhow, this is a gun, n it kin shoot, by Gawd!"

He held the gun at arm's length. Whut t hell, Ahma shoot this thing! He looked at Jenny again.

"Lissen here, Jenny! When Ah pull this ol trigger Ah don wan yuh t run n acka fool now."

Jenny stood with head down, her short ears pricked straight. Dave walked off about twenty feet, held the gun far out from him, at arm's length, and turned his head. Hell, he told himself, Ah ain afraid. The gun felt loose in his fingers; he waved it wildly for a moment. Then he shut his eyes and tightened his forefinger. Bloom! The report half-deafened him and he thought his right hand was torn from his arm. He heard Jenny whinnying and galloping over the field, and he found himself on his knees squeezing his fingers hard between his legs. His hand was numb; he jammed it into his mouth, trying to warm it, trying to stop the pain. The gun lay at his feet. He did not quite know what had happened. He stood up and stared at the gun as though it were a living thing. He gritted his teeth and kicked the gun. Yuh almos broke mah arm! He turned to look for Jenny; she was far over the fields, tossing her head and kicking wildly.

"Hol on there, ol mule!"

When he caught up with her [105] she stood trembling, walling her big white eyes at him. The plow was far away; the traces had broken. Then Dave stopped short, looking, not believing. Jenny was bleeding. Her left side was red and wet with blood. He went closer. Lawd, have mercy! Wondah did Ah shoot this mule? He grabbed for Jenny's mane. She flinched, snorted, whirled, tossing her head.

"Hol on now! Hol on."

Then he saw the hole in Jenny's side, right between the ribs. It was round, wet, red. A crimson stream streaked down the front leg, flowing fast. Good Gawd! Ah wuzn't shootin at tha mule. He felt panic. He knew he had to stop that blood, or Jenny would bleed to death. He had never seen so much blood in all his life. He chased the mule for half a mile, trying to catch her. Finally she stopped, breathing hard, stumpy tail half arched. He caught her mane and led her back to where the plow and gun lay. Then he stooped and grabbed handfuls of damp black earth and tried to plug the bullet hole. Jenny shuddered, whinnied, and broke from him.

"Hol on! Hol on now!"

He tried to plug it again, but blood came anyhow. His fingers were hot and sticky. He rubbed dirt into his palms, trying to dry them. Then again he attempted to plug the bullet hole, but Jenny shied away, kicking her heels high. He stood helpless. He had to do something. He ran at Jenny; she dodged him. He watched a red stream of blood flow down Jenny's leg and form a bright pool at her feet.

"Jenny . . . Jenny . . ." he called weakly.

His lips trembled! She's bleeding t death! He looked in the direction of home, wanting to go back, wanting to get help. But he saw the pistol lying in the damp black clay. He had a queer feeling that if he only did something, this would not be; Jenny would not be there bleeding to death.

When he went to her this time, she did not move. She stood with sleepy, dreamy eyes; and when he touched her she gave a low-pitched whinny and knelt to the ground, her front knees slopping in blood.

"Jenny . . . Jenny . . ." he whispered.

For a long time she held her neck erect; then her head sank, slowly. Her ribs swelled with a mighty heave and she went over.

Dave's stomach felt empty, very empty. He picked up the gun and held it gingerly between his thumb and forefinger. He buried it at the foot of a tree. He took a stick and tried to cover the pool of blood with dirt—but what was the use? There was Jenny lying with her mouth open and her eyes walled and glassy. He could not tell Jim Hawkins he had shot his mule. But he had to tell him something. Yeah, Ahll tell em Jenny started gittin wil n fell on the joint of the plow. . . . But that would hardly happen to a mule. He walked across the field slowly, head down.

It was sunset. Two of Jim Hawkins's men were over near the edge of the woods digging a hole in which to bury Jenny. Dave was surrounded by a knot of people; all of them were looking down at the dead mule.

"I don't see how in the world it happened," said Jim Hawkins for the tenth time.

The crowd parted and Dave's mother, father, and small brother pushed into the center.

"Where Dave?" his mother called.

"There he is," said Jim Hawkins.

His mother grabbed him.

"Whut happened, Dave? Whut yuh done?"

"Nothing."

"C'mon, boy, talk," his father said.

Dave took a deep breath and told the story he knew nobody believed.

"Waal," he drawled. "Ah brung ol Jenny down here sos Ah could do mah plowin. Ah plowed bout two rows, just like yuh see." He stopped and pointed at the long rows of upturned earth. "Then something musta been wrong wid ol Jenny. She wouldn't ack right a-tall. She started snortin n kickin her heels. Ah tried to hol her, but she pulled erway, rearin n goin on. Then when the point of the plow was stickin up in the air, she swung erroun n twisted herself back on it. . . . She stuck herself n started t bleed. N fo Ah could do anything, she wuz dead."

"Did you ever hear of anything like that in all your life?" asked Jim Hawkins.

There were white and black standing in the crowd. They murmured. Dave's mother came close to him and looked hard into his face.

"Tell the truth, Dave," she said.

"Looks like a bullet hole ter me," said one man.

"Dave, whut yuh do wid tha gun?" his mother asked.

The crowd surged in, looking at him. He jammed his hands into his pockets, shook his head slowly from left to right, and backed away. His eyes were wide and painful.

"Did he hava gun?" asked Jim Hawkins.

"By Gawd, Ah tol yuh tha wuz a gunwound," said a man, slapping his thigh.

His father caught his shoulders and shook him till his teeth rattled.

"Tell whut happened, yuh rascal! Tell whut . . ."

Dave looked at Jenny's stiff legs and began to cry.

"Whut yuh do wid tha gun?" his mother asked.

"Come on and tell the truth," said Hawkins. "Ain't nobody going to hurt you. . . ."

His mother crowded close to him.

"Did yuh shoot tha mule, Dave?"

Dave cried, seeing blurred white and black faces.

"Ahh ddinnt gggo tt sshoooot hher. . . . Ah ssswear off Gawd Ah ddint. . . . Ah wuz a-tryin t sssee ef the ol gggun would sshoot—"

"Where yuh git the gun from?" his father asked.

"Ah got it from Joe, at the sto."

"Where yuh git the money?"

"Ma give it t me."

"He kept worryin me, Bob. . . . Ah had t. . . . Ah tol im t bring the gun right back t me. . . . It was fer yuh, the gun."

"But how yuh happen to shoot that mule?" asked Jim Hawkins.

"Ah wuznt shootin at the mule, Mistah Hawkins. The gun jumped when Ah pulled the trigger . . . N for Ah knowed anything Jenny wuz there a-bleedin."

Somebody in the crowd laughed. Jim Hawkins walked close to Dave and looked into his face.

"Well, looks like you have bought you a mule, Dave."

"Ah swear for Gawd, Ah didn't go t kill the mule, Mistah Hawkins!"

"But you killed her!"

All the crowd was laughing now. They stood on tiptoe and poked heads over one another's shoulders.

"Well, boy, looks like yuh done bought a dead mule! Hahaha!"

"Ain tha ershame."

"Hohohohoho."

Dave stood, head down, twisting his feet in the dirt.

"Well, you needn't worry about it, Bob," said Jim Hawkins to Dave's father. "Just let the boy keep on working and pay me two dollars a month."

"Whut yuh wan fer yo mule, Mistah Hawkins?"

Jim Hawkins screwed up his eyes.

"Fifty dollars."

"Whut yuh do wid tha gun?" Dave's father demanded.

Dave said nothing.

"Yuh want me t take a tree lim n beat yuh till yuh talk!"

"Nawsuh!" [106]

"Whut yuh do wid it?"

"Ah thowed it erway."

"Where?"

"Ah . . . Ah thowed it in the creek."

"Waal, c mon home. N firs thing in the mawnin git to tha creek n fin tha gun."

"Yessuh."

"Whut yuh pay fer it?"

"Two dollahs."

"Take tha gun n git yo money back n carry it t Mistah Hawkins, yuh hear? N don fergit Ahma lam you black bottom good fer this! Now march yosef on home, suh!"

Dave turned and walked slowly. He heard people laughing. Dave glared, his eyes welling with tears. Hot anger bubbled in him. Then he swallowed and stumbled on.

That night Dave did not sleep. He was glad that he had gotten out of killing the mule so easily, but he was hurt. Something hot seemed to turn over inside him each time he remembered how they had laughed. He tossed on his bed, feeling his hard pillow. N Pa says he's gonna beat me. . . . He remembered other beatings, and his back quivered. Naw, naw, Ah sho don wan im t beat me tha way no mo. . . . Dam em all! Nobody ever gave him anything. All he did was work. They treat me lika mule. . . . N then they beat me. . . . He gritted his teeth. N Ma had t tell on me.

Well, if he had to, he would take old man Hawkins that two dollars. But that meant selling the gun. And he wanted to keep that gun. Fifty dollahs fer a dead mule.

He turned over, thinking how he had fired the gun. He had an itch to fire it again. Ef other men kin shoota gun, by Gawd, Ah kin! He was still listening. Mebbe they all sleepin now. . . . The house was still. He heard the soft breathing of his brother. Yes, now! He would go down an get that gun and see if he could fire it! He eased out of bed and slipped into overalls.

The moon was bright. He ran almost all the way to the edge of the woods. He stumbled over the ground, looking for the spot where he had buried the gun. Yeah, here it is. Like a hungry dog scratching for a bone he pawed it up. He puffed his black cheeks and blew dirt from the trigger and barrel. He broke it and found four cartridges unshot. He looked around; the fields were filled with silence and moonlight. He clutched the gun stiff and hard in his fingers. But as soon as he wanted to pull the trigger, he shut his eyes and turned his head. Naw, Ah can't shoot wid mah eyes closed n mah head turned. With effort he held his eyes open; then he squeezed. Bloooooom! He was stiff, not breathing. The gun was still in his hands. Dammit, he'd done it! He fired again. Bloooom! He smiled. Blooooom! Blooooom! Click, click. There! It was empty. If anybody could shoot a gun, he could. He put the gun into his hip pocket and started across the fields.

When he reached the top of a ridge he stood straight and proud in the moonlight, looking at Jim Hawkins's big white house, feeling the gun sagging in his pocket. Lawd, ef Ah had jus one mo bullet Ahd taka shot at tha house. Ahd like t scare ol man Hawkins jussa little. . . . Jussa enough to let im know Dave Sanders is a man.

To his left the road curved, running to the tracks of the Illinois Central. He jerked his head, listening. From far off came a faint hoooof-hoooof; hoooof-hoooof; hoooof-hoooof. . . . That's number eight. He took a swift look at Jim Hawkins's white house; he thought of Pa, of Ma, of his little brother, and the boys. He thought of the dead mule and heard hooof-hooof; hooof-hooof; hooof-hooof. . . . He stood rigid. Two dollahs a mont. Les see now . . . Tha means itll take bout two years. Shucks! Ahll be dam! He started down the road, toward the tracks. Yeah, here she comes! He stood beside the track and held himself stiffly. Here she comes, erroun the ben. . . . C mon, yuh slow poke! C mon! He had his hand on his gun; something quivered in his stomach. Then the train thundered past, the gray and brown boxcars rumbling and clinking. He gripped the gun tightly; then he jerked his hand out of his pocket. Ah betcha Bill wouldn't do it! Ah betcha. . . . The cars slid past, steel grinding upon steel. Ahm riding yuh ternight so hep me Gawd! He was hot all over. He hesitated just a moment; then he grabbed, pulled atop of a car, and lay flat. He felt his pocket; the gun was still there. Ahead the long rails were glinting in moonlight, stretching away, away to somewhere, somewhere where he could be a man. . . . [107]

WILLARD MOTLEY

The Almost White Boy

By birth he was half Negro and half white. Socially he was all Negro. That is when people knew that his mother was a brown-

Source: Langston Hughes, ed., *The Best Short Stories by Negro Writers* (Boston: Little, Brown and Company, 1967), pp. 134–144. Copyright © 1963 by Willard Motley. Reprinted by permission of Harold Matson Company, Inc.

skin woman with straightened hair and legs that didn't respect the color line when it came to making men turn around to look at them. His eyes were gray. His skin was as white as Slim Peterson's; his blond hair didn't have any curl to it at all. His nose was big and his lips were big—the only tip-off. Aunt Beulah-May said he looked just like "poor white trash." Other people, black and white, said all kinds of things about his parents behind their backs, even if they were married. And these people, when it came to discussing him, shook their heads, made sucking sounds with their tongues and said, "Too bad! Too bad!" And one stragglyhaired Irish woman who had taken quite a liking to him had even gone so far as to tell him, blissfully unmindful of his desires in the matter, "I'd have you marry my daughter if you was white."

One thing he remembered. When he was small his dad had taken him up in his arms and carried him to the big oval mirror in the parlor. "Come here, Lucy," his father had said, calling Jimmy's mother. His mother came, smiling at the picture her two men made hugged close together; one so little and dependent, the other so tall and serious-eyed. She stood beside him, straightening Jimmy's collar and pushing his hair out of his eyes. Dad held him in between them. "Look in the mirror, son," he said. And they all looked. Their eyes were serious, not smiling, not staring, just gloom-colored with seriousness in the mirror. "Look at your mother. . . . Look at me." His dad gave the directions gravely. "Look at your mother's skin." He looked. That was the dear sweet mother he loved. "Look at the color of my skin." He looked. That [134] was his daddy, the best daddy in the world. "We all love each other, son, all three of us," his dad said, and his mother's eyes in the mirror caught and held his father's with something shining and proud through the seriousness; and his mother's arm stole up around him and around his daddy. "People are just people. Some are good and some are bad," his father said. "People are just people. Look—and remember." He had remembered. He would never forget.

Somehow, something of that day had passed into his life. And he carried it with him back and forth across the color line. The colored fellows he palled with called him "the white nigger," and his white pals would sometimes look at him kind of funny but they never said anything. Only when they went out on dates together; then they'd tell him don't let something slip about "niggers" without meaning to. Then they'd look sheepish. Jim didn't see much difference. All the guys were swell if you liked them; all the girls flirted and necked and went on crying jags now and then. People were just people.

There were other things Jim remembered.

. . . On Fifty-eighth and Prairie. Lorenzo with white eyes in a black face. With his kinky hair screwed down tight on his bald-looking head like flies on flypaper. Ruby with her face all shiny brown and her hair in stiff-standing braids and her pipy brown legs Mom called razor-legs. Lorenzo saying, "You're black just like us." Ruby singing out, "Yeah! Yeah! You're a white nigger —white nigger!" Lorenzo taunting, "You ain't no different. My ma says so. You're just a nigger!" Lorenzo and Ruby pushing up close to him with threatening gestures, making faces at him, pulling his straight blond hair with mean fists, both yelling at the same time, "White nigger! White nigger!"

The name stuck.

. . . Women on the sidewalk in little groups. Their lips moving when he walked past with his schoolbooks under his arm. Their eyes lowered but looking at him. "Too bad! Too bad!" He could see them. He knew they were talking about him. "Too bad! Too bad!"

. . . Mom crying on the third floor of the kitchenette flat on Thirty-ninth Street. Mom saying to Dad, "We've got to move [135] from here, Jim. We can't go on the street together without everybody staring at us. You'd think we'd killed somebody."

"What do we care how much they stare or what they say?"

"Even when I go out alone they stare. They never invite me to their houses. They say—they say that I think I'm better than they are—that I had to marry out of my race—that my own color wasn't good enough for me."

Dad saying, "Why can't people mind their own business? The hell with them." Mom crying. No friends. No company. Just the three of them.

. . . Then moving to the slums near Halstead and Maxwell, where all nationalities lived bundled up next door to each other and even in the same buildings. Jews. Mexicans. Poles. Negroes. Italians. Greeks. It was swell there. People changed races there. They went out on the streets together. No more staring. No more name-calling.

He grew up there.

. . . Getting older. And a lot of the white fellows not inviting him to parties at their houses when there were girls from the neighborhood. But they'd still go out of the neighborhood together and pick up girls or go on blind dates or to parties somewhere else. He didn't like to think of the neighborhood parties with the girls and the music and everything, and the door closed to him.

. . . Only once he denied it. He had been going around with Tony for a couple of weeks over on Racine Avenue. They played pool together, drank beer together on West Madison Street, drove around in Tony's old rattling Chevy. One day Tony looked at him funny and said, point-blank, "Say, what are you anyway?"

Jim got red; he could feel his face burn. "I'm Polish," he said.

He was sorry afterwards. He didn't know why he said it. He felt ashamed.

. . . Then he was finished with school and he had to go to work. He got a job in a downtown hotel because nobody knew what he really was and Aunt Beulah-May said it was all right to "pass for white" when it came to making money but he'd better never get any ideas in his head about turning his back on his people. To him it was cheating. It was denying half himself. It wasn't a straight front. He knew how hard it was for colored [136] fellows to find decent jobs. It wasn't saying I'm a Negro and taking the same chances they took when it came to getting a job. But he did it.

Jim remembered many of these things; they were tied inside of him in hard knots. But the color line didn't exist for him and he came and went pretty much as he chose. He took the girls in stride. He went to parties on the South Side, on Thirty-fifth and Michigan, on South Park. He went dancing at the Savoy Ballroom —and the Trianon. He went to Polish hops and Italian fiestas and Irish weddings. And he had a hell of a swell time. People were just people.

He had fun with the colored girls. But some of them held off from him, not knowing what he was. These were his people. No —he didn't feel natural around them. And with white people he wasn't all himself either. He didn't have any people.

Then all of a sudden he was madly in love with Cora. This had never happened before. He had sometimes wondered if, when it came, it would be a white girl or a colored girl. Now it was here. There was nothing he could do about it. And he was scared. He began to worry, and to wonder. And he began to wish, although ashamed to admit it to himself, that he didn't have any colored blood in him.

He met Cora at a dance at the Trianon. Cora's hair wasn't as blond as his but it curled all over her head. Her skin was pink and soft. Her breasts stood erect and her red lips were parted in a queer little loose way. They were always like that. And they were always moist-looking.

Leo introduced them. Then he let them alone and they danced every dance together; and when it was time to go home Leo had disappeared. Jim asked her if he could take her home.

"I think that would be awfully sweet of you," she said. Her eyes opened wide in a baby-blue smile.

She leaned back against him a little when he helped her into her coat. He flushed with the pleasure of that brief touching of their bodies. They walked through the unwinding ballroom crowd together, not having anything to say to each other, and out onto Cottage Grove, still not having anything to say. As they passed the lighted-up plate-glass window of Walgreen's drugstore Jim asked her, "Wouldn't you like a malted milk?" She didn't answer but [137] just smiled up at him over her shoulder and he felt the softness of her arm in the doorway.

She sipped her malted milk. He sat stirring his straw around in his glass. Once in a while she'd look up over her glass and wrinkle her lips or her eyes at him, friendly-like. Neither of them said anything. Then, when Cora had finished, he held the match for her cigarette and their eyes came together and stayed that way longer than they needed to. And her lips were really parted now, with the cigarette smoke curling up into her hair.

In front of her house they stood close together, neither of them wanting to go.

"It was a nice dance," Cora said; and her fingers played in the hedge-top.

"Yes, especially after I met you."

"I'm going to see you again, aren't I?" Cora asked, looking up at him a little.

Jim looked down at the sidewalk. He hoped he could keep the red out of his cheeks. "I might as well tell you before someone else does—I'm a Negro," he said.

There was a catch in her voice, just a little noise not made of words.

"Oh, you're fooling!" she said with a small, irritated laugh.

"No, I'm not. I told you because I like you."

She had stepped back from him. Her eyes were searching for the windows of the house to see that there was no light behind the shades.

"Please, let me see you again," Jim said.

Her eyes, satisfied, came away from the windows. They looked at the sidewalk where he had looked. Her body was still withdrawn. Her lips weren't parted now. There were hard little lines at the corners of her mouth.

"Let me meet you somewhere," Jim said.

Another furtive glance at the house; then she looked at him, unbelievingly. "You didn't mean that—about being colored?"

"It doesn't matter, does it?"

"No—only—"

"Let me meet you somewhere," Jim begged.

Her lips were parted a little. She looked at him strangely, deep into him in a way that made him tremble, then down his body and [138] back up into his eyes. She tossed her head a little. "Well —call me up tomorrow afternoon." She gave him the number.

He watched her go into the house. Then he walked to the corner to wait for his streetcar; and he kicked at the sidewalk and clenched his fists.

Jim went to meet her in Jackson Park. They walked around. She was beautiful in her pink dress. Her lips were pouted a little bit, and her eyes were averted, and she was everything he had ever wanted. They sat on a bench far away from anybody. "You know," she said, "I never liked nig—Negroes. You're not like a Negro at all." They walked to the other end of the park. "Why do you tell people?" she asked.

"People are just people," he told her, but the words didn't sound real any more.

Twice again he met her in the park. Once they just sat talking and once they went to a movie. Both times he walked her to the car line and left her there. That was the way she wanted it.

After that it was sneaking around to meet her. She didn't like to go on dates with him when he had his white friends along. She'd never tell him why. And yet she put her body up close to him when they were alone. It was all right too when she invited some of her friends who didn't know what he was.

They saw a lot of each other. And pretty soon he thought from the long, probing looks she gave him that she must like him; from the way she'd grab his hand, tight, sometimes; from the way she danced with him. She even had him take her home now and they'd stand on her porch pressed close together. "Cora, I want you to come over to my house," he told her. "My mother and father are swell. You'll like them." He could see all four of them together. "It isn't a nice neighborhood. I mean it doesn't look good, but the people are nicer than—in other places. Gee, you'll like my mother and father."

"All right, I'll go, Jimmy. I don't care. I don't care."

Dad kidded him about his new flame, saying it must be serious, that he had never brought a girl home before. Mom made fried chicken and hot biscuits. And when he went to get Cora he saw Dad and Mom both with dust rags, shining up everything in the parlor for the tenth time; he heard Dad and Mom laughing quietly together and talking about their first date. [139]

He hadn't told them she was a white girl. But they never batted an eye.

"Mom, this is Cora."

"How do you do, dear. Jimmy has told us so much about you." Dear, sweet Mom. Always gracious and friendly.

"Dad, this is Cora." Dad grinning, looking straight at her with eyes as blue as hers, going into some crazy story about "Jimmy at the age of three." Good old Dad. "People are just people."

Dad and Mom were at ease. Only Cora seemed embarrassed. And she was nervous, not meeting Dad's eyes, not meeting Mom's eyes, looking to him for support. She sat on the edge of her chair. "Y-y-yes, sir . . . No, Mrs. Warner." She only picked at the good food Mom had spent all afternoon getting ready. And Jim, watching her, watching Dad and Mom, hoping they wouldn't notice, got ill at ease himself and he was glad when he got her outside. Then they were themselves again.

"Mom and Dad are really swell. You'll have to get to know them," he said, looking at her appealingly, asking for approval. She smiled with expressionless eyes. She said nothing.

On Fourteenth and Halstead they met Slick Harper. Slick was as black as they come. It was sometimes hard, because of his southern dialect and his Chicago black-belt expressions, to know just what he meant in English. He practiced jitterbug steps on street corners and had a whole string of girls—black, brownskin, high-yellow. Everybody called him Slick because he handed his bevy of girls a smooth line and because he wore all the latest fashions in men's clothes—high-waisted trousers, big-brimmed hats, bright sports coats, Cuban heels and coconut straws with gaudy bands. Slick hailed Jim; his eyes gave Cora the once-over.

"Whatcha say, man!" he shouted. "Ah know they all goes when the wagon comes but where you been stuck away? And no jive! Man, ah been lookin' for you. We're throwing a party next Saturday and we want you to come."

Jim stood locked to the sidewalk, working his hands in his pockets and afraid to look at Cora. He watched Slick's big purple lips move up and down as they showed the slices of white teeth. Now Slick had stopped talking and was staring at Cora with a black-faced smirk.

"Cora, this is Slick Harper." [140]

"How do you do." Her voice came down as from the top of a building.

"Ah'm glad to meetcha," Slick said. "You sho' got good taste, Jim." His eyes took in her whole figure. "Why don't you bring her to the party?"

"Maybe I will. Well, we've got to go." He walked fast then to keep up with Cora.

Cora never came over again.

Cora had him come over to her house. But first she prepared him a lot. "Don't ever—ever—tell my folks you're colored. Please, Jimmy. Promise me. . . . Father doesn't like colored people. . . . They aren't broad-minded like me. . . . And don't mind Father, Jimmy," she warned.

He went. There was a cream-colored car outside the house. In the parlor were smoking stands, and knickknack brackets, and a grand piano nobody played. Cora's father smoked cigars, owned a few pieces of stock, went to Florida two weeks every winter, told stories about the "Florida niggers." Cora's mother had the same parted lips Cora had, but she breathed through them heavily as if she were always trying to catch up with herself. She was fat and overdressed. And admonished her husband when he told his Southern stories through the smoke of big cigars: "Now, Harry, you mustn't talk like that. What will this nice young man think of you? There are plenty of fine upright Negroes—I'm sure. Of course I don't know any personally. . . . Now, Harry, don't be so harsh. Don't forget, you took milk from a colored mammy's breast. Oh, Harry, tell them about the little darky who wanted to watch your car—'Two cents a awah, Mistah No'the'nah!' "

Cora sat with her hands in her lap and her fingers laced tightly together. Jim smiled at Mr. Hartley's jokes and had a miserable time. And Jim discovered that it was best not to go to anybody's house. Just the two of them.

Jim and Cora went together for four months. And they had an awful time of it. But they were unhappy apart. Yet when they were together their eyes were always accusing each other. Sometimes they seemed to enjoy hurting each other. Jim wouldn't call

Willard Motley

her up; and he'd be miserable. She wouldn't write to him or would stand him up on a date for Chuck Nelson or Fred Schultz; then [141] she'd be miserable. Something held them apart. And something pulled them together.

Jim did a lot of thinking. It had to go four revolutions. Four times a part-Negro had to marry a white person before legally you were white. The blood had to take four revolutions. Mulatto—that's what he was—quadroon—octaroon—then it was all gone. Then you were white. His great-grandchildren maybe. Four times the blood had to let in the other blood.

Then one night they were driving out to the forest preserves in Tony's Chevy. "What are you thinking, Jimmy?"

"Oh, nothing. Just thinking."

"Do you like my new dress? How do I look in it?"

"Isn't that a keen moon, Cora?" The car slid along the dark, deserted highway. They came to a gravel road and Jim eased the car over the crushed stone in second gear. Cora put her cheek against the sleeve of his coat. The branches of trees made scraping sounds against the sides of the car. Cora was closer to him now. He could smell the perfume in her hair and yellow strands tickled the end of his nose. He stopped the motor and switched the lights off. Cora lifted his arm up over her head and around her, putting his hand in close to her waist with her hand over his, stroking his. "Let's sit here like this—close and warm," she whispered. Then her voice lost itself in the breast of his coat.

For a long time they sat like that. Then Jim said, "Let's take a walk." He opened the door and, half supporting her, he lifted her out. While she was still in his arms she bit his ear gently.

"Don't do that," he said, and she giggled.

Panting, they walked through the low scrub into the woods. The bushes scratched their arms. Twigs caught in Cora's hair. Their feet sank in the earth. Cora kept putting her fingers in Jim's hair and mussing it. "Don't. Don't," he said. And finally he caught her fingers and held them tight in his. They walked on like this. The moon made silhouettes of them, silhouettes climbing up the slow incline of hill.

Jim found a little rise of land, treeless, grassy. Far to the northeast, Chicago sprawled, row on row of dim lights growing more numerous but gentler.

The night was over them.

They sat on the little hillock, shoulder to shoulder; and Cora [142] moved her body close to him. It was warm there against his

80

shirt, open at the neck. They didn't talk. They didn't move. And when Cora breathed he could feel the movement of her body against him. It was almost as if they were one. He looked up at the splash of stars, and the moon clouding over. His arm went around her, shieldingly. He closed his eyes and put his face into her hair. "Cora! Cora!" The only answer she gave was the slight movement of her body.

"Cora, I love you."

"Do you, Jimmy?" she said, snuggling up so close to him that he could feel her heart beat against him.

He didn't move. But after a while she was slowly leaning back until the weight of her carried him back too and they lay full length. They lay like this a long time. He looked at her. Her eyes were closed. She was breathing hard. Her lips were parted and moist.

"Jimmy."

"What?"

"Nothing."

She hooked one of her feet over his. A slow quiver started in his shoulders, worked its way down the length of him. He sat up. Cora sat up.

"There's nobody here but us," she said. Her fingers unbuttoned the first button on his shirt, the second. Her fingers crept in on his chest, playing with the little hairs there.

"There's nobody here but us," she said, and she ran her fingers inside his shirt, over his shoulders and the back of his neck.

"We can't do this, Cora. We can't."

"Do you mean about you being colored? It doesn't matter to me, Jimmy. Honest it doesn't."

"No. Not that. It's because I love you. That's why I can't. That's why I want—"

He sat up straight then. His fingers pulled up some grass. He held it up to the light and looked at it. She had her head in his lap and lay there perfectly still. He could hear her breathing, and her breath was warm and moist on the back of his other hand where it lay on his leg. He threw the grass away, watched how the wind took it and lowered it down to the ground. He lifted her up by the [143] shoulders, gently, until they were close together, looking into each other's eyes.

"I want it to be right for us, Cora," he said. "Will you marry me?"

The sting of red in her cheeks looked as if a blow had left it there; even the moonlight showed that. She sat up without the support of his hands. Her arms were straight and tense under her. Her eyes met his, burning angrily at the softness in his eyes. "You damn dirty nigger!" she said, and jumped up and walked away from him as fast as she could.

When she was gone he lay on his face where he had been sitting. He lay full length. The grass he had pulled stuck to his lips. "People are just people." He said it aloud. "People are just people." And he laughed, hoarsely, hollowly. "People are just people." Then it was only a half-laugh with a sob cutting into it. And he was crying, with his arms flung up wildly above his head, with his face pushed into the grass trying to stop the sound of his crying. Off across the far grass Cora was running away from him. The moon, bright now, lacquered the whiteness of his hands lying helplessly above his head; it touched the blondness of his hair. [144]

RALPH ELLISON

Did You Ever Dream Lucky?

After the hurried good-bys the door had closed and they sat at the table with the tragic wreck of the Thanksgiving turkey before them, their heads turned regretfully toward the young folks' laughter in the hall. Then they could hear the elevator open and shut and the gay voices sinking swiftly beneath the floor and they were left facing one another in a room suddenly quiet with disappointment. Each of them, Mary, Mrs. Garfield, and Portwood, missed the young roomers, but in his disappointment Portwood had said something about young folks being green and now Mary was challenging him.

SOURCE: *New World Writing No. 5* (New York: The New American Library, Inc., 1954), pp. 134–145. Copyright 1954 by Ralph Ellison. Reprinted by permission of William Morris Agency, Inc., on behalf of Ralph Ellison.

"Green," she said, "shucks, you don't know nothing about green!"

"Just wait a minute now," Portwood said, pushing back from the table, "Who don't? Who you talking about?"

"I'm talking about you," Mary said. "Them chillun is gone off to the dance, so I *must* be talking 'bout you. And like I *shoulda* said, you don't even know green when you see it."

"Let me get on out of here," Portwood said, getting up. "Mrs. Garfield, she's just tuning up to lie. I can't understand why we live here with an ole lying woman like her anyway. And contentious with it too. Talking 'bout *I* don't know [134] nothing 'bout green. Why, I been meeting green folks right at the dam' station for over twenty-five years. . . ."

"Sit down, man. Just sit on back down," said Mary, placing her hand upon the heavy cut-glass decanter. "You got nowhere in this whole wide world to go—probably cause you make so much noise with your mouth . . ."

Mrs. Garfield smiled with gentle amusement. She'd been through it all before. A retired cook whose husband was dead, she had roomed with Mary almost as long as Portwood and knew that just as this was his way of provoking Mary into telling a story, it was Mary's way of introducing the story she would tell. She watched Mary cut her eyes from Portwood's frowning face to look through the window to where, far beyond the roofs of Harlem, mist-shrouded buildings pierced the sky. It was raining.

"It's gon' be cold out there on the streets this winter," Mary said. "I guess you know all about that."

"Don't be signifying at me," Portwood said. "You must aim to *lie* me into the streets. Well, I ain't even thinking about moving."

"You'll move," Mary said. "You'll be glad to move. And you still won't know nothing 'bout green."

"Then you tell us, Miss Mary," Mrs. Garfield said. "Don't pay Portwood any mind."

Portwood sat down, shaking his head hopelessly. "Now she's bound to lie. Mrs. Garfield, you done *guaranteed* she go' lie. And just look at her," he said, his voice rising indignantly, "sitting there looking like a lady preacher or something!"

"Portwood, I done tole you 'bout your way of talking," Mary began, but suddenly the stern façade of her face collapsed and they were all laughing.

"Hush, y'all," Mary said, her eyes gleaming. "Hush!"

"Don't try to laugh out of it," Portwood said, "I maintain these youngsters nowadays is green. They black and trying to git to heaven in a Cadillac. They think their education proves that we old southern folks is fools who don't know nothing 'bout life or loving or nothing 'bout living in the world. They green, I tell you! How we done come this far and lived this long if we didn't learn nothing 'bout life? Answer me that!"

"Now, Portwood," Mrs. Garfield said gently, "They're not that bad, the world just looks different to their eyes."

"Don't tell me, I see 'em when they get off the trains. Long as I been a Red Cap I've seen thousands of 'em, and dam' nigh every-one of 'em is green. And just cause these here is rooming with you, Moms, don't make 'em no different. Here you [135] done fixed this fine Thanksgiving dinner and they caint hardly finish it for rushing off somewhere. Too green to be polite. Don't even know there ain't no other ole fool woman like you renting rooms in Harlem who'll treat 'em like kinfolks. Don't tell me 'bout . . ."

"Shh," Mrs. Garfield said, as the sound of voices leaving the elevator came to them, "they might be coming back."

They listened. The voices grew gaily up the hall, then, blending with a remote peel of chimes, faded beyond a further wall. Mrs. Garfield sighed as they looked at one another guiltily.

"Shucks," Portwood said, "by now they just about beating the door down, trying to get into that dance. Like I was telling y'all . . ."

"Hush, Portwood!" Mary said. "What *green?*" She said, singing full-throatedly now, her voice suddenly folk-toned and deep with echoes of sermons and blue trombones, "Lawd, *I* was green. That's what I'm trying to tell you. Y'all hare me? *I, Me, Mary Raaaam-bo,* was green."

"You telling me?" Portwood laughed. "Is you telling *me?*" Nevertheless he leaned forward with Mrs. Garfield now, surrendering once more to Mary's once-upon-a-time antiphonal spell, waiting to respond to her stated theme: green.

"Here y'all," she said, beckoning for their glasses with one hand and lifting the decanter with the other. "Git some wine in y'all's stomachs so's it can warm y'alls' old-time blood."

They drank ceremoniously with lowered eyes, waiting for Mary's old contralto to resume its flight, its tragic-comic ascendence.

"Sho, I was green," she continued. "Green as anybody what ever left the farm and come to town. Shucks, here you criticizing those youngsters for rushing to the dance 'cause they hope to win that auto—that ain't nothing, not to what I done. Cause like them chillun and everybody else, I was after money. And I was full grown, too. Times was hard. My husband had done died and I couldn't get nothing but part-time work and didn't nobody have enough to eat. My daughter Lucy and me couldn't even afford a ten cents movies so we could go forget about it. So Lawd, this evening we're sitting in the window watching the doings down in the streets. Y'all know how it gits round here in the summertime, after it has been hot all day and has cooled off a bit: Folks out strolling or hanging on the stoops and hollering out the windows, chillun yelling and ripping and romping and begging for pennies to buy that there shaved ice with the red sirup poured over it. Dogs barking—y'all know how it is round here in the summertime. All that talk and noise and Negroes [136] laughing loud and juke boxes blaring and like-a-that. Well, it's 'bout that time on one of them kinda days, and one of them store-front churches is just beginning to jump. You can hear them clapping their hands and shouting and the tambourines is a-shaking and a-beating, and that ole levee camp trombone they has is going *Wah-wah, Wah-wah, Wah-wah-wah!* Y'all know, just like it really has something to do with the good Lawd's business—when all of a sudden two autos decides to see which is the toughest."

"A wreck?" Portwood said. "What the newspapers call a *collision?*"

"That's it," Mary said, sipping her wine, "one of the biggest smashups you ever seen. Here we is up in the window on the fourth floor and it's happening right down below us. Why, it's like two big bulls has done charged and run head-on. I tell you, Mrs. Garfield, it was something! Here they is," she said, shifting two knives upon the cloth, "one's coming thisa way, and the other's coming thata way, and when they gits right here, WHAM! They done come together and something flies out of there like a cannon ball. Then for a second it gets real quiet. It's like everybody done stopped to take a breath at the same time—all except those clapping hands and tambourines and that ole nasty-mouthed trombone (that fool was sounding like he done took over and started preaching the gospel by now). Then, Lawd," she said, rocking forward for emphasis, *"glass* is falling, *dust* is rising, *women* is screaming —Oh, such a commotion. Then all of a sudden all you can hear is Negroes' feet slapping the sidewalks . . ."

"Never mind them feet," Portwood said, "what was it that flew out of there?"

"I'm fixing to tell you now, fool. When the cars come togethe me and Lucy sees that thing bust outa there like a comet and fl off to one side somewhere. Lucy said, 'Mama, did you see what seen?' 'Come on, chile,' I says, 'Let's us get ourselfs on dow there!' And good people, that's when we started to move! Lawd, w flew down them stairs. I didn't even take time to pull off my apro or my house shoes. Just come a-jumping. Oh, it was a sight, I te you. Everybody and his brother standing round trying to see if any body was killed and measuring the skid marks and waiting for th ambulance to come—the man coulda died before that ambulanc got there————"

"Well, how about it, Moms, was anybody hurt?"

"Yes, they was, but I ain't your mama, an ole rusty Negro lik you! Sho' they was hurt. One man was all cut up and bleeding an the other knocked cold as a big deep freeze. They thought he wa dead. [137]

"But me and Lucy don't waste no time with none of that. W gets busy looking for what we seen shoot out of them cars. I whis pers, 'Chile, where did it hit?' And she points over near the curb And sho 'nough, when I starts slow-dragging my leg along the gut ter my foot hits against something heavy, and when I hears it clin together my heart almost flies out of my mouth . . ."

"My Lord, Miss Mary! What was it?" Mrs. Garfield said, he eyes intense. "You don't mean to tell me it was————"

Mary gave her a flat look. "I'm goin' to tell you," she said, tak ing a taste of wine. "I give y'all my word I'm gon' tell you— calls to Lucy, 'Gal, come over here a minute,' justa looking 'roun to see if anybody'd seen me. And she come and I whispers to her 'Now don't let on we found anything, just get on the other side o me and make like you trying to kick me on the foot. Go on, gal,' says, 'Don't argue with me—And watch out for my bunion!' An Lawd, she kicks that bag and this time I'm sho, 'cause I hear tha sweet metal-like sound. 'What you think it is' I says and she lean close to me, eyes done got round as silver dollars, says, 'Mother (always called me *mother* steada 'mama' when she was excited o trying to be proper or something) says, 'Mother, that's money! 'Shhh, fool,' I tole her, 'you don't have to tell *eve'y*body.'

" 'But, Mother, what are we going to do?'

" 'Just stand still a secon',' I says. 'Just quiet down. Don't move. Take it easy! Make out like you watching what they doing over yonder with those cars. Gimme time to figure this thing out . . .' "

She laughed. "Lawd, I was sweating by the gallon. Here I am standing in the street with my foot on a bag full of somebody's money! I don't know what to do. By now the police is all around and I don't know when whichever one of them men who was hurt is gonna rise up and start yelling for it. I tell you, I musta lost five pounds in five minutes, trying to figure out the deal."

"Miss Mary, I wish I could have seen you," Mrs. Garfield said.

"Well, I'm glad you didn't; I was having trouble enough. Oh it was agonizing. Everytime somebody walks toward us I almost faint. And Lucy, she's turning this-away and that-away, real fast, like she's trying to invent a new dance. 'Do something, Mother,' she says. 'Please hurry up and do something!' Till finally I caint stand it and just flops down on the curbstone and kicks the bag kinda up under my skirts. Lawd, today!" she sang, then halted to inspect Portwood, who, with [138] his head on his arms, laughed in silent glee. "What's the matter with you, fool?"

"Go on, tell the lie," Portwood said. "Don't mind poor me. You really had larceny in your heart that day."

"Well," Mary grinned, " 'bout this time old Miz Brazelton, a meddlesome ole lady who lived across the hall from me, she comes up talking 'bout, 'Why, Miss Mary, don't you know a woman of your standing in the community oughtn't to be sitting on the curb like some ole common nobody?' Like all Mary Rambo's got to do is worry 'bout what somebody might think about her—I looks and knows the only way to git rid of the fool is to bawl her out. 'Look here, Miz Brazelton,' I says, 'this here's my own ole rusty tub I'm sitting on and long as I can haul it 'round without your help I guess I can put it down wherever I please. . . .' "

"You a rough woman, Moms," Portwood said with deep resonance, his face a judicial frown. "Rough!"

"I done tole you 'bout calling me Moms!" Mary warned.

"Just tell the lie," Portwood said. "Then what happen?"

"I know that type," Mrs. Garfield said. "With them you do sometimes have to be radical."

"You know it too?" Mary said. "Radical sho is the word. You shoulda seen her face. I really didn't want to hurt that ole woman's feelings, but right then I had to git shed of the fool.

"Well, she leaves and I'm still sitting there fighting with myself over what I oughta do. Should I report what we'd found, or just take it on upstairs? Not that I meant to be dishonest, you know, but like everybody else in New York if something-for-nothing comes along, I wanted to be the one to git it. Besides, anybody fool enough to have that much money riding around with him in a car *deserves* to lose it."

"He sho dam' do," Portwood said. "He *dam'* sho do!"

"Well, all at once Lucy shakes me and here comes the ambulance, justa screaming.

" 'Mother, we better go,' Lucy says. And me I don't know *what* to do. By now the cops is pushing folks around and I knows soon as they see me they bound to find out what kinda egg this is I'm nesting on. Then all of a sudden it comes over me that I'm still wearing my apron! Lawd, I reaches down and touches that bag and my heart starts to going ninety miles a minute. It feels like a heapa money! And when I touches that thick cloth bag you can hear it clinking together. 'Lucy, chile,' I whispers, 'stand right in front of me while the ole lady rolls this heavy stuff up in her apron . . .' "

"Oh, Miss Mary," Mrs. Garfield said, shaking her head, "You'd given in to the devil." [139]

"I'm in his arms, girl, in his hairy arms! And Lucy in on the deal. She's hurrying me up and I picks up that bag and no sooner'n I do, here comes a cop!"

"Oh my Jesus, Miss Mary!" cried Mrs. Garfield.

"Woman," said Mary, "you don't know; you have no *idea*. He's one of these tough-looking young cops, too. One of them that thinks he has to beat you up just to prove he's in command of things. Here he comes, swinging up to Lucy like a red sledge hammer, telling folks to move along—Ain't seen *me*, cause I'm still sitting down. And when he comes up to Lucy I starts to moaning like I'm sick: 'Please, mister officer,' I says, kinda hiding my face, 'we just fixin' to leave.' Well, suh, his head shoots round Lucy like a turkey gobbler's and he sees me. Says, 'What's the matter, madam, wuz you in this wreck?'—and in a real nice voice too. Then Lucy—Lawd, that Lucy was smart; up to that time I didn't know my chile could lie. But Lucy looks the cop dead in the eye and says, 'Officer, we be going in a minute. My mother here is kinda nauchus from looking at all that blood.' "

"Oh, Miss Mary, she didn't say that!"

"She sho did, and it worked! Why the cop bends down and tries to help me to my feet and I says, 'Thank you, officer, just let me rest here a second and I be all right.' Well, suh, he leaves us and goes on off. But by now I got the bag in my apron and gets up moaning and groaning and starts out across the street, kinda bent over like, you know, with Lucy helping me along. Lawd, that bag feels like a thousand pounds. And everytime I takes a step it gets heavier. And on top of that, looks like we never going to cross the street, cause everybody in the block is stopping us to ask what's wrong: 'You sick Miss Mary?'; 'Lucy, what done happen to your mother?'; 'Do she want a doctor?'; 'Po' thing, she done got herself overexcited'—and all likea that. Shucks! I'm overexcited, all right, that bag's 'bout to give me a nervous breakdown!

"When we finally make it up to the apartment, I'm so beat that I just flops into a chair and sits there panting. Don't even take the bag outa my apron, and Lucy, she's having a fit. 'Open it up, Mother, let's see what's in it,' she says. But I figures we better wait, cause after all, they might miss the money and come searching for it. You see, after I done worked so hard gitting it up there, I had decided to keep it sho 'nough . . ."

"You had given in to the devil," Mrs. Garfield said.

"Who?" said Mary, reaching for the wine, "I'm way, *way* past the giving-in stage."

"This world is surely a trial," Mrs. Garfield mused. "It truly is." [140]

"And you can say that again," said Mary, "cause it's the agonizing truth."

"What did you do then, Miss Mary?"

"Pass me your glass, Portwood," Mary said, reaching for the decanter.

"Never mind the wine," said Portwood, covering his glass with his hand. "Get back to what *happened!*"

"Well, we goes to the bathroom—wait, don't say it!" she warned, giving Portwood a frown. "We goes to the bathroom and I gits up on a chair and drops that bag dead into the flush box."

"Now Miss Mary, really!"

"Girl, yes! I knowed wouldn't nobody think to look for it up there. It coulda been hid up in heaven somewhere. Sho! I dropped it in there, then I sent Lucy on back downstairs to see if anybody'd missed it. She musta hung 'round there for over an hour. Police and the newspaper people come and made pictures and asked a heapa questions and everything, but nothing 'bout the bag. Even after the wreckers come and dragged that pile of brand new junk away—still nothing 'bout the bag."

"Everything going in y'all's favor," Portwood said.

"Uhhuh, everything going our way."

"Y'all had it made, Moms," Portwood said, "Why you never tole this lie before?"

"The devil is truly powerful," Mrs. Garfield said, "Almost a
powerful as the Lord. Even so, it's strange nobody missed tho
much money!"

"Now that's what me and Lucy thought . . ."

Portwood struck the table, "What I want to know is how much
money was in the bag?"

"I'm coming to that in a second," Mary said.

"Yeah, but why you taking so long?"

"Who's telling this lie, Portwood, me or you?" said Mary.

"You was 'til you got off the track."

"Don't forget your manners, Portwood," Mrs. Garfield said.

"I'm not, but looks like to me y'all think money ought to be a
hard to get in a lie somebody's telling as it is to get carrying folks
bags."

"Or as 'tis to git you to hush your mouth," said Mary. "Any
way, we didn't count it right then. We was scaird. I knowed I wa
doing wrong, holding onto something wasn't really mine. But tha
wasn't stopping me."

"Y'all was playing a little finders-keepers," Portwood said, rest
ing back.

"Yeah, and concentrating on the keeping part."

"But why didn't you just *look* at the money, Miss Mary?"
[141]

"Cause we mighta been tempted to spend some of it, girl."

"Yeah, and y'all mighta give yourself away," Portwood said.

"Ain't it the truth! And that bag was powerful enough as i
was. It was really working on us. Me and Lucy just sitting 'round
like two ole hens on a nest, trying to guess how much is in it
Then we tries to figure whether it was dollars or fifty-centies. Fi
nally we decides that it caint be less'n five or ten dollar gold piece
to weigh so much."

"But how on earth could you resist looking at it?" Mrs. Garfield
said.

"Scaird, chile; scaird; We was like a couple kids who some
body's done give a present and tole 'em it would disappear if they
opened it before Christmas. And know something else, neither
one of us ever had to go to the bathroom so much as when us had
that bag up there in that flush box. I got to flushing it just to hear it
give out that fine clinking sound."

Portwood groaned, "I know you was gon' lie," he said. "I
knowed it."

"Hush, man, hush!" Mary laughed. "I know our neighbors

musta got sick and tired of hearing us flush that thing. But I tell you, everytime I pulled the chain it was like ringing up money in the cash register! I tell you, it was disintegrating! Whew! I'd go in there and stay a while and come out. Next thing I know there'd be Lucy going in. Then we got shamed and started slipping past one another. She'd try to keep hid from me, and me from her. I tell you, that stuff was working on us like a dose of salts! Why, after a few days I got so I couldn't work, just sat 'round thinking 'bout that doggone bag. And naturally, I done most of my thinking up there on the throne."

"Didn't I tell you she was tuning up to lie," Portwood laughed. "If she don't stop I'm dead gon' call the police."

"This here's the agonizing truth I'm telling y'all," said Mary.

"I wouldn't have been able to stand it, Miss Mary. I would have had to get it over with."

"They shoulda been looking for it by now," Portwood said, "all that money."

"That's what us thought," said Mary. "And we got to figuring why they didn't. First we figger maybe it was because the man who was hurt so bad had died. But then we seen in the papers that he got well . . ."

"Maybe they was gangsters," Portwood said.

"Yeah, we thought of that too; gangsters or bootleggers."

"Yeah, yeah, either one of them coulda been carrying all that money—or gamblers even."

"Sho they could. Me and Lucy figgered that maybe they [142] thought the cops had took the money or that they was trying to find it theyselves on the q.t., y'know."

"Miss Mary, you were either very brave or very reckless."

"Neither one, girl," Mary said, "just broke and hongry. And don't talk about brave, shucks, we was scaird to answer the doorbell at night. Let me tell you, we was doing some tall figuring. Finally I got so I couldn't eat and Lucy couldn't sleep. We was evil as a coupla lady bears at cubbing time."

"You just couldn't stand all that prosperity, huh, Moms?"

"It was a burden, all right. And everytime we pulled the chain it got a few dollars more so."

Mrs. Garfield smiled. "Mr. Garfield often said that the possession of great wealth brought with it the slings and arrows of outrageous responsibility."

"Mrs. Garfield," Mary mused, "you know you had you a right smart man in him? You really did. And looks like when you got stuff saved up like that you got the responsibility of keeping some of it circulating. Even without looking at it we got to figuring how to spend it. Lucy, she wants to go into business. Why she *almost* persuaded me to see about buying a building and opening a restaurant! And as if *that* wasn't enough trouble to git into, she decides, she's goin' take the third floor and open her a beauty shop. Oh, we had it all planned!" She shook her head.

"And y'all still ain't looked at it," Portwood said.

"Still ain't seen a thing."

"Dam!"

"You had marvelous self-control," Mrs. Garfield said.

"Yeah, I did," Mary said, "until that day Lucy went to the dentist. Seems I just couldn't hold out no longer. Seems like I got to thinking 'bout that bag and couldn't stop. I looked at the newspaper and all those ads. Reminded me of things I wanted to buy; looked out the window and saw autos; I tried to read the Bible and as luck would have it I opened it to where it says something 'bout 'Store ye up riches in heaven,' or 'Cast your bread upon the waters.' It really had me on a merry-go-round. I just had to take a peep! So I went and pulled down all the shades and started the water running in the tub like I was taking me a bath—turned on every faucet in the house—then I climbed up there with a pair of scissors and reached in and raised that bag up and just looked at it awhile.

"It had done got *cooold!* It come up *cooold*, with the water dripping off it like some old bucket been deep down in a well. Done turned green with canker, y'all! I just couldn't resist it no longer. I really couldn't, I took them scissors and snipped me a piece outa that bag and took me a good, *looong* [143] look. And let me tell you, dear people, after I looked I was so excited I had to get down from there and put myself to bed. My nerves just couldn't take it . . ."

"It surely must have been an experience, Miss Mary."

"Woman, you don't know. You really don't know. You hear me? *I had to go to bed!*"

"Heck, with that much money you could afford to go to bed," said Portwood.

"Wait, le'me tell you. I'm laying up there moaning and groaning when here come Lucy and she's in one of her talking moods. Soon as I seen her I knowed pretty soon she was going to want to talk 'bout that bag and I truly dreaded telling her that I'd done looked into it without her. I says, 'Baby, I don't feel so good. You talk to me later' . . . But y'all think that stopped her? Shucks, all she does is to go get me a bottle of cold beer she done brought me and start running her mouth again. And, just like I knowed she was gon' do, she finally got round to talking 'bout that bag. What ought we to buy *first,* she wants to know. Lawd, that pore chile, whenever she got her mind set on a thing! Well suh, I took me a big swoller of beer and just lay there like I was thinking awhile."

"You were really good companions," Mrs. Garfield said. "There is nothing like young people to make life rich and promising. Especially if they're your own children. If only Mr. Garfield and I . . ."

"Mrs. Garfield, let her finish this lie," Portwood said, *"then* we can talk about you and Mr. Garfield."

"Oh, of course," Mrs. Garfield said, "I'm sorry, Miss Mary, you know I didn't really mean to interrupt."

"Pay that pore fool no min'," Mary said. "I wish I had Lucy with me right this minit!"

"Is this lie about money or chillun," Portwood said. "Y'all here'bout to go serious. I want to know what you tole Lucy *then.* What did y'all start out to buy?"

"If you hadn't started monkeying with Mrs. Garfield you'da learned by now," Mary said. "Well, after I lay there and thought awhile I told her, 'Well, baby, if you want to know the truth 'bout what I think, *I* think we oughta buy us an auto.'

"Well suh, you coulda knocked her over with a feather. 'A car!' she says, 'why Mother, I didn't know you was interested in a car. We don't want to be like these ole ignorant Negroes who buy cars and don't have anything to go with it and no place to keep it,' she says. Says, 'I'm certainly surprised at you, Mother. I never would've dreamed you wanted a *car,* not the very first thing.'

"Oh, she was running off a mile a minute. And looking at [144] me like she done caught me kissing the preacher or the iceman or somebody! 'We want to be practical,' she says, 'We don't want to throw our money away . . .'

"Well, it almost killed me. 'Lucy, honey,' I says, 'that's just what your mama's trying to do, be practical. That's why I say let's git us an auto.'

" 'But, Mama,' she says, 'a car isn't practical at all.'

" 'Oh yes it is,' I says, 'Cause how else we gon' use two sets of auto chains?'—

"And do y'all know," said Mary, sitting up suddenly and balancing the tips of her fingers on her knees, her face a mask of incredulity, "I had to hop outa bed and catch that chile before she swayed dead away in a faint!"

"Yeah," Portwood laughed, falling back in his chair, "and you better hop up from there and catch me."

Mrs. Garfield's voice rose up girlishly, "Oh Miss Mary," she laughed, "you're just fooling."

Mary's bosom heaved, "I wish I was, girl," she said, "I sho wish I was."

"How 'bout that? Tire chains," Portwood said. "All that larceny for some dam' tire chain!"

"Fool," said Mary, "didn't I tell you you didn't know nothing 'bout green? There *I* was thinking I done found me a bird nest on the ground. C'mon now," she said chuckling at the gullibility of all mankind, "let's us finish the wine."

Portwood winked at Mrs. Garfield. "Hey, Moms, tell us something . . ."

"I ain't go' tell you again that I ain't yo' mama," said Mary.

"I just want you to tell us one last thing . . ."

Mary looked at him warily, "What is it? I got no more time for your foolishness now, I got to git up from here and fix for them chillun."

"Never mind them youngsters," said Portwood, "just tell us if you ever dreamed lucky?"

Mary grinned, "Ain't I just done tole you?" she said. "Sho I did, but I woke up cold in hand. Just the same though," she added thoughtfully, "I still hope them youngsters win that there auto."

"Yes," Mrs. Garfield said, "And wouldn't it be a comfort, Miss Mary? Just to know that they *can* win one, I mean . . . ?"

Mary said that it certainly would be. [145]

JOHN HENRIK CLARKE

The Boy Who Painted Christ Black

He was the smartest boy in the Muskogee County School—for colored children. Everybody even remotely connected with the

SOURCE: *Opportunity Magazine,* XVIII, 9 (1940), 264–266. Copyright 1940 by John Henrik Clarke. Reprinted by permission of the author.

school knew this. The teacher always pronounced his name with profound gusto as she pointed him out as the ideal student. Once I heard her say: "If he were white he might, some day, become President." Only Aaron Crawford wasn't white; quite the contrary. His skin was so solid black that it glowed, reflecting an inner virtue that was strange, and beyond my comprehension.

In many ways he looked like something that was awkwardly put together. Both his nose and his lips seemed a trifle too large for his face. To say he was ugly would be unjust and to say he was handsome would be gross exaggeration. Truthfully, I could never make up my mind about him. Sometimes he looked like something out of a book of ancient history . . . looked as if he was left over from that magnificent era before the machine age came and marred the earth's natural beauty.

His great variety of talent often startled the teachers. This caused his classmates to look upon him with a mixed feeling of awe and envy.

Before Thanksgiving, he always drew turkeys and pumpkins on the blackboard. On George Washington's birthday, he drew large American flags surrounded by little hatchets. It was these small masterpieces that made him the most talked-about colored boy in Columbus, Georgia. The Negro principal of the Muskogee County School said he would some day be a great painter, like Henry O. Tanner.

For the teacher's birthday, which fell on a day about a week before commencement, Aaron Crawford painted the picture that caused an uproar, and a turning point, at the Muskogee County School. The moment he entered the room that morning, all eyes fell on him. Besides his torn book holder, he was carrying a large-framed concern wrapped in old newspapers. As he went to his seat, the teacher's eyes followed his every motion, a curious wonderment mirrored in them conflicting with the half-smile that wreathed her face.

Aaron put his books down, then smiling broadly, advanced toward the teacher's desk. His alert eyes were so bright with joy that they were almost frightening. The children were leaning forward in their seats, staring greedily at him; a restless anticipation was rampant within every breast.

Already the teacher sensed that Aaron had a present for her. Still smiling, he placed it on her desk and began to help her unwrap it. As the last piece of paper fell from the large frame, the teacher jerked her hand away from it suddenly, her eyes flickering unbelievingly. Amidst the rigid tension, her heavy breathing was distinct and frightening. Temporarily, there was no other sound in the room.

Aaron stared questioningly at her and she moved her hand back to the present cautiously, as if it were a living thing with vicious characteristics. I am sure it was the one thing she least expected.

With a quick, involuntary movement I rose up from my desk. A series of submerged murmurs spread through the room, rising to a distinct monotone. The teacher turned toward the children, staring reproachfully. They did not move their eyes from the present that Aaron had brought her. . . . It was a large picture of Christ—painted black!

Aaron Crawford went back to his seat, a feeling of triumph reflecting in his every movement.

The teacher faced us. Her curious half-smile had blurred into a mild bewilderment. She searched the bright faces before her and started to smile again, occasionally stealing quick glances at the large picture propped on her desk, as though doing so were forbidden amusement.

"Aaron," she spoke at last, a slight tinge of uncertainty in her tone, "this is a most welcome present. Thanks. I will treasure it." She paused, then went on speaking, a trifle more coherent than before. "Looks like you are going [264] to be quite an artist. . . . Suppose you come forward and tell the class how you came to paint this remarkable picture."

When he rose to speak, to explain about the picture, a hush fell tightly over the room, and the children gave him all of their attention . . . something they rarely did for the teacher. He did not speak at first; he just stood there in front of the room, toying absently with his hands, observing his audience carefully, like a great concert artist.

"It was like this," he said, placing full emphasis on every word. "You see, my uncle who lives in New York teaches classes in Negro History at the Y.M.C.A. When he visited us last year he was telling me about the many great black folks who have made history. He said black folks were once the most powerful people on earth. When I asked him about Christ, he said no one ever proved whether he was black or white. Somehow a feeling came over me that he was a black man, 'cause he was so kind and forgiving, kinder than I have ever seen white people be. So, when I painted this picture I couldn't help but paint it as I thought it was."

After this, the little artist sat down, smiling broadly, as if he had gained entrance to a great storehouse of knowledge that ordinary people could neither acquire nor comprehend.

The teacher, knowing nothing else to do under prevailing circumstances, invited the children to rise from their seats and come forward so they could get a complete view of Aaron's unique piece of art.

When I came close to the picture, I noticed it was painted with the kind of paint you get in the five and ten cent stores. Its shape was blurred slightly, as if someone had jarred the frame before the paint had time to dry. The eyes of Christ were deep-set and sad, very much like those of Aaron's father, who was a deacon in the local Baptist Church. This picture of Christ looked much different from the one I saw hanging on the wall when I was in Sunday School. It looked more like a helpless Negro, pleading silently for mercy.

For the next few days, there was much talk about Aaron's picture.

The school term ended the following week and Aaron's picture, along with the best handwork done by the students that year, was on display in the assembly room. Naturally, Aaron's picture graced the place of honor.

There was no book work to be done on commencement day and joy was rampant among the children. The girls in their brightly colored dresses gave the school the delightful air of Spring awakening.

In the middle of the day all the children were gathered in the small assembly. On this day we were always favored with a visit from a man whom all the teachers spoke of with mixed esteem and fear. Professor Danual, they called him, and they always pronounced his name with reverence. He was supervisor of all the city schools, including those small and poorly equipped ones set aside for colored children.

The great man arrived almost at the end of our commencement exercises. On seeing him enter the hall, the children rose, bowed courteously, and sat down again, their eyes examining him as if he were a circus freak.

He was a tall white man with solid gray hair that made his lean face seem paler than it actually was. His eyes were the clearest blue I have ever seen. They were the only life-like things about him.

As he made his way to the front of the room the Negro principal, George Du Vaul, was walking ahead of him, cautiously preventing anything from getting in his way. As he passed me, I heard the teachers, frightened, sucking in their breath, felt the tension tightening.

A large chair was in the center of the rostrum. It had been daintily polished and the janitor had laboriously recushioned its bottom. The supervisor went straight to it without being guided, knowing that this pretty splendor was reserved for him.

Presently the Negro principal introduced the distinguished guest and he favored us with a short speech. It wasn't a very important speech. Almost at the end of it, I remember him saying something about he wouldn't be surprised if one of us boys grew up to be a great colored man, like Booker T. Washington.

After he sat down, the school chorus sang two spirituals and the girls in the fourth grade did an Indian folk dance. This brought the commencement program to an end.

After this the supervisor came down from the rostrum, his eyes tinged with curiosity, and began to view the array of handwork on display in front of the chapel.

Suddenly his face underwent a strange rejuvenation. His clear blue eyes flickered in astonishment. He was looking at Aaron Crawford's picture of Christ. Mechanically he moved his stooped form closer to the picture and stood gazing fixedly at it, curious and undecided, as though it were a dangerous animal that would rise any moment and spread destruction.

We waited tensely for his next movement. [265] The silence was almost suffocating. At last he twisted himself around and began to search the grim faces before him. The fiery glitter of his eyes abated slightly as they rested on the Negro principal, protestingly.

"Who painted this sacrilegious nonsense?" he demanded sharply.

"I painted it, sir." These were Aaron's words, spoken hesitantly. He wetted his limps timidly and looked up at the supervisor, his eyes voicing a sad plea for understanding.

He spoke again, this time more coherently. "Th' principal said a colored person have jes as much right paintin' Jesus black as a white person have paintin' him white. And he says. . . ." At this point he halted abruptly, as if to search for his next words. A strong tinge of bewilderment dimmed the glow of his solid black face. He stammered out a few more words, then stopped again.

The supervisor strode a few steps toward him. At last color had swelled some of the lifelessness out of his lean face.

"Well, go on!" he said, enragedly, ". . . I'm still listening."

Aaron moved his lips pathetically but no words passed them. His eyes wandered around the room, resting finally, with an air of hope, on the face of the Negro principal. After a moment, he jerked his face in another direction, regretfully, as if something he had said had betrayed an understanding between him and the principal.

Presently the principal stepped forward to defend the school's prize student.

"I encouraged the boy in painting that picture," he said firmly. "And it was with my permission that he brought the picture into this school. I don't think the boy is so far wrong in painting Christ black. The artists of all other races have painted whatsoever God they worship to resemble themselves. I see no reason why we should be immune from that privilege. After all, Christ was born in that part of the world that had always been predominantly populated by colored people. There is a strong possibility that he could have been a Negro."

But for the monotonous lull of heavy breathing, I would have sworn that his words had frozen everyone in the hall. I had never heard the little principal speak so boldly to anyone, black or white.

The supervisor swallowed dumfoundedly. His face was aglow in silent rage.

"Have you been teaching these children things like that?" he asked the Negro principal, sternly.

"I have been teaching them that their race has produced great kings and queens as well as slaves and serfs," the principal said. "The time is long overdue when we should let the world know that we erected and enjoyed the benefits of a splendid civilization long before the people of Europe had a written language."

The supervisor coughed. His eyes bulged menacingly as he spoke. "You are not being paid to teach such things in this school, and I am demanding your resignation for overstepping your limit as principal."

George Du Vaul did not speak. A strong quiver swept over his sullen face. He revolved himself slowly and walked out of the room towards his office.

The supervisor's eyes followed him until he was out of focus. Then he murmured under his breath: "There'll be a lot of fuss in this world if you start people thinking that Christ was a nigger."

Some of the teachers followed the principal out of the chapel, leaving the crestfallen children restless and in a quandary about what to do next. Finally we started back to our rooms. The supervisor was behind me. I heard him murmur to himself: "Damn, if niggers ain't getting smarter."

A few days later I heard that the principal had accepted a summer job as art instructor of a small high school somewhere in south Georgia and had gotten permission from Aaron's parents to take him along so he could continue to encourage him in his painting.

I was on my way home when I saw him leaving his office. He was carrying a large briefcase and some books tucked under his arm. He had already said good-by to all the teachers. And strangely, he did not look brokenhearted. As he headed for the large front door, he readjusted his horn-rimmed glasses, but did not look back. An air of triumph gave more dignity to his soldierly stride. He had the appearance of a man who has done a great thing, something greater than any ordinary man would do.

Aaron Crawford was waiting outside for him. They walked down the street together. He put his arm around Aaron's shoulder affectionately. He was talking sincerely to Aaron about something, and Aaron was listening, deeply earnest.

I watched them until they were so far down the street that their forms had begun to blur. Even from this distance I could see they were still walking in brisk, dignified strides, like two people who had won some sort of victory. [266]

FRANK YERBY

Health Card

Johnny stood under one of the street lights on the corner and tried to read the letter. The street lights down in the Bottom were so

SOURCE: Langston Hughes, ed., *The Best Short Stories by Negro Writers* (Boston: Little, Brown and Company, 1967), pp. 192–201. Copyright 1944 by Frank Yerby. Reprinted by permission of William Morris Agency, Inc.

dim that he couldn't make out half the words, but he didn't need to: he knew them all by heart anyway.

"Sugar," he read, "it took a long time but I done it. I got the money to come to see you. I waited and waited for them to give you a furlough, but it look like they don't mean to. Sugar, I can't wait no longer. I got to see you. I got to. Find a nice place for me to stay—where we can be happy together. You know what I mean. With all my love, Lily."

Johnny folded the letter up and put it back in his pocket. Then he walked swiftly down the street past all the juke joints with the music blaring out and the G.I. brogans pounding. He turned down a side street, scuffing up a cloud of dust as he did so. None of the streets down in Black Bottom were paved, and there were four inches of fine white powder over everything. When it rained the mud would come up over the tops of his army shoes, but it hadn't rained in nearly three months. There were no juke joints on this street, and the Negro shanties were neatly whitewashed. Johnny kept on walking until he came to the end of the street. On the corner stood the little whitewashed Baptist Church, and next to it was the neat, well-kept home of the pastor.

Johnny went up on the porch and hesitated. He thrust his hand in his pocket and the paper crinkled. He took his hand out and knocked on the door.

"Who's that?" a voice called.

"It's me," Johnny answered; "it's a sodjer."

The door opened a crack and a woman peered out. She was [192] middle-aged and fat. Looking down, Johnny could see that her feet were bare.

"Whatcha want, sodjer?"

Johnny took off his cap.

"Please, ma'am, lemme come in. I kin explain it t' yuh better settin' down."

She studied his face for a minute in the darkness.

"Aw right," she said; "you kin come in, son."

Johnny entered the room stiffly and sat down on a cornshuck-bottomed chair.

"It's this way, ma'am," he said. "I got a wife up Nawth. I been tryin' an' tryin' t' git a furlough so I could go t' see huh. But they always put me off. So now she done worked an' saved enuff money t' come an' see me. I wants t' ax you t' rent me a room, ma'am, I doan' know nowheres t' ax."

"This ain't no hotel, son."

"I know it ain't. I cain't take Lily t' no hotel, not lak hotels in this heah town."

"Lily yo wife?"

"Yes'm. She my sho' nuff, honest t' Gawd wife. Married in th' Baptist Church in Deetroit."

The fat woman sat back, and her thick lips widened into a smile.

"She a good girl, ain't she? An' you doan' wanta take her t' one o' these heah ho'houses they call hotels."

"That's it, ma'am."

"Sho' you kin bring huh heah, son. Be glad t' have huh. Reveren' be glad t' have huh too. What yo' name, son?"

"Johnny. Johnny Green. Ma'am—"

"Yas, son?"

"You understands that I wants t' come heah too?"

The fat woman rocked back in her chair and gurgled with laughter.

"Bless yo' heart, chile, I ain't always been a ole woman! And I ain't always been th' preacher's wife neither!"

"Thank you, ma'am. I gotta go now. Time fur me t' be gettin' back t' camp."

"When you bring Lily?"

"Be Monday night, ma'am. Pays you now if you wants it." [193]

"Monday be aw right. Talk it over with th' Reveren', so he make it light fur yuh. Know sodjer boys ain't got much money."

"No, ma'am, sho' Lawd ain't. G'night, ma'am."

When he turned back into the main street of the Negro section the doors of the joints were all open and the soldiers were coming out. The girls were clinging onto their arms all the way to the bus stop. Johnny looked at the dresses that stopped halfway between the pelvis and the knee and hugged the backside so that every muscle showed when they walked. He saw the purple lipstick smeared across the wide full lips, and the short hair stiffened with smelly grease so that it covered their heads like a black lacquered cap. They went on down to the bus stop arm in arm, their knotty bare calves bunching with each step as they walked. Johnny thought about Lily. He walked past them very fast without turning his head.

But just as he reached the bus stop he heard the whistles. When he turned around he saw the four M.P.s and the civilian policemen stopping the crowd. He turned around again and walked back until he was standing just behind the white men.

"Aw right," the M.P.s were saying, "you gals git your health cards out."

Some of the girls started digging in their handbags. Johnny could see them dragging out small yellow cardboard squares. But the others just stood there with blank expressions on their faces. The soldiers started muttering, a dark, deep-throated sound. The M.P.s started pushing their way through the crowd, looking at each girl's card as they passed. When they came to a girl who didn't have a card they called out to the civilian policemen:

"Aw right, mister, take A'nt Jemima for a little ride."

Then the city policemen would lead the girl away and put her in the Black Maria.

They kept this up until they had examined every girl except one. She hung back beside her soldier, and the first time the M.P.s didn't see her. When they came back through, one of them caught her by the arm.

"Lemme see your card, Mandy," he said.

The girl looked at him, her little eyes narrowing into slits in her black face. [194]

"Tek yo' hands offen me, white man," she said.

The M.P.'s face crimsoned, so that Johnny could see it, even in the darkness.

"Listen, black girl," he said, "I told you to lemme see your card."

"An' I tole you t' tek yo' han' offen me, white man!"

"Gawddammit, you little black bitch, you better do like I tell you!"

Johnny didn't see very clearly what happened after that. There was a sudden explosion of motion, and then the M.P. was trying to jerk his hand back, but he couldn't, for the little old black girl had it between her teeth and was biting it to the bone. He drew his other hand back and slapped her across the face so hard that it sounded like a pistol shot. She went over backwards and her tight skirt split, so that when she got up Johnny could see that she didn't have anything on under it. She came forward like a cat, her nails bared, straight for the M.P.'s eyes. He slapped her down again, but the soldiers surged forward all at once. The M.P.s fell back and drew their guns and one of them blew a whistle.

Johnny, who was behind them, decided it was time for him to

get out of there and he did; but not before he saw the squads of white M.P.s hurling around the corner and going to work on the Negroes with their clubs. He reached the bus stop and swung on board. The minute after he had pushed his way to the back behind all the white soldiers he heard the shots. The bus driver put the bus in gear and they roared off toward the camp.

It was after one o'clock when all the soldiers straggled in. Those of them who could still walk. Eight of them came in on the meat wagon, three with gunshot wounds. The colonel declared the town out of bounds for all Negro soldiers for a month.

"Dammit," Johnny said, "I gotta go meet Lily, I gotta. I cain't stay heah. I cain't!"

"Whatcha gonna do," Little Willie asked, "go A.W.O.L.?"

Johnny looked at him, his brow furrowed into a frown.

"Naw," he said, "I'm gonna go see th' colonel!"

"Whut! Man, you crazy! Colonel kick yo' black ass out fo' you gits yo' mouf open."

"I take a chanct on that." [195]

He walked over to the little half mirror on the wall of the barracks. Carefully he readjusted his cap. He pulled his tie out of his shirt front and drew the knot tighter around his throat. Then he tucked the ends back in at just the right fraction of an inch between the correct pair of buttons. He bent down and dusted his shoes again, although they were already spotless.

"Man," Little Willie said, "you sho' is a fool!"

"Reckon I am," Johnny said; then he went out of the door and down the short wooden steps.

When he got to the road that divided the colored and white sections of the camp his steps faltered. He stood still a minute, drew in a deep breath, and marched very stiffly and erect across the road. The white soldiers gazed at him curiously, but none of them said anything. If a black soldier came over into their section it was because somebody sent him, so they let him alone.

In front of the colonel's headquarters he stopped. He knew what he had to say, but his breath was very short in his throat and he was going to have a hard time saying it.

"Whatcha want, soldier?" the sentry demanded.

"I wants t' see th' colonel."

"Who sent you?"

"I ain't at liberty t' say," he declared, his breath coming out very fast behind the words.

"You ain't at liberty t' say," the sentry mimicked. "Well I'll be damned! If you ain't at liberty t' say, then I ain't at liberty t' let you see the colonel! Git tha hell outa here, nigger, before I pump some lead in you!"

Johnny didn't move.

The sentry started toward him, lifting his rifle butt, but another soldier, a sergeant, came around the corner of the building.

"Hold on there," he called. "What tha hell is th' trouble here?"

"This here nigger says he want t' see tha colonel an' when I ast him who sent him he says he ain't at liberty t' say!"

The sergeant turned to Johnny.

Johnny came to attention and saluted him. You aren't supposed to salute N.C.O.s, but sometimes it helps.

"What you got t' say fur yourself, boy?" the sergeant said, not unkindly. Johnny's breath evened. [196]

"I got uh message fur th' colonel, suh," he said; "I ain't s'posed t' give it t' nobody else but him. I ain't even s'posed t' tell who sont it, suh."

The sergeant peered at him sharply.

"You tellin' tha truth, boy?"

"Yassuh!"

"Aw right. Wait here a minute."

He went into H.Q. After a couple of minutes he came back.

"Aw right, soldier, you kin go on in."

Johnny mounted the steps and went into the colonel's office. The colonel was a lean, white-haired soldier with a face tanned to the color of saddle leather. He was reading a letter through a pair of horn-rimmed glasses which had only one earhook left, so that he had to hold them up to his eyes with one hand. He put them down and looked up. Johnny saw that his eyes were pale blue, so pale that he felt as if he were looking into the eyes of an eagle or some other fierce bird of prey.

"Well?" he said, and Johnny stiffened into a salute. The colonel half smiled.

"At ease, soldier," he said. Then: "The sergeant tells me that you have a very important message for me."

Johnny gulped in the air.

"Beggin' th' sergeant's pardon, suh," he said, "but that ain't so."

"What!"

"Yassuh," Johnny rushed on, "nobody sent me. I come on m'

Frank Yerby

own hook. I had t' talk t' yuh, Colonel, suh! You kin sen' me t' th'
guardhouse afterwards, but please, suh, lissen t' me fur jes' a minute!"

The colonel relaxed slowly. Something very like a smile was
playing around the corners of his mouth. He looked at his watch.

"All right, soldier," he said. "You've got five minutes."

"Thank yuh, thank yuh, suh!"

"Speak your piece, soldier; you're wasting time!"

"It's about Lily, suh. She my wife. She done worked an' slaved
fur nigh onto six months t' git the money t' come an' see me. An'
now you give th' order that none of th' cullud boys kin go t' town.
Beggin' yo' pahdon, suh, I wasn't in none of that trouble. I ain't
neber been in no trouble. You kin ax my cap'n, if you wants to.
All [197] I wants is permission to go into town fur one week, an'
I'll stay outa town fur two months if yuh wants me to."

The colonel picked up the phone.

"Ring Captain Walters for me," he said. Then: "What's your
name, soldier?"

"It's Green, suh. Private Johnny Green."

"Captain Walters? This is Colonel Milton. Do you have anything in your files concerning Private Johnny Green? Oh yes, go
ahead. Take all the time you need."

The colonel lit a long black cigar. Johnny waited. The clock on
the wall spun its electric arms.

"What's that? Yes. Yes, yes, I see. Thank you, Captain."

He put down the phone and picked up a fountain pen. He wrote
swiftly. Finally he straightened up and gave Johnny the slip of
paper.

Johnny read it. It said: "Private Johnny Green is given express
permission to go into town every evening of the week beginning
August seventh and ending August fourteenth. He is further permitted to remain in town overnight every night during said week,
so long as he returns to camp for reveille the following morning.
By order of the commanding officer, Colonel H. H. Milton."

There was a hard knot at the base of Johnny's throat. He
couldn't breathe. But he snapped to attention and saluted smartly.

"Thank yuh, suh," he said at last. Then: "Gawd bless you,
suh!"

"Forget it, soldier. I was a young married man once myself. My
compliments to Captain Walters."

Johnny saluted again and about-faced, then he marched out of
the office and down the stairs. On the way back he saluted

everybody—privates, N.C.O.s, and civilian visitors, his white teeth gleaming in a huge smile.

"That's sure one happy darky," one of the white soldiers said.

Johnny stood in the station and watched the train running in. The yellow lights from the windows flickered on and off across his face as the alternating squares of light and darkness flashed past. Then it was slowing and Johnny was running beside it, trying to keep abreast of the Jim Crow coach. He could see her standing up, [198] holding her bags. She came down the steps the first one and they stood there holding each other, Johnny's arms crushing all the breath out of her, holding her so hard against him that his brass buttons hurt through her thin dress. She opened her mouth to speak but he kissed her, bending her head backward on her neck until her little hat fell off. It lay there on the ground, unnoticed.

"Sugah," she said, "sugah. It was awful."

"I know," he said. "I know."

Then he took her bags and they started walking out of the station toward the Negro section of town.

"I missed yuh so much," Johnny said, "I thought I lose m' mind."

"Me too," she said. Then: "I brought th' marriage license with me like yuh tole me. I doan' wan th' preacher's wife t' think we bad."

"Enybody kin look at yuh an' see yuh uh angel!"

They went very quietly through all the dark streets and the white soldiers turned to look at Johnny and his girl.

Lak a queen, Johnny thought, lak a queen. He looked at the girl beside him, seeing the velvety nightshade skin, the glossy black lacquered curls, the sweet, wide hips and the long, clean legs striding beside him in the darkness. I am black, but comely, O ye daughters of Jerusalem!

They turned into the Bottom where the street lights were dim blobs on the pine poles and the dust rose up in little swirls around their feet. Johnny had his head half turned so that he didn't see the two M.P.s until he had almost bumped into them. He dropped one bag and caught Lily by the arm. Then he drew her aside quickly and the two men went by them without speaking.

They kept on walking, but every two steps Johnny would jerk his head around and look nervously back over his shoulder. The last time he looked the two M.P.s had stopped and were looking back at them. Johnny turned out the elbow of the arm next to Lily so that it hooked into hers a little and began to walk faster, pushing her along with him.

"What's yo' hurry, sugah?" she said. "I be heah a whole week!"

But Johnny was looking over his shoulder at the two M.P.s. They were coming toward them now, walking with long, slow strides, their reddish-white faces set. Johnny started to push Lily along faster, but she shook off his arm and stopped still. [199]

"I do declare, Johnny Green! You th' beatines' man! Whut you walk me so fas' fur?"

Johnny opened his mouth to answer her, but the military police were just behind them now, and the sergeant reached out and laid his hand on her arm.

"C'mon, gal," he said, "lemme see it."

"Let you see whut? Whut he mean, Johnny?"

"Your card," the sergeant growled. "Lemme see your card."

"My card?" Lily said blankly. "Whut kinda card, mister?"

Johnny put the bags down. He was fighting for breath.

"Look heah, Sarge," he said; "this girl my wife!"

"Oh yeah? I said lemme see your card, sister!"

"I ain't got no card, mister. I dunno whut you talkin' about."

"Look, Sarge," the other M.P. said, "th' soldier's got bags. Maybe she's just come t' town."

"These your bags, gal?"

"Yessir."

"Aw right. You got twenty-four hours to git yourself a health card. If you don't have it by then we hafta run you in. Git goin' now."

"Listen," Johnny shouted; "this girl my wife! She ain't no ho'! I tell you she ain't—"

"What you say, nigger—" the M.P. sergeant growled. "Whatcha say?" He started toward Johnny.

Lily swung on Johnny's arm.

"C'mon, Johnny," she said; "they got guns. C'mon, Johnny, please! Please, Johnny!"

Slowly she drew him away.

"Aw, leave 'em be, Sarge," the M.P. corporal said; "maybe she is his wife."

The sergeant spat. The brown tobacco juice splashed in the dirt not an inch from Lily's foot. Then the two of them turned and started away.

Johnny stopped.

"Lemme go, Lily," he said, "lemme go!" He tore her arm loose from his and started back up the street. Lily leaped, her two arms fastening themselves around his neck. He fought silently but she clung to him, doubling her knees so that all her weight was hanging from his neck. [200]

"No, Johnny! Oh Jesus no! You be kilt! Oh, Johnny, listen t' me, sugah! You's all I got!"

He put both hands up to break her grip but she swung her weight sidewise and the two of them went down in the dirt. The M.P.s turned the corner out of sight.

Johnny sat there in the dust staring at her. The dirt had ruined her dress. He sat there a long time looking at her until the hot tears rose up back of his eyelids faster than he could blink them away, so he put his face down in her lap and cried.

"I ain't no man!" he said. "I ain't no man!"

"Hush, sugah," she said. "You's a man aw right. You's my man!"

Gently she drew him to his feet. He picked up the bags and the two of them went down the dark street toward the preacher's house. [201]

JOHN OLIVER KILLENS

The Stick Up

I felt good. I think the park had something to do with it. Trees, grass, bushes—everything in brand-new togs of shining green. The warm yellow sunlight sifting down through the trees, making my face feel alive and healthy and casting shadows on the paved walks and the unpaved walks and the wooden benches. Slight breezes tickling my nostrils, caressing my face, bringing with them a good clean odor of things new and live and dripping with greenness. Such a good feeling made me uneasy.

SOURCE: Langston Hughes, ed., *The Best Short Stories by Negro Writers* (Boston: Little, Brown and Company, 1967), pp. 188–191. Copyright © 1967 by John Oliver Killens. Reprinted by permission of Ashley Famous Agency, Inc.

The park breathing with people, old and young. Playing checkers and chess, listening to portable radios—the Dodgers leading the Giants. I walked to the end of the park and stood near the wading pool where the water spurted skyward.

Little children in their underpants, splashing the water and pretending to swim, and throwing water at each other and yelling and shouting in wild childish happiness. One Negro child with a soft dark face and big brown eyes pretended to enjoy herself, but her big black eyes gave her away—anxious and uneasy. As if she were not sure that all of a sudden the other children would not turn on her and bite her like a bunch of mad dogs. I knew that feeling—even now. Barefoot women sat around the pool watching the children, reading books, trying to get brown without the expense of a Florida vacation. A little blonde-headed girl got smacked in the face and ran bawling to her black-haired mother. A double-decker Fifth Avenue bus passed to the east, with curious passengers looking from the top deck. The tall buildings of New York University looked over and down upon a noisy humanity playing in the park. *Perstando Et Praestando Utilitati*—

The kids were having loads of fun and it made me think back. I [188] substituted a country woods for the beautiful city park. I made believe the wading pool was the swimming hole on old man Gibson's forbidden grounds. And something turned over and over in my stomach and ran like a chill through the length of my body, leaving a funny taste in my mouth. I took a sudden trip into the past. Meeting kids I had known many years ago, as if they had remained kids and had never grown up. My face tight and full now as I swallowed a mouthful of cool green air. It was the first time I had been homesick in many years. Standing there trying to recall names, faces and incidents. After a moment I shrugged it off. I could never really be homesick for the country woods and the swimming holes of Georgia. Give me the city—the up-north city.

I turned and started walking back through the park, passing women, young and old, blond and brunette, and black and brown and light brown in white uniforms, pushing various types of baby carriages. I had almost reached the other end of the park, when a big lumbering giant of a white man came toward me. I tried to walk out of his way, but he maneuvered into my path and grabbed me by the shoulders. He was unshaven, his clothes were filthy and he reeked of rot-gut whiskey and days and nights without soap and water. He towered over me and coughed in my face and said in a deep rasping voice—"This is a stick up!"

I must have looked silly and startled. What was he up to, in broad open daylight? Oh—no—he must be kidding. And yet, crazier things happen every day in this crazy world of New York City. Especially in the Village.

He jabbed his big forefinger into my side, causing me to wince. Then he nudged me playfully and said, "I'm only kidding, buddy. But cheesuz christmas, I do need just four more cents for the price of a drink. How about it, professor? It's just four lousy cents. Didn't hardly take me no time at all to hustle up the rest of it this morning, but seems to me I just can't get this last four cents don't care how hard I try. It's a goddamn shame!"

I made a show of feeling in my pockets. I had no loose change and knew it. I wanted to say, Well, you sure won't get it from me, but I said instead, "Gosh, I don't have it. I'm sorry."

I started to walk away from him. He put his big arms around me, surrounding me with his foul odor. His shirt was dirty and [189] greasy, smelled like sour food and whiskey vomit. A deep gash started near his right eye and beat a trail down into his mouth. An awful cloud came between me and the springtime, blotting out the breeze, the sunshine, the freshness that had been everywhere.

"Look, buddy, I ain't no ordinary bum you meet on the street. I want you to know that. I'm just down on my luck—see?"

I wanted to shrug my shoulders, wanted to say, I don't give a damn what you are! Through the years I had built up a resistance against people like him, and I thought I was foolproof. He rambled on, "I know—you—you think I'm just one of them everyday bums, but it isn't so. I'm just as educated as the next feller. But I know what you think though. I—"

My nostrils quivered, my neck gathered sweat. I wanted to be away from him. "You don't know what I think!"

He leaned heavily on my shoulder. My body sagged under his enormous weight. My knees buckled. "You don't have to be that way, mate. Just because a feller is down on his luck. Can't never tell when you'll need a favor yourself. Listen, I'm an educated man. Look, I used to be a business man too."

I kept thinking angrily to myself, of all the people in the park, most of them white, why did he single me out? It wasn't the first time a thing like this had happened. Just a week before I was on the subway and a white drunk got on at Thirty-fourth Street. He looked around for a seat and there were plenty available next to other people. But he finally spied me, the only Negro in the half-empty car, and he came and sat down beside me, choosing me to be the benefactor of his infinite wisdom and his great liberal philosophy and his bad-liquored breath.

I tried to pull away from this one in the park but his huge hand held me by the shoulder. With his other hand he fumbled in his shirt pocket, then in the back pocket of his trousers. He fished out a dirty ragged snapshot. "Look," he said, "that's me and my family. I used to be a business man out west. Had a good business too. Yes indeed."

It would have been comical had it not been so tragic, the way pride gleamed in his eyes as he gazed at the picture. I suppose it was he, although you had to stare at it hard and stretch your imagination. He looked like a million dollars, posing with a wife and two fine-looking children. I began to wonder what had [190] happened to him along the way—what had become of his family—then caught myself going soft. Oh—no—none of that sentimental stuff. I glanced at my watch deliberately. "Look, my friend," I said, "I've got—"

His eyes were like red flint marbles. He coughed like he would strangle to death and directly into my face. My entire being came up in revolt against everything about him, but still he was a human being, and he might have gotten his four cents, maybe more, if he hadn't made his next pitch the way he did.

"Look, professor, I don't think I'm any better than you or anybody else. I want you to know that. We're all fighting together against them goddamn gooks in Viet Nam, ain't we? You look like an intelligent young man. I'm an educa— How about it, professor? Just four little old lousy cents—"

All of my inner resentment pushed outward as I squirmed and wrested myself angrily from his hold. "I've got to go! Goddamnit —I don't have any four cents for you!"

I started walking away from him toward the street corner trembling with anger, but uplifted by the fresh air rushing into my entire body. I stood at the intersection waiting for the light to change. Something made me turn and look for the big man. I saw him lumbering toward me again. My body became tense. A flock of cars were passing. Why in the hell didn't the light change to green? But then he stopped and sat down heavily on the last bench in the park. Amid a fit of coughing I heard him mumble— "Damn. This is getting to be a helluva country, when you can't chisel four lousy pennies offa prosperous-looking nigger!"

My hands clenched unconsciously. I smiled with a bitter taste in my mouth. The light changed to green. I started across the street. [191]

JAMES BALDWIN

Roy's Wound

As, in the late afternoon, John approached his home again, he saw little Sarah, her coat unbuttoned, come flying out of the house, and run the length of the street away from him, into the far drugstore. Instantly, he was frightened; he stopped a moment, wondering what could justify such hysterical haste. It was true that Sarah was full of self-importance and made any errand she was to run seem a matter of life or death; nevertheless, she had been sent on an errand, and with such speed that her mother had not had time to make her button up her coat.

Then he felt weary; if something had really happened it would be very unpleasant upstairs now, and he did not want to face it. Or perhaps it was simply that his mother had a headache and had sent Sarah to the store for aspirin. But if this were true, it meant that he would have to prepare supper and take care of the children, and be naked under his father's eye all the evening long. And he began to walk more slowly.

There were some boys standing on the stoop. They watched him as he approached, and he tried not to look at them, and to approximate their swagger. One of them said, as John mounted the low stone steps and started into the hall, "Boy, your brother was hurt real bad today."

He looked at them in a kind of dread, not daring to ask for details; and he observed that they too might have been in a battle: something hangdog in their looks suggested they had been put to flight. Then he looked down, and saw that there was blood on the

SOURCE: James Baldwin, *Go Tell It On the Mountain* (New York: The Dial Press, Inc., 1963), pp. 44–54. Copyright 1952, 1953 by James Baldwin. Reprinted by permission of the publisher.

threshold, and blood spattered on the tile floor of the vestibule. He looked again at the boys, who had not ceased to watch him, and hurried up the stairs.

The door was half open—for Sarah's return, no doubt; and he walked in, making no sound, feeling a confused impulse to flee. There was no one in the kitchen, though [44] the light was burning—the lights were on all through the house. On the kitchen table stood a shopping bag filled with groceries, and he knew that his Aunt Florence had arrived. The washtub, where his mother had been washing earlier, was open still, and filled the kitchen with a sour smell.

He had seen small, smudged coins of blood on the stairs on his way up, and there were drops of blood on the floor here too.

All this frightened him terribly. He stood in the middle of the kitchen, trying to imagine what had happened, and to prepare himself to walk into the living room, where he could hear his father's voice. Roy had been in trouble before, but this new trouble seemed the beginning of the fulfillment of a prophecy. He took off his coat, dropping it on a chair, and was about to go into the living room when he heard Sarah running up the steps.

He waited, and she burst through the door, carrying a clumsily shaped parcel.

"What happened?" he whispered.

She stared at him in astonishment, and a certain wild joy. He thought again that he really did not like his sister. Catching her breath, she said triumphantly, "Roy got stabbed with a knife!" and rushed into the living room.

Roy got stabbed with a knife. Whatever this meant, it meant that his father would be at his worst tonight. John walked slowly into the living room.

His father and mother, a small basin of water between them, knelt by the sofa where Roy lay, and his father was washing the blood from Roy's forehead. Apparently his mother, whose touch was so much more gentle, had been thrust aside by his father, who now could not bear to have anyone else touch his wounded son. And so she watched, one hand in the water, the other clenched in anguish at her waist, which was circled still by the improvised [45] apron of the morning. Her face, as she watched, was tense with fear and pity. His father muttered sweet, delirious things to Roy, and his hands, when he dipped them again in the basin and wrung out the cloth, were trembling. Aunt Florence, still wearing her hat and carrying her handbag, stood a little removed, looking down at Roy with a troubled face.

His mother looked up as Sarah bounded into the room, reached out for the package, and saw him. She said nothing, but looked at him with a strange, quick intentness, almost as though there were a warning on her tongue which she did not at the moment dare to utter. His Aunt Florence said, "We been wondering where you was, boy. This bad brother of yours done gone out and got hisself hurt."

But John understood from her tone that the fuss was, possibly, a little greater than the danger. Roy was not, after all, going to die. And his heart lifted a little. Then his father turned and looked at him.

"Where you been, boy," he shouted, "all this time? Don't you know you's needed here at home?"

More than his words, his face made John stiffen instantly with fear and malice. His father's face was terrible in anger, but now there was more than anger in his face. John saw now what he had never seen there before, except in his own vindictive fantasies: a kind of wild, weeping terror that made the face seem younger, and yet, in another way, unutterably older, and more cruel. And John knew, in the moment his father's glance swept over him, that he hated John because John was not lying on the sofa, where Roy lay. John could scarcely meet his father's eyes, and yet, briefly, he did, saying nothing; feeling in his heart an odd sensation of triumph, and hoping in his heart that Roy, to bring his father low, would die. [46]

His mother had unwrapped the package, and was opening a bottle of peroxide. "Here," she said, "you better wash it with this now." Her voice was calm, and dry, her expression closed, as she handed the bottle and the cotton to his father.

"This going to hurt," his father said—in such a different voice, so sad and tender!—turning again to the sofa. "But you just be a little man, and hold still—it ain't going to take long."

John watched, and listened, hating him. Roy began to moan. Aunt Florence moved to the mantelpiece, and put her handbag down near the metal serpent. From the room behind him, John heard the baby begin to whimper.

"John," said his mother, "go and pick her up, like a good boy." Her hands, not trembling, were still busy: she had opened the bottle of iodine, and was cutting up strips of bandage.

John walked into his parents' bedroom, and picked up the squalling baby, who was wet. The moment Ruth felt him lift her up, she stopped crying, and stared at him, wide-eyed and pathetic, as though she knew there was trouble in the house. John laughed at her so-ancient seeming distress—he was very fond of his baby sister—and whispered in her ear, as he started back to the living room, "Now, you let your big brother tell you something, baby. Just as soon as you's able to stand on your feet, you run away from *this* house, run far away." He did not quite know why he said this, or where he wanted her to run, but it made him feel better instantly.

His father was saying, as John came back into the room, "I'm sure going to be having some questions to ask you in a minute, old lady. I'm going to be wanting to know just how come you let this boy go out and get half killed."

"Oh, no, you ain't," said Aunt Florence, "you ain't going to be starting none of that mess this evening. You know right doggone well that Roy don't never ask *nobody* [47] if he can do *nothing* —he just go right ahead and do like he pleases. Elizabeth sure can't put no ball and chain on him. She got her hands full right here in this house, and it ain't her fault if Roy got a head just as hard as his father's."

"You got a awful lot to say, look like for once you could keep from putting your mouth in my business." He said this without looking at her.

"It ain't my fault," she said, "that you was born a fool, and always been a fool, and ain't never going to change. I swear to my Father you'd try the patience of Job."

"I done told you before," he said—he had not ceased working over the moaning Roy, and was preparing now to dab the wound with iodine, "that I didn't want you coming in here and using that gutter language in front of my children."

"Don't you worry about my language, brother," she said, with spirit, "you better start worrying about your *life*. What these children hear ain't going to do them near as much harm as what they *see*."

"What they *see*," his father muttered, "is a poor man trying to serve the Lord. *That's* my life."

"Then I guarantee *you*," she said, "that they going to do their best to keep it from being *their* life. *You* mark my words."

He turned and looked at her; and intercepted the look that passed between the two women. John's mother, for reasons that were not at all his father's reasons, wanted Aunt Florence to keep still. He looked away, ironically. John watched his mother's mouth tighten bitterly. His father, in silence, began bandaging Roy's forehead.

"It's just the mercy of God," he said, at last, "that this boy didn't lose his eye. Look here."

His mother leaned over and looked into Roy's face [48] with a sad, sympathetic murmur. Yet, John felt, she had seen instantly the extent of the danger to Roy's eye, and to his life, and was beyond that worry now; now she was merely marking time, as it were, and preparing herself for the moment when her husband's anger would turn, full force, against her.

His father now turned to John, who was standing near the French doors with Ruth in his arms.

"You come here, boy," he said, "and see what them white folks done done to your brother."

John walked over to the sofa, holding himself as proudly beneath his father's furious eyes, as a prince approaching the scaffold.

"Look here," said his father, grasping him roughly by one arm, "look at your brother."

John looked down at Roy; who gazed up at him with almost no expression in his dark eyes. But John knew, by the weary, impatient set of Roy's young mouth, that his brother was asking that none of this be held against him. It wasn't his fault, or John's, Roy's eyes said, that they had such a crazy father.

His father, with the air of one forcing the sinner to look down into the pit which is to be his portion, moved away slightly so that John could see Roy's wound.

Roy had been gashed by a knife, luckily not very sharp, but very jagged, from the center of his forehead where his hair began, downward to the bone just above his left eye: the wound described a kind of crazy half-moon, and ended in a violent fuzzy tail, which was the ruin of Roy's eyebrow. Time would darken the half-moon wound into Roy's dark skin, but nothing would bring together again the so violently divided hairs of his eyebrow. This crazy lift, this question, would remain with him forever, and emphasize forever something mocking and sinister in Roy's face. John felt a sudden impulse to smile, but his father's eyes were on him, and he fought the impulse back. Certainly the wound [49] was now very ugly, and very red, and must, John felt, with a quickened sympathy toward Roy, who had not cried out, have been very painful.

He could imagine the sensation caused when Roy staggered into the house, blinded with his blood; but, just the same, he wasn't dead, he wasn't changed, he would be in the streets again the moment he was better.

"You see," came now from his father. "It was white folks, some of them white folks *you* like so much, that tried to cut your brother's throat."

John thought, with immediate anger, and with a curious contempt for his father's inexactness, that only a blind man, however white, could possibly have been aiming at Roy's throat; and his mother said, with a calm insistence:

"And he was trying to cut theirs. Him and them bad boys."

"Yes," said Aunt Florence, "I ain't heard you ask that boy nary a question about how all this happened. Look like you just determined to raise cain any*how*—and make everybody in this house suffer because something done happened to the apple of your eye."

"I done ask you," cried his father, in exasperation, "to stop running your *mouth*. Don't none of this concern you—this is *my* family, and this is *my* house. You want me to slap you side of the head?"

"You slap me," she said placidly, "and I *do* guarantee you, you won't do no more slapping in a hurry."

"Hush now," said his mother, rising, "ain't no need for all this. What's done is done. We ought to be on our knees, thanking the Lord it weren't no worse."

"Amen to that," said Aunt Florence, *"tell* that foolish nigger something."

"You can tell that foolish *son* of yours something," he said to his wife, with venom, having decided, it seemed, to ignore his sister, "him standing there with them big, [50] buck eyes. You can tell him to take this like a warning from the Lord. *This* is what white folks does to niggers, I been telling you, now you see."

"He better take it like a warning?" shrieked Aunt Florence, *"He* better take it? Why, Gabriel, it ain't *him* went halfway across this city to get in a fight with white boys. This boy on the sofa went—*deliberately*—with a whole lot of other boys, all the way to the west side, just *looking* for a fight. I declare, I *do* wonder what goes on in your head."

"You know right well," his mother said, looking directly at his father, "that Johnny don't travel with the same class of boys as Roy goes with. You done beat Roy too many times, here, in this very room, for going out with them bad boys. Roy got hisself hurt this afternoon because he was out doing something he didn't have no business doing, and that's the end of it. You ought to be thanking your Redeemer he ain't dead."

"And for all the care you take of him," he said, "he might as well be dead. Don't look like you much care whether he lives, or dies."

"*Lord,* have mercy," said Aunt Florence.

"He's my son, too," she said, with heat, "I carried him in my belly for nine months, and I know him just like I know his Daddy, and they's just *exactly* alike. Now. You ain't got no *right* in the world to talk to me like that."

"I reckon you *know,*" he said, choked, and breathing hard, "all about a mother's love. I sure reckon on you telling me how a woman can sit in the house all day, and let her own flesh and blood go out and get half butchered. Don't you *tell* me you don't know no way to stop him—because I remember *my* mother, God rest her soul, and *she'd* have found a way."

"She was my mother, too," said Aunt Florence, "'and I recollect, if you don't, you being brought home many a [51] time more dead than alive. She didn't find no way to stop *you.* She wore herself *out,* beating on you, just like you been wearing yourself out, beating on this boy here."

"My, my, *my,*" he said, "you got a lot to say."

"I ain't doing a thing," she said, "but trying to talk some sense into your big, black, hard head. You better stop trying to blame everything on Elizabeth, and look to your own wrong doings."

"Never mind, Florence," his mother said, "it's all over, and done with now."

"I'm out of this house," he shouted, "every day the Lord sends, working to put the food in these children's mouths. Don't you think I got a right to ask the mother of these children to look after them, and see that they don't break their *necks* before I get back *home?*"

"You ain't got but one child," said his mother, "that's liable to go out and break his neck, and that's Roy, and you know it. And I don't know how in the world you expect me to run this house, and look after these children, and keep running around the block after Roy. *No,* I can't stop him, I done told you that, and you can't stop him neither. You don't know *what* to do with this boy, and that's why you all the time trying to fix the blame on somebody. Ain't nobody to *blame,* Gabriel. You just better pray God to stop him before somebody puts another knife in him, and puts him in his *grave.*"

They stared at each other a moment in an awful pause, a startled, pleading question in her eyes; then, with all his might, he reached out and slapped her across the face. She crumpled at once, hiding her face with one thin hand, and Aunt Florence moved to hold her up. Sarah watched all this with greedy eyes. Then Roy sat up, and said in a shaking voice:

"Don't you slap my mother. That's my *mother.* You slap her again, you black bastard, and I swear to God I'll kill you." [52]

In the moment that these words filled the room, and hung in the air like the infinitesimal moment of hanging, jagged light which precedes an explosion, John and his father were staring into each other's eyes. John thought for that moment that his father believed that those words had come from him: his eyes were so wild, and depthlessly malevolent, and his mouth was twisted into a snarl of pain. Then, in the absolute silence which followed Roy's words, John saw that his father was not seeing him, was not seeing anything, unless it were a vision. John wanted to turn and flee, as though he had encountered in the jungle some evil beast, crouching and ravenous, with eyes like hell unloosed; and exactly as though, on a road's turning, he found himself staring at certain destruction, he found that he could not move. Then his father turned away from him, and looked down at Roy.

"What did you say?" his father asked.

"I told you," said Roy, "not to touch my mother."

"You cursed me," said his father.

Roy said nothing; neither did he drop his eyes.

"Gabriel," said his mother, "Gabriel. Let us pray."

His father's hands were at his waist, and he took off his belt. Tears were in his eyes.

"Gabriel," cried Aunt Florence, "ain't you done playing the fool for tonight?"

Then his father raised his belt, and it fell with a whistling sound on Roy, who shivered and fell back, his face to the wall, but did not cry out. And the belt was raised again, and again; the air rang with the whistling, and the *crack!* against Roy's flesh. The baby, Ruth, began to scream.

"My Lord, my Lord," his father whispered, *"my Lord, my Lord."*

He raised the belt again, but Aunt Florence caught it from behind, and held it. His mother rushed over to the [53] sofa, and caught Roy in her arms, crying as John had never seen a woman, or anybody, cry before. Roy caught his mother around the neck and held on to her as though he were drowning.

His Aunt Florence and his father faced each other.

"Yes, Lord," Aunt Florence said, "you was born wild, and you's going to die wild. But ain't no need to try to take the whole world with you. You can't change nothing, Gabriel. You ought to know that by now." [54]

JOHN A. WILLIAMS

Navy Black

Dust puffed in sudden transparent brown billows from beneath the wheels of the hurtling Jeep, sped upwards and slowed abruptly, then settled upon the broad leaves of the palm trees along the narrow coral road.

The two heavily tanned officers in the Jeep pressed their overseas caps down tightly upon their heads. They approached the hairpin curve and had to slow. Their diminished speed allowed them to see, fleetingly, a basketball game in progress upon a cleared, dusty coral court. The driver who had broken down into second as they rushed into the curve, gave the Jeep gas then shifted back into third. Bouncing fiercely now, they burst out of the curve and onto the calm green expanse of the compound of the 27th Special Naval Construction Battalion. The driver shifted back into second and picked his way down the neat roadway marked off by lumps of whitewashed coral, heading toward the CO's tent where the flag snapped back and forth in a hot wind. The area was quiet. Only the *clat, clattat, clit, clatclit, bling!* of a typewriter sounded above a few muffled voices. The officers climbed out and rubbed their perspiration-stained bottoms with

SOURCE: John A. Williams, ed., *Beyond the Angry Black* (New York: Cooper Square Publishers, 1966), pp. 158–172. Copyright © 1966 by John A. Williams. Reprinted by permission of the author.

their hands. They paused and looked up and down, then started up the steps to the CO's office.

Bright had been lying down when he heard the Jeep. It had come with such a rattling rush through that hot midday that he'd raised himself automatically to see. He propped himself up with an elbow. Who after all would be running like hell through a torrid Guamanian afternoon but officers or basketball players reliving their moment of high school glory? Bright stared at the neat, tight look of the two men. Unmistakably marines. Marines, Bright thought. They vanished through the CO's door. There were momentary hearty greetings. Bright lay back down, thinking, God, it's hot. It's too damned hot. He closed his eyes and sighed. Marines.

Something was crawling on his leg. With his eyes still closed he wondered lazily what it was, if it were poisonous. He jerked his [158] leg and the crawling stopped. Bright wondered if any other sackrats had seen the marines. He jerked his leg again, this time viciously; the crawling had begun again.

Young laughter. Bright opened his eyes. "Cut the crap, Frankie." The swaggering Chamorro boy laughed again and tossed his thick black hair out of his thin, ebony eyes. Bright stared at the boy's slight, exquisitely tanned Micronesian frame, so much more attractive than the hard black of the Melanesians in the Solomons or the weak paleness of the Polynesians in the Samoas. Bright sprang to his feet. "You come here and I'll kick your butt good, you little punk," he said. He threw the twig out upon the ground then flung himself back on his cot. Frankie walked around picking up pebbles, smiling close-eyed taunts at Bright. "I wish you would!" Bright said. "I wish you would throw those at me!"

"Aw," Frankie said tentatively, "shut up." He curled his full pinkish lips.

"'Little bastard," Bright muttered so Frankie would not hear him. Then loudly: "You get away with murder around here." He glared at the boy and said softly, "Damned little gook."

Serious now, the boy approached the steps cautiously. "Where's Lyons?"

"He's a cook, isn't he?"

"Yes. . . ."

"Then he'd be in the kitchen where he always is, wouldn't he?"

Frankie opened his mouth to speak then closed it.

"And don't go around calling your father by his last name."

Frankie entered the tent and sat on Lyons' cot across from Bright. "He's no my father yet. What I call him?"

"I don't give a damn what you call him. If I was him I wouldn't adopt you; I'd leave you on this rock to rot."

Frankie sprayed the pebbles outside. "Bright, you mad for yesterday?"

"You're damned right I'm mad."

"Why you fellas no like that name when white fellas call you?"

Bright refused to hear him for several seconds. He fixed his gaze on the CO's door.

"Bright?"

Bright ignored him.

Frankie looked restlessly around the tent.

"It's not a nice name," Bright said finally. "It makes you fight." [159]

"You mad yesterday when I say it, Bright?"

"Yes."

"And Lyons, him mad too?"

"He should've kicked your butt," Bright said. He turned back to the CO's tent. "You like the white fellas better than the black fellas, huh, Frank?"

A faint shout went up from the basketball court. Bright felt sweat trickle from his armpits onto the cot.

"In America you'd be just like *us;* you wouldn't be like them. You aren't white and they'd soon make you know it."

"I not say I white."

"You act like it."

"I not." Frankie watched Bright's still, dark back.

"You think you're better than us already. Some colored guys in our outfit are *lighter* than you. Where do you get off?" Bright turned to the boy again. "Any white fellas offer to adopt you Frankie, like Lyons, and take you back to America?"

Frankie rapped his bare toes against the wooden floor.

"Did they!" Bright shouted.

Frankie jumped and edged toward the steps. Bright whirled to a sitting position. "Little *rat!* Come in here and take everything from Lyons—his money, his time, his love and then laugh at him behind his back—I've *seen you*—and call him names to his face —*get out*—" Bright charged to his feet, grasped the still thin elbow and pushed. Frankie tried to find his footing on the steps, scrambled, missed and fell, scurrying out of range in a thin cloud of coral dust at the same time, frightened . . . "Gook bastard," Bright growled. As soon as he was again on his back, staring at the crease of the tent above his cot, he knew it was all wrong. A patter of feet told him Frankie was no longer standing twenty feet away, staring at him, but running away as fast as he could.

Bright stared at the crease a long time. He heard the CO's door slam; he heard the voices and then the Jeep grinding down the road.

Frankie had been a nice kid at first; nice and grateful, the way you expected liberated kids to be. He minded then and was pleased with everything they did for him, like the clothes someone sewed together for him, sending food to his uncle, giving him money, teaching him clean habits, proving by their actions that he didn't have to be suspicious of them. *Damn him!* And then Lyons, small, fat, sweating all the time, his pocked brown face with a smile always, [160] took him over, spoke of adoption, wrote his wife, for they could have no children. Then followed all the afternoons in the offices of ComSoPac or the Provost Marshal seeing about the endless required papers and permissions and the difficult conversations with the withered old uncle, toothless, grinning all the time.

Lyons climbed heavily up the steps. Bright knew it was him by his tread; Bright looked at him. Lyons had a soiled dishcloth around his neck; his skivvy shirt was so soaked with sweat that it too looked dirty. His white pants, stained with grease and spilled foods and sweat, hung soggily over his shoetops. "Hey, ol' buddy, did I hear Frankie 'round here a while ago?"

"Man," Bright said, "I don't see how come you don't lose some weight in all this heat. It's got to be worse in that kitchen." Bright turned on his side. "Yeah, your boy was here."

Lyons sat on his cot. "Whewww!" he said. "Doc, you see them marines?"

"Yeah."

"Another push, you think?"

"I don't know."

"Maybe they're thinking about Japan. Lot of brass up around ComSoPac these days. Besides them beaches down along the highway're packed with equipment."

"Don't be so cheerful."

Lyons stretched out on his cot with a pleasurable sigh. "Where's that damned boy? Got a letter from my old lady today, Doc. She thinks Frank's a pretty good-looking cat. Like me."

"Sure."

Lyons laughed.

"Think he'll like it?"

Lyons said, "Sure, he'll like it. Best damned country in the world."

Bright peeked at Lyons and saw that he meant it. "Yeah," he said.

"Things're lookin' pretty good with the papers, Doc."

"Oh yeah?"

"Another two or three weeks."

"Great."

"Wife's started to buy things already," Lyons said with a chuckle. "They'll be too small or too big. Hell, we might not get off this rock for another five years." [161]

"You can say that again."

"Be good gettin' him used to the States. Always wanted a boy."

"Uh-huh."

"Oh, I know he's a little wild sometimes, Doc," Lyons said apologetically. "But I don't want no sissie boy. Frank lost all his folks but his uncle while the Japs were here. I mean, it's been hard on him."

"Yeah, I know."

"But you don't like him."

"I like him fine, Lyons, no crap."

"Naw you don't. You try, but you can't."

"Frank's all right with me. Honest."

Lyons said, "I guess I can handle a kid all right."

Bright sat up. "Lyons—"

"Ummm?"

Bright hesitated then lay back down. "What's for chow?"

"Es and Es."

"Christ."

"Chicken Sunday."

"Cut the crap. We have chicken *every* Sunday, just like turkey and mince pie for Thanksgiving and Christmas. It's a wonder we don't have a portable ice cream parlor for the boys."

"This is one of your good days."

"It was until those damned gyrenes showed up."

Lyons rose and stretched. He tapped his fingers against his sodden belly. "Time to get back. Trucks should be on the way. See Frankie tell him to clean up for supper."

"Okay."

Bright watched Lyons waddle back to the chow hall. On the

way he passed the basketball players on their way to the showers at the edge of the compound. "You guys take your salt pills?" Bright called out.

They grinned and nodded and Bright knew they were lying. He watched them move nude, towels clutched in their hands toward the stalls. Their brown bodies glistened with sweat. "See those marines?" one of them called back.

"Knew it was too quiet after that Iwo push," another said loudly.

Bright lit a cigarette and lay smoking until he heard the trucks coming in. From this moment until after the movie there would be noise in camp; noise and music; voices cajoling, singing; voices [162] raised in genuine and mock anger; crap shooting. There would be footsteps on crumbling coral walks; the somehow envious taunts thrown at those who would go down to the army engineers' camp looking for "Miss" Camel and his friends; Perry Como's voice, a prelude to the movie issuing from the PA from Armed Forces Radio.

Bright heard Roy singing, and when the husky, wide-shouldered man entered the tent, his Seabee baseball-type cap pulled low over his eyes, smelling of sweat which had dried in white rings on his shirt, Bright said, "You happy bastard, the marines were here looking for you."

Roy stopped singing. "What?"

"The guys from the First were here."

Roy stripped quickly to get to the showers before they became too crowded. "Jesus, I humped enough ammunition for those guys down on Peleliu to last them for fifty wars. I'm tired of white folk's wars anyway. What's the poop?"

"Haven't heard anything for real."

"Damn," Roy said, taking down his khaki towel and slipping his feet into wooden clogs. He draped the towel over one shoulder and with his cap still on, walked nude to the showers, muttering, "Home alive in '45. Crap."

II

The August morning was like any other; hot and breaking with the sun screaming bright shimmering gold off the Pacific east; shouts in the compound; the clatter of trays and stainless steel in the chowhall; the heavy thud of reluctant feet bumping the rails of the trucks. The morning sick call went quickly, as always, for the doctor, a sullen, sneering, suspicious man with a great brush mustache and a sloping, bald head, his face, like his naked torso, ugly with atabrine color, did not like mornings. He peddled up and down the line in wrinkled khaki shorts, eyes puffed from the nights of drinks and nurses and Red Cross girls, seeking the malingerers; and when they complained of backaches, he gave them ruthless prostate massages and sent them to the waiting trucks, and they, loaded with Negro Seabees, groaned off the base on the way to the docks, while the small group of white Seabees turned to their office tasks.

All this to the incessant drone of the 24's and 29's circling high above, their silver bodies reflecting the shary rays of the sun. The island [163] filled and reverberated with the sounds of their engines; the sky was violated with aircraft. They made a final sweep around and headed west, joining the groups up from Tinian and Saipan. For many moments after they had gone, the silence that seemed to creep back in, like a thief, was hard to accept.

Bright tossed out foot basins of potassium permanganate solutions which had been used for fungus rinses. He worked quickly, envying bitterly the white corpsmen who had already returned to their beds or had gone off by Jeep or ambulance to the beaches. When he finished, Bright took a handful of chlorine pills used for purifying water, but which also bleached clothes, and dropped them in a bucket of water and soap. He placed soiled underwear in next and jabbed the mass tentatively a few times, then slid it under his cot. The cleaning detail sauntered by as Bright loosened his shoes before getting into bed.

"Doc, you got it made," one named Dixon said. He was so black they sometimes called him blue.

"I earned it," Bright said, inviting the daily exchange of repartee, but the sound of trucks, great two-by-tens grumbling up the road broke it off.

Marine trucks. Marine drivers wearing low-slung fatigue caps, giving them that tough white-boy look. A clerk in the CO's waved the vehicles down the road to the peeling quonset hut that served for storage. Curious, Bright strolled through the rows of tents, past the area where the white personnel lived, to the warehouse. He watched the marines and the cleaning detail, which had been pressed into service, unload.

Helmets. Gas masks. New fatigues. New shoes. New packs. New *weapons*. New, everything new. Where were the crosses that were usually loaded in the bows of ships, all strapped together, a couple of hundred crosses and three or four Stars of David? *Cholera vaccine,* some cartons in the last truck were stenciled.

"Hey, hey, Doc," Dixon said. "Does this stuff mean what I think it means?"

"Man, I don't know."

Dixon took a handful of helmets into the hut. "Know what happened the last time we got stuff like this?"

"Yeah."

"My eighteen months were just about up," Dixon said, grabbing another handful of helmet straps, rattling the helmets like buckets. [164]

"So're mine," Bright said. He left the trucks and plodded back to the tent. Lyons lay on his cot, his eyes closed, but he spoke when Bright entered. "Seen Frank?"

"No."

Lyons stroked his forehead. "Wonder where he is?"

"New equipment's in."

"Saw it."

"I thought the damned war was just about over."

Lyons said, "I guess I'll have to get on over to his uncle's." He waited for Bright's answer.

"Hell, the kid's all right."

"You don't want to go with me?"

"No."

"Jesus, it's hot!" Lyons said, squeegeeing the sweat off his brow. "You hear about the new gun, the secret weapon?"

"What, another one?"

Lyons rose on one elbow. "All the battleships are being fitted with 'em, and when one of those special shells land, nothing'll grow there for a thousand years."

"Crap! Where'd *that* scuttlebutt come from?"

"The guys down at the docks."

"Look, if they had something special they'd a used it already, and they haven't used it which means they haven't got it. I mean doesn't that make sense?"

Lyons lay back down. "I don't know."

They didn't speak for several minutes, then Bright said, "Just wait until the guys get in at noon and see that stuff."

The Seabees bounded off the trucks before they rattled to a halt alongside the screened chowhall, and the chowline formed quickly. Most of the men would wait until after the meal to wash, if they did at all; some would eat rapidly and run for their cots and try to sleep for the balance of the hour they had in camp.

Bright leaned near the entrance thrusting his container of salt pills at each man.

"Hey, Doc, we off again?"

"What's the poop, Bright, we gonna invade Mississippi?"

"Man, will you quit shovin'—"

When Bright entered the hall, moving slowly along the clattering line, he saw Lyons standing as usual, overseeing the servers, one fist thrust into the fat of a hip, sweat dripping and spurting along [165] the furrows of his forehead, falling in murky silver drops to the dirt floor. "Seen him?" Lyons asked.

Bright shook his head. "I'll let you know if I do."

Lyons nodded.

The hall buzzed. A "push" however much feared, shattered the monotony of the daily routine at the docks; that deadly, civilian-like employment so foreign to men who reluctantly anticipate once again the glamor of war.

But for Bright there was only the weary and frightening probability of packing up, herding aboard an APA to the catacombs of the various holds to be engulfed in the stink of men placed but a foot apart, stacked from top to bottom, hanging like stalactites in the gloom. The heads would run over and smell; the men would stand for quick, half-cooked meals in the ship's chowhall. During the days on deck there would be the search for privacy; a fruitless search aboard an attack transport. And how many times a day on this one would there come the blowing out of the mike on the PA system, followed by the metallic:

"Now hear this!"

Undoubtedly there would be red and green and yellow alerts; hours of standing in the holds girded by cumbersome, reeking life jackets waiting for the planes to finish their business above, tiny and unreal in the dome of sky. And there would be times when they'd pile topside, still with those soiled and gritty life belts, standing away from the hatches waiting for the explosion of the torpedo, listening to the sea sliding past the bow, hissing all the way back into silence at the stern.

Then one fine morning the ship would rock with the waves and the sound of the screws would be absent and while you were wondering what that meant, as if you didn't know, the guns opened up, shattering at first, and then somehow conveying the idea of power and protection. Then up on deck, life belts behind, packs and guns and kits now; helmets too so that you looked like the fighters in the magazines. All over the sea there'd be a thousand other ships, but you noticed the DEs and DDs first; they would be small and fast and the sea would boil away from their bows as they charged the beach. *"Coxswains, man your boats!"* There would be the scrambling down the nets, the cough of the motors of a hundred landing barges moving in a line toward that distant soft green mound rising foolishly [166] up out of the middle of the sea, stubbornly claiming a marking on the maps, a place in history. You would tell yourself that no enemy could survive the barrage; it helped to think that, until you reached the beach, called red or orange or blue, or some sillier color when it was really black volcanic sand or brown or white coral, and the still forms of Americans would be lying there. Then you'd begin to feel naked and sacrificed.

"Bright. Bright!" the chief said, bending over the table. "Check out kits this afternoon. I think we might need a new supply of syrettes." The chief looked nervous. He was a fat, pink man with blue eyes and curly brown hair. He wore his khakis sloppily and drank a lot of beer and played a lot of cards, but he didn't press his corpsmen and stood between them and the doctor.

"When do we innoculate?" Bright asked.

"I guess tomorrow or the next day."

"So soon?"

"Yeah. Look," the chief said, straightening, "take care of those kits as soon as you can, will you, Bright?"

"Okay, chief."

The camp lapsed into a torpid silence when the last truck moved out. A Piper cub buzzed overhead. Bright sat in the shade checking the kits. The musty smell of the heavy cloth made the holds of ships suddenly more real to him.

Morphine syrettes, plastic caps securely fastened; ABDs (those great absorbent pads with straps, good for nearly any sized wound which left you still alive) sterile; Sulfa powders;—nilamide,—thiazole,—diazine,—pyridine, okay; tape, okay. Two by two, four by four bandages, sterile, okay. Bright locked up the kits and walked to the chief's tent passing two sunbathing clerks from the CO's office. Off duty chiefs sat around drinking beer, their caps and overseas hats off, the stark white upper parts of their heads showing. "Chief," Bright said, "we can use some more syrettes. Everything else's okay."

"Thanks, Bright. Take a cold beer. Go ahead."

Bright reached into the bucket filled with chipped ice and cans of beer. "Thanks," he said. One of the chiefs handed him an opener which he applied to the can; he sipped it as he walked slowly to his tent to sleep away the balance of the afternoon. He slept soundly, missing the return of the trucks, the shouting in the shower, the [167] tip-toeing Roy, who, when he first saw Bright curled in sleep, sweating, decided he would not awake him for chow. This was a delightfully malicious decision; Roy had worked extremely hard on the docks; Bright seemed to have worked even less than usual. But Bright woke up and managed to get into the chowhall before it closed. Once hunched in the nearly silent hall over his food, listening to the KPs rushing to get through, he wondered why he'd bothered.

Back in the tent he stuck a stick in his clothes in the bucket under the cot, lifted the underwear out, changed its position and pushed it back to soak some more. Bright and Roy didn't go to the movies. Lyons had borrowed a Jeep and was off to find Frankie. As the tentmates lay unspeaking, the sounds from the movie drifted over the compound; voices and music. Bright could tell from the way the music went when something exciting was going to happen. Now the planes began to return from their strike; they always came back during the movies, drowning out both voices and music. Stacked up, they circled, their lights blinking frightened red and green dots in the dark blue of the sky.

An explosion lashed out against the night; a tongue of light seared the dark palms stark white for an instant, then they each ricochetted back and forth across the island as an uneven billiard ball rolling from cushion to cushion. The undersized, almost ludicrous wail of a siren came faintly.

Roy said to Bright, "I wouldn't think there's anything left. You?"

"Can't tell." Bright stared up at a spider spinning a web in the crease of the tent above his cot. He planned to kill the spider before he turned in.

"Saw one of those babies come down three months ago," Roy said. "Saw the guys in the bubble waving, glad to be setting down, smiling and then—*Towie!*" Roy paused.

"How about the radio?" Bright asked.

Roy rolled over and snapped it on. "Why the hell don't you buy one?"

"Because you got one," Bright said, getting up to kill the spider.

III

The trucks did not go out the next morning. Shouts of glee went up from this row of tents and that; faces were happy in the chow-hall for the first time in months. The corpsmen ate a hasty break-fast and [168] retreated to the sickbay to set up for the cholera innoculations. While they were setting up, the morphine syrettes arrived from the Fleet Hospital. Bright went out to meet the truck. "You get this?" the driver asked.

"Yeah," Bright said, lifting the carton out.

"You have to sign," the driver said. His cap was snow white and crimped down. His dungarees had been bleached powder blue. He wore an earring in his left ear, a large gold one.

"Where?" Bright asked.

"Anywhere," the Fleet corpsman said, "and date it."

"What's the date?"

"August sixth."

Bright scribbled and handed the pad back and took the carton into the hut. "Chief, here's the morphine."

"Lock it up with the kits, Bright." The chief was setting out the syringes and needles. The other corpsmen broke open the serum and set the medications tables with cotton, alcohol and check-off lists.

Lyons came by and stood in a corner. He had put on his dunga-rees, the chambray shirt and the blue denim pants. His white cap, a little soiled, sat squarely upon his head. He was sweating pro-fusely.

"Find him yesterday?"

"No. Got to go back out today. Nice and cool in here," he said.

"Until you get used to it."

"Uncle hasn't seen him either," Lyons said.

"He'll show."

"I'm mad with him now," Lyons said. "That's no way for a kid to behave when you're going to adopt him."

"Maybe he doesn't want to be adopted."

"Sure he does, Doc."

"Okay."

Lyons said, "What makes you so sure?"

Bright shrugged but he wanted to remind Lyons of the fight be-tween the Negro sailors at the Naval Advanced Base and the ma-rines over the Chamarro girls at a party. One marine killed, thirty-nine sailors court-martialed for repulsing the attack. And Bright wanted to tell Lyons of the Chamarro girls who told you shyly that the white service men made them stay away from the black ones; and to recall for his friend the stories of tails and bayings at the full [169] moon, and ask had not Frankie heard and seen? "Just a feeling," Bright said.

"Well. . . ."

"What's for chow tonight?"

"Stew."

"Stew! Well, what the hell are we having for lunch?"

"Spam sandwiches. I got to go," Lyons said, not moving.

"If I see him around here. . . ." Bright's voice trailed away.

Lyons started out. Stopped, turned. "Give me my shot now."

Bright motioned toward the chief and Lyons walked toward him, rolling up his sleeve.

Now the line began to form. Bright stood in a small line of corpsmen facing a longer line of Seabees, their arms exposed. First Bright swabbed, dashing on a splash of denatured alcohol for the next corpsman to hit with the needle. Then Bright went on the needle, hitting the arm swiftly, jabbing the plunger, withdrawing the needle from under a cotton ball and replacing that needle with another, sterile one for the next in that endless line of arms, each of which took one half cc of serum. "Work your arm!" he said automatically, "Work your arm!"

From the sickbay the line stretched through sun and shade to the warehouse to receive the new equipment, and when that was deposited in the tents, the toughening up exercises began, the running, the push-ups, the jogging. Cadence calls rang out, and then faded as the men jogged off to a nearby range to practice with the carbines and the rifles.

The chowhall was relatively quiet during lunch; the shots, the equipment, the feel and sound of the guns going off, made the men sombre. Going on another push was no longer a possibility; it was fearful, unexciting fact.

The men returned to the range after lunch and fired until almost chowtime. Bright, standing at one of the intervals the corpsmen had been set at, crept into position and took a carbine and fired with the rest. At Peleliu and Kwajalein he'd managed to carry a carbine in with him; it made him feel better. No one went to see the Van Johnson movie. He played out his role to a movie area empty of people. The Seabees lay in their beds or talked in the company streets. The bombers droned back home, vibrating the night.

In their tent, Roy turned on his radio.

"Thanks," Bright said. "You want to leave that with me?" [170]

"You're goin' too, Bright, what the hell're you talking about?"

"I mean, leave it *to* me?"

"Shut up!"

"Sorry, didn't mean to make you nervous—"

At the same moment Roy hushed Bright, noise tumbled away from the entire camp, except for the movie. Radios, all tuned to the same station, delivered the message. When it was finished a shout went up around the camp. Roy turned to Bright grinning. "Did you hear *that,* man?"

Bright grinned. "Damned right I heard it."

"An atom bomb," Roy said. "What kind of bomb is that? Powerful as the sun."

"Hiroshima," Bright said.

"Surrender, bastards," Roy said, gritting his teeth. "You think they'll surrender?"

"I don't know."

"Surrender!" Roy walked around the tent pounding a fist into an open hand. "Surrender! Surrender!"

Lyons came in and sat heavily on his cot. Outside the shouts grew in intensity. They could hear beer spewing from punctured cans. There was running, and soon, singing. Voices were eager with hope. "Whew," Lyons said. "It's hot."

"Hear the news?" Bright asked.

"Yep."

"Find him?"

Lyons kicked off his shoes. "I found him."

Roy stopped walking and sat down, staring at the floor and then at his new equipment.

Dixon burst in. "The CO's called off everything for tomorrow!"

Roy gave him a smile.

"Yahooooo!" Dixon screamed, turning and racing for the next tent.

Lyons sat up suddenly and slipped on his shoes. "Doc?"

"What, man?"

"Step outside."

Roy looked quickly from Lyons to Bright. "What's wrong, Lyons?"

Lyons ignored him and tied his laces. "You gettin' ready, Doc?"

Bright raised himself. "You serious?" Stepping outside had but one meaning. He saw that Lyons was serious.

"C'mon," Lyons said. [171]

"Hey," Roy said.

"Listen, Lyons—" Bright said.

"I've already thought about it," Lyons said.

"What's this all about?" Roy asked, his arms swinging free at his sides, his chest swelling slightly.

"Frankie, I guess," Bright said, climbing slowly out of bed. He slipped on his shoes, took them off and put his sneakers on. "Ready in a minute," he said, glancing up at Lyons.

Roy said, "What about Frankie?"

"Tell him, Lyons."

"He's not going home with me," Lyons said, not looking at either of them. "He said he thought about it after—" he gestured toward Bright "—talked to him." He hesitated, his eyes still on the floor. "He said he didn't want to go back and be like *us*."

Roy laughed harshly. "Well, you're lucky."

Lyons said sadly, "Shut up, Roy."

Bright stepped past them. Roy grabbed Lyons' arm. Bright said, "It was my fault. Let him go."

"What'd you say?"

"I told the kid a little of how it was; he was always smart; he got the point."

"Aw, Lyons," Roy said. "That kid was so rotten; he was making a fool of you, man—"

Lyons shook loose and followed Bright down the steps.

"Oh, no!" Roy said, thrusting his powerful body between them. "Not over that kid. Lyons, what the hell did you think you were gonna do with him anyway? Boy, he'd run you and your wife outa house and home inside a week. I thought you'd wake up after a while." Roy had Lyons' arm again, holding tight and talking fast. The three stood alone. The night was filled with joyful running and shouting men.

Lyons started to cry. He turned away from them, and taking a soiled handkerchief from his pocket, wiped his eyes. He climbed back inside the tent, slipped off his shoes and lay down. Outside, Roy said to Bright, "Let's walk around and leave him alone for a while. He'll be all right."

"Sure," Bright said slowly, looking behind at Lyons as they moved down the company walk to where warm beer was being disbursed in celebration of what looked like the end of it. [172]

ERNEST J. GAINES

The Sky Is Gray

Go'n be coming in a few minutes. Coming 'round that bend down there full speed. And I'm go'n get out my hankercher and I'm go'n wave it down, and us go'n get on it and go.

I keep on looking for it, but Mama don't look that way no more. She looking down the road where us jest come from. It's a long old road, and far's you can see you don't see nothing but gravel. You got dry weeds on both sides, and you got trees on both sides, and fences on both sides, too. And you got cows in the pastures and they standing close together. And when us was coming out yer to catch the bus I seen the smoke coming out o' the cow's nose.

I look at my mama and I know what she thinking. I been with Mama so much, jest me and her, I know what she thinking all the time. Right now it's home—Auntie and them. She thinking if they got 'nough wood—if she left 'nough there to keep 'em warm till us get back. She thinking if it go'n rain and if any of 'em go'n have to go out in the rain. She thinking 'bout the hog—if he go'n get out, and if Ty and Val be able to get him back in. She always worry like that when she leave the house. She don't worry too much if she leave me there with the smaller ones 'cause [83] she know I'm go'n look after 'em and look after Auntie and everything else. I'm the oldest and she say I'm the man.

I look at my mama and I love my mama. She wearing that black coat and that black hat and she looking sad. I love my mama and I want put my arm 'round her and tell her. But I'm not s'pose to do that. She say that's weakness and that's cry-baby stuff, and she don't want no cry-baby 'round her. She don't want you to

Source: Ernest J. Gaines, *Bloodline* (New York: The Dial Press, Inc., 1968), pp. 83–117. Copyright © 1963, 1964, 1968 by Ernest J. Gaines. Reprinted by permission of the publisher. Originally published in *Negro Digest*.

be scared neither. 'Cause Ty scared of ghosts and she always whipping him. I'm scared of the dark, too. But I make 'tend I ain't. I make 'tend I ain't 'cause I'm the oldest, and I got to set a good sample for the rest. I can't ever be scared and I can't ever cry. And that's the reason I didn't never say nothing 'bout my teef. It been hurting me and hurting me close to a month now. But I didn't say it. I didn't say it 'cause I didn't want act like no crybaby, and 'cause I know us didn't have 'nough money to have it pulled. But, Lord, it been hurting me. And look like it won't start till at night when you trying to get little sleep. Then soon's you shet your eyes—umm-umm, Lord, look like it go right down to your heart string.

"Hurting, hanh?" Ty'd say.

I'd shake my head, but I wouldn't open my mouth for nothing. You open your mouth and let that wind in, and it almost kill you.

I'd just lay there and listen to 'em snore. Ty, there, right 'side me, and Auntie and Val over by the fireplace. Val younger 'an me and Ty, and he sleep with Auntie. Mama sleep 'round the other side with Louis and Walker. [84]

I'd just lay there and listen to 'em, and listen to that wind out there, and listen to that fire in the fireplace. Sometime it'd stop long enough to let me get little rest. Sometime it just hurt, hurt, hurt. Lord, have mercy.

II

Auntie knowed it was hurting me. I didn't tell nobody but Ty, 'cause us buddies and he ain't go'n tell nobody. But some kind o' way Auntie found out. When she asked me, I told her no, nothing was wrong. But she knowed it all the time. She told me to mash up a piece o' aspirin and wrap it in some cotton and jugg it down in that hole. I did it, but it didn't do no good. It stopped for a little while, and started right back again. She wanted to tell Mama, but I told her Uh-uh. 'Cause I knowed she didn't have no money, and it jest was go'n make her mad again. So she told Monsieur Bayonne, and Monsieur Bayonne came to the house and told me to kneel down 'side him on the fireplace. He put his finger in his mouth and made the Sign of the Cross on my jaw. The tip of Monsieur Bayonne finger is some hard, 'cause he always playing on that guitar. If us sit outside at night us can always hear Monsieur Bayonne playing on his guitar. Sometime us leave him out there playing on the guitar.

He made the Sign of the Cross over and over on my jaw, but

that didn't do no good. Even when he prayed and told me to pray some, too, that teef still hurt.

"How you feeling?" he say.

"Same," I say.

He kept on praying and making the Sign of the Cross and I kept on praying, too.

"Still hurting?" he say.

"Yes, sir."

Monsieur Bayonne mashed harder and harder on my jaw. He mashed so hard he almost pushed me on Ty. But then he stopped.

"What kind o' prayers you praying, boy?" he say.

"Baptist," I say. [85]

"Well, I'll be—no wonder that teef still killing him. I'm going one way and he going the other. Boy, don't you know any Catholic prayers?

"Hail Mary," I say.

"Then you better start saying it."

"Yes, sir."

He started mashing again, and I could hear him praying at the same time. And, sure 'nough, afterwhile it stopped.

Me and Ty went outside where Monsieur Bayonne two hounds was, and us started playing with 'em. "Let's go hunting," Ty say. "All right," I say; and us went on back in the pasture. Soon the hounds got on a trail, and me and Ty followed 'em all cross the pasture and then back in the woods, too. And then they cornered this little old rabbit and killed him, and me and Ty made 'em get back, and us picked up the rabbit and started on back home. But it had started hurting me again. It was hurting me plenty now, but I wouldn't tell Monsieur Bayonne. That night I didn't sleep a bit, and first thing in the morning Auntie told me go back and let Monsieur Bayonne pray over me some more. Monsieur Bayonne was in his kitchen making coffee when I got there. Soon's he seen me, he knowed what was wrong.

"All right, kneel down there 'side that stove," he say. "And this time pray Catholic. I don't know nothing 'bout Baptist, and don't want know nothing 'bout him."

III

Last night Mama say: "Tomorrow us going to town."

"It ain't hurting me no more," I say. "I can eat anything on it."

"Tomorrow us going to town," she say.

And after she finished eating, she got up and went to bed. [86] She always go to bed early now. 'Fore Daddy went in the Army, she used to stay up late. All o' us sitting out on the gallery or 'round the fire. But now, look like soon's she finish eating she go to bed.

This morning when I woke up, her and Auntie was standing 'fore the fireplace. She say: " 'Nough to get there and back. Dollar and a half to have it pulled. Twenty-five for me to go, twenty-five for him. Twenty-five for me to come back, twenty-five for him. Fifty cents left. Guess I get a little piece o' salt meat with that."

"Sure can use a piece," Auntie say. "White beans and no salt meat ain't white beans."

"I do the best I can," Mama say.

They was quiet after that, and I made 'tend I was still sleep.

"James, hit the floor," Auntie say.

I still made 'tend I was sleep. I didn't want 'em to know I was listening.

"All right," Auntie say, shaking me by the shoulder. "Come on. Today's the day."

I pushed the cover down to get out, and Ty grabbed it and pulled it back.

"You, too, Ty," Auntie say.

"I ain't getting no teef pulled," Ty say.

"Don't mean it ain't time to get up," Auntie say. "Hit it, Ty."

Ty got up grumbling.

"James, you hurry up and get in your clothes and eat your food," Auntie say. "What time y'all coming back?" she say to Mama.

"That 'leven o'clock bus," Mama say. "Got to get back in that field this evening."

"Get a move on you, James," Auntie say.

I went in the kitchen and washed my face, then I ate my [87] breakfast. I was having bread and syrup. The bread was warm and hard and tasted good. And I tried to make it last a long time.

Ty came back there, grumbling and mad at me.

"Got to get up," he say. "I ain't having no teef pulled. What I got to be getting up for."

Ty poured some syrup in his pan and got a piece of bread. He didn't wash his hands, neither his face, and I could see that white stuff in his eyes.

"You the one getting a teef pulled," he say. "What I got to get up for. I bet you if I was getting a teef pulled, you wouldn't be getting up. Shucks; syrup again. I'm getting tired of this old syrup. Syrup, syrup, syrup. I want me some bacon sometime."

"Go out in the field and work and you can have bacon," Auntie

Ernest J. Gaines

say. She stood in the middle door looking at Ty. "You better be
glad you got syrup. Some people ain't got that—hard's time is."

"Shucks," Ty say. "How can I be strong."

"I don't know too much 'bout your strength," Auntie say; "but
I know where you go'n be hot, you keep that grumbling up.
James, get a move on you; your mama waiting."

I ate my last piece of bread and went in the front room. Mama
was standing 'fore the fireplace warming her hands. I put on my
coat and my cap, and us left the house.

IV

I look down there again, but it still ain't coming. I almost say,
"It ain't coming, yet," but I keep my mouth shet. 'Cause that's
something else she don't like. She don't like for you to say something just for nothing. She can see it ain't coming, I can see it ain't
coming, so why say it ain't coming. I don't say it, and I turn and
look at the river that's back o' us. It so cold the smoke just raising
up from the water. I [88] see a bunch of pull-doos not too far out
—jest on the other side the lilies. I'm wondering if you can eat
pull-doos. I ain't too sure, 'cause I ain't never ate none. But I
done ate owls and black birds, and I done ate red birds, too. I
didn't want kill the red birds, but she made me kill 'em. They had
two of 'em back there. One in my trap, one in Ty trap. Me and Ty
was go'n play with 'em and let 'em go. But she made me kill 'em
'cause us needed the food.

"I can't," I say. "I can't."

"Here," she say. "Take it."

"I can't," I say. "I can't. I can't kill him, Mama. Please."

"Here," she say. "Take this fork, James."

"Please, Mama, I can't kill him," I say.

I could tell she was go'n hit me. And I jecked back, but I didn't
jeck back soon enough.

"Take it," she say.

I took it and reached in for him, but he kept hopping to the
back.

"I can't, Mama," I say. The water just kept running down my
face. "I can't."

"Get him out o' there," she say.

I reached in for him and he kept hopping to the back. Then I
reached in farther, and he pecked me on the hand.

"I can't, Mama," I say.

She slapped me again.

I reached in again, but he kept hopping out my way. Then he hopped to one side, and I reached there. The fork got him on the leg and I heard his leg pop. I pulled my hand out 'cause I had hurt him.

"Give it here," she say, and jecked the fork out my hand.

She reached and got the little bird right in the neck. I heard the fork go in his neck, and I heard it go in the ground. She brought him out and helt him right in front o' me.

"That's one," she say. She shook him off and gived me the fork. "Get the other one." [89]

"I can't, Mama. I do anything. But I can't do that."

She went to the corner o' the fence and broke the biggest switch over there. I knelt 'side the trap crying.

"Get him out o' there," she say.

"I can't, Mama."

She started hitting me cross the back. I went down on the ground crying.

"Get him," she say.

"Octavia," Auntie say.

'Cause she had come out o' the house and she was standing by the tree looking at us.

"Get him out o' there," Mama say.

"Octavia," Auntie say; "explain to him. Explain to him. Jest don't beat him. Explain to him."

But she hit me and hit me and hit me.

I'm still young. I ain't no more'an eight. But I know now. I know why I had to. (They was so little, though. They was so little. I 'member how I picked the feathers off 'em and cleaned 'em and helt 'em over the fire. Then us all ate 'em. Ain't had but little bitty piece, but us all had little bitty piece, and ever'body jest looked at me, 'cause they was so proud.) S'pose she had to go away? That's why I had to do it. S'pose she had to go away like Daddy went away? Then who was go'n look after us? They had to be somebody left to carry on. I didn't know it then, but I know it now. Auntie and Monsieur Bayonne talked to me and made me see.

V

Time I see it, I get out my hankercher and start waving. It still 'way down there, but I keep waving anyhow. Then it come closer and stop and me and Mama get on. Mama tell me go sit in the back while she pay. I do like she [90] say, and the people look at me. When I pass the little sign that say White and Colored, I start looking for a seat. I jest see one of 'em back there, but I don't take it, 'cause I want my mama to sit down herself. She come in the back and sit down, and I lean on the seat. They got seats in the front, but I know I can't sit there, 'cause I have to sit back o' the sign. Anyhow, I don't want sit there if my mama go'n sit back here.

They got a lady sitting 'side my mama and she look at me and grin little bit. I grin back, but I don't open my mouth, 'cause the wind'll get in and make that teef hurt. The lady take out a pack o' gum and reach me a slice, but I shake my head. She reach Mama a slice, and Mama shake her head. The lady jest can't understand why a little boy'll turn down gum, and she reached me a slice again. This time I point to my jaw. The lady understand and grin little bit, and I grin little bit, but I don't open my mouth, though.

They got a girl sitting 'cross from me. She got on a red over-coat, and her hair plaited in one big plait. First, I make 'tend I don't even see her. But then I start looking at her little bit. She make 'tend she don't see me neither, but I catch her looking that way. She got a cold, and ever' now and then she hist that little hankercher to her nose. She ought to blow it, but she don't. Must think she too much a lady or something.

Ever' time she hist that little hankercher, the lady 'side her say something in her yer. She shake her head and lay her hands in her lap again. Then I catch her kind o' looking where I'm at. I grin at her. But think she'll grin back? No. She turn up her little old nose like I got some snot on my face or something. Well, I show her both o' us can turn us head. I turn mine, too, and look out at the river.

The river is gray. The sky is gray. They have pull-doos on the water. The water is wavey, and the pull-doos go up and [91] down. The bus go 'round a turn, and you got plenty trees hiding the river. Then the bus go 'round another turn, and I can see the river again.

I look to the front where all the white people sitting. Then I look at that little old gal again. I don't look right at her, 'cause I don't want all them people to know I love her. I jest look at her little bit, like I'm looking out that window over there. But she know I'm looking that way, and she kind o' look at me, too. The lady sitting 'side her catch her this time, and she lean over and say something in her yer.

"I don't love him nothing," that little old gal say out loud.

Ever'body back there yer her mouth, and all of 'em look at us and laugh.

"I don't love you, neither," I say. "So you don't have to turn up your nose, Miss."

"You the one looking," she say.

"I wasn't looking at you," I say. "I was looking out that window, there."

"Out that window, my foot," she say. "I seen you. Ever' time I turn 'round you look at me."

"You must o' been looking yourself if you seen me all them times," I say.

"Shucks," she say. "I got me all kind o' boyfriends."

"I got girlfriends, too," I say.

"Well, I just don't want you to get your hopes up," she say.

I don't say no more to that little old gal, 'cause I don't want have to bust her in the mouth. I lean on the seat where Mama sitting, and I don't even look that way no more. When us get to Bayonne, she jugg her little old tongue out at me. I make 'tend I'm go'n hit her, and she duck down side her mama. And all the people laugh at us again. [92]

VI

Me and Mama get off and start walking in town. Bayonne is a little bitty town. Baton Rouge is a hundred times bigger 'an Bayonne. I went to Baton Rouge once—me, Ty, Mama, and Daddy. But that was 'way back yonder—'fore he went in the Army. I wonder when us go'n see him again. I wonder when. Look like he ain't ever coming home. . . . Even the pavement all cracked in Bayonne. Got grass shooting right out the sidewalk. Got weeds in the ditch, too; jest like they got home.

It some cold in Bayonne. Look like it colder 'n it is home. The wind blow in my face, and I feel that stuff running down my nose. I sniff. Mama say use that hankercher. I blow my nose and put it back.

Us pass a school and I see them white children playing in the yard. Big old red school, and them children jest running and playing. Then us pass a café, and I see a bunch of 'em in there eating. I wish I was in there 'cause I'm cold. Mama tell me keep my eyes in front where they blonks.

Us pass stores that got dummies, and us pass another café, and then us pass a shoe shop, and that baldhead man in there fixing on

Ernest J. Gaines

a shoe. I look at him and I butt into that white lady, and Mama jeck me in front and tell me stay there.

Us come to the courthouse, and I see the flag waving there. This one yer ain't like the one us got at school. This one yer ain't got but a handful of stars. One at school got a big pile of stars— one for ever' state. Us pass it and us turn and there it is—the dentist office. Me and Mama go in, and they got people sitting ever' where you look. They even got a little boy in there younger 'an me.

Me and Mama sit on that bench, and a white lady come in there and ask me what my name. Mama tell her, and the white lady go back. Then I yer somebody hollering in there. And soon's that little boy hear him hollering, he start [93] hollering, too. His mama pat him and pat him, trying to make him hush up, but he ain't thinking 'bout her.

The man that was hollering in there come out holding his jaw.

"Got it, hanh?" another man say.

The man shake his head.

"Man, I thought they was killing you in there," the other man say. "Hollering like a pig under a gate."

The man don't say nothing. He jest head for the door, and the other man follow him.

"John Lee," the white lady say. "John Lee Williams."

The little boy jugg his head down in his mama lap and holler more now. His mama tell him go with the nurse, but he ain't thinking 'bout her. His mama tell him again, but he don't even yer. His mama pick him up and take him in there, and even when the white lady shet the door I can still hear him hollering.

"I often wonder why the Lord let a child like that suffer," a lady say to my mama. The lady's sitting right in front o' us on another bench. She got on a white dress and a black sweater. She must be a nurse or something herself, I reckoned.

"Not us to question," a man say.

"Sometimes I don't know if we shouldn't," the lady say.

"I know definitely we shouldn't," the man say. The man look like a preacher. He big and fat and he got on a black suit. He got a gold chain, too.

"Why?" the lady say.

"Why anything?" the preacher say.

"Yes," the lady say. "Why anything?"

"Not us to question," the preacher say.

The lady look at the preacher a little while and look at Mama again. [94]

"And look like it's the poor who do most the suffering," she say. "I don't understand it."

"Best not to even try," the preacher say. "He works in mysterious ways. Wonders to perform."

Right then Little John Lee bust out hollering, and ever'body turn they head.

"He's not a good dentist," the lady say. "Dr. Robillard is much better. But more expensive. That's why most of the colored people come here. The white people go to Dr. Robillard. Y'all from Bayonne?"

"Down the river," my mama say. And that's all she go'n say, 'cause she don't talk much. But the lady keep on looking at her, and so she say: "Near Morgan."

"I see," the lady say.

VII

"That's the trouble with the black people in this country today," somebody else say. This one yer sitting on the same side me and Mama sitting, and he kind o'sitting in front of that preacher. He look like a teacher or somebody that go to college. He got on a suit, and he got a book that he been reading. "We don't question is exactly the trouble," he say. "We should question and question and question. Question everything."

The preacher jest look at him a long time. He done put a toothpick or something in his mouth, and he jest keep turning it and turning it. You can see he don't like that boy with that book.

"Maybe you can explain what you mean," he say.

"I said what I meant," the boy say. "Question everything. Every stripe, every star, every word spoken. Everything."

"It 'pears to me this young lady and I was talking 'bout God, young man," the preacher say. [95]

"Question Him, too," the boy say.

"Wait," the preacher say. "Wait now."

"You heard me right," the boy say. "His existence as well as everything else. Everything."

The preacher jest look cross the room at the boy. You can see he getting madder and madder. But mad or no mad, the boy ain't thinking 'bout him. He look at the preacher jest's hard's the preacher look at him.

"Is this what they coming to?" the preacher say. "Is this what we educating them for?"

"You're not educating me," the boy say. "I wash dishes at night to go to school in the day. So even the words you spoke need questioning."

The preacher jest look at him and shake his head.

"When I come in this room and seen you there with your book, I said to myself, There's an intelligent man. How wrong a person can be."

"Show me one reason to believe in the existence of a God," the boy say.

"My heart tell me," the preacher say.

"My heart tells me," the boy say. "My heart tells me. Sure, my heart tells me. And as long as you listen to what your heart tells you, you will have only what the white man gives you and nothing more. Me, I don't listen to my heart. The purpose of the heart is to pump blood throughout the body, and nothing else."

"Who's your paw, boy?" the preacher say.

"Why?"

"Who is he?"

"He's dead."

"And your mom?"

"She's in Charity Hospital with pneumonia. Half killed herself working for nothing."

"And 'cause he's dead and she sick, you mad at the world?" [96]

"I'm not mad at the world. I'm questioning the world. I'm questioning it with cold logic, sir. What do words like Freedom, Liberty, God, White, Colored mean? I want to know. That's why *you* are sending us to school, to read and to ask questions. And because we ask these questions, you call us mad. No, sir, it is not us who are mad."

"You keep saying 'us'?"

" 'Us' . . . why not? I'm not alone."

The preacher jest shake his head. Then he look at ever'body in the room—ever'body. Some of the people look down at the floor, keep from looking at him. I kind o' look 'way myself, but soon's I know he done turn his head, I look that way again.

"I'm sorry for you," he say.

"Why?" the boy say. "Why not be sorry for yourself? Why are you so much better off than I am? Why aren't you sorry for these other people in here? Why not be sorry for the lady who had to drag her child into the dentist office? Why not be sorry for the lady sitting on that bench over there? Be sorry for them. Not for me. Some way or other I'm going to make it."

"No, I'm sorry for you," the preacher say.

"Of course. Of course," the boy say, shaking his head. "You're sorry for me because I rock that pillar you're leaning on."

"You can't ever rock the pillar I'm leaning on, young man. It's stronger than anything man can ever do."

"You believe in God because a man told you to believe in God. A white man told you to believe in God. And why? To keep you ignorant, so he can keep you under his feet."

"So now, we the ignorant?"

"Yes," the boy say. "Yes." And he open his book again.

The preacher jest look at him there. The boy [97] done forgot all about him. Ever'body else make 'tend they done forgot 'bout the squabble, too.

Then I see that preacher getting up real slow. Preacher a great big old man, and he got to brace hisself to get up. He come 'cross the room where the boy is. He jest stand there looking at him, but the boy don't raise his head.

"Stand up, boy," preacher say.

The boy look up at him, then he shet his book real slow and stand up. Preacher jest draw back and hit him in the face. The boy fall 'gainst the wall, but he straighten hisself up and look right back at that preacher.

"You forgot the other cheek," he say.

The preacher hit him again on the other side. But this time the boy don't fall.

"That hasn't changed a thing," he say.

The preacher jest look at the boy. The preacher breathing real hard like he jest run up a hill. The boy sit down and open his book again.

"I feel sorry for you," the preacher say. "I never felt so sorry for a man before."

The boy make 'tend he don't even hear that preacher. He keep on reading his book. The preacher go back and get his hat off the chair.

"Excuse me," he say to us. "I'll come back some other time. Y'all, please excuse me."

And he look at the boy and go out the room. The boy hist his hand up to his mouth one time, to wipe 'way some blood. All the rest o' the time he keep on reading.

VIII

The lady and her little boy come out the dentist, and the nurse call somebody else in. Then little bit later they come out, and the nurse call another name. [98] But fast's she call somebody in there, somebody else come in the place where we at, and the room stay full.

The people coming in now, all of 'em wearing big coats. One of 'em say something 'bout sleeting, and another one say he hope not. Another one say he think it ain't nothing but rain. 'Cause, he say, rain can get awful cold this time o' year.

All 'cross the room they talking. Some of 'em talking to people right by 'em, some of 'em talking to people clare 'cross the room, some of 'em talking to anybody'll listen. It's a little bitty room, no bigger 'an us kitchen, and I can see ever'body in there. The little old room 's full of smoke, 'cause you got two old men smoking pipes. I think I feel my teef thumping me some, and I hold my breath and wait. I wait and wait, but it don't thump me no more. Thank God for that.

I feel like going to sleep, and I lean back 'gainst the wall. But I'm scared to go to sleep: Scared 'cause the nurse might call my name and I won't hear her. And Mama might go to sleep, too, and she be mad if neither us heard the nurse.

I look up at Mama. I love my mama. I love my mama. And when cotton come I'm go'n get her a newer coat. And I ain't go'n get a black one neither. I think I'm go'n get her a red one.

"They got some books over there," I say. "Want read one of 'em?"

Mama look at the books, but she don't answer me.

"You got yourself a little man there," the lady say.

Mama don't say nothing to the lady, but she must 'a grin a little bit, 'cause I seen the lady grinning back. The lady look at me a little while, like she feeling sorry for me.

"You sure got that preacher out here in a hurry," she say to that other boy.

The boy look up at her and look in his book again. [99] When I grow up I want be jest like him. I want clothes like that and I want keep a book with me, too.

"You really don't believe in God?" the lady say.

"No," he say.

"But why?" the lady say.

"Because the wind is pink," he say.

"What?" the lady say.

The boy don't answer her no more. He jest read in his book.

"Talking 'bout the wind is pink," that old lady say. She sitting on the same bench with the boy, and she trying to look in his face. The boy make 'tend the old lady ain't even there. He jest keep reading. "Wind is pink," she say again. "Eh, Lord, what children go'n be saying next?"

The lady 'cross from us bust out laughing.

"That's a good one," she say. "The wind is pink. Yes, sir, that's a good one."

"Don't you believe the wind is pink?" the boy say. He keep his head down in the book.

"Course I believe it, Honey," the lady say. "Course I do." She look at us and wink her eye. "And what color is grass, Honey?"

"Grass? Grass is black."

She bust out laughing again. The boy look at her.

"Don't you believe grass is black?" he say.

The lady quit laughing and look at him. Ever'body else look at him now. The place quiet, quiet.

"Grass is green, Honey," the lady say. "It was green yesterday, it's green today, and it's go'n be green tomorrow."

"How do you know it's green?"

"I know because I know."

"You don't know it's green. You believe it's green because someone told you it was green. If someone had told you it was black you'd believe it was black." [100]

"It's green," the lady say. "I know green when I see green."

"Prove it's green."

"Surely, now," the lady say. "Don't tell me it's coming to that?"

"It's coming to just that," the boy say. "Words mean nothing. One means no more than the other."

"That's what it all coming to?" that old lady say. That old lady got on a turban and she got on two sweaters. She got a green sweater under a black sweater. I can see the green sweater 'cause some of the buttons on the other sweater missing.

"Yes, ma'am," the boy say. "Words mean nothing. Action is the only thing. Doing. That's the only thing."

"Other words, you want the Lord to come down here and show Hisself to you?" she say.

"Exactly, ma'am."

"You don't mean that, I'm sure?"

"I do, ma'am."

"Done, Jesus," the old lady say, shaking her head.

"I didn't go 'long with that preacher at first," the other lady say; "but now—I don't know. When a person say the grass is black, he's either a lunatic or something wrong."

"Prove to me that it's green."

"It's green because the people say it's green."

"Those same people say we're citizens of the United States."

"I think I'm a citizen."

"Citizens have certain rights. Name me one right that you have. One right, granted by the Constitution, that you can exercise in Bayonne."

The lady don't answer him. She jest look at him like she don't know what he talking 'bout. I know I don't.

"Things changing," she say. [101]

"Things are changing because some black men have begun to follow their brains instead of their hearts."

"You trying to say these people don't believe in God?"

"I'm sure some of them do. Maybe most of them do. But they don't believe that God is going to touch these white people's hearts and change them tomorrow. Things change through action. By no other way."

Ever'body sit quiet and look at the boy. Nobody say a thing. Then the lady 'cross from me and Mama jest shake her head.

"Let's hope that not all your generation feel the same way you do," she say.

"Think what you please, it doesn't matter," the boy say. "But it will be men who listen to their heads and not their hearts who will see that your children have a better chance than you had."

"Let's hope they ain't all like you, though," the old lady say. "Done forgot the heart absolutely."

"Yes, ma'am, I hope they aren't all like me," the boy say. "Unfortunately I was born too late to believe in your God. Let's hope that the ones who come after will have your faith—if not in your God, then in something else, something definitely that they can lean on. I haven't anything. For me, the wind is pink; the grass is black."

IX

The nurse come in the room where us all sitting and waiting and say the doctor won't take no more patients till one o'clock this evening. My mama jump up off the bench and go up to the white lady.

"Nurse, I have to go back in the field this evening," she say. [102]

"The doctor is treating his last patient now," the nurse say. "One o'clock this evening."

"Can I at least speak to the doctor?" my mama say.

"I'm his nurse," the lady say.

"My little boy sick," my mama say. "Right now his teef almost killing him."

The nurse look at me. She trying to make up her mind if to let me come in. I look at her real pitiful. The teef ain't hurting me a tall, but Mama say it is, so I make 'tend for her sake.

"This evening," the nurse say, and go back in the office.

"Don't feel 'jected, Honey," the lady say to Mama. "I been 'round 'em a long time—they take you when they want to. If you was white, that's something else; but you the wrong shade."

Mama don't say nothing to the lady, and me and her go outside and stand 'gainst the wall. It's cold out there. I can feel that wind going through my coat. Some of the other people come out of the room and go up the street. Me and Mama stand there a little while and start to walking. I don't know where us going. When us come to the other street us jest stand there.

"You don't have to make water, do you?" Mama say.

"No, ma'am," I say.

Us go up the street. Walking real slow. I can tell Mama don't know where she going. When us come to a store us stand there and look at the dummies. I look at a little boy with a brown overcoat. He got on brown shoes, too. I look at my old shoes and look at his'n again. You wait till summer, I say.

Me and Mama walk away. Us come up to another store and us stop and look at them dummies, too. Then us go again. Us pass a café where the white people in there eating. [103] Mama tell me keep my eyes in front where they blonks, but I can't help from seeing them people eat. My stomach start to growling 'cause I'm hungry. When I see people eating, I get hungry; when I see a coat, I get cold.

A man whistle at my mama when us go by a filling station. She make 'tend she don't even see him. I look back and I feel like hitting him in the mouth. If I was bigger, I say. If I was bigger, you see.

Us keep on going. I'm getting colder and colder, but I don't say nothing. I feel that stuff running down my nose and I sniff.

"That rag," she say.

I git it out and wipe my nose. I'm getting cold all over now—
my face, my hands, my feet, ever'thing. Us pass another little café,
but this'n for white people, too, and us can't go in there neither.
So us jest walk. I'm so cold now, I'm 'bout ready to say it. If I
knowed where us was going, I wouldn't be so cold, but I don't
know where us going. Us go, us go, us go. Us walk clean out o'
Bayonne. Then us cross the street and us come back. Same thing I
seen when I got off the bus. Same old trees, same old walk, same
old weeds, same old cracked pave—same old ever'thing.

I sniff again.

"That rag," she say.

I wipe my nose real fast and jugg that hankercher back in my
pocket 'fore my hand get too cold. I raise my head and I can see
David hardware store. When us come up to it, us go in. I don't
know why, but I'm glad.

It warm in there. It so warm in there you don't want ever leave.
I look for the heater, and I see it over by them ba'ls. Three white
men standing 'round the heater talking in Creole. One of 'em
come to see what Mama want.

"Got any ax handle?" she say.

Me, Mama, and the white man start to the back, but [104]
Mama stop me when us come to the heater. Her and the white
man go on. I hold my hand over the heater and look at 'em. They
go all the way in the back, and I see the white man point to the ax
handle 'gainst the wall. Mama take one of 'em and shake it like
she trying to figure how much it weigh. Then she rub her hand
over it from one end to the other end. She turn it over and look at
the other side, then she shake it again, and shake her head and put
it back. She get another one and she do it jest like she did the first
one, then she shake her head. Then she get a brown one and do it
that, too. But she don't like this one neither. Then she get another
one, but 'fore she shake it or anything, she look at me. Look like
she trying to say something to me, but I don't know what it is. All
I know is I done got warm now and I'm feeling right smart better.
Mama shake this ax handle jest like she done the others, and
shake her head and say something to the white man. The white
man jest look at his pile of ax handle, and when Mama pass by
him to come to the front, the white man jest scratch his head and
follow her. She tell me come on, and us go on out and start walking again.

Us walk and walk, and no time at all I'm cold again. Look like
I'm colder now 'cause I can still remember how good it was back

there. My stomach growl and I suck it in to keep Mama from yer-ing it. She walking right 'side me, and it growl so loud you can yer it a mile. But Mama don't say a word.

X

When us come up to the courthouse, I look at the clock. It got quarter to twelve. Mean us got another hour and a quarter to be out yer in the cold. Us go and stand side a building. Something hit my cap and I look up at the sky. Sleet falling.

I look at Mama standing there. I want stand close 'side [105] her, but she don't like that. She say that's cry-baby stuff. She say you got to stand for yourself, by yourself.

"Let's go back to that office," she say.

Us cross the street. When us get to the dentist I try to open the door, but I can't. Mama push me on the side and she twist the knob. But she can't open it neither. She twist it some more, harder, but she can't open it. She turn 'way from the door. I look at her, but I don't move and I don't say nothing. I done seen her like this before and I'm scared.

"You hungry?" she say. She say it like she mad at me, like I'm the one cause of ever'thing.

"No, ma'am," I say.

"You want eat and walk back, or you rather don't eat and ride?"

"I ain't hungry," I say.

I ain't jest hungry, but I'm cold, too. I'm so hungry and I'm so cold I want cry. And look like I'm getting colder and colder. My feet done got numb. I try to work my toes, but I can't. Look like I'm go'n die. Look like I'm go'n stand right here and freeze to death. I think about home. I think about Val and Auntie and Ty and Louis and Walker. It 'bout twelve o'clock and I know they eating dinner. I can hear Ty making jokes. That's Ty. Always trying to make some kind o' joke. I wish I was right there listen-ing to him. Give anything in the world if I was home 'round the fire.

"Come on," Mama say.

Us start walking again. My feet so numb I can't hardly feel 'em. Us turn the corner and go back up the street. The clock start hit-ting for twelve.

The sleet's coming down plenty now. They hit the pave and bounce like rice. Oh, Lord; oh, Lord, I pray. Don't let me die. Don't let me die. Don't let me die, Lord. [106]

XI

Now I know where us going. Us going back o' town where the colored people eat. I don't care if I don't eat. I been hungry before. I can stand it. But I can't stand the cold.

I can see us go'n have a long walk. It 'bout a mile down there. But I don't mind. I know when I get there I'm go'n warm myself. I think I can hold out. My hands numb in my pockets and my feet numb, too, but if I keep moving I can hold out. Jest don't stop no more, that's all.

The sky's gray. The sleet keep falling. Falling like rain now—plenty, plenty. You can hear it hitting the pave. You can see it bouncing. Sometime it bounce two times 'fore it settle.

Us keep going. Us don't say nothing. Us jest keep going, keep going.

I wonder what Mama thinking. I hope she ain't mad with me. When summer come I'm go'n pick plenty cotton and get her a coat. I'm go'n get her a red one.

I hope they make it summer all the time. I be glad if it was summer all the time—but it ain't. Us got to have winter, too. Lord, I hate the winter. I guess ever'body hate the winter.

I don't sniff this time. I get out my hankercher and wipe my nose. My hand so cold I can hardly hold the hankercher.

I think us getting close, but us ain't there yet. I wonder where ever'body is. Can't see nobody but us. Look like us the only two people moving 'round today. Must be too cold for the rest of the people to move 'round.

I can hear my teefes. I hope they don't knock together too hard and make that bad one hurt. Lord, that's all I need, for that bad one to start off.

I hear a church bell somewhere. But today ain't Sunday. They must be ringing for a funeral or something. [107]

I wonder what they doing at home. They must be eating. Monsieur Bayonne might be there with his guitar. One day Ty played with Monsieur Bayonne guitar and broke one o' the string. Monsieur Bayonne got some mad with Ty. He say Ty ain't go'n never 'mount to nothing. Ty can go jest like him when he ain't there. Ty can make ever'body laugh mocking Monsieur Bayonne.

I used to like to be with Mama and Daddy. Us used to be happy. But they took him in the Army. Now, nobody happy no more. . . . I be glad when he come back.

Monsieur Bayonne say it wasn't fair for 'em to take Daddy and give Mama nothing and give us nothing. Auntie say, Shhh, Etienne. Don't let 'em yer you talk like that. Monsieur Bayonne say, It's God truth. What they giving his children? They have to walk three and a half mile to school hot or cold. That's anything to give for a paw? She got to work in the field rain or shine jest to make ends meet. That's anything to give for a husband? Auntie say, Shhh, Etienne, shhh. Yes, you right, Monsieur Bayonne say. Best don't say it in front of 'em now. But one day they go'n find out. One day. Yes, s'pose so, Auntie say. Then what, Rose Mary? Monsieur Bayonne say. I don't know, Etienne, Auntie say. All us can do is us job, and leave ever'thing else in His hand. . . .

Us getting closer, now. Us getting closer. I can see the railroad tracks.

Us cross the tracks, and now I see the café. Jest to get in there, I say. Jest to get in there. Already I'm starting to feel little better. [108]

XII

Us go in. Ahh, it good. I look for the heater; there 'gainst the wall. One of them little brown ones. I jest stand there and hold my hand over it. I can't open my hands too wide 'cause they almost froze.

Mama standing right 'side me. She done unbuttoned her coat. Smoke rise out the coat, and the coat smell like a wet dog.

I move to the side so Mama can have more room. She open out her hands and rub 'em together. I rub mine together, too, 'cause this keep 'em from hurting. If you let 'em warm too fast, they hurt you sure. But if you let 'em warm jest little bit at a time, and you keep rubbing 'em, they be all right ever' time.

They got jest two more people in the café. A lady back o' the counter, and a man on this side the counter. They been watching us ever since us come in.

Mama get out the hankercher and count the money. Both o' us know how much money she got there. Three dollars. No, she ain't got three dollars. 'Cause she had to pay us way up here. She ain't got but two dollars and a half left. Dollar and a half to get my teef pulled, and fifty cents for us to go back on, and fifty cents worse o' salt meat.

She stir the money 'round with her finger. Most o' the money is change 'cause I can hear it rubbing together. She stir it and stir it. Then she look at the door. It still sleeting. I can yer it hitting 'gainst the wall like rice.

"I ain't hungry, Mama," I say.

"Got to pay 'em something for they heat," she say.

She take a quarter out the hankercher and tie the hankercher up again. She look over her shoulder at the people, but she still don't move. I hope she don't spend the money. I don't want her spend it on me. I'm hungry, I'm [109] almost starving I'm so hungry, but I don't want her spending the money on me.

She flip the quarter over like she thinking. She must be thinking 'bout us walking back home. Lord, I sure don't want walk home. If I thought it done any good to say something, I say it. But my mama make up her own mind.

She turn way from the heater right fast, like she better hurry up and do it 'fore she change her mind. I turn to look at her go to the counter. The man and the lady look at her, too. She tell the lady something and the lady walk away. The man keep on looking at her. Her back turn to the man, and Mama don't even know he standing there.

The lady put some cakes and a glass o' milk on the counter. Then she pour up a cup o' coffee and set it 'side the other stuff. Mama pay her for the things and come back where I'm at. She tell me sit down at that table 'gainst the wall.

The milk and the cakes for me. The coffee for my mama. I eat slow, and I look at her. She looking outside at the sleet. She looking real sad. I say to myself, I'm go'n make all this up one day. You see, one day, I'm go'n make all this up. I want to say it now. I want to tell how I feel right now. But Mama don't like for us to talk like that.

"I can't eat all this," I say.

They got just three little cakes there. And I'm so hungry right now, the Lord know I can eat a hundred times three. But I want her to have one.

She don't even look my way. She know I'm hungry. She know I want it. I let it stay there a while, then I get it and eat it. I eat jest on my front teefes, 'cause if it tech that back teef I know what'll happen. Thank God it ain't hurt me a tall today.

After I finish eating I see the man go to the juke box. He [110] drop a nickel in it, then he jest stand there looking at the record. Mama tell me keep my eyes in front where they blonks. I turn my head like she say, but then I yer the man coming towards us.

"Dance, Pretty?" he say.

Mama get up to dance with him. But 'fore you know it, she

done grabbed the little man and done throwed him 'side the wall. He hit the wall so hard he stop the juke box from playing.

"Some pimp," the lady back o' the counter say. "Some pimp."

The little man jump up off the floor and start towards my mama. 'Fore you know it, Mama done sprung open her knife and she waiting for him.

"Come on," she say. "Come on. I'll cut you from your neighbo to your throat. Come on."

I go up to the little man to hit him, but Mama make me come and stand 'side her. The little man look at me and Mama and go back to the counter.

"Some pimp," the lady back o' the counter say. "Some pimp." She start laughing and pointing at the little man. "Yes, sir, you a pimp, all right. Yes, sir."

XIII

"Fasten that coat. Let's go," Mama say.

"You don't have to leave," the lady say.

Mama don't answer the lady, and us right out in the cold again. I'm warm right now—my hands, my yers, my feet—but I know this ain't go'n last too long. It done sleet so much now you got ice ever'where.

Us cross the railroad tracks, and soon's us do, I get cold. That wind go through this little old coat like it ain't nothing. I got a shirt and a sweater under it, but that wind don't pay 'em no mind. I look up and I can see us got [111] a long way to go. I wonder if us go'n make it 'fore I get too cold.

Us cross over to walk on the sidewalk. They got jest one sidewalk back here. It's over there.

After us go jest a little piece, I smell bread cooking. I look, then I see a baker shop. When us get closer, I can smell it more better. I shet my eyes and make 'tend I'm eating. But I keep 'em shet too long and I butt up 'gainst a telephone post. Mama grab me and see if I'm hurt. I ain't bleeding or nothing and she turn me loose.

I can feel I'm getting colder and colder, and I look up to see how far us still got to go. Uptown is 'way up yonder. A half mile, I reckoned. I try to think of something. They say think and you won't get cold. I think of that poem, *Annabel Lee*. I ain't been to school in so long—this bad weather—I reckoned they done passed *Annabel Lee*. But passed it or not, I'm sure Miss Walker go'n make me recite it when I get there. That woman don't never forget nothing. I ain't never seen nobody like that.

I'm still getting cold. *Annabel Lee* or no *Annabel Lee,* I'm still getting cold. But I can see us getting closer. Us getting there gradually.

Soon's us turn the corner, I see a little old white lady up in front o' us. She the only lady on the street. She all in black and she got a long black rag over her head.

"Stop," she say.

Me and Mama stop and look at her. She must be crazy to be out in all this sleet. Ain't got but a few other people out there, and all of 'em men.

"Yall done ate?" she say.

"Jest finished," Mama say.

"Yall must be cold then?" she say.

"Us headed for the dentist," Mama say. "Us'll warm up when us get there."

"What dentist?" the old lady say. "Mr. Bassett?" [112]

"Yes, ma'am," Mama say.

"Come on in," the old lady say. "I'll telephone him and tell him yall coming."

Me and Mama follow the old lady in the store. It's a little bitty store, and it don't have much in there. The old lady take off her head piece and fold it up.

"Helena?" somebody call from the back.

"Yes, Alnest?" the old lady say.

"Did you see them?"

"They're here. Standing beside me."

"Good. Now you can stay inside."

The old lady look at Mama. Mama waiting to hear what she brought us in here for. I'm waiting for that, too.

"I saw yall each time you went by," she say. "I came out to catch you, but you were gone."

"Us went back o' town," Mama say.

"Did you eat?"

"Yes, ma'am."

The old lady look at Mama a long time, like she thinking Mama might be jest saying that. Mama look right back at her. The old lady look at me to see what I got to say. I don't say nothing. I sure ain't going 'gainst my mama.

"There's food in the kitchen," she say to Mama. "I've been keeping it warm."

Mama turn right around and start for the door.

"Just a minute," the old lady say. Mama stop. "The boy'll have to work for it. It isn't free."

"Us don't take no handout," Mama say.

"I'm not handing out anything," the old lady say. "I need my garbage moved to the front. Ernest has a bad cold and can't go out there."

"James'll move it for you," Mama say.

"Not unless you eat," the old lady say. "I'm old, but I have my pride, too, you know." [113]

Mama can see she ain't go'n beat this old lady down, so she jest shake her head.

"All right," the old lady say. "Come into the kitchen."

She lead the way with that rag in her hand. The kitchen is a lit- tle bitty little thing, too. The table and the stove jest about fill it up. They got a little room to the side. Somebody in there laying cross the bed. Must be the person she was talking with: Alnest or Ernest—I forget what she call him.

"Sit down," the old lady say to Mama. "Not you," she say to me. "You have to move the cans."

"Helena?" somebody say in the other room.

"Yes, Alnest?" the old lady say.

"Are you going out there again?"

"I must show the boy where the garbage is," the old lady say.

"Keep that shawl over your head," the old man say.

"You don't have to remind me. Come, boy," the old lady say.

Us go out in the yard. Little old back yard ain't no bigger 'an the store or the kitchen. But it can sleet here jest like it can sleet in any big back yard. And 'fore you know it I'm trembling.

"There," the old lady say, pointing to the cans. I pick up one of the cans. The can so light I put it back down to look inside o' it.

"Here," the old lady say. "Leave that cap alone."

I look at her in the door. She got that black rag wrapped 'round her shoulders, and she pointing one of her fingers at me.

"Pick it up and carry it to the front," she say. I go by her with the can. I'm sure the thing 's empty. She could 'a' carried the thing by herself, I'm sure. "Set it on the sidewalk by the door and come back for the other one," she say. [114]

I go and come back, Mama look at me when I pass her. I get the other can and take it to the front. It don't feel no heavier 'an the other one. I tell myself to look inside and see just what I been hauling. First, I look up and down the street. Nobody coming.

Then I look over my shoulder. Little old lady done slipped there jest 's quiet 's mouse, watching me. Look like she knowed I was go'n try that.

"Ehh, Lord," she say. "Children, children. Come in here, boy, and go wash your hands."

I follow her into the kitchen, and she point, and I go to the bathroom. When I come out, the old lady done dished up the food. Rice, gravy, meat, and she even got some lettuce and tomato in a saucer. She even got a glass o' milk and a piece o' cake there, too. It look so good. I almost start eating 'fore I say my blessing.

"Helena?" the old man say.

"Yes, Alnest?" she say.

"Are they eating?"

"Yes," she say.

"Good," he say. "Now you'll stay inside."

The old lady go in there where he is and I can hear 'em talking. I look at Mama. She eating slow like she thinking. I wonder what 's the matter now. I reckoned she think 'bout home.

The old lady come back in the kitchen.

"I talked to Dr. Bassett's nurse," she say. "Dr. Bassett will take you as soon as you get there."

"Thank you, ma'am," Mama say.

"Perfectly all right," the old lady say. "Which one is it?" [115]

Mama nod towards me. The old lady look at me real sad. I look sad, too.

"You're not afraid, are you?" she say.

"No'm," I say.

"That's a good boy," the old lady say. "Nothing to be afraid of."

When me and Mama get through eating, us thank the old lady again.

"Helena, are they leaving?" the old man say.

"Yes, Alnest."

"Tell them I say good-by."

"They can hear you, Alnest."

"Good-by both mother and son," the old man say. "And may God be with you."

Me and Mama tell the old man good-by, and us follow the old lady in the front. Mama open the door to go out, but she stop and come back in the store.

"You sell salt meat?" she say.

"Yes."

"Give me two bits worse."

"That isn't very much salt meat," the old lady say.

"That's all I have," Mama say.

The old lady go back o' the counter and cut a big piece off the chunk. Then she wrap it and put it in a paper bag.

"Two bits," she say.

"That look like awful lot of meat for a quarter," Mama say.

"Two bits," the old lady say. "I've been selling salt meat behind this counter twenty-five years. I think I know what I'm doing."

"You got a scale there," Mama say.

"What?" the old lady say.

"Weigh it," Mama say. [116]

"What?" the old lady say. "Are you telling me how to run my business?"

"Thanks very much for the food," Mama say.

"Just a minute," the old lady say.

"James," Mama say to me. I move towards the door.

"Just one minute, I said," the old lady say.

Me and Mama stop again and look at her. The old lady take the meat out the bag and unwrap it and cut 'bout half o' it off. Then she wrap it up again and jugg it back in the bag and give it to Mama. Mama lay the quarter on the counter.

"Your kindness will never be forgotten," she say. "James," she say to me.

Us go out, and the old lady come to the door to look at us. After us go a little piece I look back, and she still there watching us.

The sleet's coming down heavy, heavy now, and I turn up my collar to keep my neck warm. My mama tell me turn it right back down.

"You not a bum," she say. "You a man." [117]

JAMES BALDWIN

My Dungeon Shook

Letter to my nephew on the one hundredth
anniversary of the Emancipation

Dear James:

I have begun this letter five times and torn it up five times. I keep
seeing your face, which is also the face of your father and my
brother. Like him, you are tough, dark, vulnerable, moody—with
a very definite tendency to sound truculent because you want no
one to think you are soft. You may be like your grandfather in
this, I don't know, but certainly both you and your father resemble him very much physically. Well, he is dead, he never saw you,
and he had a terrible life; he was defeated long before he [13]
died because, at the bottom of his heart, he really believed what
white people said about him. This is one of the reasons that he became so holy. I am sure that your father has told you something
about all that. Neither you nor your father exhibit any tendency
towards holiness: you really are of another era, part of what happened when the Negro left the land and came into what the late E.
Franklin Frazier called "the cities of destruction." You can only
be destroyed by believing that you really are what the white
world calls a *nigger*. I tell you this because I love you, and please
don't you ever forget it.

SOURCE: James Baldwin, *The Fire Next Time* (New York: The Dial Press,
Inc., 1963), pp. 13–22. Copyright © 1962, 1963 by James Baldwin. Reprinted by permission of the publisher.

I have known both of you all your lives, have carried your Daddy in my arms and on my shoulders, kissed and spanked him and watched him learn to walk. I don't know if you've known anybody from that far back; if you've loved anybody that long, first as an infant, then as a child, then as a man, you gain a strange perspective on time and human pain and effort. Other people cannot see what I see whenever I look into [14] your father's face, for behind your father's face as it is today are all those other faces which were his. Let him laugh and I see a cellar your father does not remember and a house he does not remember and I hear in his present laughter his laughter as a child. Let him curse and I remember him falling down the cellar steps, and howling, and I remember, with pain, his tears, which my hand or your grandmother's so easily wiped away. But no one's hand can wipe away those tears he sheds invisibly today, which one hears in his laughter and in his speech and in his songs. I know what the world has done to my brother and how narrowly he has survived it. And I know, which is much worse, and this is the crime of which I accuse my country and my countrymen, and for which neither I nor time nor history will ever forgive them, that they have destroyed and are destroying hundreds of thousands of lives and do not know it and do not want to know it. One can be, indeed one must strive to become, tough and philosophical concerning destruction [15] and death, for this is what most of mankind has been best at since we have heard of man. (But remember: *most* of mankind is not *all* of mankind.) But it is not permissible that the authors of devastation should also be innocent. It is the innocence which constitutes the crime.

Now, my dear namesake, these innocent and well-meaning people, your countrymen, have caused you to be born under conditions not very far removed from those described for us by Charles Dickens in the London of more than a hundred years ago. (I hear the chorus of the innocents screaming, "No! This is not true! How *bitter* you are!"—but I am writing this letter to *you,* to try to tell you something about how to handle *them,* for most of them do not yet really know that you exist. I *know* the conditions under which you were born, for I was there. Your countrymen were *not* there, and haven't made it yet. Your grandmother was also there, and no one has ever accused her of being bitter. I suggest that the innocents check with her. She isn't hard to find. [16] Your countrymen don't know that *she* exists, either, though she has been working for them all their lives.)

163

Well, you were born, here you came, something like fourteen years ago; and though your father and mother and grandmother, looking about the streets through which they were carrying you, staring at the walls into which they brought you, had every reason to be heavyhearted, yet they were not. For here you were, Big James, named for me—you were a big baby, I was not—here you were: to be loved. To be loved, baby, hard, at once, and forever, to strengthen you against the loveless world. Remember that: I know how black it looks today, for you. It looked bad that day, too, yes, we were trembling. We have not stopped trembling yet, but if we had not loved each other none of us would have survived. And now you must survive because we love you, and for the sake of your children and your children's children.

This innocent country set you down in a ghetto in which, in fact, it intended that [17] you should perish. Let me spell out precisely what I mean by that, for the heart of the matter is here, and the root of my dispute with my country. You were born where you were born and faced the future that you faced because you were black and *for no other reason*. The limits of your ambition were, thus, expected to be set forever. You were born into a society which spelled out with brutal clarity, and in as many ways as possible, that you were a worthless human being. You were not expected to aspire to excellence: you were expected to make peace with mediocrity. Wherever you have turned, James, in your short time on this earth, you have been told where you could go and what you could do (and *how* you could do it) and where you could live and whom you could marry. I know your countrymen do not agree with me about this, and I hear them saying, "You exaggerate." They do not know Harlem, and I do. So do you. Take no one's word for anything, including mine—but trust your experience. Know whence [18] you came. If you know whence you came, there is really no limit to where you can go. The details and symbols of your life have been deliberately constructed to make you believe what white people say about you. Please try to remember that what they believe, as well as what they do and cause you to endure, does not testify to your inferiority but to their inhumanity and fear. Please try to be clear, dear James, through the storm which rages about your youthful head today, about the reality which lies behind the words *acceptance* and *integration*. There is no reason for you to try to become like white people and there is no basis whatever for their impertinent assumption that *they* must accept *you*. The really terrible thing, old buddy, is that *you* must accept them. And I mean that very seriously. You must accept them and accept them with love. For these innocent people have no other hope. They are, in effect, still trapped in a history which they do not understand; and until they understand it, they cannot be released from it. They have had to believe [19] for many years, and for innumerable reasons, that black men are inferior to white men. Many of them, indeed, know better, but, as you will discover, people find it very difficult to act on what they know. To act is to be committed, and to be committed is to be in danger. In this case, the danger, in the minds of most white Americans, is the loss of their identity. Try to imagine how you would feel if you woke up one morning to find the sun shining and all the stars aflame. You would be frightened because it is out of the order of nature. Any upheaval in the universe is terrifying because it so profoundly attacks one's sense of one's own reality. Well, the black man has functioned in the white man's world as a fixed star, as an immovable pillar: and as he moves out of his place, heaven and earth are shaken to their foundations. You, don't be afraid. I said that it was intended that you should perish in the ghetto, perish by never being allowed to go behind the white man's definitions, by never being allowed to spell your proper name. You have, and [20] many of us have, defeated this intention; and, by a terrible law, a terrible paradox, those innocents who believed that your imprisonment made them safe are losing their grasp of reality. But these men are your brothers—your lost, younger brothers. And if the word *integration* means anything, this is what it means: that we, with love, shall force our brothers to see themselves as they are, to cease fleeing from reality and begin to change it. For this is your home, my friend, do not be driven from it; great men have done great things here, and will again, and we can make America what America must become. It will be hard, James, but you come from sturdy, peasant stock, men who picked cotton and dammed rivers and built railroads, and, in the teeth of the most terrifying odds, achieved an unassailable and monumental dignity. You come from a long line of great poets, some of the greatest poets since Homer. One of them said, *The very time I thought I was lost, My dungeon shook and my chains fell off.* [21]

You know, and I know, that the country is celebrating one hundred years of freedom one hundred years too soon. We cannot be free until they are free. God bless you, James, and Godspeed.

Your uncle,

James [22]

165

LE ROI JONES

The Dempsey-Liston Fight *

See?

See him dream?

See the white man dream? Which is where the whole race has gone: to the slowest. But the mass media make this dream a communal fulfillment, so that now, each man who had and has the dream in solitary can share, and grow bigger at its concrete illustration.

Sonny Liston is the big black Negro in every white man's hallway, waiting to do him in, deal him under for all the [155] hurts white men, through their arbitrary order, have been able to inflict on the world. But since the American black man has been closest to, and in *that* sense been most debased by the source and fortune of this philosophical malady, the black man is the local symbol of an entire world of hatred. Sonny Liston is "the huge Negro," the "bad nigger," a heavy-faced replica of every whipped up woogie in the world. He is the underdeveloped, have-not (politically naïve), backward country, the subject people, finally here to collect his pound of flesh.

The mock contest between Liston and Patterson was a "brush-fire" limited war (as Neo-Colonial policy) to confuse the issue. Optimistic diplomacy to obscure the balance of power. Patterson was to represent the fruit of the missionary ethic, in its use as a policy of the democratic liberal imperialist state. Patterson had found God, had reversed his underprivileged (uncontrolled) violence and turned it to work, and for this act become an object of prestige within the existing system. The tardy black Horatio

---

* Inspired by an article, "The Greatest Fights of the Century," in *Esquire* magazine, December 1963.

SOURCE: Le Roi Jones, *Home: Social Essays* (New York: William Morrow and Company, Inc., 1966), pp. 155–160. Copyright © 1962, 1963 by LeRoi Jones. Reprinted by permission of the publisher.

Alger, the glad hand of integration, to welcome those 20,000,000 chimerically, into the lunatic asylum of white America.

In this context, Liston, the unreformed, Liston the vulgar, Liston the violent (who still had to make some gesture toward the Christian ethic, like the quick trip to the Denver priest, to see if somehow the chief whitie could turn him into a regular fella) comes on as the straightup Heavy. I mean "they" painted Liston Black. They painted Patterson White. And that was the simple conflict. Which way would the black man go?

The last question traveled on all levels through the society, if anyone remembers. Pollsters wanted the colored man in the street's opinion. "Sir, who do you *hope* comes out on top in this fight?" A lot of Negroes said Patterson. (That old hope come back on you, that somehow this *is* my country, [156] and ought'n I be allowed to live in it, I mean, to make it. From the bottom to the top? Only the poorest black men have never fallen, at least temporarily, for the success story.) A lot of Negroes said Liston.

A white cab driver was turning to see me in his rear view mirror; he said, "You know that Liston has got the biggest hands of any boxer to come in the ring. You know his arms are six feet long. I mean six feet long each. He's like an animal. Jesus! He shouldn't even be allowed to fight normal guys. He's like an animal." And that's the word from that vector from polite society. Strictly, an animal.

And it meant a lot to the Liberal/Missionary syndrome that they test their handiwork against this frightening brute. So a thin-willed lower middle-class American was led to beatings just short of actual slaughter, to prove the fallibility of another artifact of American culture (which, like most of its other artifacts, suffers very seriously from built-in obsolescence). This happened twice. And each time Patterson fell, there was a vision that came to me of the whole colonial West crumbling in some sinister silence, like the across-the-tracks House of Usher.

But, dig it, there is no white man in the world who wants to fight Sonny Liston himself. (Though Cassius Clay has come from the Special Products Division of Madison Avenue to see what he can do.*)

Now the Orwell Synapse takes over. (What we cannot gain from experience, we will gain by *inperience*.) That is, as every totalitarian order has done, history is changed to correspond with what we all know reality *should* be. It's like the European painters when

* See Dempsey-Liston Addenda.

they began to paint Arab/Moorish/Semitic experience in medieval middle-European contexts. (Christ is then a blond who looks like Jeffrey Hunter. [157] Another smart Germanic type made good.) For this reason, in order to find out what really is the simple history of this country, for example, one has to go to E. Franklin Frazier and W.E.B. DuBois. *Inperience* is the positing of a fantasy "event" as what is the case. Practically speaking, for instance, if God were not white, how could he get permission from the white man to make him? If, say, God were black, there would have to be some white man somewhere to tell him what to do, right?

In the magazine, Liston beats Marciano, "the most brutal first round ever seen," and he also beats Louis, ". . . Louis flew back five feet, fell, and rolled on his face." And having set this up, Dempsey comes marching in like drunk Ward Bond whistling a cavalry tune, to straighten everything out. It was a little hectic (like in *The Spoilers,* or where John Wayne is facing a really brave Indian) but the end, I am certain, is never in doubt. Even in dirty books there has to be some moral reestablishment. As the barbarian climbs through that chink in the wall, IBM!, ". . . Liston turned and fell heavily to the floor, his right glove under his face." In the posture of sleep, like a gypsy in the desert, a *fellaheen.* "At six, he rolled over and, back now in his corner, Dempsey smiled." The muscular Neyland-Smith.

So now, forget that all this is dream and wish fulfillment, and think of it as it does now, and must necessarily, sit—as a blatant social gesture. This is how the synapse works. We erase the mad-bad big black guy by going back in time to get him in a dream, and the drop to the canvas takes nearly the whole of the dream, it is so slow and gravity-less, or maybe it is replayed, reseen, over and over again. ". . . heavily to the floor, his right glove under his face." We get the big strong likable immigrant, who has always done America's chores. He's glad to oblige. We always get to the bad niggers . . . either kill 'em, or drive 'em out of the country. [158] Jack Johnson, Henry Higland Garnet, DuBois, Paul Robeson, Robert Williams, Richard Wright, Sidney Bechet, Josephine Baker, Beauford Delaney, Chester Himes, so many others. All the black neurotic beauties trailing dumbly through the "equal" streets of hopeless European cities. All the unclaimed fugitive corpses.

But this was the calmest and most rational method. Simply going back like in a science fiction story called *By His Bootstraps,* and erasing this loud black fool. Add to the record book, just before the Tunney fight, "Liston vs Dempsey. . . . . . .Dempsey, K.O., 1:44 of the ninth." (And in the doing, of course, Louis is turned off as well.)

What kind of men are these who would practice such deception on themselves? (The will and promise of the entire society has grown just as weak, perhaps now even more so since it has lost the strong man who at least offered the fiction of its vitality.) Oh, they are simply Americans, and some years from now, perhaps there will be this short addition: "You remember them, don't you?"

Dempsey-Liston Addenda

This image, observation, was made pre-Liston-Clay, also before Mohammad Ali or Cassius X emerged. Now I think of Clay as merely a terribly stretched out young man with problems one would have hoped would have at least waited for him to reach full manhood. Clay is not a fake, and even his blustering and playground poetry are valid, and demonstrate, as far as I'm concerned, that a new and more complicated generation has moved onto the scene. And in this last sense Clay is definitely my man. However, his choosing Elijah Muhammad over Malcolm X, if indeed such is the case, means that he is still a "homeboy," embracing this folksy vector straight out of the hard spiritualism of poor [159] Negro aspiration, *i.e.,* he is right now just angry rather than intellectually (socio-politically) motivated.

The Liston-Clay fight seemed to be on the up and up to me. Liston was just way out of shape, expecting young X to be just another weak-faced American. But Cassius can box, and Liston in shape might have trouble spearing the very quick X. But poor Sonny's in jail now,* where most of the white world would have him. (Shades of Jack Johnson!) And the possibility of a return between Clay and Liston grows each day more remote.

But whoever has the heavyweight championship now, or in the future, it is an even remoter possibility that it will be Jack Dempsey, or for that matter any of his Irish progeny. Most of the Dempseys in America now don't have to knock heads for a living (except as honest patrolmen) and their new roles as just anybody, having mostly graduated from the immigrant-newcomer class, make them as weak and unfit for the task of defeating any of the black heavyweights as any other white Americans, even the honorary kind like Floyd Patterson. [160]

* 1963.

ELDRIDGE CLEAVER

To All Black Women, From All Black Men

Queen—Mother—Daughter of Africa
Sister of My Soul
Black Bride of My Passion
My Eternal Love

I greet you, my Queen, not in the obsequious whine of a cringing Slave to which you have become accustomed, neither do I greet you in the new voice, the unctuous supplications of the sleek Black Bourgeoisie, nor the bullying bellow of the rude Free Slave —but in my own voice do I greet you, the voice of the Black Man. And although I greet you *anew,* my greeting is not *new,* but as old as the Sun, Moon, and Stars. And rather than mark a new beginning, my greeting signifies only my Return.

I have Returned from the dead. I speak to you now from the Here And Now. I was dead for four hundred years. For four hundred years you have been a woman alone, bereft of her man, a manless woman. For four hundred years I was neither your man nor my own man. The white man stood between us, over us, around us. The white man was your man and my man. Do not pass lightly over this truth, my Queen, for even though the fact of it has burned into the marrow of our bones and diluted our blood, we must bring [205] it to the surface of the mind, into the realm of knowing, glue our gaze upon it and stare at it as at a coiled serpent in a baby's playpen or the fresh flowers on a mother's grave. It is to be pondered and realized in the heart, for the heel of the white man's boot is our point of departure, our point of Resolve

SOURCE: Eldridge Cleaver, *Soul On Ice* (New York: McGraw-Hill Book Company, 1968), pp. 205–210. Copyright © 1968 by Eldridge Cleaver. Reprinted by permission of the publisher.

and Return—the bloodstained pivot of our future. (But I would ask you to recall, that before we could come up from slavery, we had to be pulled down from our throne.)

Across the naked abyss of negated masculinity, of four hundred years minus my Balls, we face each other today, my Queen. I feel a deep, terrifying hurt, the pain of humiliation of the vanquished warrior. The shame of the fleet-footed sprinter who stumbles at the start of the race. I feel unjustified. I can't bear to look into your eyes. Don't you know (surely you must have noticed by now: four hundred years!) that for four hundred years I have been unable to look squarely into your eyes? I tremble inside each time you look at me. I can feel . . . in the ray of your eye, from a deep hiding place, a long-kept secret you harbor. That is the unadorned truth. Not that I would have felt justified, under the circumstances, in taking such liberties with you, but I want you to know that I feared to look into your eyes because I knew I would find reflected there a merciless Indictment of my impotence and a compelling challenge to redeem my conquered manhood.

My Queen, it is hard for me to tell you what is in my heart for you today—what is in the heart of all my black brothers for you and all your black sisters—and I fear I will fail unless you reach out to me, tune in on me with the antenna of your love, the sacred love in ultimate degree which you were unable to give me because I, being dead, was unworthy to receive it; that perfect, radical love of [206] black on which our Fathers thrived. Let me drink from the river of your love at its source, let the lines of force of your love seize my soul by its core and heal the wound of my Castration, let my convex exile end its haunted Odyssey in your concave essence which receives that it may give. Flower of Africa, it is only through the liberating power of your *re*-love that my manhood can be redeemed. For it is in your eyes, before you, that my need is to be justified, Only, only, only you and only you can condemn or set me free.

Be convinced, Sable Sister, that the past is no forbidden vista upon which we dare not look, out of a phantom fear of being, as the wife of Lot, turned into pillars of salt. Rather the past is an omniscient mirror: we gaze and see reflected there ourselves and each other—what we used to be, what we are today, how we got this way, and what we are becoming. To decline to look into the Mirror of Then, my heart, is to refuse to view the face of Now.

Eldridge Cleaver

I have died the ninth death of the cat, have seen Satan face to face and turned my back on God, have dined in the Swine's Trough, and descended to the uttermost echelon of the Pit, have entered the Den and seized my Balls from the teeth of a roaring lion!

Black Beauty, in impotent silence I listened, as if to a symphony of sorrows, to your screams for help, anguished pleas of terror that echo still throughout the Universe and through the mind, a million scattered screams across the painful years that merged into a single sound of pain to haunt and bleed the soul, a white-hot sound to char the brain and blow the fuse of thought, a sound of fangs and teeth sharp to eat the heart, a sound of moving fire, a sound of frozen heat, a sound of licking flames, a fiery-fiery sound, a sound of fire to burn the steel out of my Balls, a sound of [207] Blue fire, a Bluesy sound, the sound of dying, the sound of my woman in pain, *the sound of my woman's pain,* THE SOUND OF MY WOMAN CALLING ME, ME, I HEARD HER CALL FOR HELP, I HEARD THAT MOURNFUL SOUND BUT HUNG MY HEAD AND FAILED TO HEED IT, I HEARD MY WOMAN'S CRY, I HEARD MY WOMAN'S SCREAM, I HEARD MY WOMAN BEG THE BEAST FOR MERCY, I HEARD HER BEG FOR ME, I HEARD MY WOMAN BEG THE BEAST FOR MERCY FOR ME, I HEARD MY WOMAN DIE, I HEARD THE SOUND OF HER DEATH, A SNAPPING SOUND, A BREAKING SOUND, A SOUND THAT SOUNDED FINAL, THE LAST SOUND, THE ULTIMATE SOUND, THE SOUND OF DEATH, ME, I HEARD, I HEAR IT EVERY DAY, I HEAR HER NOW . . . I HEAR YOU NOW . . . I HEAR YOU. . . . I heard you then . . . your scream came like a searing bolt of lightning that blazed a white streak down my black back. In a cowardly stupor, with a palpitating heart and quivering knees, I watched the Slaver's lash of death slash through the opposing air and bite with teeth of fire into your delicate flesh, the black and tender flesh of African Motherhood, forcing the startled Life untimely from your torn and outraged womb, the sacred womb that cradled primal man, the womb that incubated Ethiopia and populated Nubia and gave forth Pharaohs unto Egypt, the womb that painted the Congo black and mothered Zulu, the womb of Mero, the womb of the Nile, of the Niger, the womb of Songhay, of Mali, of Ghana, the womb that felt the might of Chaka before he saw the Sun, the Holy Womb, the womb that knew the future form of Jomo Kenyatta, the womb of Mau Mau, the womb of the blacks, the womb that nurtured Toussaint L'Ouverture, that warmed Nat Turner,

nd Gabriel Prosser, and Denmark Vesey, the black womb that
urrendered up in tears that nameless and endless chain of Afri-
a's Cream, the Black Cream of the Earth, that nameless [208]
nd endless black chain that sank in heavy groans into oblivion in
he great abyss, the womb that received and nourished and held
rm the seed and gave back Sojourner Truth, and Sister Tubman,
nd Rosa Parks, and Bird, and Richard Wright, and your other
works of art who wore and wear such names as Marcus Garvey
nd DuBois and Kwame Nkrumah and Paul Robeson and Mal-
olm X and Robert Williams, and the one you bore in pain and
alled Elijah Muhammad, but most of all that nameless one they
ore out of your womb in a flood of murdered blood that splashed
pon and seeped into the mud. And Patrice Lumumba, and Em-
nett Till, and Mack Parker.

O, My Soul! I became a sniveling craven, a funky punk, a vile,
roveling bootlicker, with my will to oppose petrified by a cosmic
ear of the Slavemaster. Instead of inciting the Slaves to rebellion
with eloquent oratory, I soothed their hurt and eloquently sang the
Blues! Instead of hurling my life with contempt into the face of
ny Tormentor, *I shed your precious blood!* When Nat Turner
ought to free me from my Fear, my Fear delivered him up unto
he Butcher—a martyred monument to my Emasculation. My
pirit was unwilling and my flesh was weak. Ah, eternal ignominy!

I, the Black Eunuch, divested of my Balls, walked the earth
with my mind locked in Cold Storage. I would kill a black man or
woman quicker than I'd smash a fly, while for the white man I
would pick a thousand pounds of cotton a day. What profit is
here in the blind, frenzied efforts of the (Guilty!) Black Eunuchs
Justifiers!) who hide their wounds and scorn the truth to mitigate
heir culpability through the pallid sophistry of postulating a Universal Democracy of Cowards, pointing out that in history no one
an hide, that if not at one time then surely at another the iron
eel of the Conqueror has ground into the mud the [209] Balls of
Everyman? Memories of yesterday will not assuage the torrents of
blood that flow today from my crotch. Yes, History could pass for
a scarlet text, its jot and tittle graven red in human blood. More
armies than shown in the books have planted flags on foreign soil
eaving Castration in their wake. But no Slave should die a natural
death. There is a point where Caution ends and Cowardice begins.
Give me a bullet through the brain from the gun of the belea-
guered oppressor on the night of siege. Why is there dancing and
singing in the Slave Quarters? A Slave who dies of natural causes

cannot balance two dead flies in the Scales of Eternity. Such a one deserves rather to be pitied than mourned.

Black woman, without asking how, just say that we survived our forced march and travail through the Valley of Slavery, Suffering and Death—there, that Valley there beneath us hidden by that drifting mist. Ah, what sights and sounds and pain lie beneath that mist! And we had thought that our hard climb out of that cruel valley led to some cool, green and peaceful, sunlit place—but it all jungle here, a wild and savage wilderness that's overrun with ruins.

But put on your crown, my Queen, and we will build a New City on these ruins. [210]

JOSEPH WHITE

Old Judge Mose Is Dead

CHARACTERS

JOHN, a Negro in his late forties.
WILLIE, a young Negro.
MR. GRIFFIN, an undertaker: imperious,
   stately-looking.
MISS JANE, white woman about 35.

*The scene is the dimly lighted viewing room in a southern funeral
establishment. At opposite ends of the stage, two closed coffins
are positioned diagonally to the audience. Several chairs are in
front of both coffins. In the moment before the characters come on
stage and begin their dialogue, organ music can be heard.*

MR. GRIFFIN *enters followed by* WILLIE *and* JOHN *who are
carrying equipment for floor waxing.* Lemme put some lights on
heah so y'all can see what y'all doin'. *Flips on wall switch.* This
heah the flo I want y'all to wax. *Walks around, looks appraisingly
at the floor.* Ain't no big flo. Y'all put some elbow grease on it an'
make it shine up like a new penny, an' I'll let y'all do my flos
every time they need doin'. *With finger extended threateningly.*
Y'all got ta work fast 'cause they gon' be some 'potant folks here

SOURCE: *The Drama Review*, XII (Summer, 1968), T40, 151–156. Copyright © 1968 by *The Drama Review*. Reprinted by permission of the author and publisher. All rights reserved.

this evenin' ta see the judge over yonda. *Points to coffin.* Okay, y'all git on, an' I'll be back 'bout time y'all thu.

WILLIE, JOHN, *together.* Yessuh.

MR. GRIFFIN *turns to leave. The two men stare dumbly at each other.* WILLIE *simulates the counting of money to* JOHN.

JOHN. Mr. Griffin, Suh. MR. GRIFFIN *stops, turns around.* Suh. This flo bad. We gotta git up all that old wax 'fore we can. . . .

MR. GRIFFIN. Well, git it up boy! *Smiling.* Don't tell me 'bout it, show me! *Starts to leave again.*

JOHN. Yessuh, but . . .

MR. GRIFFIN, *hands extended in frustration.* Yessuh but what! Is y'all gon' work or is y'all gon' stand 'round chewin' the fat?

WILLIE, *walks up to* MR. GRIFFIN *and speaks almost fearfully.* Yessuh. We gon' work. What John mean ta say is, a flo like this un cost . . . twenty dollahs.

MR. GRIFFIN. Tweny dollahs! Is y'all drunk? Y'all musta been drinkin' corn. *Gestures with finger toward door.* Y'all jest git on way from here! I don't want no new flo. I want this un waxed up. Y'all take two dollahs a hour or git on way from here right now!

WILLIE, *reluctantly.* Yessuh . . . We take two dollahs a hour.

MR. GRIFFIN *leaves shaking head muttering, "tweny dollahs!"* [151]

WILLIE. Damn it! Lucille gon' be mad. I was s'pose ta give her a couple dollars. An' I was gon' keep a couple for myself. Now what ahma tell her? What ahma tell her?

JOHN. Don't tell her nuthin', jest give her yourns.

WILLIE, *kicks a pile of rags, scattering them, then seats himself on the floor.* All this heah work for two dollahs a hour. I oughta not do nothin'.

JOHN. Boy, you know you ain't 'bout to go home an' tell your woman you ain't got that money, so jest shut yo' mouth an' grab that mop.

WILLIE *stands, pours liquid solution into a bucket, dips mop in. Raises and lowers the handle, soaking the mop.* JOHN *is doing likewise in another bucket.*

WILLIE. That undertaker know good an' well this heah too much work for two dollahs a damn hour.

JOHN. Sure he know it, but he aint gon' pay me an' you what we s'pose to git.

WILLIE. A white man jest won't do right by a colored man *no how*. Ole Judge Mose layin' in that box jest as rotten as the rest of 'em.

JOHN. He rottener then the rest of 'em! He done so much dirt to us, we all oughta git together an' have a parade when they throw that dirt on him.

WILLIE *puts dripping mop in wringer, squeezes it with wringer handle.* I sure like to be the one who gon' throw that dirt on him.

JOHN. Me too.

Both laugh.

WILLIE, *motions* JOHN *to come to him.* Hey, John.

JOHN. Whut?

WILLIE. Where you think he goin'?

JOHN. Who?

WILLIE. Judge Mose! You think he goin' ta Heaven or Hail?

JOHN *stops working to make his point.* That man . . . layin' in that box . . . goin' straight to Hail, jest as sure as God make green apples!

WILLIE, *puts down his mop, walks over to* JUDGE'S *coffin, pauses several seconds.* John, you know somethin'?

JOHN. Whut?

WILLIE, *lifts lid of coffin, and speaks with seriousness.* All my life, I been wantin' ta slap a white man. Everytime one talk ta me face to face, I be thinkin' in my mind. . . . I sure like to slap your big red face—white man. Most times I don't even heah whut they sayin' I be itchin' to cut loose so bad.

JOHN, *puts down mop, walks over to coffin.* Well, there your chance; he dead. Slap 'em . . . But you better hope he really dead, and aint playing 'possum.

WILLIE. Look at Old Judge Mose layin' there wid his arms crossed, like he a angel. *Reaches in coffin, lifts corpse by the neck with one hand, slaps the limp face resoundingly several times. And lets out an ecstatic howl.* OOOooooo-whee! Come on man. Aint you gon' slap this fool?

Joseph White

JOHN. Naw, I don' wanna beat up no dead man.

WILLIE, *emphatically*. You jest scared, thas all!

JOHN, *suddenly angry*. Aint nobody scared!

WILLIE. Well hit him then!

JOHN *puts mop down and walks over to coffin*. WILLIE *raises the corpse to allow* JOHN *a better target*. JOHN *spreads his feet then strikes the corpse*. WILLIE *lets the judge's corpse fall back into the coffin*. WILLIE *laughs uproariously and then* JOHN *begins to laugh. Both men laugh several seconds; slap knees; clap* hands. WILLIE *leaps into the air. When the excitement subsides they examine the corpse*.

WILLIE, *mockingly*. Yo'Honor . . . lemme fix yo'tie suh. Can' have no big shot like you in public lookin' like that. *He reaches inside the coffin and adjusts the* [152] JUDGE'S *tie. Then, he withdraws his hands effeminately and tips his head in inspection. Both men return to their work*. WILLIE *begins mopping corner of room*.

JOHN *begins sweeping floor*. Willie, you sumpin'.

WILLIE. What you mean?

JOHN. Beatin' up Ole Judge Mose like that.

WILLIE. He lucky I din kill him! That sucka put me in jail 'bout three years ago.

JOHN, *laughs and shakes head*. He hated all colored folks, ain' no doubt about it . . . Why he put you in jail?

WILLIE. You ain't never heard 'bout it?

JOHN. I heard somethin', but I ain't got the truth 'bout it.

WILLIE, *puts the mop down and walks to the coffin, looking inside, he begins to speak*. It go back ta when I used to-go-ta church. Revival time. Ole Reverend Scott was preachin'. Them folks was gettin' happy, jumpin' up, screamin' an' carrin' on. I was feelin' pretty good myself. Jest 'bout time they took up collection, two white men come bustin' in the church wid guns in they hands an' handkerchiefs 'round they face. Reverend Scott say, "Y'all git out of the House of the Lord wid them guns!" One of 'em say, "Shut up preacher! The Holy Ghost send us for the money." An' he grab up the basket wid the collection in it. The women start screamin' an' hollerin'. Rev. Scott say, "Put that money down, you

178

heathen, scum of the earth. . . ." The other one say, "Shut up preacher, 'fore I kill you!" All them men I useta think was so bad jest sit there like they was froze an' let them two skinny white men come in and take the church money. I was gittin' madder an' madder. I knew I wasn't gon' let them two red face suckas git past me without tryin' to stop 'em. I was sittin' on the outside seat an' when they come runnin' down the aisle, pointin' them guns, I let the first one git by me, an' kicked the other on straight inta the seats. I was on him like white on rice, an' then ole Jimmy Lee Jenkins grab the other one. We was killin' them two fools 'till the women folks start fallin' out. Come ta find out, they guns wasn't even loaded.

JOHN. Then whut happen?

WILLIE. Reverend Scott call the Sheriff. When he git there, him an' his men take them fools an' put 'em in the car; then, they come back inta church and ask who beat up them white boys. Ev'rybody turn 'round an' look at me an' Jimmy Lee. I don't say nuthin'; Jimmy Lee don't say nuthin'! Sheriff mad now. He grab Fats Brown out his seat and say, "Boy! Who beat up them white men?" Fats' eyes got big as baseballs an' he 'bout ta poe on hisself from scaredness. So, I say I done it. Sheriff leggo Fats and grabs me. "Who else?" he say. I say nobody else. He say, "Don't lie ta me, boy." Then Jimmy Lee say, "I whupped one too." Reverend Scott plead with the Sheriff don't take us, but he take us anyway. When we git ta town, the Sheriff lock us up an' don't tell us nothin'. That night, Sheriff's men come an' tie us up to the beds an' let them two wha tried ta rob the church come in an' beat us half ta death. *Pauses.* Next day, this ole judge layin' in this box right here . . . give me an' Jimmy Lee 90 days for 'sault an' battry! I ain't never gon' forget that.

JOHN. One thin' sure, he ain't gon' bother no more colored folks.

WILLIE, *stops center stage and looks at the other coffin.* I wonder who in that box over yonda.

JOHN. We bettah git back ta work for he come in here. I don' want no trouble out that man.

WILLIE. What you worryin' 'bout? We gittin' paid by the hour. Ain't you never heard that song what go . . . *Improvised melody.* White man, ya think ahma workin' but I ain't.

JOHN. Yeah, but I don't like that other part what go . . . *Following same melody* . . . Black man, you think ahma pay ya but I ain't. *Begins to work.* [153]

WILLIE, *walking to other coffin*. Ahma see who in here. *Opens top of coffin*. Well looka here at Miss Ann. Ain't she sweet. Dressed all up like a *biiiig* belly doll baby. How you do Honey? My name Sweet Papa Sweet, the young girl's treat. Watcha say we step out for awhile. Oh, you tired dahlin'? Well, maybe next time. You go 'head an' git some sleep. *Bends over coffin for closer look*. Hey, John!

JOHN. Man, whut you want?

WILLIE. Look here.

JOHN *lays down his mop handle and walks to coffin*.

JOHN. Whut?

WILLIE. Ain't this that woman what work in the post office in town?

JOHN, *tips his head to get a better view. Then, looking up at* WILLIE. It damn sure is. I jest seen her day 'fore yestiddy. *In utter disbelief*. She dead?

WILLIE. Ask huh. She layin' right heah.

JOHN. 'Member how she useta make all the colored folks wait 'til the white folks had took care they business?

WILLIE. She made me wait all a time . . . Look like all them bad white folks is dyin'.

JOHN. She the one what say Benny Randolph got fresh wid huh.

WILLIE. Benny ain't bit more got fresh wid this woman then the man in the moon. 'Cause he always been half-scared of women folks.

JOHN. I 'member she tell the Sheriff Benny get fresh wid her, and Old Judge Mose lock him up an' throw 'way the key.

WILLIE, *moves across room*. Come ta think of it, I oughta go whup him some mo' for Benny.

JOHN, *restraining* WILLIE. Leave that old dead man 'lone.

WILLIE, *speaking to female corpse*. Ya tole a lie on Benny, huh? Well who you gon' tell on me! Ahma gittin' fresh wid ya. An' ya can't do nothin' 'bout it. *Reaches in coffin*. OOoooo-whee! She soft jest like cotton, 'specially right heah. Feel huh John.

JOHN. Naw, you shouldn't be doin' that to a lady.

WILLIE. Man I din know you was such a Uncle Tom.

JOHN, *noticeably angry*. Boy, I ain't no Uncle Tom. *Threateningly*. You watch yo' mouth, now.

WILLIE. Man, I don' met a whole lotta hankachief heads, but you the biggest hankachief head I evuh seen!

JOHN. I ain't no hankachief head!

WILLIE. You is.

JOHN. I ain't.

WILLIE, *slowly, emphasizing each word*. Well if you ain't, pull open the top of huh dress and look at them water melons she hidin'.

JOHN. I ain't goin do no such thing!

WILLIE, I know you ain't . . . You scared.

JOHN. I ain't scared!

WILLIE. Well, go 'head an' do it. *Several seconds lapse, as* JOHN *studies the corpse, then he puts his hands inside the coffin and unbuttons the dress*. JOHN *steps back examining his hands almost fearfully*.

JOHN. Umph!

WILLIE. Look at huh. Fat. Sloopy. An' got the nerve to be talkin' 'bout somebody got fresh wid huh. She look 'bout as good as one uh them ole fat houndogs 'round the belly. My woman Lucille look fifty time betta than huh. *Walks away, picks up mop.* Fix huh clothes back on huh, less you wanna stan' 'round lookin' at huh all night.

JOHN, *adjusts corpse's clothing and closes coffin lid quickly. Walks back to waxing equipment.* Here he come!

Both men begin to work feverishly. MR. GRIFFIN *enters with* MISS JANE. *She falters when she sees coffin, nearly sinking to her knees. He supports her, gesturing* [154] *to the two workmen to hold up their work. Taking the mops with them they move to the side and observe as* MR. GRIFFIN *steadies the distraught woman, and lifts the* JUDGE's *coffin lid. He then stands behind her with his hands clasped at his back, and his chin raised in the air like a soldier in the parade rest position. At intervals, he looks at* WILLIE *and* JOHN *who snap to attention at each glance.*

MISS JANE, *crying audibly*. Oh Daddy, Daddy, I'll miss you so much. You were such a good man. You were so good to me. Oh

Daddy, don't leave me! Don't leave me! *Smiling looking reflectively at ceiling.* It used to be so nice Daddy, just you and me, after
Mama passed away. We'd sit out on the porch after supper and
listen to the radio and talk about everything under the sun. Then
I'd get up and fix lemonade just the way you liked it—spiked with
brandy. And you would be rocking in your chair and looking, oh
so handsome, with your pipe smoke curling 'round you like a halo.
Oh Daddy, we were so happy . . . you and me . . . just you and
me . . . I don't hardly ever let myself think about that morning
years ago when you beat me for being out all night with Carter
Jessup. I know you were doing what you thought was right,
Daddy. You were doing it for my own good Daddy. You were
doing it 'cause you loved me. I never thought different. But I
wasn't lying Daddy. I . . . we . . . we hadn't done what you said
. . . I didn't do it Daddy . . . I'm thirty-four years old and I ain't
never had a man. Oh there's been times when I thought about it.
But I didn't do it Daddy because I never met any man who came
close to being like you. Your little girl is not yet a woman. *Embracing corpse, she speaks in a voice of rapid hysteria, with inter-
mittent sharp intakes of breath, building up to a crescendo.* Oh
Daddy, you can't go Daddy! Don't leave me Daddy. No Daddy.
No Daddy. Git up Daddy. Oh Daddy. I need you Daddy. I need
you Daddy. Please Daddy. Git up Daddy. Oh Daddy. I won't git
married Daddy. I'll stay with you Daddy. I'll take care of you
Daddy. You so good Daddy. Don't leave me Daddy. Don't leave
me. *High emotional pitch.* OOOOOOOOH DADDY! MR. GRIF-
FIN *touches her shoulders. She stands, and he leads her away. She
notices the two men. She stops and walks slowly over to them.
They bow their heads reverently, avoiding her gaze.* He even
treated the colored folks right, my Daddy did. He never hurt nobody . . . Did you ever hear of him treatin' colored folks bad?

WILLIE *raises his eyes and looks at* JOHN. JOHN *raises his eyes
and looks at* WILLIE.

JOHN, WILLIE, *together.* No Ma'am!

MISS JANE. He was a good man wasn't he?

Again, WILLIE *raises his eyes and looks at* JOHN; JOHN *raises
his eyes and looks at* WILLIE.

JOHN, WILLIE, *together.* Yessum!

MISS JANE. He helped to get y'all good jobs too, didn't he?

JOHN, WILLIE, *together.* Yessum!

MISS JANE. Did he ever pass by y'all without speakin'?

JOHN, WILLIE, *together.* No Ma'am!

MISS JANE *looks reflectively at coffin, then continues off stage helped by* MR. GRIFFIN. WILLIE *walks back across the stage and opens coffin lid.*

WILLIE, *to* JOHN. You hear Ole Miss Plug Ugly? *Mocking* MISS JANE *in a high-pitched voice.* Oh Daddy, Daddy, why you die and leave me? Oh Daddy, you was sooooooooo good to me. My Daddy even treat the colored folks right . . . *Looking in coffin.* Like hell you did! You baldhead ole buzzard. *Takes two steps away then returns to coffin.* An' you got a UGGGGly daughta too. She look just like uh ole roosta I useta have.

JOHN. We betta git this flo waxed for he git back heah yellin'.

WILLIE. Man, you the scaredest fool I evuh seen. All y'all old folks know how to do is hold y'alls head down talkin' about: Yes-suh, *Mimicking.* Mistah White Man. Nosuh Mistuh White Man . . . [155] He a man jest like you is? If ya act like he betta than you, thas the way he gon' treat ya. Any fool know that. Look at ya. Ya so scare-ed he gon' git mad wid ya. Ya workin' like ya got a motuh up yo' butt. *Struts around room, swinging arms.* I done took low wid white folks fo' the last time. I ain't never gon' be scare of nothin' white no mo', but a snowball!

JOHN. Go fetch the machine from out the truck, now!

WILLIE. Man, don't worry 'bout that undertaker! What he gon' do? He rather go bear huntin' wid a toothpick then start sumph 'wid me. *Begins to shadow box.* I hit that sucka with this mule kick, somebody have to put him in one of them boxes. I do him just like this mop stick. *Puts choking grip on mop stick, shakes it back and forth, then slams it into wall. Shouting.* I tole ya ta leave me 'lone! Didn't I white man, I tole ya. The next one mess wid me takin' his life in his hands. Ahm sicka runnin', bowin' and scrapin' every time one say boo. *Shaking head.* I done took all ahma take. You betta wake up man an' be like me. They ain't no betta than you is. When they dies, they's dead, jest like colored folks is. *Pointing to coffin.* If they's betta an' smarta than black people, let Ole Judge Mose git up out that box an' show me how smarta he is. *Yells at body in coffin.* Git up Mose! You so smart, git up! Git up from there an' lemme knock you back down!

JOHN, *stops mopping, looks at* WILLIE. Man, is you gon' crazy?

WILLIE. See, that go-ta show how ign'ant you is. You think 'cause I speak up for my rights ahm crazy.

JOHN. Mighty funny, you start speakin' up fo 'em when we got this flo ta do.

WILLIE. Damn this flo! I don't need the money! I got a wife an' a cigarette lighta, both workin'! *Kicks over bucket with water.*

JOHN. Now look what you done did!

WILLIE. I don't care!

MR. GRIFFIN *enters with hands propped on his hips.* What's goin' on heah?

JOHN *begins working rapidly,* WILLIE *drops to his knees and pretends to be examining the floor.*

What you s'pose ta be doin' down there, boy . . . pickin' splinters? Git up from there and git dis flo done!

WILLIE. Yessuh. *Hurries to his feet, and picks up mop.*

MR. GRIFFIN. Y'all hurry up and git thru heah. Y'all heah me?

WILLIE, JOHN, *together.* Yessuh.

MR. GRIFFIN, *pointing finger.* Y'all keep on, an' I won't pay y'all nothin'.

WILLIE, JOHN, *together.* Yessuh, we gon' hurry.

MR. GRIFFIN. Well, y'all betta.

WILLIE *looks up apprehensively as* MR. GRIFFIN *turns to look at them.* WILLIE *drops his head and concentrates on the floor again.* MR. GRIFFIN *exits.*

JOHN, *laughing at* WILLIE. Lawd ha mercy! You s'pose ta be so bad, talkin' 'bout whut you ain't gon' take no mo' from the white man. An' soons he say sumpin ta ya, ya gits jest like a baby. Boy, you is sumpin! You know that?

WILLIE, *feverishly works on in silence for a second.* I swear, one a these days ahma go up North . . . *Stops to wait for* JOHN'S *reaction.* You think ahm lyin' don'cha?

JOHN. Well, 'fore you think 'bout goin' up North, you finish this heah flo.

WILLIE *resumes working.* JOHN *sings.*

Ole Judge Mose don' gon' ta Hail; gon' ta Hail; gon' ta Hail. Old Judge Mose don' gon' ta Hail. Ole Judge Mose don' died.

WILLIE, JOHN, *together.* Ole Judge Mose don' gon' ta Hail . . . *Repeat, same as above.* [156]

JIMMY GARRETT

And We Own the Night: A Play of Blackness

CHARACTERS

JOHNNY
LIL' T
MOTHER
BILLY JOE
DOCTOR
TWO BLACK YOUTHS
TWO BODIES

The scene is an alleyway, dark, dirty, dingy. A large trashcan sits stage right next to a red brick building. The entire rear of stage right is a line of buildings shaded and faded, red or brown brick or graying white wooden frames. A dim yellow light sits above the building closest to the front of the stage. To the left of the stage is a tall white picket fence, also graying. To the right of stage front, around the trashcan, is a broom, leaning against the building. At the very rear of stage left lies a dead BODY: a black youth. In the center rear of the stage is another BODY, a white man dressed in a policeman's uniform.

The lighting should give an effect of dimness, not darkness though it is night, of muted light, of soft shadows, of a kind of gray dinginess. The time is that of the present and that of death and dying.

SOURCE: *The Drama Review*, XII (Summer, 1968), T40, 63–69. Copyright © 1968 by *The Drama Review*. Reprinted by permission of the author and publisher. All rights reserved.

From off stage there is the sound of gunfire, in short bursts, then in a long sustained burst, followed by high shrilling sirens. Then more gunfire.

VOICE, *offstage*. Johnny's been shot! Help me!

SECOND VOICE. Is he hurt bad?

FIRST VOICE. Yeah, get a doctor, Billy Joe.

SECOND VOICE. Okay. I'll try to find his mother too.

FIRST VOICE. To hell with his mother. Get a doctor, dammit. We'll be in the alley behind Central Street.

Two young black men enter from stage left as if from behind the fence. Johnny, tall and thin with fine black features, is being clutched by LIL' T *who is small-statured and has a high brown face. They move toward the building at stage right.*

LIL' T. Come on, Johnny, sit here. *He props* JOHNNY *up against the building in front of the trashcan.* JOHNNY *is clutching his left side where his shirt is covered with blood. He is holding a pistol in his right hand.*

JOHNNY, *breathing heavily*. Lil' T . . . Lil' T . . . Bad . . . Mother . . . fuckin' cops *Clutches LIL' T* . . . caught us from behind . . .

LIL' T. They won't fuck with nobody else. I blew'em away.

JOHNNY. Good . . . Good . . . *Grimaces, then clutches LIL' T.* Lil' T, find mama.

LIL' T. Cool it, Johnny. Don't talk, brother. *He touches the wound.* You're bleedin' like hell. The doctor'll be here in a little while.

JOHNNY. No . . . find Mama . . . Tell her . . . Stay away. Tell her stay home. Ain't no . . . women here . . . Tell her . . . Lil' T.

LIL' T. Don't worry Johnny. We'll keep your mother away. She knows we got a war to fight in this alley. She knows we're kickin' the white man's ass.

JOHNNY. Naw man . . . She ain't . . . She ain't . . . no good . . . that way . . . keep her away . . . til we win . . . then she'll understand. Not now . . . Not yet . . . *He nods his head from side to side.*

LIL' T. She can't stop us Johnny. Nobody can. The white man can't. Your Mama can't. Nobody. We're destroying the white man. There's wars like this in every big city . . . Harlem, Detroit, Chicago . . . all over California. Everywhere. We've held off these white motherfuckers for three days.

JOHNNY. Yeah . . . If we can keep pushin' . . . we'll win . . . we'll . . . win. Keep Mama away . . . Keep her away . . . til we win. I'm scared. I can't fight her and the white man too. *He clutches his side and grimaces.*

LIL' T. Cool it brother . . . You the leader Johnny. You ain't scared of nothing, everybody knows that. You're smart. You know how to fuck with whitey. You fight too hard to be scared of a woman.

JOHNNY. You don't know. Lil' T. You don't know . . .

LIL' T. What you mean, I don't know. I've known you for three days . . . three days of fire. I know how you fight . . .

JOHNNY. No. You don't know. On the street, in the alley, I'm a fighter. But in my Mama's house I ain't nothin.

LIL' T. What you mean? [63]

JOHNNY. She's too strong. She about killed my Daddy. Made a nigger out of him. She loves the white man . . . She'll take me home.

LIL' T. Home. This is home. This alley and those bodies. That's home. I'm your brother and you're my brother and we live and fight in alleys. This is home. And we'll win against the white man.

JOHNNY. We're brothers 'T but mama believes the white man's God. *He lapses into silence nodding his head from side to side.*

LIL' T. Cool it, Johnny. Don't be so uptight. Where's the fucking doctor?

VOICE, *offstage.* Go for soul! LIL' T *turns his head toward stage left and rises. A short, stocky, black faced young man enters. A rifle hangs loosely at his shoulder.*

LIL' T. Where's that doctor, Billy Joe?

BILLY JOE. I got him. I found him hiding at his home. Come on in the alley, Doc. A lil' dirt won't hurt you.

DOCTOR *enters, crouching low moving slowly, passes* BILLY JOE *toward* LIL' T, *who is standing. He looks around as if ex-*

pecting to be shot. He is a light-complexioned Negro in his late forties, dressed in an expensive-looking gray suit. **LIL' T** *goes over and jerks him forward.* **BILLY JOE** *leaves.*

LIL' T. Come on, Doc. We ain't got no time to be jiving. Johnny's bleeding bad.

DOCTOR, *standing above* **JOHNNY.** I don't . . . I don't know what I can do.

LIL' T, *raises his gun.* Man, you'd better do something quick. **DOCTOR** *leans over* **JOHNNY** *and kneels.*

DOCTOR. That boy rushed me so quick I didn't get a chance to get my tools. I just stuffed what I could in my pockets. *The* **DOCTOR** *presses the area where* **JOHNNY** *is bleeding.* That's a bad wound.

JOHNNY. Aw. *He slides away from the* **DOCTOR.** Be cool, man.

DOCTOR. Be still, boy, or you'll bleed to death. *Two* **BLACK BOYS** *rush on stage from the right, one carrying a pistol, the other a rifle.*

FIRST BOY. Lil' T. *He stops to catch his breath.* The cops 've broken through the barricade on Vernon.

LIL' T. Which barricade? What happened?

SECOND BOY. The one on Vernon . . . The cops come in buses, five of 'em.

FIRST BOY. Yeah, looked like 'bout fifty cops a bus. The cats saw all them cops, an' ran.

LIL' T. Where'd the cats go? Up to the park?

FIRST BOY. Yeah, they set up another barricade.

SECOND BOY. We got to think of something or them cops'll break that 'un too. We came to get Johnny. He'll know what to do.

LIL' T. He can't move. He got shot lil' while ago. *The* **TWO BOYS** *turn to go over to* **JOHNNY,** *but are held up by* **LIL' T.** Naw, man, don't bother him . . . He's been hurt bad. Wait til the Doc's finished.

FIRST BOY. Man, we can't wait. *They rush over to* **JOHNNY.** *The* **FIRST BOY** *kneels in front of the* **DOCTOR,** *the other* *stands behind him.* JOHNNY *rolls his head around.* Johnny, Johnny. Wake up brother. Hey, what's wrong?

DOCTOR. I gave him something to kill the pain.

SECOND BOY, *kneeling, grabs* JOHNNY *by the arm.* Aw, fuck. Wake up Johnny.

LIL' T. Whyn't you cats leave him alone. *Moving over to the group.*

JOHNNY. Oh. Oh. *Waking.* What. Wha . . . Lil' T. Lil' T.

LIL' T, *kneeling.* It's all right, Johnny. These cats . . .

FIRST BOY. Look, Johnny. We know you hurt but we need your help, man. Them cops're rushing the barricades in buses. Hundreds of cops. [64]

SECOND BOY. Man. We got to stop them buses or they'll wipe us out. Cats ran from Vernon. They're all the way down the park now. Got another barricade goin'. But it won't hold long!

DOCTOR, *as* JOHNNY *sits up listening.* Wait a second. I'll be through with this bandage in a minute.

JOHNNY, *to* DOCTOR. Yeah, yeah. Look here. Throw broken glass in the streets. Then pour gasoline up and down the street for a block or so. If the glass don't stop 'em, plant cats in places so they can hide with fire bombs. An' when the buses get in the middle of that gasoline, chunk them bombs under em.

FIRST BOY. Roasted cops!

SECOND BOY. Wow! Oh, man . . . outta sight. Outta sight! Come on. Let's go. We'll get 'em. Go for soul. Thanks Johnny. You're a heavy cat. *They exit.* Go for soul!

DOCTOR. Boy if you don't be still, you'll bleed to death.

LIL' T. He's right, Man. Ain't no use in you cuttin' out on a humbug. You blowin' too much soul. BILLY JOE *enters.*

BILLY JOE, *to* LIL' T. I saw Johnny's mother down at the barricade.

LIL' T *takes* BILLY JOE *to the side of the stage left.* She's not coming here is she?

BILLY JOE. Yeah, man. I told her to come. I thought Johnny might die. I thought his mother should . . .

JOHNNY. Lil' T . . . Get this dude off me.

DOCTOR, *turning to face* LIL' T. I'm just patching him. He's restless.

LIL' T. It's okay, Johnny. Take it easy Doc. *Back to* BILLY JOE. Look man . . . We got to keep his old lady away . . . She's a bitch. Johnny don't want her around. Go keep her away.

BILLY JOE. But. She's his mother . . .

LIL' T. I don't give a shit. Keep her out of here. Go on. *Pushes* BILLY JOE.

BILLY JOE. Okay man. *He rushes out.*

LIL' T *turns toward* JOHNNY *and the* DOCTOR.

VOICE, *offstage.* Look out son. You nearly knocked me down. Where's my son at? Where's Johnny at?

BILLY JOE, *backing on to stage.* You can't come in. Lil' T says you got to stay out . . .

JOHNNY'S MOTHER *enters, backing* BILLY JOE *into the alley. She is an imposing black woman, wearing a simple dress of floral design and flat shoes. She never smiles.*

MOTHER. Boy, don't you mess with me. Where is my son at? *As she speaks,* LIL' T *turns. He is blocking* JOHNNY *from his* MOTHER'S *view.*

BILLY JOE. I don't know where the dude is. *Realizes he is in the alley and stops.*

LIL' T, *walking toward them.* I told you to keep her out.

BILLY JOE. I . . .

MOTHER. Johnny! *She rushes over to* JOHNNY *and kneels, pushing the* DOCTOR *out of the way.* BILLY JOE *shrugs his shoulders and leaves.*

JOHNNY. Mama. Mama. Go back home.

DOCTOR. Don't shake him woman! He's been shot. He's bleeding inside.

MOTHER. My son. He's my son. *She speaks loudly but does not sob.* You the doctor? Will he be all right?

LIL' T, *clutching the woman by the shoulders and trying to lift her.* He's all right. Come on now. Billy Joe'll take you home.

MOTHER, *jerking loose*. Naw. Let me go. Who are you? Why'd my son get hurt like this? You're the cause of it.

LIL' T. He got shot by a white cop.

JOHNNY. Go way Mama. T get her out of here.

MOTHER. Don't you talk to me like that. You bad boys. Sinning. And this is what [65] you get. *Points at* JOHNNY'S *wound*.

LIL' T. Ain't nobody sinning but the white man. Now he's payin' for it.

MOTHER. Johnny layin' there bleedin' and the white man's payin'. Help me doctor. Help me take him to the hospital.

JOHNNY. Mama leave me alone.

LIL' T. Johnny ain't goin' to no white man's hospital. Them motherfuckers would just let him die.

MOTHER. Don't you curse white people like that. Doctor help me.

DOCTOR, *looks up at* LIL' T *who has lifted the gun*. No we shouldn't move him. I've slowed the flow but he's still bleeding internally. He'll die if he moves around too much.

MOTHER. But he can't stay here in this alley. Oh lord help me, what can I do?

DOCTOR. I've got to get that bullet out quick. I'll go back to the office and get my case.

LIL' T. Okay Doc. Billy Joe can take you and make sure you get back. Billy Joe? DOCTOR *rises*. BILLY JOE *enters*. Take the Doctor back to get his stuff.

BILLY JOE. Okay, come on, Doc. *They leave*.

MOTHER. Is it bad son? Is it bad? Oh Lord. What can I do? I need strength.

JOHNNY. Mama, don't pray. It don't do no good.

MOTHER. I told you to stay home. Out here fightin' the Police. Burnin' down white folks' businesses. I'm ashamed of you. God knows why you're doin' this.

JOHNNY. I'm bein' a man. A black man. And I don't need a white man's God to help me.

MOTHER. What you say? What you say 'bout God?

JOHNNY. Forget it.

MOTHER. Where'd you learn all that stuff. *She rises and turns to* LIL' T. Did you teach him this sacrilege?

JOHNNY. Nobody taught me.

LIL' T. He's leader. He knows how to fuck with whitey.

MOTHER, *to* LIL' T. Boy, can't you talk without cursin'? Don't no child like you need to talk that way. *To* JOHNNY. Your daddy's a man, and he don't curse.

JOHNNY. Where is he, Mama?

MOTHER. He's at home where you should be 'stead of out here in this alley.

JOHNNY. Is he hidin', Mama?

MOTHER. Naw he ain't hidin'. He's just stayin' close to his home.

LIL' T. While his woman's out on the street. Bullshit. A man don't need to hide. Can't. He'd be out here fightin' like us.

MOTHER. You're wrong boy. God knows you're wrong. You out here breakin' laws. Killin'. Look at what you've done. *She points at the bodies lying on the stage.*

LIL' T. People die when they face the white man. Better to die like a man, bringing the white man to his knees than hidin' at home under a woman's skirt.

MOTHER. My husband ain't no sinner. He don't break laws. He works hard . . . He don't bother nobody. He . . .

JOHNNY. He's still a nigger.

LIL' T. He believes what the white man says.

MOTHER. You don't know him. You don't know what he believes.

LIL' T. Be a good nigger, work hard, pray, kiss ass, and you'll make it.

MOTHER. How do you know? How do you know?

JOHNNY. I know, Mama.

MOTHER. I'm gonna take you home. Away from this sin.

JOHNNY. Don't bother me, Mama.

MOTHER. I brought you into the world. I clothed and fed you.

And now you don't want me to touch you? I'm taking you home. *She tries to lift* JOHNNY. LIL' T [66] *rushes over and grabs her by the shoulder, pulling her away.*

MOTHER. Let me go. *Breaks away from his grip.* Don't put your hands on me again.

LIL' T. Well you leave Johnny alone. Can't you understand? He's a man. He's a leader. He's my brother. We're gonna stay here in this alley and fight the white man together. Right Johnny?

JOHNNY. Yeah, brother.

MOTHER. You ain't no leader, boy. You ain't even got no mind. *Turns to* LIL' T. He's got the mind. A dirty mind. Why don't you leave him alone? He's just a boy. He didn't know about hatin' and killin' til he started running with you.

LIL' T. Killin' ain't no dirty thing to do to a white man.

MOTHER, *rising.* Murder ain't never been clean.

LIL' T. Except when the white man did it, right?

MOTHER. Who are you, the devil? I ain't speakin' of the white man as you call it. He ain't done me no harm.

LIL' T. He beat you and raped you. He made a whore out of you and a punk out of your man.

MOTHER. Naw. The white man ain't done nothing to me. But I don't know you. Where are your folks?

LIL' T. My mother and father are dead. They died the first day fightin' the cops. My brother's in jail. My sister's somewhere fightin' or dyin'! My home is this alley and Johnny is my brother. This is where I live or die.

MOTHER. You don't have nothin' left. You don't feel nothin'. You ain't found God. You don't have love.

LIL' T. That God you pray to is a lie. A punk. The last dick the white man's got to put in you.

MOTHER. You see, Johnny. He's got no heart. He's got no love.

LIL' T. Love! Love! Everybody knows that love ain't enough for the white man. He don't understand love. You got to kill him. Love! Ass suckin' love. Askin' him for forgiveness when he's done wrong. Lettin' him shoot you in the back while you're on your knees prayin' to his God.

MOTHER. Jesus said . . .

LIL' T. Another punk . . .

MOTHER. Jesus said love those who are spiteful of . . .

LIL' T. Strokin' his rod, cleanin' his shit . . .

MOTHER. Forgive those who do harm . . .

LIL' T. Blowin' up black children in churches . . . Beatin' pregnant women . . .

MOTHER. We must pray to God for salvat . . .

LIL' T. Kill that motherfucker! Cut out his heart and stuff it down his throat. Bury him in his own shit.

MOTHER, *quietly, slowly.* I will not strike out at white men. They have been good to me. Fed my son. Gave me shelter when there was no work for my husband. Gave me a job so I could care for my family. White men have done me no harm. Only niggers like you trying to take my son away and lead him to sin.

LIL' T. The white man gave you a job and took away your husband's balls. You have the money and your husband's a tramp in his own home. Ain't that right Johnny?

MOTHER, *to* JOHNNY. *She speaks quietly at first, then building to the end.* Johnny. Son. In God's name, you know how I love you and your Daddy. How I've worked and slaved for you all. And you know how white folks have always helped us. They're smart. They know what's right and what ain't. We got to trust in them. They're good. They run the whole world don't they? How come you're out here killin' white men. I don't understand. Livin' in this filth. Crawlin' around alleys bleedin' to death. You call yourselves men. Don't no men act like that. The white man don't crawl around, cussin' and stealin'! You ought to [67] be actin' like the white man stead of tryin' to kill him.

JOHNNY, *tries to rise.* Mama . . .

LIL' T. Sit still Johnny. You'll start bleedin'.

JOHNNY. I'm already bleedin'. *Tries to rise. He gets to his knees and stops, breathing heavily.* LIL' T *starts toward him, then stops.*

MOTHER. Don't try to get up son.

JOHNNY. Just stay away . . . I'll make it . . . I should try to be a white man, huh? White as snow. White as death. Don't you wish I was white Mama. Clean and white like toilet paper.

MOTHER. Johnny . . .

JOHNNY *starts to rise from his knees. He is holding the pistol with one hand and clutching his side with the other.* And daddy. Don't you wish he was white too? Daddy's smarter than I thought he was. He had to decide between bein a white man and bein nothin' and he decided to be nothin!

MOTHER. Sit down Johnny, you're bleedin!

JOHNNY. So I'm bleedin'. Its a blood comin' from a black body shot by a white cop. Or don't that matter?

MOTHER. You were doing wrong.

JOHNNY. The white man decides what's wrong. The white man's right no matter what he's done. Right Mama. I'm wrong from the time I was born. You love the white man. And I kill the white man.

MOTHER. You made yourself into a criminal.

JOHNNY. My name is criminal. I steal and kill. I am black and that is my greatest crime. And I am proud of that crime.

MOTHER. I didn't raise you to be no criminal.

JOHNNY. You raised me to be white, but it didn't work. The white man is my enemy. I wait in alleys to stab him in the back or cut his throat.

MOTHER. But that is heathen.

JOHNNY. I have been a heathen for three days. He has for three hundred years. But I am not guilty. I feel passion when I kill. Love. He don't give a shit for nobody. He kills efficiently. I kill passionately. He is your God and I have sworn to kill God. Can't you understand, Mama? We're gonna build a whole new thing after this. After we destroy the white man. Black people don't want to kill. We want to live. But we have to kill first. We have to kill in order to win.

MOTHER. But you can't win. They've got guns and bombs. *Loud explosion. They all stop—startled.* God, what is it?

JOHNNY. It's the police buses, they got to the police buses.

LIL' T. Blow them motherfuckers away! I'll go see. *He leaves stage right. As soon as he is out of sight a second explosion roars. He rushes back on stage jumping wildly.* Boom! Man, Johnny, you should have seen that scene.

JOHNNY. Are they gettin' to 'em?

Jimmy Garrett

LIL' T. Goin' for soul. Gimme five brother. *He extends his open palm to* JOHNNY *who takes his bloody left hand away from his side and slaps* LIL' T's *palm.*

JOHNNY. See. See mama. We're winnin! *Dabbing his side.*

MOTHER, *quietly.* I don't see nothing boy 'cept you lost your mind. There's nothin' I can do with you. *A third explosion.*

LIL' T, *rushes up to* JOHNNY *and spins him around seemingly not remembering that* JOHNNY *has been shot.* Forget her, Johnny. She's too old. JOHNNY *spins around with* LIL' T, *stumbling but trying to acquiesce to the dance.* This is judgment day, and we're the judges. Motherfuck the police. Motherfuck the white man. JOHNNY *is stumbling, holding the gun and clutching his side.*

JOHNNY. And motherfuck daddy and mama and all them house niggers. Death to the house niggers! *A fourth explosion.* JOHNNY *tries to dance and falls to his knees.* It's all over for the white man, huh T? [68]

LIL' T. You damn right. *He picks up his rifle.* I'm going out to the barricade. I ain't gonna stay and wait for that Doctor no more. We got a war to fight.

JOHNNY. Okay, brother, be cool.

LIL' T. *Walks up to* JOHNNY *who is breathing very heavily while his body falters.* I hope you don't die brother . . . But you know how death is. It's over with. Ain't no more after that. Gimme five. *He extends his hand.*

JOHNNY *slaps it with his last expression of strength.* LIL' T *wipes the blood onto his shirt, and leaves, not looking back.*

JOHNNY. Mama . . .

MOTHER. You ain't my son. I don't know you. You rejoice when you kill white people and don't even feel sympathy for each other when you dying. That boy did more toward killin' you than any white man but you love him.

JOHNNY *falls forward bracing himself by his elbow.*

JOHNNY. Mama . . .

MOTHER. Don't Mama me. I don't care about that no more. You steal and kill and curse God. You call yourselves criminals and feel no remorse. You hide in alleys cuttin' throats. You blow up buses and burn down property. That boy left here knowin' you'd die and he was smilin'. I don't understand. He'll probably be dead himself in a few minutes. I just can't see it. I know you're wrong. The white people would never do those things. You must be wrong. I don't understand. But they'll know. They'll understand. They'll make it right. They'll explain it to me. They'll show me the way. I trust in them. Ain't no nigger never been right. *She turns slowly and walks toward the stage left.* And never will be right.

JOHNNY, *points the gun at her back.* We're . . . new men, Mama . . . Not niggers. Black men. *He fires at her back. She stops still, then begins to turn.* JOHNNY *fires again and she stumbles forward and slumps to the stage.* JOHNNY *looks at her for a moment, then falls away. There is a loud explosion followed by gunfire.* [69]

II: SELECTED CRITICISM

ARTHUR P. DAVIS

The Harlem of Langston Hughes' Poetry

In a very real sense, Langston Hughes is the poet-laureate of Harlem. From his first publication down to his latest, Mr. Hughes has been concerned with the black metropolis. Returning to the theme again and again, he has written about Harlem oftener and more fully than any other poet. As Hughes has written about himself:

I live in the heart of Harlem. I have also lived in the heart of Paris, Madrid, Shanghai, and Mexico City. The people of Harlem seem not very different from others, except in language. I love the color of their language: and, being a Harlemite myself, their problems and interests are my problems and interests.

Knowing how deeply Langston Hughes loves Harlem and how intimately he understands the citizens of that community, I have long felt that a study of the Harlem theme in Hughes' poetry would serve a twofold purpose: it would give us insight into the growth and maturing of Mr. Hughes as a social poet; it would also serve as an index to the changing attitude of the Negro during the last quarter of a century.

When Mr. Hughes' first publication, *The Weary Blues* (1926), appeared, the New Negro Movement was in full swing; and Harlem, as the intellectual center of the movement, had become the Mecca of all aspiring young Negro writers and artists. This so-called Renaissance not only encouraged and inspired the black

Source: *Phylon,* XIII (1952), 276–283. Reprinted by permission of *Phylon.*

creative artist, but it served also to focus as never before the attention of America upon the Negro artist and scholar. As a result of this new interest, Harlem became a gathering place for downtown intellectuals and Bohemians—many of them honestly seeking a knowledge of Negro art and culture, others merely looking for exotic thrills in the black community. Naturally, the latter group was much the larger of the two; and Harlem, capitalizing on this new demand for "primitive" thrills, opened a series of spectacular cabarets. For a period of about ten years, the most obvious and the most sensational aspect of the New Negro Movement for downtown New York was the night life of Harlem. The 1925 Renaissance, of course, was not just a cabaret boom, and it would be decidedly unfair to give that impression. But the Harlem cabaret life of the period was definitely an important by-product of the new interest in the Negro created by the movement, and this life strongly influenced the early poetry of Langston Hughes.

Coming to Harlem, as he did, a twenty-two-year-old adventurer who [276] had knocked around the world as sailor and beachcomber, it was only natural that Hughes should be attracted to the most exotic part of that city—its night life. The Harlem of *The Weary Blues* became therefore for him "Jazzonia," a new world of escape and release, an exciting never-never land in which "sleek black boys" blew their hearts out on silver trumpets in a "whirling cabaret." It was a place where the bold eyes of white girls called to black men, and "dark brown girls" were found "in blond men's arms." It was a city where "shameless gals" strutted and wiggled, and the "night dark girl of the swaying hips" danced beneath a papier-mâché jungle moon. The most important inhabitants of this magic city are a "Nude Young Dancer," "Midnight Nan at Leroy's," a "Young Singer" of *chansons vulgaires,* and a "Black Dancer in the Little Savoy."

This cabaret Harlem, this Jazzonia is a joyous city, but the joyousness is not unmixed; it has a certain strident and hectic quality, and there are overtones of weariness and despair. "The long-headed jazzers" and whirling dancing girls are desperately trying to find some new delight, and some new escape. They seem obsessed with the idea of seizing the present moment as though afraid of the future: "Tomorrow . . . is darkness / Joy today!" "The rhythm of life / Is a jazz rhythm" for them, but it brings only "The broken heart of love / The weary, weary heart of pain." It is this weariness and this intensity that one hears above the laughter and even above the blare of the jazz bands.

There is no daytime in Jazzonia, no getting up and going to work. It is wholly a sundown city, illuminated by soft lights, spotlights, jewel-eyed sparklers, and synthetic stars in the scenery. Daylight is the one great enemy here, and when "the new dawn / Wan and pale / Descends like a white mist," it brings only an "aching emptiness," and out of this emptiness there often comes in the clear cool light of morning the disturbing thought that the jazz band may not be an escape, it may not be gay after all:

> Does a jazz-band ever sob?
> They say a jazz-band's gay . . .
> One said she heard the jazz-band sob
> When the little dawn was gray.

In this respect, the figure of the black piano player in the title poem is highly symbolic. Trying beneath "the pale dull pallor of an old gas light" to rid his soul of the blues that bedeviled it, he played all night, but when the dawn approached:

> The singer stopped playing and went to bed
> While the Weary Blues echoed through his head.
> He slept like a rock or a man that's dead.

It is hard to fool oneself in the honest light of dawn, but sleep, like dancing and singing and wild hilarity, is another means of escape. Unfortunately, it too is only a temporary evasion. One has to wake up sometime and face the harsh reality of daylight and everyday living. [277]

And in the final pages of *The Weary Blues,* the poet begins to sense this fact; he realizes that a "jazz-tuned" way of life is not the answer to the Negro's search for escape. The last poem on the Harlem theme in this work has the suggestive title "Disillusionment" and the even more suggestive lines:

> I would be simple again,
> Simple and clean . . .
> Nor ever know,
> Dark Harlem,
> The wild laughter
> Of your mirth . . .
> Be kind to me,
> Oh, great dark city.
> Let me forget.
> I will not come
> To you again.

Evidently Hughes did want to forget, at least temporarily, the dark city, for there is no mention of Harlem in his next work, *Fine Clothes to the Jew,* published the following year. Although several of the other themes treated in the first volume are continued in this the second, it is the only major production [1] in which the name Harlem does not appear.

But returning to *The Weary Blues*—it is the eternal emptiness of the Harlem depicted in this work which depresses. In this volume, the poet has been influenced too strongly by certain superficial elements of the New Negro Movement. Like too many of his contemporaries, he followed the current vogue, and looking at Harlem through the "arty" spectacles of New Negro exoticism, he failed to see the everyday life about him. As charming and as fascinating as many of these poems undoubtedly are, they give a picture which is essentially false because it is one-dimensional and incomplete. In the works to follow, we shall see Mr. Hughes filling out that picture, giving it three-dimensional life and being.

The picture of Harlem presented in *Shakespeare in Harlem* (1942) has very little in common with that found in *The Weary Blues*. By 1942 the black metropolis was a disillusioned city. The Depression of 1929, having struck the ghetto harder than any other section of New York, showed Harlem just how basically "marginal" and precarious its economic foundations were. Embittered by this knowledge, the black community had struck back blindly at things in general in the 1935 riot. The riot brought an end to the New Negro era; the Cotton Club, the most lavish of the uptown cabarets, closed its doors and moved to Broadway; and the black city settled down to the drab existence of WPA and relief living.

In the two groups of poems labeled "Death in Harlem" and "Lenox Avenue," Hughes has given us a few glimpses of this new Harlem. There [278] are no bright colors in the scene, only the sombre and realistic shades appropriate to the depiction of a community that has somehow lost its grip on things. The inhabitants of this new Harlem impress one as a beaten people. A man loses his job because, "awake all night with loving," he cannot get to work on time. When he is discharged, his only comment is "So I went on back to bed . . ." and to the "sweetest dreams" ("Fired"). In another poem, a man and his wife wrangle over the family's last

[1] The *Dream Keeper* (1932) is not considered a major publication and will not be examined here. It is a collection of Mr. Hughes' poems edited by Miss Effie L. Powers and designed for young readers.

dime which he had thrown away gambling ("Early Evening Quarrel"). Harlem love has lost its former joyous abandon, and the playboy of the cabaret era has become a calculating pimp who wants to "share your bed / And your money too" ("50-50"). In fact all of the lovers in this section—men and women alike—are an aggrieved lot, whining perpetually about being "done wrong." Even the night spots have lost their jungle magic, and like Dixie's joint have become earthy and sordid places: "Dixie makes his money on two-bit gin"; he also "rents rooms at a buck a break." White folks still come to Dixie's seeking a thrill, but they find it unexpectedly in the cold-blooded shooting of Bessie by Arabella Johnson, in a fight over Texas Kid. As Arabella goes to jail and Bessie is taken to the morgue, Texas Kid, the cause of this tragedy, callously "picked up another woman and / Went to bed" ("Death in Harlem"). All of the fun, all of the illusion have gone from this new and brutal night life world; and as a fitting symbol of the change which has come about, we find a little cabaret girl dying forlornly as a ward of the city ("Cabaret Girl Dies on Welfare Island").

There is seemingly only one bright spot in this new Harlem—the spectrum-colored beauty of the girls on Sugar Hill ("Harlem Sweeties"); but this is only a momentary lightening of the mood. The prevailing tone is one of depression and futility:

> Down on the Harlem River
> > Two A.M.
> > Midnight
> > By yourself!
> Lawd, I wish I could die—
> But who would miss me if I left?

We see here the spectacle of a city feeling sorry for itself, the most dismal and depressing of all spectacles. Hughes has given us a whining Harlem. It is not yet the belligerent Harlem of the 1943 riot, but it is a city acquiring the mood from which this riot will inevitably spring.

The Harlem poems in *Fields of Wonder* (1947) are grouped under the title "Stars Over Harlem," but they do not speak out as clearly and as definitely as former pieces on the theme have done. The mood, however, continues in the sombre vein of *Shakespeare in Harlem,* and the idea of escape is stated or implied in each of the poems. In the first of the group, "Trumpet Player: 52nd Street," we find a curious shift in the African [279] imagery used.

205

Practically all former pieces having an African background tended to stress either the white-mooned loveliness of jungle nights or the pulse-stirring rhythm of the tom-tom. But from the weary eyes of the 52nd Street musician there blazes forth only "the smoldering memory of slave ships." In this new Harlem even the jazz players are infected with the sectional melancholy, and this performer finds only a vague release and escape in the golden tones he creates.

In "Harlem Dance Hall" there is again an interesting use of the escape motif. The poet describes the hall as having no dignity at all until the band began to play and then: "Suddenly the earth was there, / And flowers, / Trees, / And air." In short, this new dignity was achieved by an imaginative escape from the close and unnatural life of the dance hall (and of Harlem) into the freedom and wholesomeness of nature and normal living.

Although it is rather cryptic, there is also the suggestion of escape in "Stars," the last of these poems to be considered here:

> O, sweep of stars over Harlem streets . . .
> Reach up your hand, dark boy, and take a star.

One Way Ticket (1949) and *Montage of a Dream Deferred* (1951), especially the latter work, bring to a full cycle the turning away from the Harlem of *The Weary Blues*. The Harlem depicted in these two works has come through World War II, but has discovered that a global victory for democracy does not necessarily have too much pertinence at home. Although the Harlem of the 1949–51 period has far more opportunity than the 1926 Harlem ever dreamed of, it is still not free; and the modern city having caught the vision of total freedom and total integration will not be satisfied with anything less than the ideal. It is therefore a critical, a demanding, a sensitive, and utterly cynical city.

In *One Way Ticket,* for example, Harlem remembers "the old lies," "the old kicks in the back," the jobs it never could have and still cannot get because of color:

> So we stand here
> On the edge of hell
> In Harlem
> And look out on the world
> And wonder
> What we're gonna do
> In the face of
> What we remember.

But even though Harlem is the "edge of hell," it still can be a refuge for the black servant who works downtown all day bowing and scraping to white folks ("Negro Servant"). Dark Harlem becomes for him a "sweet relief from faces that are white." The earlier Harlem was a place to be shared with fun-seeking whites from below 125th Street; the new city is a sanctuary from them. [280]

So deep is the unrest in this 1949–51 Harlem it may experience strangely conflicting emotions. Like aliens longing sentimentally for the "old country," it may feel momentarily a nostalgia for the South, even though it has bought a one way ticket from that region. In "Juice-Joint: Northern City," we find sad-faced boys who have forgotten how to laugh:

> But suddenly a guitar playing lad
> Whose languid lean brings back the sunny South
> Strikes up a tune all gay and bright and glad
> To keep the gall from biting in his mouth,
> > Then drowsy as the rain
> > Soft sad black feet
> > Dance in this juice joint
> > On the city street.

The deepest tragedy of a disillusioned city is the cruelty it inflicts on its own unfortunates, and this bitter Harlem wastes no pity on a poor lost brother who was not "hep":

> Harlem
> Sent him home
> In a long box—
> Too dead
> To know why:
> The licker
> Was lye.

The longest and most revealing Harlem poem in *One Way Ticket* is the thumping "Ballad of Margie Polite," the Negro girl who "cussed" a cop in the lobby of the Braddock Hotel and caused a riot when a Negro soldier taking her part was shot in the back by a white cop. In these thirteen short stanzas, Langston Hughes has distilled, as it were, all of the trigger-sensitiveness to injustice—real or imagined; all of the pent-up anti-white bitterness; and all of the sick-and-tired-of-being-kicked-around feelings which characterize the masses of present-day Harlem. It is indeed a provocative analysis of the frictions and the tensions in the black ghetto, this narrative of Margie Polite, who

Arthur P. Davis

> Kept the Mayor
> And Walter White
> And everybody
> Up all night!

In *Montage of a Dream Deferred,* Mr. Hughes' latest volume of poems, the Harlem theme receives its fullest and most comprehensive statement. Devoting the whole volume to the subject he has touched on many aspects of the city unnoticed before. His understanding is now deep and sure, his handling of the theme defter and more mature than in any of the previous works. In this volume, the poet makes effective use of a technique with which he has been experimenting since 1926—a technique he explains in a brief prefatory note:

> In terms of current Afro-American popular music . . . this poem on contemporary Harlem, like be-bop, is marked by conflicting [281] changes, sudden nuances, sharp and impudent interjections, broken rhythms, and passages sometimes in the manner of the jam session, sometimes the popular song, punctuated by the riffs, runs, breaks, and distortions [*sic*] of the music of a community in transition.

According to this scheme, we are to consider the whole book of ninety-odd pieces as really one long poem, marked by the conflicting changes, broken rhythms, and sudden interjections characteristic of a jam session. This "jam session" technique is highly effective because, tying together as it does fragmentary and otherwise unrelated segments in the work, it allows the poet, without being monotonous, to return again and again to his overall-theme, that of Harlem's frustration. Like the deep and persistent rolling of a boogie bass—now loud and raucous, now soft and pathetic—this theme of Harlem's dream deferred marches relentlessly throughout the poem. Hughes knows that Harlem is neither a gay nor healthy but basically a tragic and frustrated city, and he beats that message home. Because of the fugue-like structure of the poem, it is impossible for the reader to miss the theme or to forget it.

This 1951 Harlem is a full and many-sided community. Here one finds the pathos of night funerals and fraternal parades: "A chance to let / the whole world see / old black me!"; or the grim realism of slum-dwellers who like war because it means prosperity; or the humor of a wife playing via a dream book the number suggested by her husband's dying words. This is the Harlem of black celebrities and their white girl admirers, the Harlem of vice squad detectives "spotting fairies" in night spots, the Harlem of bitter anti-Semitism, and the Harlem of churches and street corner orators, of college formals at the Renaissance Casino and of Negro students writing themes at CCNY. It is now definitely a class-conscious Harlem, a community of dicties and nobodies; and the Cadillac-riding professional dicties feel that they are let down by the nobodies who "talk too loud / cuss too loud / and look too black." It is a Harlem of some gaiety and of much sardonic laughter; but above all else, it is Harlem of a dream long deferred; and a people's deferred dream can "fester like a sore" or "sag like a heavy load."

Whatever else it may or may not believe, this Harlem has no illusion about the all-inclusiveness of American democracy. Even the children know that there is still a Jim Crow coach on the Freedom Train.

> What don't bug
> them white kids
> sure bugs me;
> We knows everybody
> ain't free.

Perhaps the dominant over-all impression that one gets from *Montage of a Dream Deferred* is that of a vague unrest. Tense and moody, the inhabitants of this 1951 Harlem seem to be seeking feverishly and forlornly for some simple yet apparently unattainable satisfaction in life: [282] "one more bottle of gin"; "my furniture paid for"; "I always did want to study French"; "that white enamel stove"; "a wife who will work with me and not against me." The book begins and ends on this note of dissatisfaction and unrest. There is "a certain amount of nothing in a dream deferred."

These then are the scenes that make up the Harlem of Langston Hughes' poetry. The picture, one must remember, is that of a poet and not a sociologist; it naturally lacks the logic and the statistical accuracy of a scientific study, but in its way the picture is just as revealing and truthful as an academic study. As one looks at this series of Harlems he is impressed by the growing sense of frustration which characterizes each of them. Whether it is in the dream fantasy world of *The Weary Blues* or in the realistic city of *Montage of a Dream Deferred,* one sees a people searching—and searching in vain—for a way to make Harlem a part of the American dream. And one must bear in mind that with Langston Hughes Harlem is both place and symbol. When he depicts the hopes, the aspirations, the frustrations, and the deep-seated discontent of the New York ghetto, he is expressing the feelings of Negroes in black ghettos throughout America. [283]

STANLEY EDGAR HYMAN

American Negro Literature and the Folk Tradition

By "American Negro Literature" I do not mean any special body of writing, like Petrarchan sonnets, but only that varied American literature produced by Negroes. It is my contention that it has, or that some of it has, a relation to a living folk tradition that is rare in American writing, and very much worth our study. At the same time, I would insist that this special criterion of analysis does not involve any special criteria of evaluation, and that the writing of Negro authors must be judged by the same standards we use to judge the writing of any other authors. Such standards have not always been the case. One Negro critic has charged that white reviewers discriminate against Negro writing. This is obviously so in isolated instances, although even here it would probably be more accurate to say that white reviewers are often deaf to many of the resonances of Negro writing. I am sure that for the most part, however, the bias has gone the other way, and that there has been almost a concerted leaning-over-backward to welcome as masterworks one ultimately unimpressive Negro book after another. Some of this is the unconscious guilt of white Americans, some of it is an odd sort of romantic primitivism, and some of it surely is the general shape of our marketing culture, [295] which heralds masterworks everywhere, daily. In any case, it is an insult to every serious Negro writer, as to every serious writer of any complexion.

SOURCE: Stanley Edgar Hyman, *The Promised End* (Cleveland and New York: The World Publishing Company, 1963), pp. 295–315. Copyright © 1963, 1962, 1960, 1959, 1958, 1957, 1956, 1955, 1953, 1951, 1950, 1949, 1946, 1942 by Stanley Edgar Hyman. Reprinted by permission of the author.

In discussing Negro writing in relation to a folk tradition, I do not mean a folksy tradition. I have in mind the dependence of writers like Yeats and Synge on Irish folk culture, not of James Whitcomb Riley or Edgar Guest on Hoosier corn. There is a whole spectrum of possible relations to a folk tradition, ranging from such unpromising connections as simple imitation and fakery, archaism or sentimentalizing, to a number of complicated, ironic, and richly rewarding connections. I propose as much as possible to confine myself to some of the latter.

Without attempting any sort of historical survey of Negro writing, I would suggest that several obviously different strains are visible. One is a body of writing largely indistinguishable from white writing, with no specifically Negro character at all, which exists in an unbroken line from the poems of Phillis Wheatley, an eighteenth-century slave and apologist for slavery, to the historical novels of Frank Yerby. A second strain has a specifically Negro character, or at least subject matter. It is the naturalism of the social protest or documentary, the account of lynching, passing, discrimination, or varieties of resistance, and its examples are legion. A third is the naturalism of the regional or folksy, which was once about watermelon eating on the old plantation, and now seems to be mostly about hair straightening and razor fighting in Harlem. It is my intention to bypass these populous avenues, and to discuss the half-dozen or so Negro writers who seem to me largely to have gone beyond any sort of mimicry or naturalism, and to have joined the mainstream of modern literature in its symbolist and ironical flowing, who use literary form as an act of the moral imagination with Melville and Dostoevsky, Kafka and Joyce, Eliot and Baudelaire. These Negro writers, although not all of them are from the South, clearly relate to the renaissance of white Southern writing we have seen in our day, particularly in fiction, from Faulkner to Flannery O'Connor. I intend to discuss this small band of Negro writers, and to mention a few others, in relation to three forms of Negro folk literature: the folk tale, the blues, and the sermon. Other forms, among them [296] spirituals and ballads, rhymes and games, have comparable literary extensions, but three should suffice to show some of the possibilities.

To talk about the folk tale, oddly enough, we have to begin with the familiar figure of the "darky" entertainer: Stepin Fetchit, Rochester, the Kingfish of the Amos 'n' Andy program. His role is to parody the familiar stereotype of the Negro: stupid, ignorant, lazy, fraudulent, cowardly, submoral, and boundlessly good-na-tured. The comic point of the act is that the performer is not really this subhuman grotesque, but a person of intelligence and skill, in other words, a performer. Assuming this role, a smart man playing dumb, is a characteristic behavior pattern of Negroes in the South (and often in the North) in a variety of conflict situa-tions. *No Day of Triumph,* the reporting by a brilliant and sensi-tive Negro, J. Saunders Redding, of a trip through the South in 1940, gives us a typical example. He was driving into Kentucky with a Negro hitchhiker he had picked up, when they were stopped in a strikebound mining town by a guard with an auto-matic rifle. Before Redding could say anything, the hitchhiker shifted automatically into just such a "coon" act:

"Cap'n, we'se goin' to Kintucky. See all dat stuff back dere, Cap'n? Well, dat stuff 'longs ter Mista Rob French, an' he sho' will raise hell ef we don' git it to him," Bill lied convincingly.

"That gittar too?" the guard questioned, already softened to a joke.

Bill grinned. "No, suh, Cap'n. Dis yere box is mine. Dis yere's ma sweetheart! If we-all hed time an' you hed time, I'd beat one out fer you," Bill said.

"G'on. But don' stop nowheres. Don' even breathe hard," the guard said, grinning.

"No, suh, Cap'n. I ain't much of a breever noway. Jus' 'nough ter live on. No, suh. I don' want no mo' o' white folks' air den I just got ter have."

One of the memorable characters in Richard Wright's autobiog-raphy *Black Boy* is a Memphis elevator operator called Shorty, who specializes in playing what Wright calls "the role of a clown of the most debased and degraded type." Shorty gets quarters [297] from white passengers by an obsequious clown act that cul-minates in his inviting the white man to kick his rump. When Wright, full of "disgust and loathing," asks him, "How in God's name can you do that?" Shorty answers simply, "Listen, nigger, my ass is tough and quarters is scarce." Wright's fictional use of the stereotype constitutes something like Shorty's revenge. In Wright's latest novel, *The Outsider,* the hero, Cross Damon, is a Negro intellectual and existentialist criminal of terrifying literacy and paranoia. At one point in his criminal career he needs a false birth certificate, and gets it by the same "darky" act. Cross thinks: "He would have to present to the officials a Negro so scared and ignorant that no white American would ever dream that he was up to anything deceptive." He does so, batting his eyes stupidly, asking for "the paper that say I was born," explaining in answer to every question only that his white boss said he had better have it right away. Of course he gets it immediately. The novel explains:

And as he stood there manipulating their responses, Cross knew exactly what kind of man he would pretend to be to kill suspicion if he ever got into trouble. In his role of an ignorant, frightened Negro, each white man—except those few who were free from the race bias of their group—would leap to supply him with a background and an identity; each white man would project out on him his own conception of the Negro and he could safely hide behind it. . . . He knew that deep in their hearts those two white clerks knew that no human being on earth was as dense as he had made himself out to be, but they wanted, needed to believe it of Negroes and it helped them to feel racially superior. They were pretending, just as he had been pretending.

A comically related use of the "darky" act appears in Rudolph Fisher's *The Conjure-Man Dies,* which so far as I know is the only Negro detective story. Here there are no whites at all: victim, murderer, detective, police, and all the other characters are Negroes. The "darky" act is thus directed not at a character in the book, but at the white reader. Shortly after the murder, an uncouth kinky-haired buffoon appears, exclaiming:

"Great day in the mornin'! What all you polices doin' in this place? Policeman outside d' front door, policeman in d' hall, policeman on d' stairs, and hyer's another one. 'Deed I mus' be in [298] d' wrong house! Is this Frimbo the conjure-man's house, or is it the jail?"

He turns out, of course (and I hope the reader will forgive me for giving away the plot of a twenty-five-year-old mystery), to be the murderer, an intelligent and literate man, disguised in a wig and a "coon" act. The point here seems to be that for a Negro reader, no Negro ever talked like that to his fellows, and the character is immediately suspicious. To a white reader, Fisher apparently assumes (and probably with justice), the disguise would be impenetrable because it fits white stereotypes. Writing a mystery that would mystify whites but convey essential hints to Negro readers seems an odd burlesque equivalent to Cross Damon's power manipulations.

The fullest development I know of the darky act in fiction is Ralph Ellison's *Invisible Man,* where on investigation every important character turns out to be engaged in some facet of the smart-man-playing-dumb routine. The narrator's grandfather, who was "the meekest of men," confesses on his deathbed:

"Son, after I'm gone I want you to keep up the good fight. I never told you, but our life is a war and I have been a traitor all my born days, a spy in the enemy's country ever since I give up my gun back in the Reconstruction. Live with your head in the lion's mouth. I want you to overcome 'em with yeses, undermine 'em with grins, agree 'em to death and destruction, let 'em swoller you till they vomit or bust wide open."

Dr. Bledsoe, the president of the college, a tough and unscrupulous autocrat, pretends to be a simple pious Negro for the school's white trustees, explaining to the narrator: "I had to be strong and purposeful to get where I am. I had to wait and plan and lick around. . . . Yes, I had to act the nigger!" Tod Clifton, a young intellectual in the Brotherhood, perversely turns to peddling black Sambo dolls on the street, singing and making them dance, and is thus himself a kind of Sambo doll when he is shot down. Rinehart, like his prototype, Melville's Confidence-Man, has so many disguises—from the Reverend B. P. Rinehart, Spiritual Technologist, to Rine, the sweet man and numbers runner—that we see only comic masks, and have to conjecture the master illusionist [299] behind them. And so on, from character to character, with the narrator himself the ultimate darky act, an invisible blackness that conceals a sentient human being.

The origins of this figure in clown make-up are many. He comes immediately from vaudeville, burlesque, and the minstrel show, but behind those sources he is an authentic figure of folk tale, in fact the major figure of Negro folk tale. In one form, he is Brer Rabbit (more accurately, "Ber" or "Buh" Rabbit), who appears an innocent but can outwit fox and wolf; in another form he is John, who appears an ignorant slave but can always outwit Ole Massa. When Richard M. Dorson was collecting folk tales in Michigan, an informant told him, "Rabbit always the schemey one," and an informant in Florida similarly told Zora Neale Hurston, "John was too smart for Ole Massa. He never got no beatin'!" Behind both figures in American Negro tales there is the prototype of the West African trickster hero of so many cycles: Spider on the Gold Coast, Legba the creator god's son in Dahomey, Rabbit or Tortoise elsewhere. Like other trickster heroes in other folklores, he is not quite animal, man, or god, but partakes of all three natures.

If Wright, Fisher, and Ellison get the darky act from the realities (and travesties) of Negro life in America, from folk tales of Buh Rabbit and John, and ultimately from West African mythology, those are still not the only sources. The same mocking figure dances through Western literature from the *Eiron* in Greek old comedy and the Fool in *Lear* down to Holden Caulfield in J. D. Salinger's *The Catcher in the Rye* and Kingsley Amis' Jim in *Lucky Jim*. We see a related figure called into being by the hard doctrine of 1 Corinthians 3:19, "For the wisdom of this world is foolishness with God," and 4:10, "We are fools for Christ's sake."

In other words, when the Negro writer retreats furthest from white models and deepest into Negro folk tradition, back in fact to African myth, he is paradoxically not furthest from Western literature but finds himself sharing a timeless archetype with Aristophanes, Shakespeare, and St. Paul, who in turn derived it from *their* folk sources in myth and ritual. High Western culture and the Negro folk tradition thus do not appear to pull the [300] writer in opposite directions, but to say the same thing in their different vocabularies, to come together and reinforce insight with insight. Prince Myshkin in *The Idiot* derives identically from the *Eiron* and Fool of drama, the Fool in Christ, and a folk figure of wisdom-in-stupidity out of Russian peasant life and lore instead of Negro life and lore.

The relationship of Negro writing to the blues is, if anything, even more immediately visible than its relationship to the folk tale, although it is much harder to describe, since the blues is an extraordinarily complicated and subtle form, much of it depending on the music, which I shall have to ignore here. Most blues songs seem to divide readily into two types, a slow lament and a faster and gayer form. The slow lament says, with Ma Rainey:

> C.C. rider, see what you done done, Lord Lord Lord,
> Made me love you, now your gal done come,
> You made me love you, now your gal done come.

or with Bessie Smith:

> I was with you, baby, when you didn't have a dime,
> I was with you, baby, when you didn't have a dime;
> Now since you got plenty money you have throwed your
>   good gal down.

The fast blues says, with Joe Turner:

> You so beautiful, but you gotta die someday,
> Oh, you so beautiful, but you gotta die someday;
> All I want's a little lovin', baby, before you pass away.

or with Jabo Williams:

> Please, fat mama, keep them great big legs off of me,
> Please, fat mama, keep them great big legs off of me. . . .
> Them great big legs gonna keep me away,
> Them big legs keep me away.

or with Rosetta Crawford:

> I'm gonna get me a razor and a gun,
> Cut him if he stand still, shoot him if he run;
> 'Cause that man jumped salty on me. [301]

Superficially, the choice seems to be the impossible pair of alternatives Freud gave us in *Beyond the Pleasure Principle,* destroy others or turn the destruction inward. Yet beyond it in the memorable blues performance there seems always to be some resolution, transcendence, even catharsis and cure.

The themes of the blues appear everywhere in Negro literature. One of the most predominant is the theme of leaving, travel, journey: "I'm gonna move to Kansas City"; "Some day, some day, I'll shake your hand goodbye"; "Well, babe, goin' away and leave you by yourself"; "Pick up that suitcase, man, and travel on." Walter Lehrman, in an unpublished study of the blues (to which I am considerably indebted), finds some sort of movement away from "here" in eighty-three out of one hundred lyrics. This sort of aimless horizontal mobility is a constant in American Negro life, substituting for frustrated possibilities of vertical mobility: if a Negro cannot rise in a job, he can change jobs; if he cannot live well here, he can try elsewhere. The major theme of Wright's *Native Son* is Bigger's aimless running; in *The Outsider* it is the journey from Chicago to New York to start a new life that proves the impossibility of any such rebirth. In Ellison's *Invisible Man* the movement is first the great Exodus out of the South, north to the Promised Land. Then, when that fails its promises, it is a random skittering up and down Manhattan, between Harlem and "downtown," until the narrator achieves his only possible vertical mobility, significantly *downward,* into a sewer (an ironic verticality already anticipated in Wright's story "The Man Who Lived Underground").

The dramatic self-pity of the blues, as we hear it in Billie Holiday's:

> My man don't love me, treats me oh so mean,
> My man he don't love me, treats me awful mean;
> He's the lowest man that I've ever seen.

or Pine Top Smith's:

> Now my woman's got a heart like a rock cast down in the sea,
> Now my woman's got a heart like a rock cast down in the sea;
> Seems like she can love everybody and mistreat poor me. [302]

is the constant note in the work of such a writer as James Baldwin. In *Go Tell It on the Mountain,* the adolescent hero, John, is ugly, friendless, and always the smallest boy in each class. When he encounters *Of Human Bondage* he identifies (almost inconceivably) with Mildred. In Baldwin's "Autobiographical Notes" in *Notes of a Native Son,* the author identifies himself with Caliban, and says to white Prospero, "You taught me language, and my profit on't is I know how to curse." In *Giovanni's Room,* the book's most contemptible-pathetic character, Jacques, retires "into that strong self-pity which was, perhaps, the only thing he had which really belonged to him."

Self-pity is a compensatory grandiose fantasy. In the blues, Bessie Smith sings:

> Say, I wisht I had me a heaven of my own,
> Say, I wisht I had me a heaven of my own;
> I'd give all the poor girls a long lost happy home.

In Negro writing, the grandiose fantasy is often upward, but rarely so otherworldly as a private heaven. The nameless Negro protagonist of "The Man Who Lived Underground," after a casual and pointless robbery, papers the walls of his sewer cavern with hundred-dollar bills, hangs gold watches and rings from nails all around him, and makes the dirt floor a mosaic of diamonds. The narrator of *Invisible Man* wires *his* hole in the ground with 1,369 light bulbs covering every inch of the ceiling, and plans on five phonographs simultaneously playing Louis Armstrong's record of "Black and Blue" while he eats pink and white—vanilla ice cream covered with sloe gin. In *Go Tell It on the Mountain,* John lives in a fantasy world where he is "beautiful, tall, and popular." In his daydreams he feels "like a giant who might crumble this city with his anger; he felt like a tyrant who might crush this city beneath his heel; he felt like a long-awaited conqueror at whose feet flowers would be strewn and before whom multitudes cried, Hosanna!" Sometimes John fancies, in the direct imagery of the blues, that he has "a closet full of whisky and wine," at other times, in his family's imagery, that he is the John of Revelation, or St. Paul. His identification with Maugham's [303] Mildred is not only self-pity but power fantasy. Baldwin writes: "He wanted to be like her, only more powerful, more thorough, and more cruel; to make those around him, all who hurt him, suffer as she made the student suffer, and laugh in their faces when they asked pity for their pain."

The long monologue by "Flap" Conroy in Redding's *No Day of Triumph,* in its combination of bitter misery with high-spirited defiance, is almost an extended blues. Flap opposes reality to blues fantasy, *"White folks* got the world in a jug an' the stopper in their hand," and then immediately denies it, "That's what *they* think." Bigger and his friend Gus in *Native Son* daydream of flying planes and dropping bombs on the white world. In *The Outsider,* this has become a vision, by a Negro in a bar, of flying saucers landing from Mars and disembarking *colored* men, come to put the white overlords of earth in their place. In Langston Hughes's *Simple Speaks His Mind,* Simple, who alternates between feeling "like I got the world in a jug and the stopper in my hand" and varieties of depression, also alternates between fury that Negroes are not allowed to run trains and fly planes, and fantasies of space flight:

Why, man, I would rock so far away from this color line in the U.S.A., till it wouldn't be funny. I might even build me a garage on Mars and a mansion on Venus. On summer nights I would scoot down the Milky Way just to cool myself off. I would not have no old-time jet-propelled plane either. My plane would run on atom power. This earth I would not bother with no more. No, buddy-o! The sky would be my roadway and the stars my stopping place. Man, if I had a rocket plane, I would rock off into space and be solid gone. Gone. Real gone! I mean *gone!"*

Balancing this complex of misery and compensation in the slow blues, we have the abuse and bawdry of the fast blues. Georgia White sings:

When we married, we promised to stick through thick and thin,
When we married, we promised to stick through thick and thin;
But the way you thinnin' out is a lowdown dirty sin.

"Speckled Red" sings: [304]

Now you're a dirty mistreater, a robber and a cheater,
I slip you in the dozen, your pappy is your cousin,
Your mama do the Lordy-Lord.

(The reference is to "the dozens," a formalized Negro game, particularly common among children, creating what John Dollard calls "a pattern of interactive insult" by chanting slurs on the cleanliness, odor, legitimacy, fidelity, and heterosexuality of the opponent's immediate family, particularly his mother.) Simple and Hughes's narrator slip each other repeatedly in the dozens, as do the college boys in Redding's novel *Stranger and Alone,* along with the characters in many other Negro works. There is a particularly interesting example in *Invisible Man.* The nameless protagonist, brought up on charges before a committee of the Brotherhood, is asked indignantly where he got the "personal responsibility" he claims, and automatically answers, "From your ma," before he corrects himself.

Related to the theme of obscenity and abuse in the blues is a pervasive cynicism, the cynicism of "If you don't like my peaches, don't shake my tree; I ain't after your woman, she's after me," or "Papa, papa, you in a good man's way; I can get one better than you any time of day." The Negro poet who has made this note uniquely his own is Fenton Johnson. I quote part of his poem "Tired," which catches the fast blues' mingled tones of despair and mean comedy:

I am tired of work; I am tired of building up somebody else's civilization.
Let us take a rest, M'Lissy Jane.
I will go down to the Last Chance Saloon, drink a gallon or two of gin, shoot a game or two of dice and sleep the rest of the night on one of Mike's barrels.
You will let the old shanty go to rot, the white people's clothes turn to dust, and the Calvary Baptist Church sink to the bottomless pit.
You will spend your days forgetting you married me and your nights hunting the warm gin Mike serves the ladies in the rear of the Last Chance Saloon.
Throw the children into the river; civilization has given us too many. [305]

Along with the themes and attitudes of the blues, their techniques and diction are equally pervasive in Negro writing. In the folk blues, the formal unit is not the song but the individual stanza (what in ballad study is called the "commonplace"), and the composer or singer strings traditional stanzas together to produce his own composition. The formal organization of the blues is associative, like a good deal of modern poetry. A typical folk blues is "Little Brother's Blues," recorded by the Lomaxes, for the Library of Congress, at Texas State Penitentiary in 1934 (I will not bother repeating the first lines of each stanza):

> Lord, you light weight skinners, you better learn to skin,
> Old Mister Bud Russell, I tell you, he wants to starve the men.
>
> O my mama, she called me, I'm gonna answer "Mam?"
> "Lord, ain't you tired of rollin' for that big-hat man?"
>
> She's got nine gold teeth, long black curly hair,
> Lord, if you get on the Santa Fe, find your baby there.
>
> I been prayin' Our Father, Lord, Thy kingdom come,
> Lord, I been prayin' Our Father, let Your will be done.
>
> One, two, three, four, five, six, seven, eight, nine,
> I'm gonna count these blues she's got on her mind.

Here motifs of work, compulsion and hunger, mother and rebellion, nine gold teeth and long black curly hair, train journey and baby, God's will and counting the digits, all associate thematically with doing time in a prison camp and the contrasted pole of freedom and gratifications, as T. S. Eliot associates garlic and sapphires in the mud.

The Negro poet most obviously identified with this sort of thematic and associative organization is Melvin B. Tolson, in his remarkable long poem *Libretto for the Republic of Liberia.* Allen Tate in a preface places the poem "in the direct succession" from Hart Crane's *The Bridge,* and other critics have identified its techniques with those of Eliot's *Waste Land* or Pound's *Cantos.* Reinforcing rather than denying these analogies, I would insist on its kinship to the associative organization of the blues. In any [306] case, it is an intricate and sophisticated work, and the advance in complexity it represents can best be shown by comparing a stanza with one from its obvious predecessor, Paul Laurence Dunbar's "Ode to Ethiopia." Dunbar writes:

> On every hand in this fair land,
> Proud Ethiope's swarthy children stand
>   Beside their fairer neighbor;
> The forests flee before their stroke,
> Their hammers ring, their forges smoke—
>   They stir in honest labor.

Tolson writes:

> And now the hyenas whine among the barren bones
> Of the seventeen sun sultans of Songhai,
> And hooded cobras, hoodless mambas, hiss

> In the gold caverns of Falémé and Bambuk,
> And puff adders, hook scorpions, whisper
> In the weedy corridors of Sankoré. *Lia! Lia!*

The language of the blues is rich in the sort of irony and ambiguity to which the modern criticism of poetry has heightened our consciousness. Pine Top Smith sings:

> Now I combed her hair, even manicured her fingernails,
> Now I combed her hair, even manicured her fingernails;
> Every time I get in trouble, she let me go to jail.

Robert Johnson sings:

> She's a kind-hearted mama, studies evil all the time.

The poetry of Gwendolyn Brooks shows something of this range of irony, from the mockery of a folk tradition in "The Ballad of Late Annie" to the poignant Dickinsonian cadences of poem IV of "The Womanhood" in *Annie Allen,* which I must quote entire:

> A light and diplomatic bird
> Is lenient in my window tree.
> A quick dilemma of the leaves
> Discloses twist and tact to me.
>
> Who strangles his extremest need
> For pity of my imminence [307]
> On utmost ache and lacquered cold
> Is prosperous in proper sense:
>
> He can abash his barmecides;
> The fantoccini of his range
> Pass over. Vast and secular
> And apt and admirably strange.
>
> Augmented by incorrigible
> Conviction of his symmetry
> He can afford his sine die.
> He can afford to pity me
>
> Whose hours at best are wheats or beiges
> Lashed with riot-red and black.
> Tabasco at the lapping wave.
> Search-light in the secret crack.
>
> Oh open, apostolic height!
> And tell my humbug how to start

> Bid balance, bleach: make miniature
> Valhalla of my heart.

Negro writers have ceaselessly attempted to define the emotional ambivalence of the blues: "grief-gaiety," "melancholy-comic," "wistfulness-laughter," "making light of what actually is grave," or the blues line itself, "I'm laughing just to keep from crying." In his *Libretto,* that treasure ship of plunder from the world's cultures and languages, Tolson uses a Yiddish phrase for this ambivalence, *"lachen mit yastchekes,"* which he translates in the notes as " 'laughing with needles being stuck in you'; ghetto laughter." "As for the laughter," a character in Redding's *Stranger and Alone* thinks, "unless one had experienced it, he cannot imagine how it rips and tears you with pain." In an interview in the *New York Times,* Baldwin stated what are clearly his intentions as a writer: "I have always wondered why there has never, or almost never, appeared in fiction any of the joy of Louis Armstrong or the really bottomless, ironic and mocking sadness of Billie Holiday." His own books display a comparable ambivalence everywhere. Florence in *Go Tell It on the Mountain* "did not want his touch, and yet she did: she burned with longing and froze with rage." Gabriel "hated his sins—even as he ran towards sin," and [308] "prayed, as his mother had taught him to pray, for loving kindness; yet he dreamed of the feel of a white man's forehead against his shoe." John, the young protagonist, is ambivalent toward his stepfather, his mother, his aunt, his idol Elisha, even to God. In *Notes of a Native Son,* Baldwin generalizes from the irony of his father's death on the day the father had a child: "Life and death so close together, and love and hatred, and right and wrong, said something to me which I did not want to hear concerning man, concerning the life of man." *Giovanni's Room,* as befits a novel about sexual ambivalence, shows both sides of every coin: the narrator yields to Giovanni, "With everything in me screaming *No!* yet the sum of me sighed *Yes*"; he later feels "a hatred for Giovanni which was as powerful as my love and which was nourished by the same roots"; when he intends to desert him for a girl, "I really felt at that moment that Judas and the Saviour had met in me"; when he has his final battle with Giovanni, "He grasped me by the collar, wrestling and caressing at once, fluid and iron at once: saliva spraying from his lips and his eyes full of tears."

Ellison made the first critical attempt I know to relate the blues to specific Negro literature in an article on *Black Boy* entitled "Richard Wright's Blues" in *The Antioch Review,* Summer, 1945. He began by defining the form as a symbolic action:

The Blues is an impulse to keep the painful details and episodes of a brutal experience alive in one's aching consciousness, to finger its jagged grain, and to transcend it, not by the consolation of philosophy, but by squeezing from it a near-tragic, near-comic lyricism.

and concluded:

Let us close with one final word about the Blues: Their attraction lies in this, that they at once express both the agony of life and the possibility of conquering it through sheer toughness of spirit. They fall short of tragedy only in that they provide no solution, offer no scapegoat but the self.

This conception did not really fit Wright's *Black Boy* very well (it would apply much more aptly to "The Man Who Lived Underground"), but it turned out to be a remarkably accurate manifesto for Ellison's own novel, *Invisible Man,* published seven [309] years later. If we want "a near-tragic, near-comic lyricism" in a fictional image we need go no further than its final tableau of the Harlem riot of 1943. Here Ras the Exhorter, a bitter Negro nationalist, arrays himself as an Abyssinian chieftain, armed with spear and shield, and rides out against the police guns. We see the scene through the eyes of an anonymous Harlem citizen:

"Hell, yes, man, he had him a big black hoss and a fur cap and some kind of old lion skin or something over his shoulders and he was raising hell. Goddam if it wasn't a *sight,* riding up and down on this ole hoss, you know, one of the kind that pulls vegetable wagons, and he got him a cowboy saddle and some big spurs."

"Aw naw, man!"

"Hell, yes! Riding up and down the block yelling, 'Destroy 'em! Drive 'em out! Burn 'em out! I, Ras, commands you.' You get that, man," he said, " 'I *Ras,* commands you—to destroy them to the last piece of rotten fish!' And 'bout that time some joker with a big ole Georgia voice sticks his head out the window and yells, 'Ride 'em, cowboy. Give 'em hell and bananas.' "

Finally, "riding like Earl Sande in the fifth at Jamaica," Ras charges to his death.

If the blues is the ancestor of the low rhetoric in Negro writing, the sermon is the ancestor of the high. Oratory has a surprisingly prominent place in American Negro life: Redding notes that the children in his family "were all trained at home in the declining art of oratory and were regular contestants for prizes at school"; Baldwin was a preacher in a Harlem store-front church for several years in his teens; when Ellison decided not to make his protagonist a writer, making him a speaker was the obvious choice. Their books are inevitably full of oratorical set pieces: *No Day of Triumph* reproduces a Negro funeral sermon and *Stranger and Alone* a Southern governor's campaign speech; the effective end of *Native Son* is Max's impassioned defense of Bigger in court; a whole chapter of *Invisible Man* is devoted to blind Barbee's sermon on the Founder of the school, and the narrator makes several eloquent political speeches; *Go Tell It on the Mountain* includes two of Gabriel's remarkable sermons. Listen to such an example [310] of the Negro folk sermon as "The Man of Calvary," by "Sin-Killer" Griffin, which John Lomax recorded in 1934 during an Easter Sunday service at a Texas penitentiary, and which the Library of Congress issues on a record. The three principal ingredients seem to be: a Biblical violence of acting and suffering ("Roman soldiers came riding in full speed and splunged Him in the side"); apocalyptic, almost surrealist imagery like that of the Book of Revelation (the sun "clothed itself in sack cloth-ing and went down," the moon sank in blood and "done bled away," "each little star leaped out of its silver orbit" and became a funeral torch); and a contrasting tone of concentrated wisdom, like that of the Book of Proverbs.

All three of these tones are markedly evident in Negro writing. The violence, like so much else, is overdetermined: it comes not only from the Bible, but from all the harsh realities of American Negro life, and it relates to the mock-violence of the blues ("Cut him if he stand still, shoot him if he run"). Our most extreme example is Richard Wright, whose writings are almost indescribably violent: *Native Son* from the beating of the rat to death in the first pages to the imminent electrocution of Bigger in the last; the innumerable whippings, bone-smashings, rapes, murders, and burnings in the stories. The tone of *Black Boy* is set in the first pages when Wright is almost beaten to death by his mother; the poems are a dreadful tissue of mobs "battering my teeth into my throat till I swallowed my own blood" and "the tall flames that cooked and charred the black flesh." This overreaches itself to the point of Grand Guignol horror in *The Outsider*. Cross frees himself in a subway wreck, to give one moderate example, by smashing a corpse's head to a bloody pulp. He then escapes out the window by standing on the chest of a dead woman, "feeling his shoes sinking into the lifeless flesh and seeing blood bubbling from the woman's mouth as his weight bore down on her breast." And so on for four hundred pages.

The apocalyptic imagery of the sermon appears in Negro writing at least as far back as the fantasies of W. E. B. DuBois, particularly *Darkwater* in 1919, with its black Christ born in Georgia and the destruction of Manhattan by a comet. Jean Toomer's *Cane,* published in 1923, displays a lower-keyed, rather whimsical surrealism [311]: "Her mind is a pink mesh-bag filled with baby toes." In our time, two principal exemplars of these juxtapositions have been Ellison and Baldwin. Open *Invisible Man* at any page: here is a stag smoker entertained by a combination of Negro boys fighting a battle royal, a graduation address, and a naked white dancer with a small American flag tattooed on her belly; there, an artificial eye in a glass of water staring intently at the narrator everyone else finds invisible. *Go Tell It on the Mountain* is full of the same wild imagery: John hears the sounds of his parents in bed together "over the sound of rat feet, and rat screams"; after his conversion at the end he sees the Devil on the streets of Harlem, disguised as a lean cat eying him from behind a garbage can, or a gray bird perched on the metal cornice of a roof.

Baldwin talks of "something ironic and violent and perpetually understated in Negro speech," and complains that despite the "force and precision" of the spoken language, Negro writing "has been generally speaking so pallid and harsh." This force and precision is the third strain of the sermon, its gnarly eloquence. The same quality is common to the Bible, West African speech forms (Tolson quotes a number of remarkable African proverbs), and American Negro folklore. Zora Neale Hurston was told, "Hard work in de hot sun done called many a man to preach." "You ain't the only frog done fattened hisself for snakes," says a character in *No Day of Triumph.* "Any time a nigger with white folks," remarks a figure in Redding's novel, "he alone." "Reach and draw back a nub," taunts the narrator in *Invisible Man.* "Me and the Lord," Florence's husband remarks in *Go Tell It on the Mountain,* "Don't always get along so well. He running the world like He thinks I ain't got good sense."

Negro writing, because of the special vulnerabilities and resources of Negro writers, is in a position to deal with certain ironies and ambivalences of the American condition as most white writers (at least outside the South) are not. Negro writers are, as it were, a special kind of radar to extend our vision. Wright in "The Ethics of Living Jim Crow" and *Black Boy,* Tolson in the *Libretto,* Ellison in the Prologue and Epilogue to *Invisible Man,* Baldwin in *Notes of a Native Son,* have all tirelessly articulated [312] this peculiar role, with its consequent responsibilities. The social and racial relations of America are changing radically. In 1900 almost three-quarters of the Negroes in America had lived in the rural South; by 1950, fewer than one-fifth of them did. Where one out of three Negroes over sixty-five is illiterate, fewer than one out of twenty is, in the younger generation. The seventeen million Negroes in the United States now earn a sum about equal to the national income of Canada. Not long ago the Cotton Club in Harlem would not admit Negroes unless they were celebrities, now Broadway and 52nd Street night clubs advertise eagerly for the Negro trade. One has only to read Toomer's 1923 portrait of Negro life in the South in *Cane,* and its 1942 equivalent, Redding's *No Day of Triumph,* to see the changes wrought by two decades, and a comparable 1957 book would show changes about again as great. Nor does this process go on only in the United States. Any daily paper will show the varieties of ferment of the world's Negro peoples, and we can see its articulate consciousness in such fiction as *In the Castle of My Skin* by George Lamming of the Barbados, or *The Palm-Wine Drinkard* and *My Life in the Bush of Ghosts* by the Nigerian writer Amos Tutuola.

"The artist must lose such lesser iden.tities [as Negro] in the great well of life," Waldo Frank says in his foreword to *Cane.* That has not been the view of many Negro artists of our time. In Paris, Baldwin reports, the American Negro "finds himself involved, in another language, in the same old battle: the battle for his own identity," and this turns out to be part of a larger American quest: "The American in Europe is everywhere confronted with the question of his identity." There is a Negro character in Claude McKay's *Home to Harlem* for whom identity is largely a matter of cuisine: "He would not eat watermelon, because white people called it 'the niggers ice-cream'. Pork chops he fancied not. Nor corn pone. And the idea of eating chicken gave him a spasm." Ellison has written exhaustively on the identity problem in "Richard Wright's Blues" and elsewhere, but his most graphic account of it is a similarly culinary identification in *Invisible Man.* The narrator had always scorned Negro food, along with other backward "darky" trappings, in his effort to rise in the white

world, until a moment in the middle of the book when on impulse
[313] he buys a yam from a peddler and eats it on the street. At
that moment, in the magical equation of "yam" with "I am," he
comes to terms with his Negro identity and folk tradition, while
maintaining his quest for a fully developed human consciousness.
In other words, he wants yams, but he wants to be a twentieth-
century Western man eating them. It is in just this fashion that the
blues, say, develop in significance; starting with the specific lament
for lost love, calamity, or hard times, and ending with these events
metaphoric for the most universal human condition.

The folk tradition, for the Negro writer, is like Ellison's yams,
not the regression or reversion it appears to be, but another path
to the most ironic and sophisticated consciousness. Tate's preface
to *Libretto for the Republic of Liberia* finds that full utilization of
the resources of modern poetry and language has made Tolson
"not less but more intensely *Negro.*" There is an almost unavoida-
ble unconscious pun in dealing with Negro culture. A silly white
Negrophile in Fisher's *The Walls of Jericho* says she prefers Negroes to whites because "You see, they have so much color." Margaret Just Butcher, the Negro author of *The Negro in American
Culture,* makes the pun continually in what I am sure is entire innocence: "The Negro observably colored the general temper and
folkways of the American south"; Negro comedy "richly colored
Southern local and regional culture, and eventually that of the
whole nation"; a work typifies "the well-meaning, somewhat color-
less accounts by white authors"; *Uncle Tom's Cabin* is written in
"sharp blacks and whites, no shadings." The reality behind the
pun is that Negro life in America, Negro folk literature, and some
Negro writing does have color in every sense; not only skin pigment, but all the rich pigmentation of the fullest possible awareness. The best Negro literature and folk literature extends our perception to a far wider range. "Who knows," the narrator of
Invisible Man asks in the book's last line, "but that, on the lower
frequencies, I speak for you?" Perhaps, we can add, on the very
highest, the almost inaudible frequencies as well?

NOTE [1963]: This was originally written as the first Ludwig Lew-
isohn Lecture at Brandeis. When I finished the manuscript I
[314] sent it to my friend Ralph Ellison for an opinion. He replied with a long eloquent letter arguing the other half of the
truth, the indebtedness of American Negro literature to the Euro-

pean literary tradition. As a result we produced a rather contrived
debate in *Partisan Review,* Spring, 1958. A shortened version of
my lecture was followed by his rejoinder, "Change the Joke and
Slip the Yoke"; the two constituting "The Negro Writer in America: an Exchange." Ellison's article is particularly interesting for
its statements about the influences on his own work. [315]

RALPH ELLISON

Change the Joke and Slip the Yoke

Stanley Edgar Hyman's essay on the relationship between Negro
American literature and Negro American folklore concerns matters in which my own interest is such that the very news of his
piece aroused my enthusiasm. Yet after reading [45] it I find that
our conceptions of the way in which folk tradition gets into
literature—and especially into the novel; our conceptions of just
what is *Negro* and what is *American* in Negro American folklore;
and our conceptions of a Negro American writer's environment
—are at such odds that I must disagree with him all along the
way. And since much of his essay is given over so generously to
aspects of my own meager writings, I am put in the ungrateful—
and embarrassing—position of not only evaluating some of his
statements from that highly dubious (but privileged) sanctuary
provided by one's intimate knowledge of one's personal history,
but of questioning some of his readings of my own novel by con-
sulting the text.

Archetypes, like taxes, seem doomed to be with us always, and
so with literature, one hopes; but between the two there must
needs be the living human being in a specific texture of time,
place, and circumstance; who must respond, make choices, achieve
eloquence, and create specific works of art. Thus I feel that Hy-

SOURCE: Ralph Ellison, *Shadow and Act* (New York: Random House, Inc.,
1964), pp. 45–59. Copyright © 1958 by Ralph Ellison. Reprinted by permission of Random House, Inc.

man's fascination with folk tradition and the pleasure of archetype-hunting leads to a critical game that ignores the specificity of literary works. And it also causes him to blur the distinction between various archetypes and different currents of American folklore, and, generally, to oversimplify the American tradition.

Hyman's favorite archetypical figure is the trickster, but I see a danger here. From a proper distance *all* archetypes would appear to be tricksters and confidence men; part-God, part-man, no one seems to know he-she-its true name, because he-she-it is protean with changes of pace, location, and identity. Further, the trickster is everywhere and anywhere at one and the same time, and, like the parts of some dismembered god, is likely to be found on stony as well as on fertile ground. Folklore is somewhat more stable, in its identity if not in its genealogy; but even here, if we are to discuss [46] *Negro* American folklore let us not be led astray by interlopers.

Certainly we should not approach Negro folklore through the figure Hyman calls the " 'darky' entertainer." For even though such performers as he mentions appear to be convenient guides, they lead us elsewhere, into a Chthonic labyrinth. The role with which they are identified is not, despite its "blackness," *Negro* American (indeed, Negroes are repelled by it); it does not find its popularity among Negroes but among whites; and although it resembles the role of the clown familiar to Negro variety-house audiences, it derives not from the Negro but from the Anglo-Saxon branch of American folklore. In other words, this " 'darky' entertainer" is white. Nevertheless, it might be worthwhile to follow the trail for a while, even though we seem more interested in interracial warfare than the question of literature.

These entertainers are, as Hyman explains, professionals, who in order to enact a symbolic role basic to the underlying drama of American society assume a ritual mask—the identical mask and role taken on by white minstrel men when *they* depicted comic Negroes. Social changes occurring since the 1930's have made for certain modifications (Rochester operates in a different climate of rhetoric, say, than did Stepin Fetchit) but the mask, stylized and iconic, was once required of anyone who would act the role— even those Negroes whose natural coloration should, for any less ritualistic purposes at least, have made it unnecessary.

Nor does the role, which makes use of Negro idiom, songs, dance motifs, and word-play, grow out of the Negro American sense of the comic (although we too have our comedy of blackness), but out of the white American's Manichean fascination with the symbolism of blackness and whiteness expressed in such contradictions as the conflict between the white American's Judeo-Christian morality, his democratic [47] political ideals and his daily conduct—indeed in his general anti-tragic approach to experience.

Being "highly pigmented," as the sociologists say, it was our Negro "misfortune" to be caught up associatively in the negative side of this basic dualism of the white folk mind, and to be shackled to almost everything it would repress from conscience and consciousness. The physical hardships and indignities of slavery were benign compared with this continuing debasement of our image. Because these things are bound up with their notion of chaos it is almost impossible for many whites to consider questions of sex, women, economic opportunity, the national identity, historic change, social justice—even the "criminality" implicit in the broadening of freedom itself—without summoning malignant images of black men into consciousness.

In the Anglo-Saxon branch of American folklore and in the entertainment industry (which thrives on the exploitation and debasement of all folk materials), the Negro is reduced to a negative sign that usually appears in a comedy of the grotesque and the unacceptable. As Constance Rourke has made us aware, the action of the early minstrel show—with its Negro-derived choreography, its ringing of banjos and rattling of bones, its voices cackling jokes in pseudo-Negro dialect, with its nonsense songs, its bright costumes and sweating performers—constituted a ritual of exorcism. Other white cultures had their gollywogs and blackamoors but the fact of Negro slavery went to the moral heart of the American social drama and here the Negro was too real for easy fantasy, too serious to be dealt with in anything less than a national art. The mask was an inseparable part of the national iconography. Thus even when a Negro acted in an abstract role the national implications were unchanged. His costume made use of the "sacred" symbolism of the American flag—with red and white striped pants and coat and with stars set in a field of blue for a collar—but he could [48] appear only with his hands gloved in white and his face blackened with burnt cork or greasepaint.

This mask, this willful stylization and modification of the natural face and hands, was imperative for the evocation of that atmosphere in which the fascination of blackness could be enjoyed, the comic catharsis achieved. The racial identity of the performer was unimportant, the mask was the thing (the "thing" in more ways than one) and its function was to veil the humanity of Negroes thus reduced to a sign, and to repress the white audience's awareness of its moral identification with its own acts and with the human ambiguities pushed behind the mask.

Hyman sees the comic point of the contemporary Negro's performance of the role as arising from the circumstance that a skilled man of intelligence is parodying a subhuman grotesque; this is all very kind, but when we move in from the wide-ranging spaces of the archetype for a closer inspection we see that the specific rhetorical situation involves the self-humiliation of the "sacrificial" figure, and that a psychological dissociation from this symbolic self-maiming is one of the powerful motives at work in the audience. Motives of race, status, economics, and guilt are always clustered here. The comic point is inseparable from the racial identity of the performer—as is clear in Hyman's example from Wright's *Black Boy*—who by assuming the group-debasing role for gain not only substantiates the audience's belief in the "blackness" of things black, but relieves it, with dream-like efficiency, of its guilt by accepting the very profit motive that was involved in the designation of the Negro as national scapegoat in the first place. There are all kinds of comedy: here one is reminded of the tribesman in *Green Hills of Africa* who hid his laughing face in shame at the sight of a gun-shot hyena jerking out its own intestines and eating them, in Hemingway's words, "with relish."

Down at the deep dark bottom of the melting pot, where [49] the private is public and the public private, where black is white and white black, where the immoral becomes moral and the moral is anything that makes one feel good (or that one has the power to sustain), the white man's relish is apt to be the black man's gall.

It is not at all odd that this black-faced figure of white fun is for Negroes a symbol of everything they rejected in the white man's thinking about race, in themselves and in their own group. When he appears, for example, in the guise of Nigger Jim, the Negro is made uncomfortable. Writing at a time when the blackfaced minstrel was still popular, and shortly after a war which left even the abolitionists weary of those problems associated with the Negro, Twain fitted Jim into the outlines of the minstrel tradition, and it is from behind this stereotype mask that we see Jim's dignity and human capacity—and Twain's complexity—emerge. Yet it is his source in this same tradition which creates that ambivalence between his identification as an adult and parent and his "boyish" naivete, and which by contrast makes Huck, with his street-sparrow sophistication, seem more adult. Certainly it upsets a Negro reader, and it offers a less psychoanalytical explanation of the discomfort which lay behind Leslie Fiedler's thesis concerning the relation of Jim and Huck in his essay "Come Back to the Raft Ag'in, Huck Honey!"

A glance at a more recent fictional encounter between a Negro adult and a white boy, that of Lucas Beauchamp and Chick Mallison in Faulkner's *Intruder in The Dust,* will reinforce my point. For all the racial and caste differences between them, Lucas holds the ascendency in his mature dignity over the youthful Mallison and refuses to lower himself in the comic duel of status forced on him by the white boy whose life he has saved. Faulkner was free to reject the confusion between manhood and the Negro's caste status which is sanctioned by white southern tradition, but Twain, standing [50] closer to the Reconstruction and to the oral tradition, was not so free of the white dictum that Negro males must be treated either as boys or "uncles"—never as men. Jim's friendship for Huck comes across as that of a boy for another boy rather than as the friendship of an adult for a junior; thus there is implicit in it not only a violation of the manners sanctioned by society for relations between Negroes and whites, there is a violation of our conception of adult maleness.

In Jim the extremes of the private and the public come to focus, and before our eyes an "archetypal" figure gives way before the realism implicit in the form of the novel. Here we have, I believe, an explanation in the novel's own terms of that ambiguity which bothered Fiedler. Fielder was accused of mere sensationalism when he named the friendship homosexual, yet I believe him so profoundly disturbed by the manner in which the deep dichotomies symbolized by blackness and whiteness are resolved that, forgetting to look at the specific form of the novel, he leaped squarely into the middle of that tangle of symbolism which he is dedicated to unsnarling, and yelled out his most terrifying name for chaos. Other things being equal he might have called it "rape," "incest," "parricide," or—"miscegenation." It is ironic that what to a Negro appears to be a lost fall in Twain's otherwise successful wrestle with the ambiguous figure in black face is viewed by a critic as a symbolic loss of sexual identity. Surely for literature there is some rare richness here.

Although the figure in black face looks suspiciously homegrown, Western, and Calvinist to me, Hyman identifies it as being related to an archetypical trickster figure, originating in Africa. Without arguing the point I shall say only that it *is* a trickster; its adjustment to the contours of "white" symbolic needs is far more intriguing than its alleged origins, for it tells us something of the operation of American values [51] as modulated by folklore and literature. We are back once more to questions of order and chaos; illusion and reality, nonentity and identity.

The trickster, according to Karl Kerenyi (in a commentary included in Paul Radin's study, *The Trickster*), represents a personification of the body

"which is . . . never wholly subdued, ruled by lust and hunger, forever running into pain and injury, cunning and stupid in action. Disorder belonging to the totality of life . . . the spirit of this disorder is the trickster. His function in an archaic society, or rather the function of his mythology, of the tales told about him, is to add disorder to order and to make a whole, to render possible, within the fixed bounds of what is permitted, an experience of what is not permitted. . . ."

But ours is no archaic society (although its archaic elements exert far more influence in our lives than we care to admit), and it is an ironic reversal that, in what is regarded as the most "open" society in the world, the license of the black trickster figure is limited by the rigidities of racial attitudes, by political expediencies, and by the guilt bound up with the white compulsion to identify with the ever present man of flesh and blood whose irremediable features have been expropriated for "immoral" purposes. Hyman, incidentally, would have found in Louis Armstrong a much better example of the trickster, his medium being music rather than words and pantomime. Armstrong's clownish license and intoxicating powers are almost Elizabethan; he takes liberties with kings, queens, and presidents; emphasizes the physicality of his music with sweat, spittle, and facial contortions; he performs the magical feat of making romantic melody issue from a throat of gravel; and some few years ago was recommending to all and sundry his personal physic, "Pluto Water," as a purging way to health, happiness, and international peace. [52]

When the white man steps behind the mask of the trickster his freedom is circumscribed by the fear that he is not simply miming a personification of his disorder and chaos but that he will become in fact that which he intends only to symbolize; that he will be trapped somewhere in the mystery of hell (for there is a mystery in the whiteness of blackness, the innocence of evil, and the evil of

233

innocence, though, being initiates, Negroes express the joke of it in the blues) and thus lose that freedom which, in the fluid, "traditionless," "classless," and rapidly changing society, he would recognize as the white man's alone.

Here another ironic facet of the old American problem of identity crops up. For out of the counterfeiting of the black American's identity there arises a profound doubt in the white man's mind as to the authenticity of his own image of himself. He, after all, went into the business when he refused the king's shilling and revolted. He had put on a mask of his own, as it were; and when we regard our concern with identity in the light of what Robert Penn Warren has termed the "intentional" character of our national beginnings, a quotation from W. B. Yeats proves highly meaningful:

There is a relation between discipline and the theatrical sense. If we cannot imagine ourselves as different from what we are and assume the second self, we cannot impose a discipline upon ourselves, though we may accept one from others. Active virtue, as distinct from the passive acceptance of a current code, is the wearing of a mask. It is the condition of an arduous full life.

For the ex-colonials, the declaration of an American identity meant the assumption of a mask, and it imposed not only the discipline of national self-consciousness, it gave Americans an ironic awareness of the joke that always lies between appearance and reality, between the discontinuity of social tradition and that sense of the past which clings to the mind. And perhaps even an awareness of the joke that [53] society is man's creation, not God's. Americans began their revolt from the English fatherland when they dumped the tea into the Boston Harbor, masked as Indians, and the mobility of the society created in this limitless space has encouraged the use of the mask for good and evil ever since. As the advertising industry, which is dedicated to the creation of masks, makes clear, that which cannot gain authority from tradition may borrow it with a mask. Masking is a play upon possibility and ours is a society in which possibilities are many. When American life is most American it is apt to be most theatrical.

And it is this which makes me question Hyman's designation of the "smart man playing dumb" role as primarily Negro, if he means by "conflict situations" those in which racial pressure is uppermost. Actually it is a role which Negroes share with other Americans, and it might be more "Yankee" than anything else. It is a strategy common to the culture, and it is reinforced by our anti-intellectualism, by our tendency toward conformity and by the related desire of the individual to be left alone; often simply by the desire to put more money in the bank. But basically the strategy grows out of our awareness of the joke at the center of the American identity. Said a very dark southern friend of mine in laughing reply to a white business man who complained of his recalcitrance in a bargaining situation, "I know, you thought I was colored, didn't you." It is across this joke that Negro and white Americans regard one another. The white American has charged the Negro American with being without past or tradition (something which strikes the white man with a nameless horror), just as he himself has been so charged by Europeans and American critics with a nostalgia for the stability once typical of European cultures; and the Negro knows that both were "mammy-made" right here at home. What's more, each secretly believes that he alone knows what is valid in the American experience, and that [54] the other knows he knows but will not admit it, and each suspects the other of being at bottom a phony.

The white man's half-conscious awareness that his image of the Negro is false makes him suspect the Negro of always seeking to take him in, and assume his motives are anger and fear—which very often they are. On his side of the joke the Negro looks at the white man and finds it difficult to believe that the "grays"—a Negro term for white people—can be so absurdly self-deluded over the true interrelatedness of blackness and whiteness. To him the white man seems a hypocrite who boasts of a pure identity while standing with his humanity exposed to the world.

Very often, however, the Negro's masking is motivated not so much by fear as by a profound rejection of the image created to usurp his identity. Sometimes it is for the sheer joy of the joke; sometimes to challenge those who presume, across the psychological distance created by race manners, to know his identity. Nonetheless, it is in the American grain. Benjamin Franklin, the practical scientist, skilled statesman, and sophisticated lover allowed the French to mistake him for Rousseau's Natural Man. Hemingway poses as a non-literary sportsman, Faulkner as a farmer; Abe Lincoln allowed himself to be taken for a simple country lawyer—until the chips were down. Here the "darky" act makes brothers of us all. America is a land of masking jokers. We wear the mask for purposes of aggression as well as for defense; when we are projecting the future and preserving the past. In short, the motives hidden behind the mask are as numerous as the ambiguities the mask conceals.

My basic quarrel with Hyman is not over his belief in the importance of the folk tradition; nor over his interest in archetypes, but that when he turns to specific works of literature he tends to distort their content to fit his theory. Since he refers so generously to my own novel, let us take it as a case in point. So intense is Hyman's search for archetypical [55] forms that he doesn't see that the narrator's grandfather in *Invisible Man* is no more involved in a "darky" act than was Ulysses in Polyphemus' cave. Nor is he so much a "smart-man-playing-dumb" as a weak man who knows the nature of his oppressor's weakness. There is a good deal of spite in the old man, as there comes to be in his grandson, and the strategy he advises is a kind of jiu jitsu of the spirit, a denial and rejection through agreement. Samson, eyeless in Gaza, pulls the building down when his strength returns; politically weak, the grandfather has learned that conformity leads to a similar end, and so advises his children. Thus his mask of meekness conceals the wisdom of one who has learned the secret of saying the "yes" which accomplishes the expressive "no." Here too is a rejection of a current code and a denial become metaphysical. More important to the novel is the fact that he represents the ambiguity of the past for the hero, for whom his sphinx-like deathbed advice poses a riddle which points the plot in the dual direction which the hero will follow throughout the novel.

Certainly B. P. Rhinehart (the P. is for "Proteus," the B. for "Bliss") would seem the perfect example of Hyman's trickster figure. He is a cunning man who wins the admiration of those who admire skulduggery and know-how; an American virtuoso of identity who thrives on chaos and swift change; he is greedy, in that his masquerade is motivated by money as well as by the sheer bliss of impersonation; he is god-like, in that he brings new techniques—electric guitars, etc.—to the service of God, and in that there are many men in his image while he is himself unseen; he is phallic in his role of "lover"; as a numbers runner he is a bringer of manna and a worker of miracles, in that he transforms (for winners, of course) pennies into dollars, and thus he feeds, (and feeds on), the poor. Indeed, one could extend this list in the manner of much myth-mongering criticism until the fiction dissolved into anthropology, but Rhinehart's [56] role in the formal structure of the narrative is to suggest to the hero a mode of escape from Ras, and a means of applying, in yet another form, his grandfather's cryptic advice to his own situation. One could throw Rhinehart among his literary betters and link him with Mann's Felix Krull, the Barron Clappique of Malraux's *Man's Fate* and many others, but that would be to make a game of criticism and really say nothing.

The identity of fictional characters is determined by the implicit realism of the form, not by their relation to tradition; they are what they do or do not do. Archetypes are timeless, novels are time-haunted. If the symbols appearing in a novel link up with those of universal myth they do so by virtue of their emergence from the specific texture of a specific form of social reality. The final act of *Invisible Man* is not that of a concealment in darkness in the Anglo-Saxon connotation of the word, but that of a voice issuing its little wisdom out of the substance of its own inwardness —after having undergone a transformation from ranter to writer. If, by the way, the hero is pulling a "darky act" in this, he certainly is not a smart man playing dumb. For the novel, his memoir, is one long, loud rant, howl, and laugh. Confession, not concealment, is his mode. His mobility is dual; geographical, as Hyman points out, but, more importantly, it is intellectual. And in keeping with the reverse English of the plot, and with the Negro American conception of blackness, his movement vertically downward (not into a "sewer," Freud notwithstanding, but into a coal cellar, a source of heat, light, power and, through association with the character's motivation, self perception) is a process of *rising* to an understanding of his human condition. He gets his restless mobility not so much from the blues or from sociology but from the circumstance that he appears in a literary form which has time and social change as its special province. [57] Besides, restlessness of the spirit is an American condition that transcends geography, sociology, and past condition of servitude.

Discussions of folk tradition and literature which slight the specific literary forms involved seem to me questionable. Most of the writers whom Hyman mentions are novelists, workers in a form which has absorbed folk tradition into its thematic structures, its plots, symbolism and rhetoric; and which has its special way with folklore as it has with manners, history, sociology and psychology. Besides, novelists in our time are more likely to be inspired by reading novels than by their acquaintance with any folk tradition.

I use folklore in my work not because I am Negro, but because writers like Eliot and Joyce made me conscious of the literary value of my folk inheritance. My cultural background, like that of most Americans, is dual (my middle name, sadly enough, is Waldo).

I knew the trickster Ulysses just as early as I knew the wily rabbit of Negro American lore, and I could easily imagine myself a pint-sized Ulysses but hardly a rabbit, no matter how human and resourceful or Negro. And a little later I could imagine myself as Huck Finn (I so nicknamed my brother) but not, though I racially. identified with him, as Nigger Jim, who struck me as a white man's inadequate portrait of a slave.

My point is that the Negro American writer is also an heir of the human experience which is literature, and this might well be more important to him than his living folk tradition. For me, at least, in the discontinuous, swiftly changing and diverse American culture, the stability of the Negro American folk tradition became precious as a result of an act of literary discovery. Taken as a whole, its spirituals along with its blues, jazz, and folk tales, it has, as Hyman suggests, much to tell us of the faith, humor, and adaptability to reality necessary to live in a world which has taken [58] on much of the insecurity and blues-like absurdity known to those who brought it into being. For those who are able to translate its meanings into wider, more precise vocabularies it has much to offer indeed. Hyman performs a service when he makes us aware that Negro American folk tradition constitutes a valuable source for literature, but for the novelist, of any cultural or racial identity, his form is his greatest freedom and his insights are where he finds them. [59]

CHARLES I. GLICKSBERG

The Alienation of Negro Literature

Even in the republic of letters, Negroes work under a crippling handicap. The poison of racial prejudice subtly pervades the cultural atmosphere so that even the language of criticism is influenced by unconscious but nonetheless invidious value-judgments

SOURCE: *Phylon,* XI (1950), 49–58. Reprinted by permission of *Phylon.*

which set the colored people apart from the American folk and its native culture. The brutal lynching of the Negro has given way to a more refined form of cultural segregation. Negro writers are praised and encouraged for possessing talent that is authentically "Negroid." They are not *American* writers. They are Negroes, and that makes all the difference. Only those elements of their work which differentiate it *racially* from "white" art are praised and encouraged, and since the whites for the most part control the aesthetic norms of appreciation as well as the channels of public recognition, they have helped to lay the foundation of what has been called "Negro literature."

There would be little objection to such a designation if it were nothing but a descriptive label. The connotations of the label, however, are more significant than the denotative aspect. What is usually implied by the term? It is hard to say, since no two "white" critics would agree *in toto,* but the prevailing theme seems to be that "Negro literature" is racial at heart, a "primitive" product. "Negroid" in substance and spirit, Negro literature and art give expression to the soul of the black folk: their exuberance, their earthy sensuousness, their childlike mind and innocent eye, their African sense of rhythm. It is the art of a separate race within America.

Thus the term "Negro literature" reveals the pattern of cultural [49] segregation in which Negro writers are being confined. Since they are Negroes, not Americans, their work must somehow be identified as "alien." The linguistic impasse springs from a contradiction in the mind and heart of the whites. Everything is either honorifically white or damnably black. There is American literature and "Negro literature." There is American culture, and an alien sector reserved exclusively for Negroes. The reservation is not altogether exclusive. The whites hold a mortgage even on this segregated sector and dictate the terms of the lease. (Not *all* whites to be sure, but that is where the difficulty comes in: the sharp black-white dualism distorts the perspective of discourse.) They decide what is unique in Negro genius: the blues, the spirituals, jazz, primitive music, neo-African art, racial poetry and fiction. If a Negro poet were to write on universal rather than specifically racial themes he would most likely be ignored by the whites, and the colored folk would probably regard him as a traitor, trying to "pass." It is rare to find a Negro novelist dealing with anything but themes of racial conflict and oppression. Even the Negro social scientists are obsessed with this subject.

Remarkable indeed is the fact that Negro writers have adjusted themselves to this state of affairs. In fact, they have transformed it into a militant crusade. Cultural alienation manifests itself as racialism, the Negro writers betraying an almost pathological pride in their separateness, their "difference," their achievements as a people. Racialism is a fetish, a source of inspiration and strength, a philosophy of aesthetics, a creative religion.

The race war is on. Because the "whites" exalt "whiteness" as the mark of superiority, the source and standard of all that is truly excellent in the world of letters, the Negroes are constrained to take exaggerated pride in the contrasting fact of "blackness." "Color" thus becomes a category of culture, and Negro writers are driven into a cultural Black Belt. As a result of being thus segregated and of segregating themselves, they find it extremely difficult to reach the plane of the universal. Too much Negro fiction and poetry is of an aggressive racial cast, dealing obsessively and often monotonously with the theme of racial discrimination. This is the basic reason for the limitations of Negro literature in the United States. That is why, alas, it so often falls short of greatness. It cannot view the condition of humanity objectively, only through the "colored" lens of the racial problem. Cosmic tragedy—the precariousness and unutterable pathos of human fate quite apart from the frustrations and failures of social life—lies entirely outside its scope. Not that the Negro writers are unaware of these tragic implications, but that these are overshadowed, in some cases completely, by the race psychosis. Negro poets may be bitter, but they do not voice the philosophical pessimism of a Thomas Hardy or an A. E. Housman; no Negro novelist with [50] the possible exception of Richard Wright betrays the profound social insight of a Theodore Dreiser, a James T. Farrell, a John Dos Passos. It is not without considerable aesthetic significance that those who are able to see beyond the racial motif are, by and large, those who have been deeply influenced by the philosophy of Communism. As a result of serving his literary apprenticeship in left-wing groups and identifying himself with the struggles of the proletariat, white and black, Richard Wright came to perceive that injustice and exploitation are not confined to the Negro masses but are the logical evolution and inevitable outcome of a particular economic system.

For the great majority of Negro writers, however, Communism is no solution. They must work out their creative salvation in terms of the American scene. Recoiling from the painful experience of rejection, they return with intensified love to the security offered by their own racial group, focusing their hatred against the "white" oppressor. The price of cultural alienation is racial identification. Since they are judged as a race rather than as individuals, as Americans, they will ally themselves unreservedly with their own people. Creative Negroes voice the aspirations and resentments, the hurts and traumatic hatreds, the desires and dreams and terrible frustrations, of their own race. They know what it means to be a Negro in "white America," and they protest with all the force of their being against the myth of innate racial inferiority.

Consequently, they attack the vicious stereotypes the whites have created about their race, by endeavoring to prove that Negroes are uniquely talented in this or that artistic field. This belief, namely, that in music, rhythm, and in spirituals, the Negro is exceptionally well endowed by virtue of his primitive African ancestry, deepens and confirms his cultural alienation. The whites are delighted to welcome any contribution which can be conspicuously and generically labeled "Negroid." By stressing the "Negroid" quality of his art, the whites strengthen the dualism in the heart of the Negro writer. After pushing him into a Black Ghetto, they say: "Go to it, boy. That is your distinctive racial talent. You will succeed best to the extent that you are most truly yourself: a Negro." Buell G. Gallagher, who in *American Caste and the Negro College* had written sanely on this aspect of cultural alienation, points out that the reversion of the Negro to "specifically 'Negroid' themes and modes of expression is in a sense a tacit admission that the Negro is giving up the struggle for acceptance as part of a white world—he is accepting cultural segregation, a symbol of social status as well." There is the inexorable dilemma: if the Negro writer retreats into himself and develops his "racial" potentialities he is departing from the norms of "American" culture; if he imitates that culture, he may cease to be himself and destroy both his uniqueness and his creative vitality.

Negro literature is thus handicapped by its very virtues. It is a literature [51] of passionate protest, intense in feeling but narrow in scope. Its hatred of racial injustice assumes at times the shrill, incoherent character of an obsessional neurosis. The writer has his eyes fixed broodingly on one sector of experience, the suffering of his people, the fatality of "color," and he can think and write of nothing else. He must drink this cup of gall and wormwood to the lees. In novel and drama and lyric, the Negro writer voices in bitter and poignant accents the Golgotha his folk must tread.

There is an element of singular fascination in the tales of horror and the poems of suffering and violent protest that Negro writers publish. That is often the single, cumulative impression left on the mind by a great deal of Negro fiction and poetry: horror drawn to the breaking-point, protests that swell to a frenzied, almost vengeful climax. There are passages of unbearable tension in *Native Son,* scenes of melodramatic horror in *The White Face.* It is as if these writers, Richard Wright and Carl Ruthven Offord respectively, worked under a compulsion they could not resist, the unconscious dictating the script of the nightmare they have known. Richard Wright has told us of the struggle that went on within him while he was trying to project the character of Bigger Thomas, the protagonist of *Native Son.* Though he concentrated all his energies on showing Bigger Thomas in the Negro slums of Chicago, he was aware of another life that Bigger led, and this dualism pictured the alienation of the American Negro in all its tragic nakedness. "He was an American," declares Richard Wright of Bigger Thomas, "because he was a native son; but he was also a Negro nationalist in a vague sense because he was not allowed to live as an American. Such was his way of life and mine; neither Bigger nor I resided fully in either camp." The nationalist emphasis came first, Wright decided, because that corresponded most truly with Bigger's fierce hatred of the whites and also because that hate served as a symbol of the alienation of the black race in America.

In other words, his nationalist complex was for me a concept through which I could grasp more of the total meaning of his life than I could in any other way. . . . What made Bigger's social consciousness most complex was the fact that he was hovering unwanted between two worlds—between powerful America and his own stunted place in life —and I took upon myself the task of trying to make the reader feel this No Man's Land.

Whenever Richard Wright came across people who had suffered from the sense of alienation, his critical faculty was sharpened. How would Bigger Thomas have reacted under such circumstances? Everything he read or heard or experienced shed some light on the problem of the American Negro. Gradually came the realization that as the Negroes in the South and in many parts of the North lived so had other oppressed peoples in the past until they revolted against their oppressor, and that unless the intolerable burden of the American Negro was lifted, [52] in time the inner flood of resentment would break forth. If Richard Wright was fascinated by the history of the Russian Revolution, he was equally intrigued by the Fascist movement in Germany, for in that land he recognized behavior patterns similar to those in the Bigger Thomases among his own people. For Negroes, too, yearned for a messianic leader who would give them all the redeeming answers, lead them out of the wilderness of oppression, weld them into a nation. Listening to such remarks from the Bigger Thomases among his own people, Wright came to understand

that the civilization which had given birth to Bigger contained no spiritual sustenance, had created no culture which could hold and claim his allegiance and faith, had sensitized him and had left him stranded, a free agent to roam the streets of our cities, a hot and whirling vortex of undisciplined and unchannelized impulses. The results of these observations made me feel more than ever estranged from the civilization in which I lived, and more than ever resolved toward the task of creating with words a scheme of images and symbols whose direction could enlist the sympathies, loyalties, and yearnings of the millions of Bigger Thomases in every land and race. . . .

Richard Wright had no illusions about the kind of civilization money-grubbing, industrial, heartless America had created nor about the way this civilization had treated the Negro people. He declares most revealingly:

But we do have in the Negro the embodiment of a past tragic enough to appease the spiritual hunger of even a James; and we have in the oppression of the Negro a shadow athwart our national life dense and heavy enough to satisfy even the gloomy broodings of a Hawthorne. And if Poe were alive, he would not have to invent horror; horror would invent him.

Richard Wright, in the most powerful work of naturalistic fiction an American Negro has yet produced, sought to explore his horror-haunted No Man's Land. *Native Son* is a detailed study of the tragic effects of alienation upon a Negro lad who is the symbol of the Negroes in America: the rejected, the scorned, the frustrated, the hate-tormented, who turn into killers. In these race-thwarted personalities the pattern of hate and fear culminates in murderous violence. *Black Boy* is the autobiographical elaboration of the same environmental thesis. Through this story of Wright's life runs the same obsessive note of fear and hate: fear of monstrous white men, the Ku Klux Klan, and hate of the sadists who demand that Negroes "keep their place."

The result is very much what one might expect. After the mind sups full on such concentrated horrors, one of two things is bound to happen: either the mind is rendered callous, insensitive to the suffering involved, or its appetite for more sensational fare is whetted. The Negro cannot, of course, avoid painting reality as *he* sees it, the ugliness as well as the beauty, the horror as well as the redeeming humanity of life, but as a writer he should at least be objectively aware of the psychological [53] effect he produces. By stressing the tragic plight of his people, he misses the note of universality and fails to capture in words the amazing variety of experiences to which man is exposed during his pilgrimage on earth. The racial obsession shuts him out from dealing with the cosmic tragedy and divine comedy of man, the intrusion of ironic chance and malign accident into the warp and woof of fate, the sense of mystery that rounds out our little life.

Hemmed in as they are by a psychological as well as physical Black Ghetto, for the Negro writers, race is fate. Everything that happens to the Negro is interpreted in the light of the racial struggle. The individual scarcely appears in all his uniqueness and emotional complexity. Instead he appears almost invariably as a race man, his conflicts and his personal development conditioned by his environment and the persecutory hostility of the whites. The Negro who becomes a killer is a cultural product, fighting against overwhelming odds, filled with ineffectual resentments that explode in hot murderous impulses.

Then, too, Negro writers have been so preoccupied with the immediate racial issue that they have failed to develop a true historical sense. As a rule, their work reveals little trace of their native cultural past. It is singularly deficient in historical perspective. This arises from the curious circumstance that the Negro regards himself in a sense as a man without a history. Since he is treated not as an American but as a Negro, he feels himself cut off from the cultural heritage of this land. True, he is a most earnest believer in the American Creed, but he is forced to view the American past with a divided mind. Fundamentally he is ashamed of the past of slavery and ashamed to confess that he is ashamed. He simply keeps silent about it. There are few Negro novels or poems or dramas which deal realistically and yet understandingly with this extraordinary phase of the American past. Yet here is epic material for those with the imaginative courage and the talent and the fierce insight to develop it to the full.

If one sought a common denominator in Negro poetry he would

find it in its single-minded preoccupation with the racial problem. When Paul Laurence Dunbar first came on the American scene, few critics recognized the creative potentialities of the Negro. The publication of Dunbar's poetry was therefore an event of considerable importance. Here was Negro humor, here was Negro dialect. Here was a writer blazing a new tradition, writing about the experiences of his own people in their own "peculiar" tongue. Dunbar's aesthetic philosophy was basically sound, even though his poetic strategy was mistaken. He strove scrupulously to attain the ideal of universality. For him there was but one road to salvation: the Negro must be acknowledged as a man. Only after his humanity was recognized did the secondary identifying characteristics of color and race enter in. [54]

Admirable as such a theory is when considered in the abstract, it was unfortunately out of alignment with the facts of life as they then functioned in American society. As Benjamin Brawley points out in his study of Dunbar, this was a way of blinding himself to the truth of social reality. Dunbar hypnotized himself into the belief that he was primarily a man when the rest of the world continued to look upon him only as a Negro. Because of this contradiction, his poetry, written for a predominantly white audience and completely divorced from the racial conflict, was born of a divided will and a split personality. He once told a reporter: "For two hundred and fifty years the environment of the Negro has been American, in every respect the same as that of all other Americans." His great hope was that his people would in time be permitted to share as equals in the cultural life of this country. Yet he unwittingly lent himself to the writing of poetry in dialect, which popularized many of the ugly stereotypes concerning the Negro. It is poetry steeped in sentimentality, nostalgic, romantically idealized.

Contemporary poetry has tended to steer away from dialect verse, since it fails to do justice to the spirit of the Negro folk and is out of touch with the facts of modern life. James Weldon Johnson saw that no matter how sincere the Negro poet writing in the conventionalized dialect might be, he was really expressing "only certain conceptions about Negro life that his audience was willing to accept and ready to enjoy," and that audience consisted of whites who knew what they wanted. That is it precisely: dialect for the Negro writer is a trap. He thinks he is being "racial" whereas he is in reality conforming to white stereotyped conceptions of Negro life and speech, Negro character and sentiment. Dialect poetry has had to be discarded by poets who wished for freedom in their choice of subject matter and mode of treatment. It is James Weldon Johnson's considered opinion that *"traditional* Negro dialect as a form for Aframerican poets is absolutely dead." Whatever compromises Paul Laurence Dunbar had to make, he was definitely on the right track in asserting that the Negro was first and foremost an American, and that he must write as an American, not as a segregated Negro with a peculiar, caste-conditioned culture of his own.

No writer can function vitally without sinking his roots deep into native soil. The past is always with us; the Negro writer is the organic summation of his past. Whatever the Negro people are now is the evolutionary result of all they have been. If they fight for full freedom today, it is because they were once denied freedom in the American past. But what past should the Negro writer resurrect? If human beings trace their biological evolution back far enough, they come to the primordial slime. The past exists for the writer only in so far as it is viable. Shall the Negro rediscover Africa and make common cause with black people the world over or shall he confine himself to his cultural past in [55] the United States so that eventually he may become creatively and culturally identified with America? If he chooses the former alternative, he is doomed. If the latter, the question arises, how shall this be accomplished?

For the Negro writer is not permitted to sink his roots into the cultural soil of his native land. He cannot identify himself with what passes for American culture because it is a "white" man's culture, just as he has failed in his attempts to transcend discrimination within the heart of Christianity by creating images of a "black" Christ and "black" saints. Whereas Negro writers still appeal to the tradition embodied in the Declaration of Independence and the Bill of Rights, the work of John Brown and Abraham Lincoln and Thaddeus Stevens, and the writings of the Abolitionist poets, their usable past must be sought elsewhere. It is to be found in the history and martyrdom of their own people, in the insurrections of poorly armed and loosely organized slaves who attempted to break the chains that bound them. The Negroes need no longer be ashamed of their past; their primary need as writers is to understand it and put it creatively to use.

Dangerous in its implications is the tendency to amalgamate with African culture, to return to primitive fountainheads of feeling, tradition, and myth. If "white" America rejects Negroes, they will look for salvation to their ancestral "homeland." On the cultural plane, this back-to-Africa movement represents the sublimated equivalent of the old discarded plan to have Negroes transplanted to Africa. That way is forever closed to American Negroes. True enough, investigations of life in Africa at the time the Negroes were brought to these shores point to the existence of a rich ancient culture and disprove the Southern stereotype that the imported Negro slaves were ignorant savages. They had been part of a proud, flourishing native culture. But what ideological castles can be built on such historical foundations? The Negro, after all, belongs to America. His art is genuinely American in inspiration and content, untutored and underivative, uninfluenced by African as well as European models. As Gunnar Myrdal concludes in *An American Dilemma:* "Negro art will continue to be American because its creators are American and American influences continually mold it."

Negro writers cannot have it both ways: if they oppose racialism as a meaningless as well as dangerous term when applied to politics, they must, if they are to remain consistent in their thinking, oppose it with equal firmness when they encounter it, however camouflaged, on the cultural front. They cannot, on the one hand, maintain that they are American born and bred, native sons of this land, and, on the other, propose to alienate themselves from the American cultural tradition on the ground of racial solidarity with the people of Africa or black folk throughout the world. As Countee Cullen asks in troubled introspection, [56] what is Africa to the American Negro? How much does he know of its history, tribal composition, folklore, collective life, indigenous culture? Even if he studied it, what creative value would it have for him as a writer? What is it he hopes to find in Africa that is denied him in America? Nothing but the hope that in this land and among these people, his ancestors, he will discover the sources of a pure, primitive, autochthonous art.

That hope is foredoomed to failure. As the result of his acculturation in America, he is as much a stranger to Africa as the African is a stranger to America. By spiritually migrating to Africa, he abandons the struggle for freedom and equality in order to retreat to a mythical paradise in the tropics, an idyllic jungle of primitivism. He repudiates his creative citizenship in the body of Western culture for the sake of a pseudo-primitivism which fundamentally has no appeal and no meaning for him. There is no reason why he must make such a choice. He can still support the

Charles I. Glicksberg

cause of the colored people, whether in India or Indonesia or China or Africa, without seeking artistic inspiration and cultural roots in the heart of Africa. He will not find them there.

When the Negro renaissance finally got under way in the twentieth century, what the "white" critic singled out for praise was this very element of the primitive. The curious feature of it all was that Negro writers began to believe it was so. African art was lauded to the skies as the art of pure feeling, the spontaneous product of a primitive mentality. Some Negro intellectuals even argued that Negro writers and artists could find a fruitful source of inspiration in African art. Alain Locke, who beat the drum loudly in this cause, then declared that there is "a real and vital connection between this new artistic respect for African heritage and the natural ambition of Negro artists for a racial idiom in their art expression." Albert C. Barnes, writing on "Negro Art and America" in *The New Negro,* calls the artistic contribution of the American Negro sound "because it comes from a primitive nature upon which a white man's education has never been harnessed." To analyze the psychological character of the Negro in terms of his primitive ancestry and to maintain that he is still subject to its racial influence is an example of the cult of the primitive at its worst. The belief that reintegration into the African cultural background will make for a renaissance of Negro art in America is not only pure superstition, it also reveals in what devious ways the process of cultural alienation acts on the Negro.

What then is the Negro writer to do? To imitate the "white" American culture is damnable, a confession of a lack of originality. To exploit his unique "racial" soul is to cut himself off from the taproot of universality and the culture of his own land. Negro literature is American literature or it is nothing. Langston Hughes once argued earnestly that the assimilative tendency was the mountain standing in the way of true [57] Negro art in America —"this urge within the race toward whiteness, the desire to pour racial individuality into the mold of American standardization, and to be as little Negro and as much American as possible." Though Hughes speaks of racial individuality, this is different from postulating a racial creative spirit, a racial mentality. Even at that the statement is fallacious. Why this false antithesis between "Negro" and "American"? Why can't the Negro write as a full-fledged American and still retain his individuality, the precious amalgam of all his experiences, intuitions, and insights?

On this issue the Negro writer cannot afford to compromise. By surrendering uncritically to the insidious appeal of "Negroid" or "racial" art, he is in effect accommodating himself to the ethics and aesthetics of a "segregated" literature; he is impoverishing his art and deepening his sense of alienation, confining the Negro genius within the dark and narrow walls of caste. The major task of the Negro writer at present is to destroy the stereotypes that keep him in mental as well as physical bondage. He must break down both the practice of cultural exclusion and the barriers of economic discrimination. At all costs he must find a way out of the trap of cultural alienation if he is to take his rightful place in American literature. All of life, all that is distinctively human, should be included within his creative province. Then Negro comedy as well as tragedy will be born: the gift of irony and laughter. Is it not significant that the Negroes have not yet produced an outstanding humorist? That will surely come in the fullness of time, and when it does Negro literature, having come of age, will cease to be "Negroid" or racial; it will be truly American in spirit and substance, instinct with overtones of the universal. [58]

HAROLD R. ISAACS

Five Writers and Their African Ancestors *

PART I

Immediately after World War I when W. E. B. DuBois was speaking for Pan-Africanism in his cultured tones, and Marcus Garvey was raising his loud plebeian clamor for Negroes to go back to Africa, a school of new Negro poets appeared who also, in their own way, sang of Africa. They were partly influenced by DuBois

* A paper read before the American Society of African Culture in June, 1960. It is drawn from a larger study of the impact of world affairs on race relations in the United States.
SOURCE: *Phylon*, XXI, 3 and 4 (1960), 243–265, 317–336. Reprinted by permission of *Phylon*.

—many of their poems first appeared in *Crisis*. Like DuBois they were romantics, but they were Bohemian poets, not strait-laced geopoliticians. They looked back, not ahead. They preferred their dreams of an idyllic past to his intercontinental visions of the future. They also felt the emotions that surged up around Marcus Garvey, but they were too sophisticated to join his simple-minded followers or take part in his mad pageantry. Their dreams were much less literal, and their flights of romantic imagination could take them much more swiftly to Africa—and much more safely back to Bohemia again—than the Black Star Line ever would.

Back to (*Literary*) *Africa*

This reaching out to Africa as a "literary homeland" was one of the features of the so-called Negro Renaissance of the 1920's, the birthtime of the "New Negro," the emergence of new Negro voices in literature. This outburst of high creativity was a product of the many moods and circumstances of the time. It was part of the world-wide postwar shake-out of hopes and values, part of the response of Negroes in America to the postwar despair, part of their resistance to the re-establishment of the supremely white order of things. It was also part of the larger literary stirrings of the period. Among the many new preoccupations, new modes, new subjects, some white writers had begun to "rediscover" the Negro, Eugene O'Neill (*Emperor Jones*), Sherwood Anderson (*Dark Laughter*), DuBose Heyward (*Porgy*), and Harlem's rediscoverer-in-chief, Carl Van Vechten (*Nigger Heaven*). In various tangible and intangible ways, this school of white writing helped open the way for a whole new school of Negro writing about Negroes. Much has been written of the Harlem Bohemia of the time, of the young Negro writers who began to flash, to flicker, and sometimes to shine, the best-remembered [243] among them now Countee Cullen, Claude McKay, and Langston Hughes, but also figures like Jean Toomer, who fell so quickly silent, and Wallace Thurman and Rudolph Fisher, who died so soon, and many others now to be found only in the literary histories. Some of these writers discovered the "New Negro" in the postwar turmoil or rediscovered "old" values in the folklore, a few discovered themselves, and all of them discovered Africa. It is this African thread in the pattern that we want here, without quite absenting ourselves from the rest, to trace awhile.

In a way it can be said that what began to take place was a new exchange in the old dialogue. Just a few years earlier, in 1917, the

poet and humanist, the gifted James Weldon Johnson, summoning
Negroes to face down their adversity, chose these words:

> Far, far the way we have trod
> From heathen kraal and jungle dens
> To freedmen, freemen, sons of God,
> Americans and citizens . . .
> No, stand erect and without fear
> And for our foes let this suffice—
> We've bought a rightful kinship here
> And we have more than paid the price.

But in hardly any time at all, the poet-aesthetes of Harlem were
trooping back to the kraals and the jungle dens, going "back-to-
Africa" in their own way, just like the despairing black masses
who lined up behind Garvey to reach the homeland on his steam-
ship line. The poets had an international current of their own to
drift in; among other things the world of the white literati had developed a new interest in primitivism, Picasso taking up African
sculpture, Gide writing of the Congo, and a great vogue for African naturalism followed the award of the 1921 Prix Goncourt to
Batouala, a novel of African tribal life by René Maran, a Marti-
nique-born Negro. Some of this was in an old tradition; despairing
of nobility in modern white civilization, sentimentalists began to
look for virtue in black primitivism. But there was also a fascinated reach for the primeval mysteries, the jungle depths, for the
abysmal brute, for the Freudian id personified in the naked black
man in his natural state and setting. Books about voodooism, wild
rites, and magic in the black Caribbean and Africa helped to set
this style. So did Vachel Lindsay's poem "The Congo," which he
subtitled "A Study of the Negro Race" and whose first section he
called "Their Basic Savagery," illustrating the theme with tomtom
rhythms and bloody doings along the black river. With Brutus
Jones, Sterling Brown remarked, O'Neill did move the Negro from
comic relief to the tragic center, but did so by relying on "tomtoms, superstition and atavism." Brown remembers "the discovery
of Harlem as a new African colony" as cheap faddism: [244]

Wa-wa trumpets, trap drums (doubling for tomtoms) and shapely
dancers with bunches of bananas girdling their middles in Bamboo Inns
and jungle cabarets nurtured tourists' illusions of 'the Congo cutting
through the black'. . . .[1]

[1] Sterling Brown, "The New Negro in Literature," in *The New Negro
Thirty Years Afterward* (Washington, D.C., 1955), pp. 58–59.

Harold R. Isaacs

Much was made of primitive sculpture and there was ample white patronage for all sorts of alleged Africanisms among Negroes, in poets, in nightclubs, and in individual behavior. The idea of the Negro as savage, whether noble or brute, had a peculiarly exploitable appeal, and it was played for all it was worth in the short-lived, high-temperature Harlem Bohemia, in that time, when, as Langston Hughes has put it, "the Negro was in vogue."

On the other hand, Alain Locke, the critic-philosopher and chronicler of the "New Negro," thought that "the current mode of idealizing the primitive and turning toward it in the reaction from the boredom of ultra-sophistication," was only the "Caucasian strain in the Negro poet's attitude toward Africa at the present time," and, fortunately, was "not dominant." He thought he saw in all the ferment "the most sophisticated of all race motives—the conscious and deliberate threading back of the historic sense of group tradition to the cultural backgrounds of Africa." [2]

This was not easy to find. Negroes finding their voices were either trying to express their angry defiance of the wave of lynchings across the country at that time, or else seeking an escape from it. The most famous and most often quoted cry of anger was Claude McKay's "If we must die, let it not be like hogs/Hunted and penned in an inglorious spot. . . ." In another poem, called "To The White Fiends," McKay wrote:

> Think you I am not fiend and savage too?
> Think you I could not arm me with a gun
> And shoot down ten of you for every one
> Of my black brothers murdered, burnt by you?
> Be not deceived, for every deed you do
> I could match—out-match: am I not Afric's son,
> Black of that black land where black deeds are done?

Of Africa itself, McKay wrote in sorrow and loss:

> The sun sought the dim bed and brought forth light,
> The sciences were sucklings at thy breast;
> When all the world was young in pregnant night,
> Thy slaves toiled at thy monumental best . . .
> Honor and Glory! Arrogance and Fame!
> They went. The darkness swallowed thee again.
> Thou art the harlot, now thy time is done,
> Of all the mighty nations of the sun.

[2] Alain Locke, "The Negro In American Culture," in *Anthology of American Negro Literature*, V.F. Calverton, ed. (New York, 1929), p. 264.

And he yearned in despair in a sonnet he called "Outcast":

> For the dim regions whence my fathers came
> My spirit, bondaged by the body, longs. [245]
> Words felt, but never heard, my lips would frame;
> My soul would sing forgotten jungle songs.
> I would go back to darkness and to peace.
> But the great western world holds me in fee,
> And I may never hope for full release
> While to its alien gods I bend my knee.
> Something in me is lost, forever lost,
> Some vital thing has gone out of my heart,
> And I must walk the way of life a ghost
> Among the sons of earth, a thing apart.
>
> For I was born, far from my native clime,
> Under the white man's menace, out of time.

Among the Negroes interviewed for the larger study from which this article is extracted, the best-remembered poem of this theme and of this time was Countee Cullen's "Heritage." Cullen, writer of romantic lyrics, had used many lines to idealize Africa, "the dusky dream-lit land" where black men and women had been kingly and queenly. But in "Heritage" he both dreams and chides himself for dreaming. It begins:

> What is Africa to me:
> Copper sun or scarlet sea,
> Jungle star or jungle track,
> Strong bronzed men, or regal black
> Women from whose loins I sprang
> When the birds of Eden sang?
> *One three centuries removed*
> *From the scene his fathers loved,*
> *Spicy grove, cinnamon tree,*
> *What is Africa to me?*

The italics are Cullen's. He goes on to dream of lying in the jungle, of "great drums throbbing through the air," of dancing a lover's dance naked in the rain, of remembering the "quaint, outlandish, heathen gods," and wishing that the God he did serve were black. "One three centuries removed," he repeats, "what is Africa to me?" Because, as Alain Locke observed, his poem "dramatized the conflict so brilliantly," his readers could and did take his intent either way; some cited the poem to me to say that it expressed their feeling of kinship with Africa; some quoted it to say

Harold R. Isaacs

that to them, as to the poet, Africa was too far removed to mean anything at all. But the poet is seeing Africa as a dream to which he can flee from anguish. "Africa?" he asks, "a book one thumbs / Listlessly, till slumber comes." In another poem, "The Shroud of Color," in his dream he flies free:

> Now suddenly a strange wild music smote
> A chord long impotent in me; a note
> Of jungles, primitive and subtle, throbbed
> Against my echoing breast, and tom-toms sobbed
> In every pulse beat of my frame. The din [246]
> A hollow log bound with a python's skin
> Can make wrought every nerve to ecstasy
> And I was wind and sky again, and sea,
> And all sweet things that flourish, being free.[3]

The dreamland Africa of the "Renaissance" poets and the nightclub Africa of the Harlem faddists receded, just like the Africa in the dream dreamed by Marcus Garvey. What is remembered now about the Negro writers of the 1920's is not how they languished over Africa, but how they asserted themselves in America, as in the memorably wishful words of the 1926 manifesto of Langston Hughes:

We younger Negro artists who create now intend to express our individual dark-skinned selves without fear or shame. If white people are pleased, we are glad. If they are not, it doesn't matter. . . . If colored people are pleased, we are glad. If they are not, their displeasure doesn't matter either.

Langston Hughes has proved to be the hardiest of all these literary figures. He was among those yearning after the ancestral home way back then, and he is helping to exult in its new eminence now. This makes his work the logical place to begin an effort to trace variations on the Africa theme in the works of certain Negro writers as they have appeared in the years from the "Renaissance" of the 1920's until now.

For this purpose I have chosen five writers whose lives overlap each other's by five to ten years, a difference sufficient in each case to mark a passage into another literary—and political—generation. Only Langston Hughes' writing life spans the whole

[3] For relevant discussion of Countee Cullen, see Saunders Redding *To Make a Poet Black* (Chapel Hill, 1939), pp. 108–112. Redding calls Cullen the "Ariel of Negro poets" who could "not beat the tomtom above a faint whisper." Also Arthur P. Davis, "The Alien-and-Exile Theme in Countee Cullen's Racial Poems." *Phylon,* XIV (Fourth Quarter, 1953), 390–400.

time; he was born in 1902, the year before DuBois' *Souls of Black Folk* appeared, published his first poem in 1921, and has been going strong ever since. Richard Wright was born in 1909, his first book appeared in 1936 and *Native Son,* the work for which he is famous, in 1940. Ralph Ellison followed Wright closely enough—he was born in 1914—to share many common experiences with him, but his novel, *Invisible Man,* did not appear until 1952, and he writes now of a world that Wright has left. James Baldwin, born in 1924, is wholly the product of a different era. His first work, *Go Tell It On the Mountain,* was published in 1953. Finally, born only yesterday in 1930, Lorraine Hansberry completes the group, not because she has made her way as yet to any solid small summit of her own, but because her play, *A Raisin In the Sun,* was a hit of the 1959 season, because it dramatizes in its freshest form some of the old dilemmas with which we are dealing, and finally because by the very title of her play, taken from one of his poems, she will enable us to end our essay, as it begins now, with Langston Hughes.

Langston Hughes

Of all the poets in Harlem who sang of Africa in the 1920's, Langston [247] Hughes was the only one who had been there. Perhaps this was why he sometimes sang of Africa in a key different from the rest:

> We cry among the skyscrapers
> As our ancestors
> Cried among the palms in Africa
> Because we are alone,
> It is night,
> And we're afraid.

Or, in a different mood:

> We should have a land of trees
> Bowed down with chattering parrots
> Brilliant as the day
> And not this land where birds are grey.

It was more common to sing about happy Africans long dead or imaginary Africans who never lived, but Langston Hughes saw himself trying to shake hands with live Africans, now:

> We are related—you and I.
> You from the West Indies,

Harold R. Isaacs

> I from Kentucky.
> We are related—you and I.
> You from Africa,
> I from these States.
> We are brothers—you and I.

As he tells it, the young poet's trip to Africa happened to him like an odd chance, as unpremeditated as a line of poetry coming unbidden into his head. He had wanted simply to get away, to break from all his young life up to then, and like a lot of young people who had this urge, he tried to do it by going to sea and to any far place he could reach. On his first try he got a job on a freighter tied up among the war-weary discards in the Hudson, going nowhere. He stayed aboard her for a long season, excursioning to Bear Mountain and only a few times back to Harlem. Come spring, he tried again, took the first job offered and only afterward learned that the ship was sailing for Africa. In telling this story in his autobiography, *The Big Sea,* Hughes does not even add an exclamation point to this discovery of his unplanned destination. The exclamations came later. At the moment what mattered was not where he was going but what he was leaving. That night, sailing out of New York, in a scene that can stand forever as an image of youth declaring its manhood, twenty-one year old Hughes dumped all his books into the bay, and felt that it was like dropping all his burdens, "everything unpleasant and miserable out of my past . . . like throwing a million bricks out of my heart."

Langston Hughes tried to take Africa as he tried to school himself to take most things: casually, on the surface, and wherever possible, with a laugh, even a sad laugh. With Hughes this was more than a device or a literary style; it was a way of functioning, of coping with life. There [248] was so much on the Negro surface, after all, hardly noted by anyone until he came along. Langston Hughes achieved real uniqueness as a poet by describing the life and people of the Negro ghetto, catching them by their sights and sounds, by some of their sorrows and some of their angers, but mostly by their sardonic humors. He achieved his effect mostly by peeling off a layer of the surface, hardly ever more than a single layer, and then usually leaving what he found there undescribed, for the reader to see and hear if he could. He modelled his emotional patterns on the blues whose rhythms he adopted. This mood, as he explained in a prefatory note to an early volume of his poems, "is almost always despondency, but when they are sung people laugh." In addition to this, Hughes set out to do what few, regardless of race, creed, or color, have succeeded in doing, to earn his living by his writing alone. The result has been a body of work that has given us a rich, varied, and often vivid picture of the tops of a lot of things about Negroes and Negro life in America, but rather little at depth about any one person, especially about himself.

Still, even under that single layer, and even in his Africa, so briefly glimpsed through young eyes bright with adventure, we do learn something about Hughes if we look hard enough at what he has shown us. The exclamation points about Africa came on that first voyage when Hughes, fresh (he said) from a gay night in a love palace in Las Palmas, kept watching for the first sight of the African coast:

And when finally I saw the dust-green hills in the sunlight, something took hold of me inside. My Africa, Motherland of the Negro peoples! And me a Negro! Africa! The real thing, to be touched and seen, not merely read about in a book.

Dakar was too French and too Mohammedan, but

. . . farther down the coast it was more like the Africa I had dreamed about—wild and lovely, the people dark and beautiful, the palm trees tall, the sun bright, and the rivers deep. The great Africa of my dreams!

But here, in the Africa of his dreams, the young Hughes almost immediately finds again the heaviest of the burdens that, for a heady moment, he had imagined dropping with his books into New York Bay. Here in Africa, where everything was dark and beautiful, we come upon Hughes touching—lightly as always—on one of the central themes of his life:

There was one thing that hurt me a lot when I talked with the people. The Africans looked at me and would not believe I was a Negro. You see, unfortunately, I am not black.[4]

And this is where Hughes goes back to tell the story of his life, of his family with all its mixtures of bloods and colors, of white great grandparents, of strains of poets and statesmen and Indian chiefs, Cherokee, [249] Jewish, Scotch, French, and Negro forebears, of his "olive-yellow" mother and his "darker brown" father, whom he saw once when he was six, and not again until he was

[4] *The Big Sea* (New York, 1945), pp. 10–11.

seventeen. He tells of his wandering life, with his mother, with an aunt, with a stepfather, and with his father who had migrated to Mexico to make his way because there was no color line or jim crow there. His father hated "niggers" and "hated himself too, for being a Negro," had great contempt for all poor people and valued only money made to keep.

It was while he was bound for Mexico to see his father that Hughes, just out of high school, wrote one of the best known of all his poems, "The Negro Speaks of Rivers." This act of creation came out of a fusing of thoughts about his father, Negroes, himself, slavery, and his ancestors in dim and distant Africa. He was on the train out of St. Louis, he relates, and was feeling bad over his parting from his mother (his "best poems," he adds in a parenthesis, "were all written when I felt the worst. When I was happy, I didn't write anything."). He goes on:

It came about in this way. All day on the train I had been thinking about my father, and his strange dislike of his own people. I didn't understand it, because I was a Negro, and I liked Negroes very much. . . . Now it was just sunset, and we crossed the Mississippi, slowly, over a long bridge. I looked out the window of the Pullman at the great muddy river flowing down toward the heart of the South, and I began to think what that river, the old Mississippi, had meant to Negroes in the past . . . how Abraham Lincoln had made a trip down the Mississippi on a raft to New Orleans, and how he had seen slavery at its worst, and had decided within himself that it should be removed from American life. Then I began to think about other rivers in our past—the Congo, and the Niger, and the Nile in Africa—and the thought came to me: "I've known rivers," and I put it down on the back of an envelope I had in my pocket, and within the space of ten or fifteen minutes, as the train gathered speed in the dusk, I had written this poem, which I called "The Negro Speaks of Rivers." [5]

[5] *The Big Sea,* pp. 54–55. The poem, his first to be published outside of his high school paper, appeared in DuBois' *Crisis* in June, 1921:

I've known rivers;
I've known rivers as ancient as the world and older than the flow of human blood in human veins.
My soul has grown deep like the rivers.
I bathed in the Euphrates when dawns were young.
I built my hut near the Congo and it lulled me to sleep.
I looked upon the Nile and raised the Pyramids above it.
I heard the singing of the Mississippi when Abe Lincoln went down to New Orleans, and I've seen its muddy bosom turn all golden in the sunset.
I've known rivers:
Ancient, dusky rivers.
My soul has grown deep like the rivers.

Much of what made up the inner life of Langston Hughes stares out at us from the telling of this story of how he made a poem. He has told us here and elsewhere of some of its separate parts. It is of their inner connections that he has never written.

In Mexico he experienced a great crisis of hate of his father. He fell into a deep illness that no doctor could diagnose, much less cure, because [250] Hughes preferred to lie in his expensive hospital bed—his father was paying the bills—and not to tell them what was the matter with him. It was two years after this, following a try at student life at Columbia, a series of odd jobs and his winter with the dead fleet in the Hudson, that he crossed the sea and saw Africa as he said he had dreamed of it:

A long sandy coastline, gleaming in the sun. Palm trees sky-tall. Rivers darkening the sea's edge with the loam of their deltas. People black and beautiful as the night. The bare, pointed breasts of women in the market places. The rippling muscles of men loading palm oil and cocoa beans and mahogany on the ships of the white man's world. . . .

It was 1923, and the Africans Hughes met had heard of Marcus Garvey and they "hoped that what they had heard about him was true—that he really would come and unify the black world and free and exalt Africa."

"Our problems in America are very much like yours," I told the Africans, "especially in the South. I am a Negro, too."

But they only laughed at me and shook their heads and said: "You, white man!"

It was the only place in the world where I've ever been called a white man. They looked at my copper-brown skin and straight black hair—like my grandmother's Indian hair, except a little curly—and they said: "You—white man."

One of the laborers aboard, a Kru from Liberia who knew about these things, explained to Hughes that most non-whites who came to Africa from abroad came to help the white man, whether as missionary or as clerk or helper in colonial governments, "so the Africans call them all *white* men."

"But I am not white," I said.

"You are not black either," the Kru man said simply. "There is a man of my color," and he pointed to George, the pantryman, who protested loudly.

"Don't point at me," George said. "I'm from Lexington, Kentucky, U.S.A. And no African blood nowhere."

Harold R. Isaacs

"You black," said the Kru man.

"I can part my hair," said George, "and it ain't nappy."

But to tell the truth, George shaved a part of his hair every other week, since the comb wouldn't work. The Kru man knew this, so they both laughed loudly, for George's face was as African as Africa.

And then Langston Hughes adds this astonishing parenthesis:

(Yet dark as he was George always referred to himself as brown-skin, and it was not until years later, when a dark-skinned minister in New Jersey denounced me to his congregation for using the word *black* to describe him in a newspaper article, that I realized that most dark Negroes in America do not like the word *black* at all. They prefer to be referred to as *brownskin,* or at the most as *darkbrownskin*— no matter how dark they really are.) [6] [251]

In this remarkable statement Langston Hughes, the poet whose appeal and repute was based on his sensitive awareness of the common mores of Negroes, asks his readers to believe that until the late 1920's, he had no idea that Negroes had any special feelings about the word "black." We are asked to imagine a youthful Hughes—the same one who wrote *Weary Blues* and *Fine Clothes to the Jew*—equipped with a selective soundproofing device which kept out all Negro talk of blackness but let in all the other words and sounds and feelings out of which he made his poems. Whether this is what Hughes really remembered about himself when he wrote these words (in 1945), or whether he was deliberately "mis-remembering," the effect is much the same: it reveals a block so deep and so important that one's first impulse is to step away from it. But his statement is so extravagantly absurd that it becomes a revelation in itself; Hughes the writer is violently signalling, all bells ringing, that Hughes the man had some super-special feelings himself on this subject of blackness. This becomes even clearer as we go on, because this curious little parenthesis is sandwiched in between the story of how Africans had called him a "white man" and the story of a golden-skinned boy who came aboard at one port looking for reading matter in English. He was the son, he told Hughes, of an African woman and an Englishman who had gone back to England. Now he and his mother were ignored by the whites and shunned by the blacks. "Was it true," the boy wanted to know, "that in America the black people were friendly to the mulatto people?" Hughes later had a letter from the boy but never answered it "because I have a way of not answering

[6] *The Big Sea,* pp. 102–104.

260

letters when I don't know what to say." Instead Hughes wrote a short story about the encounter, called "African Morning." He says he had always been "intrigued" with this problem of mixed blood which was, he added, "a minor problem." On this minor problem he also wrote "several other short stories," a poem called "Mulatto" about which he says: "I worked harder on that poem than on any other that I have ever written," and a play, also called "Mulatto," which ran successfully on Broadway.

Langston Hughes never did write a poem about Africans calling him "a white man." Instead he wrote lots of poems about being black, black, black.

> I am a Negro:
>> Black as the night is black,
>> Black like the depths of my Africa.

In "Dream Variation":

>> To fling my arms wide
>> In the face of the sun,
>> Dance! Whirl! Whirl!
>> Till the quick day is done.
>> Rest at pale evening . . .
>> A tall slim tree . . .
>> Night coming tenderly
>>> Black like me. [252]

Again in "Me and My Song," a poem eighty words long, the word black appears nine times. A sample:

>> Black
>> As the gentle night,
>> Black as the kind and quiet night,
>> Black as the deep and productive earth,
>> Body
>> Out of Africa,
>> Strong and black . . .
>> Kind
>> As the black night
>> My song
>> From the dark lips
>> Of Africa . . .
>> Beautiful
>> As the black night . . .
>> Black
>> Out of Africa,
>> Me and my song.

Hughes had also joined in the popular poetic pastime of beating the tomtoms:

> The low beating of the tomtoms
> The slow beating of the tomtoms,
>   Low . . . slow
>   Slow . . . low
> Stirs your blood . . .

But in the end he was badly tripped himself by the vogue for primitivism, noble savage department. When the bright "Renaissance" was fading into the gay depression, Hughes had got himself a patron, a rich old lady who lived on Park Avenue. She fed him well, sent him around town in her chauffeured limousine, and generally made his life comfortable and pleasant so that he could write "beautiful things." But one day he wrote a crude and angry poem contrasting the lushness of the newly opened Waldorf Astoria with the toil and growing deprivation outside. His benefactor did not like it at all. She wanted him to write out of his simple primitive soul and poor Hughes did not know how.

> She wanted me to be primitive, and know and feel the intuitions of the primitive. But, unfortunately, I did not feel the rhythms of the primitive surging through me, and so I could not live and write as though I did. I was only an American Negro—who had loved the surface of Africa and the rhythms of Africa—but I was not Africa. I was Chicago and Kansas City and Broadway and Harlem. And I was not what she wanted me to be.[7]

His parting from his patron threw Hughes into the second great emotional crisis of his life. As he had in Mexico in the crisis of his hate of [253] his father, he now again fell violently ill. It was a complicated shame and anger he felt, and an even more complicated loss. What he did was to go home to Cleveland, to his own mother, who had always demanded much of him and given him little. In Cleveland he took to the bed which his mother and stepfather vacated for him, and stayed sick until he had spent what was left of his Park Avenue money, mostly on doctors who did not know what was wrong and could do nothing for him.

Hughes was, in truth, "not Africa" at all. Africa had become another one of the world's places he had liked and left. During the next ten years he circled the world and saw much of its busy surface—Russia, China, Japan, Spain. In a second volume of his autobiography chronicling these travels up to 1938,[8] nowhere in

[7] *The Big Sea*, p. 325.
[8] *I Wonder As I Wander* (New York, 1956).

all the pages filled with the sights he had seen and the names endlessly dropping does he again revert to the subject of Africa except in one or two incidental mentions. Africa remained locked away among his old poems and old thoughts and he did not bring them out and dust them off until recent years when new Negro and world interest in Africa rose so sharply. Then he revived them all, full of their drumbeats and ancestral memories and sad yearning, and wrote some new ones in the new mood, and made them all part of "The Poetry of Jazz," a sequence of readings that he performs for large audiences, reciting to the accompaniment of beating drums. His new tone on Africa sounds like this:

> Africa,
> Sleeply giant,
> You've been resting awhile.
> Now I see the thunder
> And the lightning
> In your smile.
>
> Now I see
> The storm clouds
> In your waking eyes:
> The thunder,
> The wonder
> And the new
> Surprise
>
> Your every step reveals
> The new stride
> In your thighs.

"Big roll," says the direction to the accompanying drummer, as this poem ends.

Richard Wright

Unlike Langston Hughes, Richard Wright has never beat any tomtoms, never yearned after a dead past, nor sentimentalized about a primitive [254] present. Nor does it appear that any of his particular personal problems are wrapped up in the shades of color, in what it means to be light, not dark, tan, not brown, brown, not black. There is no mystique about blackness in Wright's pages. His mystiques are ideological and about these he tries to be as explicit as he can. He is not a man to touch a deep matter and, like Hughes, after brushing it lightly with a short poem, dance away until another day. Wright wrestles long and hard with the problems of world society and has never found the art of fiction adequate to his need. Even in *Native Son,* the novel on which his fame mainly rests, he gives over fifteen pages at the end to the courtroom summation in which Bigger Thomas' lawyer explains the sociology of Bigger's crime. Wright has published eleven books, of which only three are novels and one autobiography. The bulk of his work has been reportage, lectures, and essays, earnest and urgent explanations, exclamations, and exhortations. One of these books, *Black Power,* is the story of Wright's trip to Africa, to what was still the Gold Coast, in 1953. From this book we learn that Wright, like Langston Hughes, went through an experience of rejection and repulsion in Africa, though it was of quite a different kind. It is this experience that will concern us here. But to begin to see the individual Wright in Africa, we have to try to see where the politician-ideologist Wright locates Africa in his own larger setting.

As he constantly reminds his readers, Richard Wright spent twelve years, from 1932 to 1944, in the Communist Party. The cost of this experience was heavy. Though the Communist gods failed him, they did make him sufficiently over in their image to make him more of a political being than an artist. It was mainly to win back his identity as an artist that Wright, by his own account,[9] finally broke from the Communist grip. But he did not do so before they had more than half-shaped him permanently in their ideological mold. The effects kept appearing in many of his ideas and in much of his writing in the years after he struck out on his own. But Wright did not only leave the Communist movement in which he had lived so long. Soon afterward, the native son also quit his native land to live in exile in France. Thus Wright left all his familiar places and chose to live, intellectually and physically, in limbo. Now anyone who tries to be heard from limbo has to shout loudly, and whether in these conditions Wright will grow or wither as an artist still remains to be seen. Except for a few bravely whistling passages,[10] he has not yet tried to deal with the stuff of his life-in-exile. In his third and most recent (1958) novel, *The Long Dream,* Wright [255] goes back to the

[9] In *The God That Failed* (New York, 1950).

[10] "I'm a rootless man, but I'm neither psychologically distraught or in any wise disturbed because of it. Personally I do not hanker after, and seem not to need, as many emotional attachments, sustaining roots, or idealistic allegiances as most people. I declare unabashedly that I like and even cherish the state of abandonment, of aloneness: it does not bother me. . . ." (*White Man, Listen!* [New York, 1957] p. 17).

Mississippi setting of his early years where his own apartness from the world began. A few topical references (e.g., to the Korean war) fix the time in the mid-1950's, but Wright unfolds his story as if it were happening a full generation earlier, never referring to the changes in the larger society which have made Mississippi part of a shrinking last stronghold of the white supremacy system. At the end, when his protagonist finally leaves there, Wright has him board a train in his deep Southern town, then picks him up soaring over the land, never allowing us to see him set foot for an instant in any of the places where so much has changed since Wright went away. He has him continue instead, aloft in his plane, straight on across the sea bound for . . . Paris.

On the other hand, besides being a gifted writer, Richard Wright is also an honest and serious man who clings hard to the idea of some larger commonwealth for human society than the tribe, the nation, or the race. From his French exile he has restlessly wandered to far corners in search of this larger identity. His thoughts on these matters appear in books like *The Color Curtain,* the story of his journey to the Bandung Conference in 1955, and *White Man, Listen!,* a collection of lectures given in Europe between 1950 and 1956. In these works, Wright is often strident and naive, and stretches some of his points until they snap. Too often, also, he seems to see himself as the first to discover what many before him have seen and said about the history of the West in Asia and Africa and about the emergent Asian and African elites. But even if he is not Balboa looking out over this turbulent sea, Wright brings special perceptions and emotions to bear upon his discoveries. They take him swiftly, unhindered by too much encumbering knowledge, to the sharp edges of many an Asian-African dilemma.

In the place of traditional cultures in the changing scene, about which so much loose talk passes, Wright sees clearly, for example, that the West was "irrevocably triumphant in its destruction of [the old] culture" of the lands it despoiled, and that in the very act of spoliation, "white Europeans set off a more deep-going and sudden revolution in Asia and Africa than had ever obtained in all the history of Europe." [11] The present task is one of total reorganization of all aspects of life and culture in these countries, and in this process Wright sees, with deep apprehension, the surviving power among these peoples of "race and religion, two of the most

[11] *The Color Curtain* (New York, 1956), p. 73; *White Man, Listen!,* p. 95.

Harold R. Isaacs

powerful and irrational forces in human nature." [12] In the matter of race, Wright sees dark and dangerous crevices ahead and illustrates with an anecdote about being served out of turn, ahead of a white American, by an Indonesian official: [256]

Well, there it was . . . I was a member of the master race! I'm not proud of it. It took no intelligence, no courage. . . . It was racism. And I thought of all the times in the American South when I had had to wait until the whites had been served before I could be served. . . . All you have to do in a situation like that is relax and let your base instincts flow. And it's so easy, so natural, you don't have to think; you just push that face that is of an offensive color out of your mind and forget about it. You are inflicting an emotional wound that might last for years . . . but why worry about that! You are safe; there are thousands around you of your color, and if the man who's been offended should object, what the hell can he do? . . . That was how the whites had felt about it when they had had all the power . . . and now I saw that same process reversed. Will Asians and Africans, being as human as white men, take over this vicious pattern of identification when they become, as they will, masters of this earth? Racism is an evil thing and breeds its own kind. [13]

Wright has described himself as being "numbed and appalled" by Asian and African religion:

The teeming religions gripping the minds and consciousness of Asians and Africans offend me. I can conceive of no identification with such mystical visions of life that freeze millions in static degradation, no matter how emotionally satisfying such degradation seems to those who wallow in it. [14]

He ponders uneasily over what could happen in the world if these outlooks ever become welded to the techniques and power instruments of the twentieth century. These countries will not progress, he argues, "until such religious rationalizations have been swept from men's minds," and the world will not be safe until the narrow "secular and rational base of thought and feeling" developed in the West fuses successfully with the similar base that "shaky and delicate as yet, exists also in the elite of Asia and Africa."

And those two bases of Eastern and Western rationalism must become one! And quickly, or else the tenuous Asian-African secular, rational attitudes will become flooded, drowned in irrational tides of racial and religious passions. [15]

[12] *The Color Curtain*, p. 140.
[13] *Ibid.*, pp. 14–15.
[14] *White Man, Listen!*, p. 80.
[15] *The Color Curtain*, p. 219.

So here is Richard Wright, unwilling to lean on desiccated tradition and rejecting all superstition (in which he includes all religion, from Anabaptism to Zoroastrianism) and everything else that he thinks hobbles the free human mind. He looks, in his own way, for new reaches of the human spirit. He does not want an identity made up of what he sees as the useless baggage of the past, and in his own past sees little that he wants to carry forward with him at all. This is his pain and trouble, and this is what drives him apart not only from most of the white world, but from much of the non-white world as well, because in both worlds most men still reach back for the buttressing comfort of tradition, even when it is hollow. This is the lonely man [257] who in 1953 journeyed to Africa, wondering what he would find there that would link him to Africans in a common legacy from the ancestral past.

Richard Wright went to the Gold Coast in 1953, four years before it became the independent state of Ghana. Nkrumah was already "Leader of Government Business," but the British were still in control. The new shape of things was present in outline but as yet had little substance. Wright has much to say about Gold Coast politics and Nkrumah's politics. He ends up by urging Nkrumah to be "hard," to "militarize" his people for the leap, in one generation, out of the past. "Our people must be made to walk, forced draft, into the twentieth century!" But such views are not unique to Wright and are, in any case, another subject. For our purposes here, we will bypass Wright's thinking about the politics of Africa and pick up instead the thread of his reactions to Africans, his painful exploration of the real or imagined elements of kinship between him and the Africans among whom he came as a black American stranger. This was, in fact, the principal theme that raced through his mind at the outset when it was first suggested to him that he go to Africa:

I heard them, but my mind and feelings were racing along another and hidden track. Africa! Being of African descent, would I be able to feel and know something about Africa on the basis of a common "racial" heritage? Africa was a vast continent full of "my people." . . . Or had three hundred years imposed a psychological distance between me and the "racial stock" from which I had sprung? . . . My emotions seemed to be touching a dark and dank wall. . . . . Am I African? Had some of my ancestors sold their relatives to white men? What would my feelings be when I looked into the black face of an African, feeling that maybe his great-great-great-grandfather had sold my great-great-great-grandfather into slavery? Was there something in

Harold R. Isaacs

Africa that my feelings could latch onto to make all of this dark past clear and meaningful? Would the Africans regard me as a lost brother who had returned? . . . According to popular notions of "race" there ought to be something of "me" down there in Africa. Some vestige, some heritage, some vague but definite ancestral reality that would serve as a key to unlock the hearts and feelings of the Africans whom I'd meet. . . . But I could not feel anything African about myself, and I wonder, "What does being *African* mean?" [16]

The meeting between Richard Wright and Africa produced something less than love-at-first-sight. At first sight what did strike him—as it has other Negroes—was the fact that "the whole of life that met the eyes was black," but instead of being enthralled by it, Wright was full of the grim thought that these were the people whose so-and-so [258] ancestors had sold his ancestors down the river and across the sea into slavery. In his first minutes ashore he was exchanging hostilities on this score with the second African he met, a clerk in a store who pressed Wright to explain why he did not know where in Africa his ancestors had lived. "You know," he said "softly" to the startled clerk, "you fellows who sold us and the white men who bought us didn't keep any records." It is characteristic of Wright that of all the possible reasons for avowed or unavowed Negro constraint toward Africans, this should be the one to float free and first at the top of his mind. He brings it up again several times during his stay, and when, just before leaving, he makes the pilgrimage to the great grim castles from which the slaves had been fed out to the ships riding offshore, again this is first among the images in his mind. At Christianborg Castle he tries to imagine a decked-out chief leading his prisoners into the castle to be sold, but "my mind refused to function." At Elmina Castle, he looked into the slave dungeons through the slits from neighboring rooms where "African chiefs would hide themselves while their captives were being bid for by Europeans." Wright thinks of this as a principal source for American Negro alienation from Africans, but only once in all my interviews did anyone even mention this particular view of Africans as guilty participants in the historic crimes of enslavement. Whatever else it might prove to be at more obscure depths, this thought is at least part of an effort to be evenhandedly honest. In Wright it is also a defense against sentimentality, or worse, racism.

[16] *Black Power* (New York, 1954), pp. 3–4. All following quotations from Wright are from this source until otherwise indicated.

Actually as a "race man," or more correctly, an "anti-race man," Wright confronted Africa with all sorts of harsh and complicated questions in his mind. But Wright reacted at the same time at several different levels. He reacted also, to begin with, as a Western man, a man of Paris, New York, Chicago, a comer to Africa from a different world, a different century. As he rode into town from the shorefront where he landed, "the kaleidoscope of sea, jungle, nudity, mud huts, and crowded market places induced in me . . . a protest against what I saw . . . [not] against Africa or its people [but] against the unsettled feeling engendered by the strangeness of a completely different order of life . . . a world whose laws I did not know . . . faces whose reactions were riddles to me." Wright not only felt the familiar revulsion of the Western man at the sights and smells of non-Western backwardness and poverty; he was also overcome by a strong sense of its impenetrability. "Faced with the absolute otherness and inaccessibility of this new world, I was prey to a vague sense of mind panic, an oppressive burden of alertness which I could not shake off." It was not merely that the lack of modern sanitation assailed his Western-style fastidiousness. It was more the lack of modern thinking that assailed his Western-style intelligence. For Wright reacted most of all as a rationalist who had put [259] his faith in the power of the mind to conquer ignorance and violence. He made a positively heroic effort to explore and understand African religious notions and superstitions as he came upon them, trying to discuss them with ordinary people, with intellectuals, trying to make sense out of what he could find to read about the matter. Going by his own rules, he tried to banish the thought that this was all "irrational," and to get at "the underlying assumptions of the African's beliefs." He dived in, and then had to "come up for air, to take a deep breath," and while he came up musing with the thought that the African's religious dreams might be better suited to his old ways, might indeed be "the staunchest kind of reality," his strong sense of history told him that this could not ever be the stuff of life in the twentieth century world that the white man had irrevocably made over in his image. It appalled him to find that belief in *juju* or magic was by no means confined to the uneducated. He ran into it even in Nkrumah's anteroom where the chief minister's secretary warned him not to underestimate its power.

At the end of his journey, Wright wrote to Nkrumah that he had "felt an odd kind of at-homeness, a solidarity that stemmed not from ties of blood or race, or from my being of African descent," but from "the deep hope and suffering imbedded in the lives of your people, from the hard facts of oppression. . . ." Again, Wright is trying to be as truthful as he can. But by his own account, Wright never did get to feel at home at all in the Gold Coast. He left the country as he had come, full of his broad, general bonds of political solidarity and sympathy, but still a stranger. He was confounded by what he saw of the psychological and cultural havoc wreaked by the whites, especially by their missionaries. But he was also shaken by what he discovered about the nature of surviving African culture. Wright was at home in none of this, either with any part of the society or with individuals. As he travelled about, questing, probing, asking, he never did find it easy to open channels of communication with Africans. On this score, in fact, he delivers some whopping generalizations:

> I found the African an oblique, hard-to-know man who seems to take a kind of childish pride in trying to create a state of bewilderment in the minds of strangers.

Or again:

> I found that the African almost invariably underestimated the person with whom he was dealing; he always placed too much confidence in an evasive reply, thinking that if he denied something, then that something ceased to exist. It was childlike.

His most qualified statement:

> Most of the Africans I've met have been, despite the ready laughter, highly reserved and suspicious men. . . . [260]

He found the attitude of distrust to be universal:

> I could feel [the] distrust of me; it came from no specific cause; it was general. I was a stranger, a foreigner, and, therefore, must be spoken to cautiously, with weighed words. Distrust was in full operation before any objective event had occurred to justify it. A stranger confronting an African and feeling this distrust would begin to react to it and he'd feel himself becoming defensively distrustful himself. Distrust bred distrust; he'd begin to watch for evasion; he'd begin to question a flattering phrase. . . . In the end what had begun as a stranger's apprehension of the African's wariness would terminate in a distrust created out of nowhere, conjured up out of nothing. This fear, this suspicion of nothing in particular came to be the most predictable hallmark of the African mentality that I met in all the Gold Coast, from the Prime Minister down to the humblest "mammy" selling *kenke* on the street corners.

Wright thought for awhile that "this chronic distrust arose from their centuries-long exploitation by Europeans," but after he had wandered farther, especially into the Ashanti country to the north, he came to think that the "African's doubt of strangers" was "lodged deep in the heart of African culture." He thought he discovered its source deep in the patterns of fear and guilt that he found in the ancestor worship and blood sacrifices that dominated traditional African beliefs. "Men whose hearts are swamped by such compounded emotional problems," he concluded, "must needs be always at war with reality. Distrust is the essence of such a life."

Restlessly, Wright took his questions to all sorts of people. He was relieved to find a quality of relative directness in one of the Gold Coast's leading intellectuals, author of a work he'd consulted on the country's religion. But he was left again at a loss when this man assured him that if he would stay longer in Africa he would come to feel his race.

> *"What?"*
> "You'll feel it," he assured me. "It'll all come *back* to you."
> "What'll come back?"
> "The knowledge of your race. . . ."
> . . . I knew that I'd never feel an identification with Africans on a "racial" basis. "I doubt that," I said softly.

Again and again Wright remarks that his blackness, his African descent, did not help him at all in achieving communication with Africans. After being caught up one day in a funeral procession and trying to learn what it meant, he wrote: "I had understood nothing. I was black and they were black, but my blackness did not help me." He found it the same with young black officials, with young nationalists, with Nkrumah himself. Something of their nature as he found it, or something about his unrelenting inquisitiveness, or both together, threw up a barrier that baffled him. "I'm of African descent and I'm in the midst of Africans, yet I cannot tell what they are thinking and feeling." [261]

But in this matter of kinship linking Africans and American Negroes, Wright did have one experience that pulled him up sharply and left him in the end, again, baffled. On one of his first days in Accra he rode around town with Nkrumah. Crowds gathered around their car, shouting and singing their greetings to the leader, the women dancing, "a sort of weaving, circular motion with their bodies, a kind of queer shuffling dance. . . ."

And then I remembered: I'd seen these same snakelike, veering dances before. . . . Where? Oh, God, yes, in America, in storefront churches, in Holy Roller tabernacles, in God's Temples, in unpainted wooden prayer-meeting houses in the plantations of the Deep South. . . . And here I was seeing it all again against a background of a surging nationalistic political movement. How could that be? . . . What I was now looking at in this powerfully improvised dance of these women, I'd seen before in America. How was that possible?

He had always rejected the ideas of "some American anthropologists" about "what they had quaintly chosen to call 'African survivals,' a phrase which they had coined to account for exactly what I had observed."

I understood why so many American Negroes were eager to disclaim any relationship with Africa . . . first, it was a natural part of his assimilation of Americanism; second, so long had Africa been described as something shameful, barbaric, a land in which one went about naked, a land in which his ancestors had sold their kith and kin as slaves—so long had he heard all this that he wanted to disassociate himself in his mind from all such realities.

The bafflement evoked in me by this new reality did not spring from any desire to disclaim kinship with Africa, or from any shame of being of African descent. My problem was how to account for this "survival" of Africa in America when I stoutly denied the mystic influence of "race," when I was as certain as I was of being alive that it was only, by and large, in the concrete social frame of reference in which men lived that one could account for men being what they were . . . that "racial" qualities were but myths of prejudiced minds. . . . I sighed. This was a truly big problem. . . .

Wright kept churning this matter in his mind and finally produced a lumpy sort of answer: where he was free to do so, the transplanted African adapted to his new environment and, like any other human being, changed to meet its demands; but where he was barred from fitting himself fully into his new setting, he retained some of his "basic and primal attitudes toward life," including "his basically poetic apprehension of existence." This does not appear to shed much light on the question of "African survivals," but the episode does sharpen our picture of Richard Wright. For he also tells us that instead of making him feel any closer to Africans, the sight of the dancing women had made him feel his apartness all the more: [262]

This African dance today was as astonishing and dumbfounding to me as it had been when I'd seen it in America. Never in my life had I been able to dance more than a few elementary steps and the carrying even of the simplest tune had always been beyond me. So, what had bewildered me about Negro dance expression in the United States now bewildered me in the same way in Africa.

Here, perhaps, is the ultimate clue to Richard Wright's experience in Africa, indeed to his experience anywhere. For Wright reacted to Africa not only as a Western man, a rationalist, a twentieth-century man, an American Negro, but also as a man whose chosen life-style was outsiderness, the source of his chief pains and anxieties and also of his chief satisfactions. Unlike Langston Hughes, Wright does not feel "outside" merely because he is neither wholly white nor wholly black. But more like DuBois, in his mind's eye he sees himself standing out in the open spaces of history that time has not yet filled; his limbo again. In Africa Wright, already separated by so much from the Europeans, found himself also apart from Africans, because Europeans and Africans alike carried with them too much of the burden of the past that he wants to see left behind.

Three years later, at a conference of black artists and writers in Paris, convened under the mystic aura of the concept of *negritude,* Wright was described (in an account by James Baldwin) as being claimed as a spokesman both by American Negroes and by Africans, but when it came his turn to speak, Wright could only speak for himself. He had been listening to the proceedings with a troubled ear. He was both a black man and a Westerner, he said, and this made for painful contradictions. "I see both worlds from another, and third, point of view." [17] This meant that while he shared the black man's rejection of the white world's power and prejudices, he also insisted upon recognizing that Europe, though seeking its own selfish ends and acting quite blindly, had also freed Africans from the "rot" of their past, and that this was a good thing. For the American Negroes who were trying to establish contact with the Africans at the conference, this was, at the very least, tactless, and they were embarrassed by it. As for the Africans, most of them were either politically intent on using their sticks to beat all white beasts, including the American, or they were deep in the dark pool of *negritude,* trying to recreate a racial mystique as the basis for making the unique African presence known, at last, to the world. The result was that both for Americans and Africans, Wright succeeded only in making alien noises. This left him where he always chose to be, outside.

[17] James Baldwin, "Princess and Powers," *Encounter,* January, 1957, p. 58.

But Wright's experience did bring the subject of Africa back into his thinking about the problems of American Negroes and their endless effort [263] to identify themselves. All of Wright's books have been about the shaping of Negro identities, including his own. But the thought of Africa in this connection had not come to the top before this, neither in the life of Bigger Thomas, nor in his own early years, as told in *Black Boy,* nor in his 1953 novel, *The Outsider.* It appears for the first time in Wright's fiction in *The Long Dream,* published in 1958, blowing in on wisps of talk among four teen-age boys in a small Mississippi town. One of them is the son of a strong race-man type who thinks Negroes ought to acquire as African the identity denied them as American. He brings the matter to his friends, and they try it out on Fishbelly:

> "Fish, you want to go to *Africa?*"
> Fishbelly blinked, looking from black face to black face.
> "Hunh? To *Africa?*" Fishbelly asked. *"What for?"*
> Zeke and Tony stomped their feet with glee, Sam scowled.
> *"I told you."* Zeke screamed triumphantly.
> "Fish, you sure looked funny when you heard that word 'Africa.' " Tom whooped.
> "But who's going to Africa?" Fishbelly asked, seeking the point of the debate.
> "Nobody but damn fools!" said Zeke emphatically.
> "Nobody but fatheads!" Tony growled.
> "You niggers don't know nothing!" Sam railed at Zeke and Tony.
> "Who's a nigger?" Zeke asked, fists clenched. . . .
> "A nigger's a black man who don't know who he *is,*" Sam made the accusation general.

Sam goes on to charge them with wanting to be white, and when the others indignantly deny it, he taxed them with trying to straighten their hair, "like white folks' hair." But it was not to make it look white but to look nice, the boys answered. Sam sneered back that this was because white folks thought straight hair was nice and the others screamed that he was lying. Sam then makes Fishbelly admit that if he went back far enough, he had to agree that his folks had come from Africa.

> "Okay, they came from Africa." Fishbelly tried to cover up his hesitancy. . . . Sam now fired his climactic question.
> "Now, just stand there and tell me, what *is* you?"
> Before Fishbelly could reply, Zeke and Tony set up a chant: "Fishbelly's a African! Fishbelly's a African!"

Sam then tries to prove to the confused and uncomfortable Fishbelly that if he was no longer African he certainly could not say he was American:

"All I know about Africa's what I read in the geography book at school," Fishbelly mumbled, unwilling to commit himself.

"Sam wants us to git naked and run wild and eat with our hands and live in mud huts!" Zeke ridiculed. . . . [264]

"Okay," Sam agreed sarcastically. "Nobody wants to go to Africa. Awright. Who wants to go to America? . . ."

"We awready in America, you fool!"

"Aw, naw you ain't," Sam cried hotly. "You niggers ain't *nowhere*. You ain't in Africa, 'cause the white man took you out. And you ain't in America. . . . You can't live like no American, 'cause you ain't no American. And you ain't African neither! So what is you? Nothing! *Just nothing!*"

Wright had gone to Africa to find out, among other things, whether a black man who was nothing could become something there. He had come away knowing that Africans were on the way to becoming something, but he did not know what, and he was not sure he liked it. As for black Americans, Wright has no word. As we have already remarked, his novel ends with the boy Fishbelly leaping, in a sentence or two, from Mississippi to France. There is no hint that there is an answer for Fishbelly in France, or in Africa. We do not know whether Fishbelly could have carried any message to Paris that might bring Wright back to America to see if any new answers were forming here. [265]

PART II

Ralph Ellison

"Richard Wright," said Ralph Ellison, "has a passion for ideology and he is fascinated by power. I have no desire to manipulate power. I want to write imaginative books." The books Ellison wants to write are books that will come out of the American Negro's own culture and as works of art become part of the culture of man. He has made it his problem to identify that culture and preserve it in literature, while Wright's problem, he said, is that "he has cut his ties to American Negroes" and is more concerned with world politics and world sociology. "People who want to write sociology," Ellison has written, "should not write a novel."

Like Wright, Ellison rejects racial mysticism and he also strongly rejects the idea that there is any significant kinship be-

Harold R. Isaacs

tween American Negroes and Africans. But unlike Wright, Ellison feels this so strongly that he has not even allowed himself any curiosity about the matter. He was offered a trip to Africa in 1955 but turned it down. "I said I had no interest in it," he told me, "no special emotional attachment to the place. I don't read much on Africa nowadays. It is just a part of the bigger world picture to me."

At the time we talked, events in Africa had already begun to make a visible impact among Negroes, but Ellison had remained quite unimpressed by it. In years past, he remarked, "Negroes either repeated all the very negative cliches, or else laughed at Africa, or, in some cases, related to it as a homeland." As an example of the latter type he mentioned the black nationalists, like the character Ras the Exhorter in *The Invisible Man,* and he also remembered that he had felt involved in the Ethiopian war. "Back in the 1930's, I was for Ethiopia too, of course, but I did not identify with the Ethiopians as people. I remember being amused when Haile Selassie denied any identity with American Negroes." At the present time, Ellison went on, the rise of nationalism in Africa has made many Negroes feel good. "The man-on-the-street might say now that Africa is justifying Garvey. He might say: 'They said Garvey was a boob, but look now, just watch, they'll go right on to South Africa and kick those crackers out of there.' There is a lot of this pride, predicting things, putting the bad mouth on the whites, now that things are finally moving in Africa." Middle-class Negroes might share [317] this pride to some extent, but Ellison said he did not know much about middle-class Negroes. As for intellectuals, he was contemptuous. He thought that there was a lot of "fakery" in some of the new organizations springing up to exploit the new feeling about Africa and he scornfully referred to a certain well-known Negro intellectual who "had taken to wearing African robes at Alabama State."

Ellison himself had been unable to respond in any direct way to Africans and the experience had been mutual. "The Africans I've met in Paris and Rome have seen me as an alien. They see most American Negroes this way. I never really got into contact. I won't have anything to do with racial approaches to culture." His only point of contact, he said, was an interest in African art. He had read Malraux's new interpretations of it, and gone to some exhibitions, but that was all. Not having any political interests like Wright's, and believing that the African origins had only the most remote place in the making of a distinctively American Negro culture, Ellison has not written at all on the subject, alluding to it only in glancing remarks in some of his essays. Hence what I report here on the way in which Ellison sees Africa (as well as himself) comes out of a long day's talk during which he freely and generously and with cool candor answered a great many questions.

As we spoke of Wright and other Negro writers who have chosen to live as expatriates in Europe, Ellison showed me a clipping from *Time* in which he had been included among the exiles because he had just spent two years in Rome on a fellowship. In a letter sharply correcting the report, Ellison said that "While I sympathize with those Negro Americans whose disgust with the racial absurdities of American life leads them to live elsewhere, my own needs—both as citizen and as artist, make the gesture of exile seem mere petulance." He said he thought for a writer the key question was where he could work well, adding that Faulkner did all right in Mississippi and Hemingway and Henry James in Europe, while "Richard Wright wrote better in Chicago and Brooklyn than he has in Paris." As for himself: "Personally I am too vindictively American, too full of hate for the hateful aspects of this country, and too possessed by the things I love here to be too long away."

Ralph Ellison came up just behind Richard Wright—he is five years younger—and for a few years in the 1930's they travelled together in the orbit of the Communist movement, with Wright serving as a help and an inspiration to the younger man. But Ellison had come up by a different path, from Oklahoma via Tuskegee, and out of a life that eventually shaped him into becoming a different kind of writer. Like Wright, Ellison had lost his father at an early age, but to death, not desertion. His father had been a construction foreman, served in the army in the Philippines and the Orient, had read widely, and had named [318] his son after Ralph Waldo Emerson. Ellison's mother was a strong-minded woman who worked as a servant in a white home, but also helped canvass Negro voters for Eugene Debs' Socialist Party and was in touch with "liberal whites who tried to keep Oklahoma from becoming like Texas, but failed." His mother bought her two sons a phonograph and records, electrical sets and chemical sets, and a toy typewriter, and told them the world would get to be a better place if they fought to change it. Oklahoma was jim crow and "you knew about the villainies of white people, yet in Oklahoma it was possible to realize that it was not a blanket thing. . . . We had some violence, there was fighting between Negro and white boys, but it was not too deeply fixed in the traditions or psychology of people." Ellison's mother had encouraged him to read and at Tuskegee he "blundered onto T. S. Eliot's *Wasteland,* and started to follow up all the footnotes, reading all those books. . . ." Ellison came to New York, then, not as Wright had come to Chicago, out of a seared childhood and with a parched mind. He did not come escaping, but seeking, and this difference laid its mark on their preoccupations and their work as writers. Wright became the restless ideologue, pulling away from the near, small things, and looking for the large solutions, while Ellison, as he began to write *The Invisible Man,* asked himself: "Could you present the Negro in his universal aspects and not keep your imagination in the leash of sociology? How do you do this and have it understood?"

In trying to think his way through to expressing what he believes to be a distinctive American Negro culture, Ellison has little or no thought at all of any African influence on this culture, past or present, or on himself. "I have great difficulty associating myself with Africa," Ellison said. "I suppose this is because so many people insist that I have a special tie to it that I could never discover in any concrete way. I mean the sociologists, Negro friends of mine who are trying to find some sort of past beyond the previous condition of servitude. I have always felt very Western. I can't find that in Africa in any way. I think now of Ghana, new countries, their problems, their need to bridge the gap between tribal patterns and the needs of modern government and life."

As we began to talk of his awarenesses of Africa and began to move back in time, all the familiar experiences quickly turned up in his memories. He brought them in and flicked them away: "the usual crap" in geography class, "the African villain in jungle movies." By his account, these had simply rolled off his hard surfaces:

"As a small boy, I remember the Garvey movement. We had some enthusiasts out there in Oklahoma. People wanted to go to Africa. The people I knew thought this was very amusing, going back to a place they had never been. The other association I can remember was in geography class, the usual crap, Africans as lazy people, living in the [319] sun. I always knew we were partially descended from African slave stock. I knew that Negroes were black and that blacks came from Africa. . . . There were expressions, the fist, for example, was called 'African soupbone.' No"—

he dismissed my question shortly—"I don't think this was an allusion to cannibalism."

"You ran into the African villain in jungle movies," he went on, "I suppose that like all other kids I identified with the white heroes. I have no vivid memories of them or the feelings they aroused. I don't remember being repelled. You might have related to the blacks in some way, but you identified with the hero, not with the villains. I do remember a Negro named Noel Johnson who always played Indian roles, and all Indians, of course, were villains. We always went for him, though, and when they would be coming after him, the kids in the movie would shout: 'Look out, Noel, here they come after you!' "

In his reading, Ellison came across it quite incidentally, as in Countee Cullen's poem "Heritage." At the time, 1931, he said, "I felt it to be artificial and alien. I was reading all these people very intensely and I felt something missing in them that I ran into in Eliot, the folk tradition they had and didn't know what to do with." This was at Tuskegee where "we had African princes walking around the campus. There was a girl from Sierra Leone and West Indians—we tended to link them all together. The sense of the alien was strong. It was not antagonism but a matter of totally different cultural backgrounds. I didn't share much of the interest in these people. . . . Usually I thought them quite British. I had no cultural identification with them. I rejected any notion of a link, just as I later rejected Herskovits' ideas [about African cultural survivals]. Lorenzo Turner on African survivals in American speech interested me. But I did not—and I do not—feel a lack in my cultural heritage as an American Negro. I think a lot of time is wasted trying to find a substitute in Africa. Who was it that saw Americans as 'a people without a history but with a new synthesis'? The thing to do is to exploit the meaning of the life you have."

In *The Invisible Man,* the African theme appears only in the person of Ras the Exhorter, leader of the ultra-racist black nationalists in Harlem, patterned on one of several successors to Marcus Garvey in the Harlem of the 1930's. In Ellison's novel, Ras, a West Indian black man, contests the streets of Harlem with the Communists. During a fracas caused by Ras' attempt to break up a Communist street meeting, Ras, knife in hand, makes a passionate appeal to a black Communist:

You *my* brother, mahn. Brothers are the same color; how the hell you call these white men *brother?* . . . Brothers the same color. We

sons of Mama Africa, you done forgot? You black. BLACK! You—
Godahm, mahn!" he said, swinging the knife for emphasis. "You got
bahd *hair.* You got thick *lips!* They say you stink! They hate you,
mahn. You African. AFRICAN! Why you with them? [320]

The two Communists, one of them Ellison's protagonist, listen
fascinated despite themselves as Ras tells them the only allies to
seek were not white men, but black and yellow and brown allies,
and that the white men would only betray and betray and betray
them in the end. "This man's full of pus," says Ellison's hero as
he pulls his friend away, "black pus." At the novel's end, in the
wild and bloody rage of a Harlem riot, Ras the Exhorter appears
on a black horse in the midst of his followers, dressed "in the costume of an Abyssinian chieftain, a fur cap upon his head, his arm
bearing a shield, a cape made of the skin of some animal around
his shoulders." Ras confronts Ellison's hero on the dark street just
as he has come to realize the perfidy involved in bringing on the
bloodshed. He tries to reason with Ras, he wants to say: "Look,
we're all black folks together. . . ." But Ras is blood mad and
they fight, and it is in fleeing from Ras the Destroyer that Ellison's
hero descends into the deep cellar where he begins to reorder everything he has learned in his life. His principal discovery seems
to be that not only the black man but every man shares the common plight: "None of us seems to know who he is or where he's
going." He decides ultimately that he must shake off the "old
skin," leave it in the hole behind him, and re-emerge into a world
of "infinite possibilities"—"a good phrase and a good view of life
and a man shouldn't accept any other."

Thus while Richard Wright wandered over the world holding
fast to his outsiderness, Ellison, clinging hard to his home ground,
began trying to reach for a new sense of Negro insiderness, for a
distinctive cultural personality that asserted its legitimacy within
the American society and, for that matter, within the total human
culture. Ellison, trying to look beyond the threshold of the conquest of civil rights and equality of status for Negroes, asks himself: what does the Negro become when he has shed his second-
classness? "What part of Negro life has been foisted on us by jim
crow and must be gotten rid of; what part of Negro life, expression, culture do we want to keep? We will need more true self-
consciousness. I don't know what values, what new tragic sense
must emerge. What happens to the values of folk life, of church
life? Up to now it has been a matter of throwing things off. But
now we have to get conscious of what we do not want to throw

off." Ellison believes that the Negro identity of the future will be shaped out of the unique Negro folk tradition. He believes this can be preserved—though he is not sure how—and that the Negro is not struggling to become free simply in order to disappear.

"To the question, *what am I?,*" Ellison said, "I answer that I am a Negro American. That means far more than something racial. It does not mean race, it means something cultural, that I am a man who shares a dual culture. For me, the Negro is a member of an America-bound [321] cultural group with its own idiom, its own psychology, growing out of its preoccupations with certain problems for hundreds of years, out of all its history. The American Negro stock is *here,* a synthesis of various African cultures, then of slavery, and of all the experience of Negroes since."

Of all these ingredients, the African is the least: "The African content of American Negro life is more fanciful than actual," Ellison said, and this is why he has such a minimum interest in it. He thinks that it is the novelist's business to translate the unique Negro experience into literature. "As long as Negroes are confused as to how they relate to American culture," he said, "they will be confused about their relationship to places like Africa."

James Baldwin

What would you say, I asked James Baldwin, if a man from Mars appeared suddenly before you and asked: "What are you?" Baldwin looked at the question quizzically. "At the time I left the country in 1948," he said, "I would have answered your man from Mars by saying: 'I am a writer'—with an edge in my voice while thinking: 'I am a nigger, you green bastard.' Now I think I'd say to him: 'I'm a writer with a lot of work to do and wondering if I can do it.'"

Both Richard Wright and Ralph Ellison had something to do with this change in Baldwin's concept of himself over this space of years. In 1948, Baldwin was twenty-four years old, born and grown in Harlem, already full of knowing he had to write and already full of bile and desperation. He followed Richard Wright's example and left this country for France. "I knew I would die if I stayed here," he said, "that I would never be a writer." In 1952, Baldwin came back to America for a brief visit and while he was here he met Ralph Ellison. He came away from that encounter with the impression of a tough-minded man who already took it for granted that great changes had come and that it was time for a

Negro writer to learn a new job, "to help Negroes destroy their habits of mind of inferiority, those crushing habits, to become men and women, not to use 'black' as a crutch, but to get past it, to become a person with no special privilege and no special handicap." Baldwin went back to exile with habits of mind and handicaps of his own to overcome, but with this new idea also turning slowly within him. As he thought and wrote searchingly about the problems of his identity, as a man, as a man with African ancestors, as a Negro, an American, a writer, Baldwin was already beginning to look around him with a fresh eye, though it was some time before he was able to bring what he saw into focus. When he finally did so—it took another six years—new emotions of assertion of self had displaced his hatred for whites, and Baldwin came home. [322]

"I began to be oppressed in Europe by the American colony talking about how awful America was," Baldwin said. "It made no sense, it made me mad, there in France, with its own injustice and corruption, the Algerian thing, people just as small-minded as everywhere else. It just wasn't *that* much better! Sitting on a cafe terrace and trying to explain Little Rock made me feel as though I was letting the best years of my life go to nothing." Baldwin looked critically at Richard Wright who, he said, he "admired and liked" but "who has gotten caught between his habits of rage and what is going on in the world, so he doesn't understand it very well. He is frightened by the Africans he knows in Paris who have such different attitudes than he had, and by the things which have happened in America, depriving him of his role of being the celebrated victim." Through a long and painful process, Baldwin came as new to an old conclusion: "You have to go far away to find out that you never do get far away." He also came to realize: "I couldn't get to *know* France. The key to my experience was *here,* in America. Everything I could deal with was *here.*" From a pile of papers, Baldwin pulled out an article he had just written that was to have appeared that very week in the strikebound *New York Times Book Review,* in which he reviewed his rediscovery of his identity as an American:

For even the most incorrigible maverick had to be born somewhere. He may leave the group which produced him—or he may be forced to—but nothing will efface his origins, the marks of which he carries with him everywhere. I think it is important to know this and even find it a matter for rejoicing, as the strongest people do, regardless of their station. On this acceptance, literally, the life of a writer depends.

Baldwin could not come to this acceptance easily. He had much to weigh, including some acutely important personal considerations. But he chose, finally, one day in the tenth year of his exile, to quit Wright's path for Ellison's in order, ultimately, to find his own.

This is a personal day [he had written] a terrible day, the day to which his entire sojourn has been tending. It is the day he realizes that there are no untroubled countries in this fearfully troubled world, that if he has been preparing himself for anything in Europe, he has been preparing himself—for America. In short, the freedom that the American writer finds in Europe brings him full circle back to himself, with the responsibility for his development where it always was: in his own hands.

So Baldwin came back from exile, after ten years, and went on a journey of discovery to the American South, which he had never seen. "That was when I realized what tremendous things were happening," he told me, "and that I did have a role to play, that I was part of it, could work for it." Baldwin looked away. "I can't be happy here," he said, "but I can work here."

In James Baldwin's story of himself and his rediscoveries, we come [323] upon Africa at several different levels and in several different guises. It appears most directly in the persons of the Africans he met in Paris during the years of his exile. Baldwin found them difficult to get on with, difficult to talk to, and had a sense of a great gulf of difference between them and himself. In a 1950 essay [1] he describes this difference:

The African before him has endured privation, injustice, medieval cruelty; but the African has not yet endured the utter alienation of himself from his people and his past. His mother did not sing "Sometimes I Feel Like a Motherless Child," and he has not, all his life long, ached for acceptance in a culture which pronounced straight hair and white skin the only acceptable beauty. They face each other, the Negro and the African, over a gulf of three hundred years—an alienation too vast to be conquered in an evening's goodwill. . . .

In our talk about these matters, Baldwin added these details:

I think these Africans admired white more than I did, and thought the white world was worth getting into. I thought they were naive. They liked American things, cigarettes, clothes. I suppose they frightened me. They illustrated all the things I had been running away

[1] Reprinted in *Notes of a Native Son* (Boston, 1955) with the title "Encounter on the Seine: Black Meets Brown."

from. All my clothes were dark. I would run from wearing bright clothes. They went around in outrageous getups. They were terribly goodnatured, but did not seem to have, really, any understanding of the world or of how society is put together. I say this of the students, not of people like [the West African poet] Senghor. . . . Senghor frightened me because of his extraordinary way of being civilized and primitive at the same time. . . . This frightened me. I thought this meant sooner or later a great clash between myself and someone like that. I was committed to Western society in a way he could not be. . . . All discussions were on politics. You could never get into anything else. They disgusted me, I think. They thought I had money, but I didn't. Maybe I was insufficiently intransigent against America. I couldn't really hate America the way they did. They hated America, were full of racial stories, held their attitudes largely on racial grounds. Politically, they knew very little about it. Whenever I was with an African, we would both be uneasy. On what level to talk? The terms of our life were so different, we almost needed a dictionary to talk. . . .

At quite a different level, as he searched out the terms of his elusive identity, Baldwin for a long time saw Africa as the blank and empty backdrop of his past. It was the edge of the world over which he dropped, he thought, into nothingness as he backed away, an unwanted and unsharing alien, from the rich and busy world of non-African culture:

I was a kind of bastard of the West; when I followed the line of my past I did not find myself in Europe but in Africa. And this meant that in some subtle way, in a really profound way, I brought to Shakespeare, Bach, Rembrandt, to the stones of Paris, to the cathedral at Chartres, and to the Empire State Building a special attitude. These were not really my creations; they did not contain my history; I might search in them in vain forever for any reflection of myself. I was an interloper; this was not my heritage. At the same time I had no other [324] heritage which I could possibly hope to use—I had certainly been unfitted for the jungle or the tribe. I would have to appropriate these white centuries, I would have to make them mine—I would have to accept my special attitude, my special place in this scheme— otherwise I would have no place in *any* scheme.[2]

At one time, Baldwin went (to work and to recover from a "species of breakdown") to a tiny village in Switzerland where he was the first black man any of the villagers had ever seen. The children ran after him calling "Neger! Neger!" and touched his hair or

[2] *Notes of a Native Son*, p. 7.

tried to see if his color came off when they rubbed it. He told them he came from America, but they did not really believe it because they knew that "black men come from Africa." The village made an annual pre-Lenten collection to "buy" African natives into Christ's grace. Two village children blackened their faces, put horsehair wigs on their blond heads and solicited money for the missionaries in Africa. Baldwin was proudly informed that the last year they had raised enough to "buy" six or eight Africans out of hell's grasp.

Baldwin tried vainly to imagine "white men arriving for the first time in an African village" and the astonishment with which the black villagers might exclaim over the white men's hair and skin.

But there is a great difference between the first white man to be seen by Africans and being the first black man to be seen by whites. The white man takes the astonishment as tribute, for he arrives to conquer and convert the natives, whose inferiority in relation to himself is not even to be questioned; whereas I, without a thought of conquest, find myself among a people whose culture controls me, has even, in a sense, created me, people who have cost me more in anguish and rage than they will ever know. . . . The astonishment with which I might have greeted them, should they have stumbled into my African village a few hundred years ago, might have rejoiced their hearts. But the astonishment with which they greet me can only poison mine.[3]

Baldwin saw the villagers possessing "an authority which I shall never have" and saw himself as a latecomer without right to any part of everything they have inherited—in which Baldwin included the whole of Western culture. Once again, Baldwin divorced himself from Chartres and the Empire State Building:

For this village, even were it incomparably more remote and incredibly more primitive, is the West, the West onto which I have been so strangely grafted. These people cannot be, from the point of view of power, strangers anywhere in the world; they have made the modern world, even if they do not know it. The most illiterate among them is related in a way that I am not, to Dante, Shakespeare, Michelangelo, Aeschylus, Da Vinci, Rembrandt, and Racine; the cathedral at Chartres says something to them which it cannot say to me, as indeed would the Empire State Building, should anyone here ever see it. Out of their hymns and dances come Beethoven and Bach. Go back a

[3] *Ibid.*, pp. 163–64.

few [325] centuries and they are in their full glory—but I am in Africa, watching the conquerors arrive.[4]

These were the matters that Baldwin eventually resolved by coming around to a clearer view of American culture, and a more inclusive view of human culture and his place in it. He came to see, for one thing, that his sense of lostness, far from distinguishing him from white Americans, made him kin with them, that they were just as lost and alienated as he was, and that "this depthless alienation from oneself and one's people is, in sum, the American experience." Baldwin also resolved, with a reassertion of his intelligence, the problem of his sense of divorcement from the stream of culture. "No matter where our fathers had been born," he wrote in the same *Times* article quoted earlier, "or what they had endured, the fact of Europe had formed us both, was part of our identity, part of our inheritance." This discovery helped Baldwin to stop thinking that he had no share of Chartres, Beethoven, or the Empire State Building. In fact, by the time we talked of this, he had forgotten he had ever cut himself off from these monuments of human achievement and was struck anew to discover how far he had come since he had unhappily walked the streets of that village in the Swiss Alps. He had stopped seeing himself as waiting, empty-handed and empty-minded, for the white conqueror in Africa while Western man created his glories. Now he saw that in all time all people had exchanged and appropriated cultures and in doing so reshaped them. "Henry James said somewhere," Baldwin said, "that a novelist has to be someone on whom nothing is lost. When you've taken it in, it is yours!" Baldwin had come to see, in great liberating excitement, that the world was his if he made it so: "All that has ever been done in the world speaks to a basic human experience that is constant. What the Greeks did, what the people did who built Chartres, what they were all doing is what *I* am doing now, coming up with something out of human experience, plunging into that great sea where there are no barriers at all, of race or of any other kind."

Thus Baldwin regained a sense of American identity by realizing that it is the search for an identity that makes all Americans kin, and he won his way through to share in Rembrandt and Bach by striking out boldly from his remote African shore and making his own path through the great sea of the common human experience. But while this did begin to settle Baldwin's problem of cul-

[4] *Ibid.,* p. 165.

tural identity and brought him back home for a fresh beginning, it
did not mean that he left Africa abandoned behind him. On the
contrary, Baldwin still carried something of Africa within him at
a deeper and much more obscure level than we have yet explored,
continuing to haunt and bedevil his search for an understanding of
who and what he is.

As anyone can know who reads Baldwin's novel *Go Tell It on
the* [326] *Mountain,* or the title essay of *Notes of a Native Son,*
his father—or more correctly his stepfather [5]—was the most important person in his young life. As anyone can also know by
reading his second novel, *Giovanni's Room,* Baldwin is deeply
preoccupied with the problems of homosexuality. Baldwin himself
has linked these two concerns, for to the hero of *Giovanni's Room*
he gave his stepfather's name. And through all of this, not always
visible or traceable, runs a dark little African thread.

Twice in *Notes of a Native Son,* Baldwin associates Africa with
his stepfather. At one point he tells of thinking of his father as he
was being told how the Swiss children, blackfaced and with wigs
on their blond hair, collected money to "buy" black Africans for
Christ. The second time, in the fuller account of the man he called
his father, he makes the association more directly:

Handsome, proud . . . he looked to me, as I grew older, like pictures I had seen of African tribal chieftains; he really should have
been naked, with war paint on and barbaric mementos, standing
among spears. He could be chilling in the pulpit and indescribably
cruel in his personal life and he was certainly the most bitter man I
have ever met; yet it must be said that there was something else in
him. . . . It had something to do with his blackness, I think—he was
very black—with his blackness and his beauty, and with the fact that
he knew he was black but did not know that he was beautiful. . . .[6]

When we talked of Africa and carried it back in time, much
more appeared about the link in Baldwin's mind between his
father and Africa. Africa, he said first, made him think of: "A

[5] In *Go Tell It on the Mountain,* Baldwin's hero is brought, the infant
son of another man, into his mother's May–December marriage with the
preacher, an angry man full of hate who becomes the principal influence in
the boy's life. In the autobiographical essay in *Notes of a Native Son,*
Baldwin writes of such a man as his actual father. It seemed reasonable to
think that the literalness of the essay was exact: that in the novel Baldwin
had used his license to deny blood kinship with the man he came to hate
so mortally. But my literalness was simpleminded; the fictional version was
the true one.
[6] *Notes of a Native Son,* p. 37.

very black man, much blacker than me, naked, very romantic, very banal, sweat, something very sensual, very free, something very mysterious. Africa's mental and emotional structure," he added, "is hard for me to imagine. It intrigues me. Also frightens me."

There was certainly nothing about Africa before he went to school, he first said, but then went on:

But there is something vague tied up with the image of my father before I ever went to school, seeing his face over my mother's shoulder. What this has to do with Africa I don't know, but somehow my first association with Africa comes through him. I compared the people in my father's church to African savages. This was because of my relation to my father. . . . I was ten or twelve. The church and my father were synonymous. Music and dancing, again sweat, out of the jungle. It was contemptible because it appeared to be savage. But this was also my image of my father. I guess I was hipped on being American and the things they did seemed so common, so vulgar. My image of [327] myself was of not having anything to do with my father or anything my father represented.

Baldwin talked then about going to the movies.

I hardly ever went, but every once in a while I did see savages. There was something painful, sort of embarrassing about it. I suppose it was because that savage was black like me and was making a fool of himself in front of the whole white world which laughed at him and exploited him. I wanted not to be identified with that. I know the general attitude about Africans was uneasy contempt, embarrassment, a little fear. I think also of Stepin Fetchit rolling his eyes. African savages did that too. "You're acting like a nigger," you were told if you rolled your eyes, if your nails were not brushed, or you used bad language. These attitudes about Africans did not become explicit.

Then he returned again to the subject of his father: "I don't know when Africa came in first. It *must* have been from my father. My associations. . . ." Baldwin stopped for a long moment. "My father thought of himself as a king," he went on, "and he would have said something like we were descended from kings in Africa." There was another agitated silence. Then he talked of a clash that had taken place between himself and his father over a white school teacher who had been kind to him—he tells this story also in *Notes of a Native Son*—and the deep way in which the issue of blackness and his father and the church and Africa got all mixed up in his mind. "When I joined the church at fourteen . . ." he began, and stopped again. "This gets very complicated. In church I imagined myself as an African boy, dancing as I might have danced thousands of years ago. It really was a mystical experience and did something permanent to my sense of time. . . . But I wasn't in the least prepared to deal with Africa. I gave a kind of lip service to it as the land of my forebears, and tried to find out things about it, mainly through the sculpture. . . . But I don't know where any of this left me or my father, or the church. . . ."

We moved away, then, from this territory toward the more open spaces where other people were reacting to Africa, and Baldwin described the man-in-the-street reaction to Africa this way:

A few years ago he would have laughed and said: "A bunch of funky Negroes." "Funky" has to do with the odor of sweat, I think. I don't know what he'd say now, but he wouldn't say that. He might say: "They're showing, they're doing all right." I'd be astonished if anybody reacted to newsreels or movies of Africans the way I did. Now there is pride. The shot of Nkrumah getting off his plane has an effect on all the other images. It takes a certain sting out of those pictures of the African savage. I am presumably not talking about myself now, but of others, like my baby sister who's fifteen.

We talked of the "new" Africa and the "new" Negro reaction to it and then at the end Baldwin said: "I want to go to Africa one of these days. I think there is a great deal I can discover about myself there. There is something beautiful about it. I want to find out. It is at the gateway of the modern world, and I could help be a guide, I've been [328] here, I know some of the goat tracks. I might also find that part of me I had to bury when I grew up, the capacity for joy, of the sense, and something almost dead, real good-naturedness. I think they still believe in miracles there and I want to see it."

Lorraine Hansberry

James Baldwin was six years old when the Depression set in, but by the time Lorraine Hansberry was six, the Depression was nearly over. This was a divide great enough in itself to mark off two quite different generations. But the difference between the two is marked by more than time, for Lorraine Hansberry came of a comfortably situated family, and though she knew what life was like for most people on Chicago's South Side, in the department of economic well-being, her pangs were all vicarious. Miss Hansberry, born in 1930, is old enough to have footholds of memory back in the world of pre-1945. She remembers newsreels about It-

aly's invasion of Ethiopia and the strong feelings in her home over
that event. She was nine when Europe went to war in Poland and
eleven when Pearl Harbor was bombed, and she remembers her
father's ambivalent emotions over the conflict between the non-
white Japanese and the white Americans. Her adult years did not
begin until after that war ended. When she came from two years
in college in Wisconsin to make her way in New York, it was
1950. All of this makes Lorraine Hansberry old enough to feel
some share in the experience of her elders, but leaves her young
enough to accept the present climate of great change as her natural environment. She is also so new as a writer that her hit play of
1959, *A Raisin in the Sun,* was the first and only work of hers
that anybody knew. It is precisely because of her youth and her
newness, and the way in which the subject of Africa appears in
her play, that Lorraine Hansberry turns up here at the end of our
progression of Negro writers and our scrutiny of the ways in
which they have dealt with the matter of their African ancestors.

Lorraine Hansberry took the title of her play from a line by
Langston Hughes: "What happens to a dream deferred? / Does it
dry up / Like a raisin in the sun?" Her success was the winning of
a dream that first came upon her in her young girlhood when she
first read the poetry of Langston Hughes and others. Much of this
poetry, as we have seen, was about Africa, and on this subject too,
curiously enough, Miss Hansberry also in a way completes a circle
begun by Hughes. In a new and much more realistic setting, she
too has had a vision of a romantic reunion between Negro American and black African. But her vision is shaped by new times,
new outlooks. It is no longer a wispy literary yearning after a lost
primitivism, nor does she beat it out on synthetic tomtoms. Nor is
it any longer a matter of going back-to-Africa as the ultimate op-
tion [329] of despair in America. In Lorraine Hansberry's time it
has become a matter of choice between new freedoms now in the
grasp of black men, both African and American.

This idea appears only glancingly in *A Raisin in the Sun,* going
largely unnoticed by raving critics and applauding audiences alike.
The play is about the drive of the members of a poor Negro family to better their estate. Against this strong and sober central
theme, the subtheme of Africa appears only in incidental passages
and is used mainly to lighten the play's main emotional burdens.
The action turns on the use to be made of the insurance money of
the hard-working father who has just died, the son's ill-judged and
costly effort to get ahead quick, and the mother's intentness on

lifting them out of the black slums. The daughter of the family, oddly named Beneatha, is the real symbol of its passage from lower-classness; she is already at the university and wants to become a doctor. She has two beaux, one the son of a successful Negro businessman, the other an African, a student from Nigeria. On these two the author's biases are laid with a heavy hand, for the rich man's son is presented as a well-advanced case of bourgeois American decay who offers the girl a future of mink coats and Cadillacs. The Nigerian, by heavy contrast, brings a new look and a new sound to the African theme in American Negro life. He is the most literate, the most self-possessed, the most sophisticated, most purposive, I-know-where-I'm-going character in the play. He offers the girl a life of dedication, work, and self-realization in emergent Africa.

The imminent arrival of this young African brings on this colloquy between mother and daughter: [7]

Mama—I don't think I never met no African before.
Beneatha—Well, do me a favor and don't ask him a lot of ignorant questions about Africans. I mean, do they wear clothes and all that—
Mama—Well, now, I guess if you think we so ignorant 'round here maybe you shouldn't bring your friends here.
Beneatha—It's just that people ask such crazy things. All anyone seems to know about it when it comes to Africa is Tarzan—
Mama—(Indignantly) Why should I know anything about Africa?

When the young African, also oddly named as Asagai (which sounds more like the Zulu word *assegai,* a sawed-off spear, than like a Nigerian name), finally appears, Mama acquits herself, as always, with dignity. He comes bearing a Nigerian robe as a gift for the girl. He teasingly reminds her that she had first approached him at school to say: "I want very much to talk with you. About Africa. You see, Mr. Asagai, I am looking for my *identity!*" It is clear that this is no joking matter to the girl, and it becomes even less so when he gently but sharply reproves her for "mutilating" her hair by trying to straighten it. She hotly denies [330] that she is "assimilationist," which is one of Miss Hansberry's favorite words.

In a later scene, Beneatha appears in her Nigerian robe and headdress. She flicks off the "assimilationist junk" on the radio and goes into what she imagines to be a Nigerian tribal dance.

[7] All quotations from the play are from the published text, *A Raisin in the Sun* (New York, 1959).

Brother Walter comes in drunk, full of the angers and confusions arising out of the main business of the play. He enters into her mood. "And Ethiopia shall stretch forth her hands again!" he shouts, and together they go into a wild and noisy and hilarious caper punctuated by what are supposed to be African shouts. Walter leaps on the table and begins to address his imaginary tribesmen, summoning them to battle. In the stage directions we discover that he is seeing himself as "a great chief, a descendant of Chaka," the great Zulu chief—and the creator, incidentally, of the weapon called the *assegai*. It is hard to tell from the text how seriously the author intended all this to be taken; the night I saw the play it convulsed the house with laughter. At its height, George, the rich man's son, walks in. Walter holds forth his hand: "Black brother!" he cries. George looks amazed and disgusted. "Black brother, hell!" he says, and demands that Beneatha go in at once and change to go out. She accuses him of being "ashamed of his heritage," and when she is asked to explain, she goes on:

Beneatha—It means someone who is willing to give up his culture and submerge himself completely in the dominant, and in this case, oppressive culture!

George—Oh dear, dear, dear! Here we go! A lecture on the African past! On our great West African Heritage! In one second we will hear all about the great Ashanti empires, the great Songhay civilizations, and the great sculpture of Benin—and some poetry in the Bantu—and the whole monologue will end with the word *heritage!* (Nastily) Let's face it, baby, your heritage is nothing but a bunch of raggedy-assed spirituals and some grass huts!

Beneatha retorts that he is slandering the people who were "the first to smelt iron on the face of the earth" and who "were performing surgical operations when the English . . . were still tattooing themselves with blue dragons!" But she changes all the same and dutifully goes out with George.

The last act also opens on a relieving bit about Africa. The main action of the play has just come to climax. Walter has stupidly lost the money, and Beneatha sits in crushed defeat and despair, when young Mr. Asagai appears. He tries to comfort her with philosophy, and she turns on him in anger, predicting that things will be just as bad in Africa when the black man takes over. He retorts that for better or worse, it will be the black man's own fate, determined by himself. Then abruptly, he invites her to come home with him. At first she misunderstands.

Asagai—I mean across the ocean, home—to Africa. [331]

Beneatha—To—to Nigeria?

Asagai—Yes! (Smiling and lifting his arms playfully) Three hundred years later, the African prince rose up out of the seas and swept the maiden back across the middle passage over which her ancestors had come—

Beneatha—(Unable to play) Nigeria?

Asagai—Nigeria. Home. (Coming to her with genuine romantic flippancy) I will show you our mountains and our stars; and give you cool drinks from gourds and teach you the old songs and the ways of our people—and, in time, we will pretend that you have only been away for a day. . . .

Beneatha is shaken and confused by all that has been happening and wants time to think. Asagai, gently and sweetly understanding, looks back at her from the door: "How often I have looked at you and said, 'Ah—so this is what the New World hath finally wrought . . .' " and makes a graceful exit.

In the play's last moments, the main issue happily resolved, again after a scene of the highest tension, the unresolved subject of Africa reappears to help break the strain. To make talk to cut in on the insupportable emotion of the moment, Beneatha announces that Asagai had asked her to marry him. Mama is barely able to hear what she says.

Beneatha—(Girlishly and unreasonably trying to pursue the conversation) To go to Africa, Mama—be a doctor in Africa . . .

Mama—(Distracted) Yes, baby.

Walter—Africa! What he want you to go to Africa for?

Beneatha—To practice there—

Walter—Girl, if you don't get them silly ideas out of your head! You better marry yourself a man with some loot . . .

And the two of them go out, still arguing, George versus Asagai, as their voices fade away, leaving the issue, America or Africa, hanging in the air, rustling and sounding there after they'd gone, like the theme of another play to come.

In *A Raisin in the Sun,* the new form of an old fact, the new shape of the African idea in the American Negro universe, made its first appearance, I believe, in any play or story of wide public notice. If it appeared only incidentally, as a secondary theme to a much more moving main story, this too was appropriate, since this was just about where the subject of Africa stood in the thinking of

Negroes at the time the play was produced. The play's audiences were moved by its dramatization of an American problem, by the classic figure of the strong mother, by the son's struggle to find his manhood, by the endurance of the son's wife, and by the fresh forthrightness of the daughter. But few, it seemed, were quite ready to tune in on the new sounds and sights of Africa that also came into view in Miss Hansberry's play. They will no doubt reappear at higher and stronger levels, as time goes on, and will be counterposed to something more substantial than Miss Hansberry's [332] idea of decadent bourgeois affluence in America. Still, she had opened the subject to a new and higher visibility than it had yet enjoyed, and I found, when I sought her out to talk about it, that she was grateful to have someone notice it. She was being praised so highly for creating "real" people in the play that hardly anybody had given her credit, she said ruefully, for also trying to deal symbolically with some important ideas.

These ideas, I found as we talked on, had been assembled out of a series of sources and exposures going back to her childhood and were sometimes expressed in a string of broad generalizations somewhat eclectically tied together. Thus Miss Hansberry described herself as "a strong Negro nationalist" who also believed that all peoples and cultures must eventually merge in a common humanity: "It will be a great day when people merge biologically and in culture," she said, "but until that day, oppressed peoples must express themselves," and this has to be done by stressing one's special identity. "I want all to assimilate in all," she said at one point, "but now one must identify." It sometimes seemed during our conversation that a kind of shape-as-you-go quality had been imposed on Miss Hansberry's thinking by the need, in her sudden celebrity, to answer a lot of questions about herself that she had never been asked before or, for that matter, asked herself. Because she had so successfully created some "real" people on the stage, she was having the wonderful but rather unseating experience of discovering that her opinions about all sorts of things had overnight become important. Inevitably, some of her opinions and perhaps some memories had to be put together on the spur of the moment. But Lorraine Hansberry was not only a polite and decent young woman trying hard to keep her balance in the storm of a Broadway success. She was also a bright and thoughtful person, and almost every thread of her thought did lead back to some significant life experience.

Talking about the changes in the world, she described how

sometime after World War II she had begun to feel not so much a member of an American minority as of a "world majority" of oppressed people who were beginning to throw off the systems that oppressed them. "As a fairly self-conscious Negro," she said, "I began to feel this kinship, the feeling from the past summed up in 'Aren't we all miserable' passing to a new and happier feeling: 'Aren't we all moving ahead!' " For herself, she thought, this was not a change, "just a logical progression. Why ever since I was three years old," she exclaimed, "I knew that somebody somewhere was doing something to hurt black and brown peoples. Little as I was I remember the newsreels of the Ethiopian war and the feeling of outrage in our Negro community. Fighters with spears and our people in a passion over it, my mother attacking the Pope blessing the Italian troops going off to slay Ethiopians. When the Pope died [333] that was the thought of him that came to my mind. I didn't know a thing about Spain but I certainly did know about Ethiopia. I didn't know about Hitler, but I certainly did know about Leopold cutting off the hands of the people in the Congo. Japan's war in China? Vague, very vague. I don't remember people talking about it. In 1941, though, many people saw the Japanese as a colored nation, and this affected their feelings, certainly in Chicago, and this was reflected even in my own home. But we just expected that things would change. We had been saying for a long time: 'Ethiopia will stretch forth her hands!' This always meant that *they* were going to pay for all this one day."

Miss Hansberry said she remembered the verse about Ethiopia's hands "because I am the granddaughter of an AME minister." She was also the daughter of a strong-minded man who evidently devoted himself, with considerable success, to winning just the kind of bourgeois affluence she deprecates in her play. Besides being a well-to-do businessman and a power in the Chicago Negro community, her father was also a strongly race-conscious man. "My father was a student of history," said Miss Hansberry, "and we were always taught pride in our Negro heritage." Her father gave her a strong sense of the positive virtues of Negro-ness but these all had to do, she remembers, with Negroes in America. "It was all in terms of the United States," she said, "nothing in particular about Africa." At the same time, her family also had certain prejudices about color. "My people had the stereotyped attitudes," she said. "They thought blacker people were less attractive, and we were a dark-skinned family! Nowadays nobody would admit ever having such feelings. We assumed, of course, that *our* color was the marking-off point. . . . The prejudices in my family were very, very complicated. We were never proud of its attitudes." Some combination of these factors, involving attitudes about Africa and color, doubtless had something to do with the odd fact that by her own account Lorraine Hansberry had never even heard about Marcus Garvey until after she came to New York in 1950. But little Lorraine took in a great deal about Africa nonetheless. Her father's house "was full of books," and when she was about nine she started reading the Negro poets, and got some of her first and more enduring images of Africa from their lines, so much so that when I first asked her what came to her mind when she thought of Africa she instantly said:

"Beautiful mountains, plateaus, beautiful dark people." And these pictures came, she added, "from the poets I grew up reading, Langston Hughes, Countee Cullen, Waring Cuney. I was deeply influenced by them and their images of Africa were marvelous and beautiful."

Out in the hard world of the Chicago South Side, in its schools and on its streets, Lorraine had ample opportunity to summon up the resources of pride she had acquired from her father and from Langston [334] Hughes' poetry. She ran into all the familiar hateful images and she fought them back with all she had:

In school in the lower grades, primitive peoples, hot, animals, mostly negative, how good it was we were saved from this terrible past. Most of the kids reflected this. To call a kid an African was an insult. It was calling him savage, uncivilized, naked, something to laugh at. A naked black savage with a spear and war paint. It was equivalent to ugliness. Everything distasteful and painful was associated with Africa. This came from school, from the movies, and from our own people who accepted this. In common talk, the term was always derogatory—"you are acting like a wild African!" This meant heathen, un-Christian. Most children absorbed this and acquired a deep shame of their African past. But I resented what I saw in the movies and I resented the teachers who couldn't give a more positive view. This too was mainly about our own American Negro past. We were very sensitive to such things as how the slavery issue was discussed, even in grade school. I resented all of it. I was very unique in that I extended this [resentment] to the African thing too. The others didn't do this, but I made the connection. . . . I really don't know why this was so, but I was very aware, and even when kids said "you look like an African" as a form of insult, this hurt me, it brought me pain. At the movies when one white man was holding off thousands of Africans with a gun, all the kids were with the hero, but I ,was with the Africans. When I was thirteen or fourteen I was more sophisticated. I had begun to read Carter Woodson. My brothers and I talked about Hannibal, we had passion, if not information, and we thought Africa was a great thing in the world. . . .

Lorraine Hansberry, then, got her early defensive race-consciousness from her father and her romantic view of Africa quite largely from the poems of Langston Hughes. These two influences in her young life were further linked by a curiously arresting set of coincidences that I mark here because of their obvious relevance not only to our grasp of these two individual writers, but also to our general subject. I can do so, however, only in scantiest outline, for they involve the two fathers about whom neither writer has yet told us quite enough.[8] Lorraine Hansberry's father and Langston Hughes' father were evidently in many ways very similar men, both hard-driving and ambitious and intent on wealth and recognition. As the reader will recall from our brief account of Hughes, his father quite early in his life quit the United States because it did not allow a Negro to be a man and migrated to Mexico where he made his fortune in business. Lorraine's father made his fortune here, in Chicago, after coming up empty-handed out of Mississippi. He fought personally to wring recognition of Negro rights out of the white world. At his own expense he carried a restricted covenants case right up to the Supreme Court, and he won. But he came finally to the despairing conclusion, like Hughes' father and others before him, that the United [335] States was no place for a self-respecting black man to live out his life, and he decided to migrate. It was not Africa, however, that he had in view. As Miss Hansberry's own account intimates, her father had something less than a romantic view of Africa. Remember, she never even had heard of Marcus Garvey in her father's race-conscious home—the only version of back-to-Africa that had ever reached her, she told me, was Senator Bilbo's race-baiting bill in Congress to ship all Negroes back where they came from—and there were also the elder Hansberry's views about blackness. These views and attitudes were somehow linked, but we will not ever know their inwardness unless Miss Hansberry one day chooses to explain why her father's color attitudes were so

[8] My information about Hughes' father comes entirely out of Hughes' autobiographical volume, *The Big Sea*. I know about Hansberry Senior only what Miss Hansberry herself told me. Essentially the same details appear in the autobiographical account she gave of herself in *The New Yorker*, May 9, 1959.

"very, very complicated." In any case, when he planned to migrate, the elder Hansberry fixed his eye not on Africa, but like the elder Hughes some forty years before, on Mexico. In 1945 he took the step, actually bought a house in a Mexico City suburb, and put Lorraine and her sister in school there. But he had waited too long. Within a short time Mr. Hansberry died, and the family resumed its life in the United States.

Her brothers, Lorraine Hansberry told me, have been moved to follow in their father's path, and they now see West Africa, not Mexico, as a more promising land since, with the changing times, they have been able to develop business interests there. But Lorraine herself chose quite differently. Like Langston Hughes in a far-gone year, she decided that she was not Africa, or Mexico, but Chicago and New York. She went even further and by marrying a non-Negro added to her vision of the far future the ultimate end of all troubling race distinctions. At the same time she has clung hard in her near view to a strong insistence on racial and national identifications. She thinks it an absurd idea that persons of African descent should return to Africa because of that; Africans have their own national identities, and American Negroes have—or must now shape—their own. And this, again, is the rub. Here Lorraine Hansberry in her turn arrives, behind Ralph Ellison and James Baldwin, at the new edge of time and looks with them out over the same confusions: as he emerges from his second classness, what does the American Negro become? And in this process of new becoming, what is he to Africa, and what is Africa to him? "I don't know about the future," answered Lorraine Hansberry, "or what role Africa will have in it. One thing, though, the shame about Africa among Negroes is actively disintegrating. I don't think this change should be so difficult. Most people are glad to replace a negative view with an affirmative view." [336]

BLYDEN JACKSON

The Negro's Negro in Negro Literature

There was a time when all Negro literature seemed designed to demonstrate to white Americans how very much Negroes were just like them. As a matter of fact, it was with this earnest exercise that Negro writing in fiction began. "Look," it seemed to say, "at us Negroes as we actually are. We are no different from white people. We are as good as you because we are just like you." And so, at their beginning, Negro novels swarmed with octoroons or light-skinned Negroes with Nordic features. Twenty-eight of the eighty-two novels in Gloster's standard bibliography of Negro fiction, the majority of them before the Harlem Renaissance, have prominent characters light enough in skin color to pass for white. Thus it is with Clotel, the titular heroine of the earliest Negro novel in 1853. Thus, too, is the state of affairs in many another Negro novel through Jessie Fauset's pallid assemblage of marionettes in her would-be chronicles of the Negro upper crust (1924–1933) and Walter White's *Flight* (1926) and Nella Larsen's parable on passing which is named just that: *Passing* (1929). For many weary years, indeed, the Negro writer harped on his twin themes of passing as a white, and the tragic mulatto, negligible though the relative percentage of Negroes who could pass has ever been and inconsequential as such themes ultimately can be to the basic issues of xenophobia in America. When the Negro writer presented Negroes who could not pass, they tended to be white in everything but color, even to their strictures on Negroes of the wrong kind. And so, repeatedly and repeatedly, these white Negroes of Negro fiction, a large number of them brought before the world in some of the very poorest of Negro novels, and all of them, incidentally, dedicated to a proposition which was, and is,

SOURCE: *The Michigan Quarterly Review*, IV (1965), 290–295. Copyright © 1965 by the University of Michigan. Reprinted by permission of the publisher.

essentially true—that Negroes and whites *are* alike—signally failed if their mission was to prove how like anyone were these strange creatures from the dubious overlapping worlds of melodrama and pastiche.

Then came the 1920's and the Harlem Renaissance. There was a new Negro. And he was not like white folks. He was better than they were. He had retained some primitive quality which contributed, in a way too ineffable for definition, to the joy of living, and which the scientific orientation and mass culture of the twentieth century had somehow removed from the spiritual capacities of white people. White people may, indeed, have been the first to notice this superiority of the Negro. But Negroes became aware of it quickly enough. In *Home to Harlem* (1928) the Negro writer Claude McKay turned the capital of the Negro world, which Harlem certainly was by the 1920's, into the capital of Negro joy, in the process, moreover, at least calling into question that old notion of the agrarian South as the Negro's home to which Richard Wright was to pay [290] his respects within a decade.

Some Negro writers managed, in effect, to join the cult of the superior Negro without relinquishing their argument that Negroes were only unacknowledged white people. A clear instance of this feat of carrying water on both shoulders appears in Walter White's *Flight.* The heroine of *Flight,* an octoroon of course, passes, and passes well, in the opulent world of New York women's shops. But one day she revisits the Negro ghetto. The special something there, so poignantly absent from her white wasteland, recalls her to her right mind and she, as it were, comes home, to stay in her own real (as well as figurative) Harlem, never returning to her well-to-do white husband and her affluent job in the dreary world of white success.

Other writers of the Harlem Renaissance, however, had at least the simple good sense of McKay. They saw, as did he, the elementary logic demanded of the cult of the superior Negro. One can hardly argue a unique virtue deriving directly and exclusively from Negroness and then support his argument with Negroes who are white. Jake Brown, the expatriate who makes the literal return to Harlem in McKay's fable, is a Negro-looking product of the Negro masses. So is Aunt Hager's family in *Not Without Laughter* (1930) except for the daughter, Tempy, who acts like white people and lives in Philistine gloom. So are the Damon-and-Pythias pair of *The Walls of Jericho* (1928). So is Sam Lucas of Countee Cullen's *One Way to Heaven* (1932), the ultimate proof that Negroes are beautiful people. Lucas has spent a lifetime faking his own abandonment of sin, going from one big revival meeting to another, flinging down, in a well-practiced routine, his razor and his cards at the mourners' bench and enjoying, from a host of deeply moved congregations, the sweet and lavish charity which rises to reward his repentance and conversion. But then, of a day too suddenly come upon him, he arrives at an abandonment he can not fake, his own translation from the here into the hereafter. Yet, out of his unquenchable capacity to out-Mercutio Mercutio, his Negro superiority over the bleakness of this world and the next, in his dying he plays again his counterfeit repentance and pretends to see the opening of heaven's gates, giving thus his supreme performance in a final debonair gesture of atonement to the wife, and the devout church woman, he calculatingly married and has indifferently mistreated.

Beyond a Sam Lucas the doctrine of Negro buoyancy could hardly go. Moreover, the years of the Harlem Renaissance blended almost imperceptibly into the years of American depression, when joy was hardly compatible with the spirit of the time. Meanwhile the campaign strategy of Negro writing changed its front, aided by the circumstance that the Harlem Renaissance, if it had done nothing else, had at least introduced a new literary respect for the Negro masses. On this new front the Negro writer challenged America. He appealed to its compassion, its sense of guilt, its enlightened self-interest. But, also, he played upon its fears for its personal security. For he emphasized the Negro now as a creature so embittered and so brutalized by the experience of life forced upon him by America, and so full to bursting of pent-up violence and venom, that every moment he existed he was a menace to any civilized community.

Bigger Thomas, of course, was far and away the most celebrated exemplar of this doctrine of the Negro as a menace to white Americans. It was a flash of rare genius for his creator to open the book about him, *Native Son* (1940), with the unforgettable episode in which Bigger Thomas, his younger brother crouching by, in the one-room apartment occupied by their family, smashes to death a cornered rat. For the story of Bigger Thomas is the story of a cornered rat. Time after time in his novel, Bigger is physically cornered: in the Negro restaurant by the white man and woman, Jan and Mary; in Mary's room by the blind Mrs. Dalton; in his own room by white inquisitors; beside the furnace by white reporters; at long last on an icy rooftop by the white police and the white vigilante horde who have been pursuing him for Mary's murder; and always, in a larger concept, by his own mode of existence in the land of his own birth. Always, too, by this same token, he is a rat, a nauseating human rodent, created so [291] by the society that must bear full responsibility for making him the vicious, repulsive, furtive individual he is.

Native Son opens with Bigger Thomas, in a frenzy of fear and resentment, beating a hated animal to death. *The Street* (1946) closes with Lutie Johnson transformed into a fury by the same emotions, beating another hated animal to death. It is incidental that Bigger Thomas's animal is only a rat, and that Lutie Johnson's is a man. Lutie is like Bigger Thomas, like the protagonist of *If He Hollers Let Him Go* (1946), like the black rioters in *Invisible Man* (1952) and the Negro soldier who wants to kill his captain in *Last of the Conquerors* (1948). Lutie has endured a lifetime of abuse with no saving grace of relief. The wondrous thing is that she has not killed before. Her environment has battered her. It is only an inevitable reflex, as well as a poetic justice, that she should batter her environment.

We still have in Negro fiction the sick Negro, the human individual so full of trauma that he is bound to hurt someone if his precarious equilibrium of emotions is but slightly tipped by chance. But latterly, at this moment of our literary history, this Negro differs from Bigger Thomas in one extremely portentous respect. This Negro is a menace now, not so much to others as to himself. His hate and bitterness at his own defilement by an unjust world have eaten out the inner resources we all should have for establishing social relations with others and a permanent amity with ourselves. He is, this Negro, pre-eminently Rufus Scott of *Another Country* (1962), whom no overtures of good will and understanding, and no attempts at aid from his white associates, nor even the genuine love of his white girl-friend, can absolve from his own traumas, nor rescue from his own suicide. But he is also Richie Stokes, the Eagle of John Williams's *Night Song* (1961), a burnt-out case in his thirties, whose death of an overdose of heroin, however the drug was administered, constitutes as surely a suicide as Rufus Scott's leap into the Hudson from the George Washington Bridge. This newest Negro of the Negroes who have succeeded each other in Negro fiction was foreshadowed by the Invisible Man, whose physical withdrawal to subterranean depths paralleled the beginning of a similar burrowing into his own mind;

by the garrulous, but also existentialist, Cross Damon of Richard Wright's *The Outsider* (1953); by the musings of Hayes Dawkins in *Last of the Conquerors;* and by the whole strange, pensive, non-conformist life and death of Lincoln Williams in *The Narrows* (1953). But he is also part of a literary wave of fashion which is operative in all fiction now, and of which, therefore, it is only natural for Negro fiction to be a part. This newest Negro belongs, that is, to the search for identity in which the typical character of the typical current writer of serious fiction is altogether likely to find himself involved.

In great probability, fewer coincidences could be happier for Negro fiction. You could hardly have failed to notice that this new Negro's Negro is a person, and yet is not, in the sense that is final and compelling and meaningful to us when we measure characters of fiction against people as we actually know them. So far, I have been outlining the literary history associated with this Negro. I have not taken individual Negro characters and looked inside of them and tried to see what makes them tick. My description has been historical and quite sociological. It has not been adequately aesthetic. What does the fictional Negro feel deep within? How does he think? What are his qualities as an inner man? All such issues I have not completely avoided, of course. No one, for example, but an angry and a fear-filled man could be a cornered rat. Yet I have not talked about the fictive people whom I have cited as living people tend to talk of Hamlet when they wonder why he did not kill the king. Of course, I have been generalizing. Still, is there not some other kind of generalizing that I can perform about the Negro's Negro closer to the private workings of his mind and heart than anything I have said hitherto? I think there is. I think, moreover, that all I have said thus far should be only preparation for this nearer, and in our case, final, understanding.

It was once an article of American folklore that Negroes lived, to borrow a phrase [292] from Paul Laurence Dunbar, "in the heart of Happy Hollow." They were creatures, that is, who were well adjusted—I call your attention to the "Hollow" in "Happy Hollow"—to their environment, and, I suppose also in love with it. This article of American folklore Negro literature was never verified. Dunbar himself, who wrote verse and fiction often in dialect, complained because the world would not listen to him when he used the English language with a proper accent. He was never well adjusted to the refusal of white America to recognize in him what he wished to have recognized. He was not contented. He was discontented. And the constant burden of the Negro in America has been, not contentment, but discontent.

This discontent, as has already been intimated here, is very evident in Negro literature. It shows itself in a variety of ways, all eloquent, all insistent, all sincere. There are, for instance, in the entirety of Negro fiction, at most only four or five novels set in the agrarian South. Virtually every Negro character in Negro fiction is urban, or migrant, or both, as if the Negro writer, even for that long period of time when the bulk of the Negro folk were still domiciled in the land of magnolias and cotton-tenancy, could not bring himself to contribute the smallest modicum of comfort to the Plantation Legend of Stephen Foster and *So Red the Rose*. It is, indeed, a Book of Revelation of the Negro writer's consciousness to read Richard Wright's novella, "Big Boy Leaves Home" (1936), a title in which not a word is wasted as a testament of acid bitterness. For Big Boy does not leave home in the approved American fashion. Nor is Big Boy, really, big enough when he does leave home to be striking forth into an adult world under his own responsibility. He is, truly enough, big for his age, an adolescent with a powerful physique. But he is still a boy on a morning when he plays truant in the woods with three other adolescents who seem to be his boon companions. He is cruelly adult, however, before the next day dawns. He has been initiated into a precocious manhood. And his home has performed the ceremony with a special set of rites which it apparently kept in reserve only for innocents like Big Boy. From noon to midnight he has seen two of his companions shot to death and the third one lynched. And he is himself, as the southern sun rises above the smoldering embers of his lynched friend's corpse, being spirited north in a truck.

All of these things happen to Big Boy because he and his companions go swimming. True, they go swimming on property that is posted, and, true, when they finish their sportive trespass a stranger lady who happens to be white happens to see them nude. Who would expect, however, to lose his home and his friends from such a chain of relatively trivial and innocuous incidents? That Big Boy should is an outcome incongruous to a reasonable expectation. Moreover, his own emotions must be mixed as he rides north the morning after. He must be pained. Yet he must also be amused. For he has been a victim, the victim of a joke.

To say that there has been complexity of character construction in Negro literature would be something of an overstatement. To say that there has been little richness of character realization there would be something less. To say, however, that every Negro character of any consequence in Negro literature shares with Big Boy, Big Boy's pain and Big Boy's laughter is to proclaim a fact and, possibly, to make as sweeping a generalization about the Negro's literary Negro as the evidence up to this time will warrant. For there seem to be no Negroes in America, except those too young to receive impressions and then sort them out, who are apparently unaware of color caste. Furthermore, there seem to be no Negroes in America, except those still too young after this sorting out to consider their own relative well-being, who have not become passionately attached to the doctrine of equalitarianism in the American creed. Certainly there are no Negro writers who do not know that they are Negro or have not learned the slogans of American democracy. And so Negro character after Negro character is presented to us in Negro literature just as Big Boy is. That is, virtually every Negro character in Negro literature is a sentimental ironist. For, of course, to experience an outcome [293] incongruous to an expectation and to react to that experience with pain and laughter is, at some level of sensitivity and sophistication, to enter into the realm of irony.

It is a great realm, this realm of irony, a realm of infinite possibilities to the artist. One cannot pretend that Negro artists have exhausted its El Dorado. Indeed, the pity is that Negroes have explored so little in a kingdom so magnificent. For every Negro character, unfortunately, although quite understandably, is experiencing the self-same irony. He is measuring his own life, or some portion of it, against his tantalizing vision of what he supposes that life would be in an America free of color caste. He is Lutie Johnson, colored maid, walking down a street in Connecticut exurbia on an errand for her mistress, checking in her mind the tree-lined thoroughfare against the streets on which she has to live. Or he is friendly Harrietta Williams, growing up in a Kansas town, absorbing the cumulative affront of the progressive withdrawal of association with her by her classmates as they advance in age through high school. Or he is Bob Jones, the Negro leaderman in *If He Hollers Let Him Go,* unable to secure the materials and personnel he urgently needs for the successful performance of his crew in the arsenal of democracy because he is a Negro in a supervisory capacity. It seems fairly well understood by many observers of Negro literature that Negro fiction has only one theme. And it follows, therefore, that a large percentage of Negro writers write their one book and are heard from no more. But it would do no harm, perhaps, if it were likewise understood that Negro literature has, in effect, also only one character, who does one thing— and does that one thing, even, within only fairly narrow limits.

But a group's literature needs more than a single character. For no group, in a universe as much a blooming welter as the one men inhabit, profits any more from a circumscribed perspective than it does from a circumscribed existence. I think you and I both know why the Negro in Negro literature has changed without really changing; why, whether as tragic mulatto, or *bel-esprit,* or bogeyman or artist *manqué,* he is still Big Boy leaving home. The Negro character in Negro literature is, to a certain extent, autobiographical, as, of course, what character is not. We have yet no serious Negro writers who are emancipated from their racial consciousness, even should such an emancipation be desirable. We have as yet, also, no serious Negro writers who have so sublimated their racial consciousness that it may coalesce with the rigorous disciplines of irony at the highest levels of invention and execution.

This lecture is one of a series the University of Michigan has entitled "The American Negro in Transition," and I suppose the transition therein intended is a change of status for the Negro in American life. Surely, in such a sense the title is highly justifiable. But it is highly justifiable in some other senses also. The Negro in transition today is, I pause to remind you happily, the white man in transition today. But the Negro in transition outwardly is also the Negro in transition inwardly. This lecture series could not be, had there not already been a change within the Negro mentality, a change which, in spite of my caution just stated that Negro writers are very Negro, is, incidentally, increasingly manifest in the work of the Negro writer. It is not a sudden change. The Negro mentality has, of course, in America always been in a state of transition. Negro writing, for example, has been improving steadily ever since, with the end of slavery, it became legal over all of the United States for Negroes to read and write. As a breed, Negro writers of the Harlem Renaissance in the nineteen-twenties were superior to their Negro predecessors. Negro writers of today, as a group, are better than their Renaissance forerunners. But there has come, I think, within the very last few years in America, especially on the upper levels of the Negro's collective consciousness, in those portions of the uncommitted cortex where expansion of the self may occur with the most opulent results, an unprecedented furor of beneficent activity. Negroes who, a generation ago, would never have lifted their horizons beyond the fields they tended and the rural church at which they worshipped [294] with fundamentalist fervor have children who, even in the Negro colleges of the South, have learned to think with informed concern of the outer world as if the Cow Palace were across the street and Asia and Africa around some nearby corner. There has been, and continues at, I would hope, an accelerating pace, a corresponding transition in the Negro's artistic consciousness. This consciousness, that is, seems markedly also to have adopted wider horizons, although this adoption has evinced itself in what seems to be a paradox, but is not, in the production in Negro literature of characters who are more sensitive at the same time that they are more convincing. And this is why the search for identity of the characters in Negro literature comes now at such a fortuitous moment. It blends its might and impetus with those of sets of processes intrinsically similar as it interacts with a group culture becoming less parochial and a group art becoming less inartistic. For one cannot create characters whose validity is convincing unless one lives out of one's self and deeply into an infinite variety of people and experiences. I have thought long over the white Vivaldo Moore of *Another Country.* He may well have limitations a white person would detect that are not apparent to me. He has, for that matter, some limitations of which I think I could be aware were I to search for them. But I esteem him as a white man in Negro fiction who puts to shame most of the white people in Negro fiction before his incarnation. Vivaldo is a serious study in character, a man whose desire to write a book and whose judgments on his white friends and American civilization, as well as on the business of living in general, are made real to us even while his role in the tragedy of Rufus Scott and the averted tragedy of Ida, Rufus's sister, assumes in the novel's propagandistic aims the proportions both of imaginative vitality and of humane letters. I would assert, too, that Vivaldo Moore is not alone. Equal to him, in recent Negro literature, is David Hillary, the stricken deer of *Night Song,* who recovers his will to live and to resume his career as an intellectual —to rediscover, in other words, his own identity—largely through his abrasive intimacies with Keel Robinson and Richie Stokes, the two Negro bohemians, comrades in spite of their differences, of John Williams's account of a double resurrection. For Hillary also

is no mere bundle of dogma and doctrine. He thinks and suffers in
ways that invite our suspension of disbelief in the illusion he supports and often, I would hope, our empathic concurrence in his reactions. I would argue that the mere act of creating white characters like Vivaldo and Hillary conveys the Negro writer along the
path of an overdue escape from his ubiquitous one theme and one
character. It does not make the Negro writer whole, of course, but
it does make him less fractional, whether the identity he is seeking
to incorporate into a fictive essence is intended to represent a
white man or a Negro. And thus it enlists the Negro writer, even
more than may have previously been the case for Negro literature,
in the benign cavalcade of the great tradition in our culture and
our literature, the cavalcade which is itself the church militant of
our one American transition most devoutly to be wished, the ref-
ormation of our social order into that New Jerusalem of justice
and opportunity which all men of good will proclaim as the purpose and the end of our democratic dream. [295]

LE ROI JONES

The Myth of a "Negro Literature" *

The mediocrity of what has been called "Negro Literature" is one
of the most loosely held secrets of American culture. From Phyllis
Wheatley to Charles Chesnutt, to the present generation of American Negro writers, the only recognizable accretion of tradition
readily attributable to the black producer of a formal literature in
this country, with a few notable exceptions, has been of an almost
agonizing mediocrity. In most other fields of "high art" in America, with the same few notable exceptions, the Negro contribution
[105] has been, when one existed at all, one of impressive medioc-

* An address given at the American Society for African Culture, March
14, 1962.
SOURCE: LeRoi Jones, *Home: Social Essays* (New York: William Morrow
and Company, Inc., 1966), pp. 105–115. Copyright © 1962, 1963 by LeRoi
Jones. Reprinted by permission of the publisher.

rity. Only in music, and most notably in blues, jazz, and spiritu-als, *i.e.,* "Negro Music," has there been a significantly profound contribution by American Negroes.

There are a great many reasons for the spectacular vapidity of the American Negro's accomplishment in other formal, serious art forms—social, economic, political, etc.—but one of the most per-sistent and aggravating reasons for the absence of achievement among serious Negro artists, except in Negro music, is that in most cases the Negroes who found themselves in a position to pur-sue some art, especially the art of literature, have been members of the Negro middle class, a group that has always gone out of its way to cultivate *any* mediocrity, as long as that mediocrity was guaranteed to prove to America, and recently to the world at large, that they were not really who they were, *i.e.,* Negroes. Negro music alone, because it drew its strengths and beauties out of the depth of the black man's soul, and because to a large extent its traditions could be carried on by the lowest classes of Negroes, has been able to survive the constant and willful dilutions of the black middle class. Blues and jazz have been the only consistent exhibitors of "Negritude" in formal American culture simply be-cause the bearers of its tradition maintained their essential identi-ties as Negroes; in no other art (and I will persist in calling Negro music, Art) has this been possible. Phyllis Wheatley and her pleasant imitations of 18th century English poetry are far and, finally, ludicrous departures from the huge black voices that splin-tered southern nights with their *hollers, chants, arwhoolies,* and *ballits.* The embarrassing and inverted paternalism of Charles Chesnutt and his "refined Afro-American" heroes are far cries from the richness and profundity of the blues. And it is impossi-ble to mention the achievements of the Negro in any area of artis-tic endeavor [106] with as much significance as in spirituals, blues and jazz. There has never been an equivalent to Duke El-lington or Louis Armstrong in Negro writing, and even the best of contemporary literature written by Negroes cannot yet be com-pared to the fantastic beauty of the music of Charlie Parker.

American Negro music from its inception moved logically and powerfully out of a fusion between African musical tradition and the American experience. It was, and continues to be, a natural, yet highly stylized and personal version of the Negro's life in America. It is, indeed, a chronicler of the Negro's movement, from African slave to American slave, from Freedman to Citizen. And the literature of the blues is a much more profound contribution to Western culture than any other literary contribution made by American Negroes. Moreover, it is only recently that formal literature written by American Negroes has begun to approach the literary standards of its model, *i.e.,* the literature of the white middle class. And only Jean Toomer, Richard Wright, Ralph Ellison, and James Baldwin have managed to bring off examples of writing, in this genre, that could succeed in passing themselves off as "serious" writing, in the sense that, say, the work of Somerset Maugham is "serious" writing. That is, serious, if one has never read Herman Melville or James Joyce. And it is part of the tragic naïveté of the middle class (brow) writer, that he has not.

Literature, for the Negro writer, was always an example of "culture." Not in the sense of the more impressive philosophical characteristics of a particular social group, but in the narrow sense of "cultivation" or "sophistication" by an individual within that group. The Negro artist, because of his middle-class background, carried the artificial social burden as the "best and most intelligent" of Negroes, and usually entered into the "serious" arts to exhibit his familiarity [107] with the social graces, *i.e.,* as a method or means of displaying his participation in the "serious" aspects of American culture. To be a writer was to be "cultivated," in the stunted bourgeois sense of the word. It was also to be a "quality" black man. It had nothing to do with the investigation of the human soul. It was, and is, a social preoccupation rather than an aesthetic one. A rather daring way of status seeking. The cultivated Negro leaving those ineffectual philanthropies, Negro colleges, looked at literature merely as another way of gaining prestige in the white world for the Negro middle class. And the literary and artistic models were always those that could be socially acceptable to the white middle class, which automatically limited them to the most spiritually debilitated imitations of literature available. Negro music, to the middle class, black and white, was never socially acceptable. It was shunned by blacks ambitious of "waking up white," as low and degrading. It was shunned by their white models simply because it was produced by blacks. As one of my professors at Howard University protested one day, "It's amazing how much bad taste the blues display." Suffice it to say, it is in part exactly this "bad taste" that has continued to keep Negro music as vital as it is. The abandonment of one's local (*i.e.,* place or group) emotional attachments in favor of the abstract emotional response of what is called "the general public" (which is notoriously white and middle class) has always been the great diluter of any Negro culture. "You're acting like a nigger," was the standard disparagement. I remember being chastised severely for daring to eat a piece of watermelon on the Howard campus. "Do you realize you're sitting near the highway?" is what the man said, "This is the capstone of Negro education." And it is too, in the sense that it teaches the Negro how to make out in the white society, using the agonizing overcompensation [108] of pretending he's also white. James Baldwin's play, *The Amen Corner,* when it appeared at the Howard Players theatre, "set the speech department back ten years," an English professor groaned to me. The play depicted the lives of poor Negroes running a store-front church. Any reference to the Negro-ness of the American Negro has always been frowned upon by the black middle class in their frenzied dash toward the precipice of the American mainstream.

High art, first of all, must reflect the experiences of the human being, the emotional predicament of the man, as he exists, in the defined world of his being. It must be produced from the legitimate emotional resources of the soul in the world. It can *never* be produced by evading these resources or pretending that they do not exist. It can never be produced by appropriating the withered emotional responses of some strictly social idea of humanity. High art, and by this I mean any art that would attempt to describe or characterize some portion of the profound meaningfulness of human life with any finality or truth, cannot be based on the superficialities of human existence. It must issue from *real* categories of human activity, *truthful* accounts of human life, and not fancied accounts of the attainment of cultural privilege by some willingly preposterous apologists for one social "order" or another. Most of the formal literature produced by Negroes in America has never fulfilled these conditions. And aside from Negro music, it is only in the "popular traditions" of the so-called lower class Negro that these conditions are fulfilled as a basis for human life. And it is because of this "separation" between Negro life (as an emotional experience) and Negro art, that, say, Jack Johnson or Ray Robinson is a larger cultural hero than any Negro writer. It is because of this separation, even evasion, of the emotional experience of Negro life, that Jack Johnson is a more modern political symbol than most Negro writers. [109] Johnson's life, as proposed, certainly, by his career, reflects much more accurately the symbolic yearnings for singular values among the great masses of Negroes than any black novelist has yet managed to convey. Where is the Negro-ness of a literature written in imitation of the meanest of social intelligences to be found in American culture, *i.e.,* the white middle class? How can it even begin to express the emotional predicament of black Western man? Such a literature, even if its "characters" *are* black, takes on the emotional barrenness of its model, and the blackness of the characters is like the blackness of Al Jolson, an unconvincing device. It is like using black checkers instead of white. They are still checkers.

The development of the Negro's music was, as I said, direct and instinctive. It was the one vector out of African culture impossible to eradicate completely. The appearance of blues as a native *American* music signified in many ways the appearance of American Negroes where once there were African Negroes. The emotional fabric of the music was colored by the emergence of an American Negro culture. It signified that culture's strength and vitality. In the evolution of form in Negro music it is possible to see not only the evolution of the Negro as a cultural and social element of American culture, but also the evolution of that culture itself. The "Coon Shout" proposed one version of the American Negro—and of America; Ornette Coleman proposes another. But the point is that both these versions are accurate and informed with a legitimacy of emotional concern nowhere available in what is called "Negro Literature," and certainly not in the middlebrow literature of the white American.

The artifacts of African art and sculpture were consciously eradicated by slavery. Any African art that based its validity on the production of an artifact, *i.e.,* some *material* manifestation [110] such as a wooden statue or a woven cloth, had little chance of survival. It was only the more "abstract" aspects of African culture that could continue to exist in slave America. Africanisms still persist in the music, religion, and popular cultural traditions of American Negroes. However, it is not an African art American Negroes are responsible for, but an American one. The traditions of Africa must be utilized within the culture of the American Negro where they *actually* exist, and not because of a defensive rationalization about the *worth* of one's ancestors or an attempt to capitalize on the recent eminence of the "new" African nations. Africanisms do exist in Negro culture, but they have been so translated and transmuted by the American experience that they have become integral parts of that experience.

The American Negro has a definable and legitimate historical tradition, no matter how painful, in America, but it is the only place such a tradition exists, simply because America is the only place the American Negro exists. He is, as William Carlos Williams said, "A pure product of America." The paradox of the Negro experience in America is that it is a separate experience, but inseparable from the complete fabric of American life. The history of Western culture begins for the Negro with the importation of the slaves. It is almost as if all Western history before that must be strictly a learned concept. It is only the American experience that can be a persistent cultural catalyst for the Negro. In a sense, history for the Negro, before America, must remain an emotional abstraction. The cultural memory of Africa informs the Negro's life in America, but it is impossible to separate it from its American transformation. Thus, the Negro writer if he wanted to tap his legitimate cultural tradition should have done it by utilizing the entire spectrum of the American experience from the point of view of [111] the emotional history of the black man in this country: as its victim and its chronicler. The soul of such a man, as it exists outside the boundaries of commercial diversion or artificial social pretense. But without a deep commitment to cultural relevance and intellectual purity this was impossible. The Negro as a writer, was always a social object, whether glorifying the concept of white superiority, as a great many early Negro writers did, or in crying out against it, as exemplified by the stock "protest" literature of the thirties. He never moved into the position where he could propose his own symbols, erect his own personal myths, as any great literature must. Negro writing was always "after the fact," *i.e.,* based on known social concepts within the structure of bourgeois idealistic projections of "their America," and an emotional climate that never really existed.

The most successful fiction of most Negro writing is in its emotional content. The Negro protest novelist postures, and invents a protest quite amenable with the tradition of bourgeois American life. He never reaches the central core of the America which *can* cause such protest. The intellectual traditions of the white middle class prevent such exposure of reality, and the black imitators reflect this. The Negro writer on Negro life in America postures, and invents a Negro life, and an America to contain it. And even most of those who tried to rebel against that *invented* America were trapped because they had lost all touch with the reality of their experience within the *real* America, either because of the hidden emotional allegiance to the white middle class, or because they did not realize where the reality of their experience lay. When the serious Negro writer disdained the "middlebrow" model, as is the case with a few contemporary black American writers, he usually rushed headlong into the groves of the Academy, perhaps the most insidious and clever dispenser of middlebrow standards of excellence under [112] the guise of "recognizable tradition." That such recognizable tradition is necessary goes without saying, but even from the great philosophies of Europe a contemporary usage must be established. No poetry has come out of England of major importance for forty years, yet there are would-be Negro poets who reject the gaudy excellence of 20th century American poetry in favor of disembowelled Academic models of second-rate English poetry, with the notion that somehow it is the only way poetry should be written. It would be better if such a poet listened to Bessie Smith sing *Gimme A Pigfoot,* or listened to the tragic verse of a Billie Holiday, than be content to imperfectly imitate the bad poetry of the ruined minds of Europe. And again, it is this striving for *respectability* that has it so. For an American, black or white, to say that some hideous imitation of Alexander Pope means more to him, emotionally, than the blues of Ray Charles or Lightnin' Hopkins, it would be required for him to have completely disappeared into the American Academy's vision of a Europeanized and colonial American culture, or to be lying. In the end, the same emotional sterility results. It is somehow much more tragic for the black man.

A Negro literature, to be a legitimate product of the Negro experience in America, must get at that experience in exactly the terms America has proposed for it, in its most ruthless identity. Negro reaction to America is as deep a part of America as the root causes of that reaction, and it is impossible to accurately describe that reaction in terms of the American middle class; because for them, the Negro has never really existed, never been glimpsed in anything even approaching the complete reality of his humanity. The Negro writer has to go from where he actually is, completely outside of that conscious white myopia. That the Negro does exist is the point, and as an element of American culture he is completely misunderstood by Americans. The [113] middlebrow, commercial Negro writer assures the white American that, in fact, he doesn't exist, and that if he does, he does so within the perfectly predictable fingerpainting of white bourgeois sentiment and understanding. Nothing could be further from the truth. The Creoles of New Orleans resisted "Negro" music for a time as raw and raucous, because they thought they had found a place within the white society which would preclude their being

Negroes. But they were unsuccessful in their attempts to "disappear" because the whites themselves reminded them that they were still, for all their assimilation, "just coons." And this seems to me an extremely important idea, since it is precisely this bitter insistence that has kept what can be called "Negro Culture" a brilliant amalgam of diverse influences. There was always a border beyond which the Negro could not go, whether musically or socially. There was always a possible limitation to any dilution or excess of cultural or spiritual reference. The Negro could not ever become white and that was his strength; at some point, always, he could not participate in the dominant tenor of the white man's culture, yet he came to understand that culture as well as the white man. It was at this juncture that he had to make use of other resources, whether African, sub-cultural, or hermetic. And it was this boundary, this no-man's-land, that provided the logic and beauty of his music. And this is the only way for the Negro artist to provide his version of America—from that no-man's-land outside the mainstream. A no-man's-land, a black country, completely invisible to white America, but so essentially part of it as to stain its whole being an ominous gray. Were there really a Negro literature, now it could flower. At this point when the whole of Western society might go up in flames, the Negro remains an integral part of that society, but continually outside it, a figure like Melville's Bartleby. He is an American, capable [114] of identifying emotionally with the fantastic cultural ingredients of this society, but he is also, forever, outside that culture, an invisible strength within it, an observer. If there is ever a Negro literature, it must disengage itself from the weak, heinous elements of the culture that spawned it, and use its very existence as evidence of a more profound America. But as long as the Negro writer contents himself with the imitation of the useless ugly inelegance of the stunted middle-class mind, academic or popular, and refuses to look around him and "tell it like it is"—preferring the false prestige of the black bourgeoisie or the deceitful "acceptance" of *buy and sell* America, something never included in the legitimate cultural tradition of "his people"—he will be a failure, and what is worse, not even a significant failure. Just another dead American. [115]

DAVID LITTLEJOHN

from *Black On White*

There is, obviously, no "Negro experience" in America, though some Negro polemicists among our authors may try to make one think so. There are twenty million separate experiences. To take every Negro author, foolish or wise, as a spokesman for the Negro is absurd. It is simply to foster the lumping dehumanization, the stereotyping that has been one of the race's most frustrating debasements. If sophisticated white Americans (and Europeans) have outgrown the singing-and-dancing-fool concept of the Negro, they have not learned a great deal in the process if they now rush to adopt each Negro novelist's new agonized, hate-filled hero as the norm. There may be, realistically speaking, some minimal unity of experience and heritage partaken in by great numbers of American Negroes, although what Lena Horne has in common with an Alabama tenant farmer must be so small as to dissolve into the metaphysical. [157] But to presume anything further, to make any generalization for the Negro race on the basis of these works without the most scrupulous qualification, is to debase new knowledge into something worse than ignorance, to fall back on the We-They simplifications that prolong the war.

All sociological or "race-psychological" interpretations of literature are to some degree illicit, insofar as they discard the essential element of the author's private experience. They must be conducted with exceptional delicacy, with constant reservations, with an implicit confession of their partial, tentative, and fictional nature. All this granted, what can one learn, if not of The American Negro, then of American Negroes from the literature surveyed?

One can learn, first, a great deal about the quality of life in the urban ghettoes of the North, in particular those of Harlem and

SOURCE: David Littlejohn, *Black On White* (New York: Grossman Publishers, Inc., 1966), pp. 157–170. Reprinted by permission of the publisher.

Chicago's South Side. (Our picture of Negro life in the rural or village South today, on the other hand, is dim and distorted. Decreasing numbers of this generation of Negro authors know it firsthand.) One comes to know the crumbling, smelly tenements with their rats and roaches and garbagey, urinous halls; the ubiquitous rent men and numbers runners; the elaborate underground codes of dress and conversation and behavior. In this dismal world, where the only legal jobs open are maid or scrub woman or kitchen help, shoeshine boy, porter, elevator operator, day laborer, or bellboy, the reader is seized with the awareness of a life style so barbarically limited that its only comforts are alcohol, crime, dope, and, especially, sex and religion.

It is clear that sex, for better or worse, becomes something quite open and unashamed, something un-American, [158] in the straitened conditions of the ghetto. The slum-dwelling Negro child is fully and frankly aware of casual sex, of bastardy, of the various manifestations of human depravity to a degree unimaginable by most carefully cushioned white puritans. It seems further clear, however, that most "upstanding," illiberal Negro citizens are as (publicly) unenthusiastic about interracial sex as their paler-faced counterparts.

The fervid, evangelical variety of Negro Christianity ("a fairly desperate emotional business," according to Baldwin) has produced a marvelous subliterature all its own. It has dominated Negro writing from the anonymous spirituals and the poems of James Weldon Johnson to the Harlem store-front congregation stories by Baldwin and Hughes. Tour-de-force imitations of the Negro preacher's sermon abound in American Negro writing, an incantatory progression of Scriptural echoes and images, moving through an associative emotional crescendo. The elaborate Negro funeral is a stock-in-trade setting. There is no question, despite Wright's militant atheism and Baldwin's recantation, of the still dominant place of religion in many Negro lives.

Beyond this, the white reader acquires a great deal of inside information about Negro life. The obsession, for example, with shades of darkness as an index of acceptability continues to torment scores of characters, even in the "freer" literature of the past generation. It is the high-yellow or ivory-beige girls who are always the more desired; a few are even light enough to "pass," which shows where the values come from. Similar is the concern for "good" hair, which writers like John A. Williams have attacked. Langston Hughes writes in his memoirs of [159] A'lelia

Walker, a Gatsby-like party giver of the twenties, who inherited millions from "the pride and glory of the Negro race," Madame Walker's Hair-Straightening Formula.

The Negro caste system, one learns from these works, is elaborate and unique. At the top (not counting international-class athletes and entertainers) is the small group of professional positions still open to the Negro in America—doctors, dentists, and lawyers to the Negro community; undertakers, burial-society and insurance agents; preachers, barbers, and beauticians. One learns something, too, of the Negro Establishment—of the colleges and professors, the organizations and their leaders, the potent Negro press, a Society with its own debutante balls; of the *Amsterdam News, Ebony,* the Theresa Hotel Smart Set.

One learns much, too, of the aggressive enmity of Black against Black. "Assimilationists" fight with Black Nationalists of various breeds—Purlie Victorious with his "ten thousand Queens of Sheba," Assagai of *A Raisin in the Sun,* Ras the Destroyer from *Invisible Man.* Defenders of Booker T. Washington fight the partisans of W. E. B. DuBois. Angry young black men, usually author surrogates, curse the realists, the accommodationists—the Uncle Toms, the White Men's Niggers, the dickty Sugar Hill bourgeoisie with its downtown tastes and manners (and hair). The despised and distrusted Negro Leaders—the term is meant to suggest a white-approved, self-serving type of leader in the Booker Washington tradition, like Ellison's magnificent Dr. Bledsoe, President Wimbush of Redding's *Stranger and Alone*—come in for particular abuse.

At a more urgent level, the white observer is taught [160] a good deal about what Richard Wright called, coolly and acutely, "the ethics of living Jim Crow." There is perhaps no Negro character in the recent works discussed in this survey except Walker Vessels, the gunman in *The Slave,* and Richard Henry in *Blues for Mister Charlie* who is not forced at some time to adopt the degrading role of "nigger" before white men. To get a job, to avoid arrest, to ward off a blow, to buy a ticket, to beg charity or mercy or even justice, the Negro character must forever cringe and grin and play the ignominious part invented for him by white Americans. Some (the Negro Leaders, the operators, the professional Uncle Toms: Gitlow in *Purlie Victorious*) so perfect their acting as to capitalize on it.

A Negro learns to gauge precisely what reaction the alien person facing him desires, and he produces it with disarming artlessness.

(James Baldwin, *Notes of a Native Son*)

Others derive compensation from the useful wedge of moral superiority they achieve over the harassed, blustering whites, who never know when Negroes are acting and when they are not.

Other aspects of peculiarly "racial" psychology are dramatized and discussed as well. The first childhood discovery of one's "inferior" racial status often assumes the stature of a traumatic event. "Race men," Negroes who impulsively "talk race," are regarded in their own society as unhealthy. The more doctrinaire varieties of race men consider hatred of whites as a categorical imperative, as useful as it is necessary. Race pride is encouraged or mocked, depending on one's cynical temperature. Among the lower orders and the populist [161] poets, Joe Louis and Louis Armstrong and Negro History Week and the African heritage may be very important; to the rising black bourgeoisie, jazz and sweet potatoes and all things "Negro" are to be avoided at all possible costs. The existentialist hero and his contemporary creator may scorn them both, but still find a home with Miles Davis and the "authentic" Bessie Smith blues.

At the deepest, most fundamental level, one can note certain psychological obsessions, certain fixations, certain recurring myths that loom very large in Negro literature. Here we are dealing with indirect communication. What one learns is what he intuits and interprets from certain constantly repeated types and patterns, certain ritual events in the writings of American Negroes. It is not important at this level whether or not the myths are true in fact. It *is* important that they seem to be necessary.

One is the myth of Negro endurance I have referred to, a supposed racial duty or trait of Going On Nevertheless, exemplified in the bitter affirmations of the blues and in many Negro poems, or in the work of Langston Hughes. Related to this is the mythical figure of the Negro Mammy or Grandma, all bosom and lap and folk wisdom and stability—Faulkner's Dilsey (*The Sound and the Fury*) is the classic representative, or Ethel Waters on stage or screen. Ellison's Mary, Hughes' Aunt Hager, Lorraine Hansberry's Mama, many others maintain the tradition in Negro writing —a counterpart figure to the lost and angry male.

American Negroes would seem, from this sampling, to be as obsessed by interracial sex myths as stupid Southern white men are supposed to be. More interestingly, [162] they seem to be obsessed by white men's versions of the myths. The whole issue is darkly confusing, but it is astonishing how often Negro authors feel compelled to create scenes in which their heroes are purposely tempted by white women; or by white men *using* their own women to tempt; or scenes of white men who try to force or fake an interracial rape, who put the black hero up to it, compel him to it, and then accuse him of the deed whether he accomplishes it or not. Now, white men may well do such things, or want to do them, for heaven knows what reasons of racial-sexual insecurity. Interracial rape is the South's great symbolic sin, its unspeakable desire (and "The spirit of the South is the spirit of America," according to James Baldwin). It is the professed occasion of two thousand lynchings and the obvious occasion of many millions of brown Negroes. But why Negro writers should want to dramatize this sordid white desire is not altogether clear.

Similar to this is the use by Negro writers of white men's abuse; many seem to enjoy "playing white men," and cursing out their "nigger" heroes with obscene and excessive abandon. The use of murder as the symbolic act, for a final example, is also fairly frequent: murder, *real* murder, by Negro of white as a kind of alternative to love—as if it were the only possible honest communication between the races. This is all distinctly race-war material. As to what, specifically, it may signify, although I have my theories like anyone else, I am incompetent to speculate in print.

Finally, this reading can be for the white reader an education in the history and folklore, the suffering and dreams of American Negroes. What one gains will be in direct measure to his ignorance at the start: the story [163] of the slave ships, the character of the American police, and the intraracial Negro codes were among my lessons. It could all have been acquired, I suppose, from the vast library of non-fictional texts about the Negro in America; but this, for me, was a livelier, a less forgettable way to learn.

This, then, is a glimpse of what one can learn from the writings of American Negroes. And as there is no one "Negro experience," there is also, obviously, no "Negro writer." Most writers who are Negroes hate the deindividuation, the "Groupthink" such essays as this propose (though they themselves—e.g., Negro writers' conferences, etc.—are among the first to use the category). Most writers of any breed would despise it—a writer is by definition a solitary being. Everything one says about "the Negro writer" is false to some degree. There are personalities subtle and obvious, mean and magnanimous, imaginative and dense, narrow and far-seeing, self-deluded and self-aware among Negro writers, just as there are among all manner of human beings. There are stunted, clumsy, crayon-scrawl "artists" with their primitive morality-play stories. There are untrained and undisciplined scandal-drooling naturalists. There are many non-thinkers. The range of possibility includes Ellison and Brooks; and Willard Motley, Baldwin at his best, and Baldwin at his worst. Literary history is too full already of formulaic generalizations about groups of writers for us to add any more about Negroes.

And yet, and yet—a few conclusions, a very few, may be drawn about "the Negro writer" in America, present and future. He *is* different, both because he is black and [164] because he is a writer. "His" experience has been different—both from that of the white writers and from that of his non-writing fellows.

As an American writer, first of all, he will be, of course, lonely and introverted. He will be misunderstood by other people (black and white), misread by critics, harassed or unappreciated by his publishers, and bragged about by his mother. He will feel, much of the time, cut off from other men. As a Negro, he may blame this on his color; but it is only the condition of most serious American writers. His heroes are likely to be egotists like himself, "strangers and alone"; their Negroness may only symbolize or intensify *his* dilemma as a writer. The ranks of Negro authors, like the ranks of white authors, will have their quota of "first novelists," of family-thwarted, college-bred, sexually insecure solipsists who feel driven to make books out of their own unimportant stories and fantasies. They should be taken no more seriously for being Negro. A Negro author *will* be, of course, atypical of his race; there is something very "white middle class" in the very notion of wanting to publish a book. The profession of writing (whether practiced full or part time, whether remunerative or not) is by definition cerebral, Western, leisured, and leisure-class oriented. All Negroes who do not write, even relatives and friends, are going to seem alien to a Negro who does.

The Negro writer, moreover—especially the novelist—stands the same risk as every other American writer of losing his openness and honesty, the more a professional he becomes; of losing his original purpose and identity; of turning from writer to Writer. His first book, let us say, is done: *Native Son, Invisible Man, Go* [165] *Tell It on the Mountain.* Gradually, he becomes a Commodity, then a Celebrity; he attends press parties, signs autographs, reads from his works, participates in college symposia (on the Negro), gives largely of his Opinions, talks literary gossip, writes about writers (Ellison on Wright, Baldwin on Mailer).

David Littlejohn

It can happen to anyone, and there is reason in their last or latest works to fear that it has happened to each of America's three leading Negro novelists. The Negro writer may be no *more* susceptible than the white, but he is no less.

But as a writer who is also a Negro, he may have special problems as well, obstacles to overcome that no white writer will ever know. The problems, moreover, are rarely those discussed at Negro writers' conferences: whether to identify with America or Africa, whether to write of Negroes or whites, for what audience he should write, his place in the democratic myth, the nature of America, *négritude,* and so forth. The man to whom such questions are real questions is probably more a *conférencier* than a writer.

Consider: how many Negro authors have ever been able to create, alive from within, a convincing, living white man—except as a ritual, negative self-projection, or a crude stick figure? Some, perhaps: Baldwin, Ann Petry. How many, to take it further, have created *any* person, black or white, wholly other than themselves? Ann Petry again, Owen Dodson in his Deaconess Quick; a few others. Consider then, the central place of autobiography in Negro literature. Richard Wright's and Katherine Dunham's are small classics. James Weldon Johnson's, Langston Hughes', and Saunders Redding's are all richly full, and readable. The most recent — [166] Claude Brown's, Horace Cayton's, Malcolm X's—are among the most moving of all. But there are scores of others, and more coming out every year: *every* Negro who achieves the most marginal degree of fame feels compelled to tell his story, however little it may differ from the next man's. This autobiographical insistence, this locked-in-the-self imprisonment, suggests that, for most American Negroes, the day of artistic objectivity and detachment has not yet arrived. (The finest, most understanding piece of race war literature ever written—*A Passage to India*—was composed by an upper class Englishman in 1924.) Just how many Negro imaginations, given the environmental limits of American prejudice, *can* make the break and soar free? Or have their owners perhaps other, more necessary things to do first?

The Negro writer may feel, honestly and honorably, that he has quite a number of tasks to fulfill that a white writer would never dream of: a deal of seeking, searching, puzzling out answers about himself, of ritual attacking and exorcising. There is still, he may vividly feel, a war on.

From this racial war that is America most white writers, even

Southern white writers, can opt out; that is the privilege of the comfortably more powerful combatant. For the embattled under-dog, it is not so easy, even if he is a pacifist at heart. He may feel obliged, like some demon-driven character out of Faulkner, to talk about his history, his sufferings, his burden, to play over and over his oppressively limited range of theme.

These may be for him ritual stages, psychologically or sociolog-ically necessary, that must be gotten through. The Negro writer has, in addition to every writer's burden of mother, father, frustra-tions, nightmares, and [167] shames, burdens all of his own, im-posed by America, that he has to deal with or be dishonest—which is to say, or not be a writer. (All things considered, it is astonishing not that there are so *few* Negro writers in the United States, but so many.)

He *may* still overcome them. Some already have, to quiet de-grees. One Negro (two, three) may soon come to terms with him-self, with his undefinable, unbalanced, senseless American "place"; and then find himself able to sit down and concentrate on something more objective than his own unfortunate story.

We will then, I hope, have less of the frenzied war literature, the now necessary dramatizations of The Problem, with their apocalyptic insistence on the ritual battling of Black vs. White, of We vs. They; and more unfrenzied, sympathetic renderings of the total life of non-militant, non-warring Americans who happen to be Negroes. It would help us all. The great Irish writers, for a precedent, oppressed, militant, suffering, did themselves and their readers immortal service in defining so completely the life style, the inner necessity of their people.

But most Negroes—including most Negro writers—seem still to be too uncertain of, too unhappy about their own racial identity to be able to celebrate the Life of their People. Many still half-want to deny their people (which is understandable, when the ma-jority despises them), to become white, in fact, to adopt white val-ues, to "assimilate." So they cannot, will not write of Negro life *except* as a war against the envied and hated white majority. It is one thing to want to be free; it is quite another, and sick, to want to be a different color. It makes for neurosis, not for art. But America, all of it, [168] goes on hating blackness, fosters the neurosis, and holds off the day of a true Negro art.

But if no Negro yet has achieved sufficient stability and content to write fully and comfortably of Negro life, this is no reason to conclude that none will. Faulkner had, at least, ambivalent feelings about the South, but yet was able to become, sympathetically, a whole world full of Southerners.

Still, Faulkner was not consciously waging a hopeless war. He was relatively content with what he was. He did not, one assumes, have to go on night and day fighting the battle of himself. The Dostoevskys and Joyces and Bellows and Faulkners are (were) *pleased,* one infers, to be Russian and Irish and Jewish and Southern American. It seems almost insanely difficult for a Negro in America to come to this stage of self-acceptance, self-contentment. Ralph Ellison protests that *he* has; but his protest is so exceptional that one tends (unfairly) to doubt.

Ideally, I think he will come, a Negro pleased to be a Negro in America, despite all; one willing to love, live, and recreate for the world the lives of his people. It is a stirring thought that one man could affect the necessary self-redefinition for millions of people, the acceptance of a racial identity.

Then—and only then—after that as yet unreached stage is attained, we can hope, after perhaps another generation, for a Negro writer who can turn his sympathies outward, and acquire an understanding of suffering whites or Orientals, people everywhere; a man who can reach out and know by sympathy the sufferings of others, possessed (like the mythical twentieth-century Jew) of a unique and world-wide sympathy for [169] suffering, for the inner frustrations of all manner of men. He, this unborn Negro writer, may teach the rest of America—James Baldwin has served, after all, as a crude, first-stage national conscience—what suffering, endurance, uncertainty, desperation, fury, communal understanding, and pity are like. Like the American Jew, he may retain of his racial identity then little more than an impulsive sense of universal moral justice.

As some men are bettered by oppression, so the real humanists of a future America, Richard Wright predicted (in *White Man, Listen!*), will be the Negroes who can love. As the American Dilemma makes clear, the Negro is already far freer of psychological burdens than his puzzled white master, and will be far readier to assume the role of national conscience, "after the war."

To sum up: we wait, still, for a Negro writer who can tell us, truly, what it is like to be a Negro. But they have other things to do, first: they have a war to fight. The Jews became no one's conscience-dictators until after Hitler, who came after more than a thousand years of only slightly less holocaustic and dehumanizing oppression. American Negro writers must first find themselves, and rest content with what they find, before they can tell us about it—or about ourselves. [170]

LARRY NEAL

The Black Arts Movement

1

The Black Arts Movement is radically opposed to any concept of the artist that alienates him from his community. Black Art is the aesthetic and spiritual sister of the Black Power concept. As such, it envisions an art that speaks directly to the needs and aspirations of Black America. In order to perform this task, the Black Arts Movement proposes a radical reordering of the western cultural aesthetic. It proposes a separate symbolism, mythology, critique, and iconology. The Black Arts and the Black Power concept both relate broadly to the Afro-American's desire for self-determination and nationhood. Both concepts are nationalistic. One is concerned with the relationship between art and politics; the other with the art of politics.

Recently, these two movements have begun to merge: the political values inherent in the Black Power concept are now finding concrete expression in the aesthetics of Afro-American dramatists, poets, choreographers, musicians, and novelists. A main tenet of Black Power is the necessity for Black people to define the world in their own terms. The Black artist has made the same point in the context of aesthetics. The two movements postulate that there are in fact and in spirit two Americas—one black, one white. The Black artist takes this to mean that his primary duty is to speak to the spiritual and cultural needs of Black people. Therefore, the main thrust of this new breed of contemporary writers is to confront the contradictions arising out of the Black

Source: *The Drama Review*, XII (Summer, 1968), T40, 29–39. Copyright © 1968 by *The Drama Review*. Reprinted by permission of the author and publisher. All rights reserved.

man's experience in the racist West. Currently, these writers are re-evaluating western aesthetics, the traditional role of the writer, and the social function of art. Implicit in this re-evaluation is the need to develop a "black aesthetic." It is the opinion of many Black writers, I among them, that the Western aesthetic has run its course: it is impossible to construct anything meaningful within its decaying structure. We advocate a cultural revolution in art and ideas. The cultural values inherent in western history must either be radicalized or destroyed, and we will probably find that even radicalization is impossible. In fact, what is needed is a whole new system of ideas. Poet Don L. Lee expresses it:

. . . We must destroy Faulkner, dick, jane, and other perpetuators of evil. It's time for DuBois, Nat Turner, and Kwame Nkrumah. As Frantz Fanon points out: destroy the culture and you destroy the people. This must not happen. Black artists are [29] culture stabilizers; bringing back old values, and introducing new ones. Black Art will talk to the people and with the will of the people stop impending "protective custody."

The Black Arts Movement eschews "protest" literature. It speaks directly to Black people. Implicit in the concept of "protest" literature, as Brother Knight has made clear, is an appeal to white morality:

Now any Black man who masters the technique of his particular art form, who adheres to the white aesthetic, and who directs his work toward a white audience is, in one sense, protesting. And implicit in the act of protest is the belief that a change will be forthcoming once the masters are aware of the protestor's "grievance" (the very word connotes begging, supplications to the gods). Only when that belief has faded and protestings end, will Black art begin.

Brother Knight also has some interesting statements about the development of a "Black aesthetic":

Unless the Black artist establishes a "Black aesthetic" he will have no future at all. To accept the white aesthetic is to accept and validate a society that will not allow him to live. The Black artist must create new forms and new values, sing new songs (or purify old ones); and along with other Black authorities, he must create a new history, new symbols, myths and legends (and purify old ones by fire). And the Black artist, in creating his own aesthetic, must be accountable for it only to the Black people. Further, he must hasten his own dissolution as an individual (in the Western sense)—painful though the process may be, having been breast-fed the poison of "individual experience."

When we speak of a "Black aesthetic" several things are meant. First, we assume that there is already in existence the basis for such an aesthetic. Essentially, it consists of an African-American cultural tradition. But this aesthetic is finally, by implication, broader than that tradition. It encompasses most of the usable elements of Third World culture. The motive behind the Black aesthetic is the destruction of the white thing, the destruction of white ideas, and white ways of looking at the world. The new aesthetic is mostly predicated on an Ethics which asks the question: whose vision of the world is finally more meaningful, ours or the white oppressors'? What is truth? Or more precisely, whose truth shall we express, that of the oppressed or of the oppressors? These are basic questions. Black intellectuals of previous decades failed to ask them. Further, national and international affairs demand that we appraise the world in terms of our own interests. It is clear that the question of human survival is at the core of contemporary experience. The Black artist must address himself to this reality in the strongest terms possible. In a context of world upheaval, ethics and aesthetics must interact positively and be consistent with the demands for a more spiritual world. Consequently, the Black Arts Movement is an ethical movement. Ethical, that is, from the viewpoint of the oppressed. And much of the oppression confronting the Third World and Black America is directly traceable to the Euro-American cultural sensibility. This sensibility, anti-human in nature, has, until recently, dominated the psyches of most Black artists and intellectuals; it must be destroyed before the Black creative artist can have a meaningful role in the transformation of society.

It is this natural reaction to an alien sensibility that informs the cultural attitudes of the Black Arts and the Black Power movement. It is a profound ethical sense that [30] makes a Black artist question a society in which art is one thing and the actions of men another. The Black Arts Movement believes that your ethics and your aesthetics are one. That the contradiction between ethics and aesthetics in western society is symptomatic of a dying culture.

The term "Black Arts" is of ancient origin, but it was first used in a positive sense by LeRoi Jones:

> We are unfair
> And unfair
> We are black magicians

> Black arts we make
> in black labs of the heart
>
> The fair are fair
> and deathly white
>
> The day will not save them
> And we own the night

There is also a section of the poem "Black Dada Nihilismus" that carries the same motif. But a fuller amplification of the nature of the new aesthetics appears in the poem "Black Art":

> Poems are bullshit unless they are
> teeth or trees or lemons piled
> on a step. Or black ladies dying
> of men leaving nickel hearts
> beating them down. Fuck poems
> and they are useful, would they shoot
> come at you, love what you are,
> breathe like wrestlers, or shudder
> strangely after peeing.We want live
> words of the hip world, live flesh &
> coursing blood. Hearts and Brains
> Souls splintering fire. We want poems
> like fists beating niggers out of Jocks
> or dagger poems in the slimy bellies
> of the owner-jews . . .

Poetry is a concrete function, an action. No more abstractions. Poems are physical entities: fists, daggers, airplane poems, and poems that shoot guns. Poems are transformed from physical objects into personal forces:

> . . . Put it on him poem. Strip him naked
> to the world. Another bad poem cracking
> steel knuckles in a jewlady's mouth
> Poem scream poison gas on breasts in green berets . . .

Then the poem affirms the integral relationship between Black Art and Black people:

> . . . Let Black people understand
> that they are the lovers and the sons [31]
> of lovers and warriors and sons
> of warriors Are poems & poets &
> all the loveliness here in the world

It ends with the following lines, a central assertion in both the Black Arts Movement and the philosophy of Black Power:

> We want a black poem. And a
> Black World.
> Let the world be a Black Poem
> And let All Black People Speak This Poem
> Silently
> Or LOUD

The poem comes to stand for the collective conscious and unconscious of Black America—the real impulse in back of the Black Power movement, which is the will toward self-determination and nationhood, a radical reordering of the nature and function of both art and the artist.

2

In the spring of 1964, LeRoi Jones, Charles Patterson, William Patterson, Clarence Reed, Johnny Moore, and a number of other Black artists opened the Black Arts Repertoire Theatre School. They produced a number of plays including Jones' *Experimental Death Unit # One, Black Mass, Jello,* and *Dutchman.* They also initiated a series of poetry readings and concerts. These activities represented the most advanced tendencies in the movement and were of excellent artistic quality. The Black Arts School came under immediate attack by the New York power structure. The Establishment, fearing Black creativity, did exactly what it was expected to do—it attacked the theatre and all of its values. In the meantime, the school was granted funds by OEO through HAR-YOU-ACT. Lacking a cultural program itself, HARYOU turned to the only organization which addressed itself to the needs of the community. In keeping with its "revolutionary" cultural ideas, the Black Arts Theatre took its programs into the streets of Harlem. For three months, the theatre presented plays, concerts, and poetry readings to the people of the community. Plays that shattered the illusions of the American body politic, and awakened Black people to the meaning of their lives.

Then the hawks from the OEO moved in and chopped off the funds. Again, this should have been expected. The Black Arts Theatre stood in radical opposition to the feeble attitudes about culture of the "War On Poverty" bureaucrats. And later, because of internal problems, the theatre was forced to close. But the Black Arts group proved that the community could be served by a valid and dynamic art. It also proved that there was a definite need for a cultural revolution in the Black community.

With the closing of the Black Arts Theatre, the implications of what Brother Jones and his colleagues were trying to do took on even more significance. Black Art groups sprang up on the West Coast and the idea spread to Detroit, Philadelphia, [32] Jersey City, New Orleans, and Washington, D.C. Black Arts movements began on the campuses of San Francisco State College, Fisk University, Lincoln University, Hunter College in the Bronx, Columbia University, and Oberlin College. In Watts, after the rebellion, Maulana Karenga welded the Blacks Arts Movement into a cohesive cultural ideology which owed much to the work of LeRoi Jones. Karenga sees culture as the most important element in the struggle for self-determination:

Culture is the basis of all ideas, images and actions. To move is to move culturally, i.e. by a set of values given to you by your culture.

Without a culture Negroes are only a set of reactions to white people.

The seven criteria for culture are:

1. Mythology
2. History
3. Social Organization
4. Political Organization
5. Economic Organization
6. Creative Motif
7. Ethos

In drama, LeRoi Jones represents the most advanced aspects of the movement. He is its prime mover and chief designer. In a poetic essay entitled "The Revolutionary Theatre," he outlines the iconology of the movement:

The Revolutionary Theatre should force change: it should be change. (All their faces turned into the lights and you work on them black nigger magic, and cleanse them at having seen the ugliness. And if the beautiful see themselves, they will love themselves.) We are preaching virtue again, but by that to mean NOW, toward what seems the most constructive use of the word.

The theatre that Jones proposes is inextricably linked to the Afro-American political dynamic. And such a link is perfectly consistent with Black America's contemporary demands. For theatre is potentially the most social of all of the arts. It is an integral part of the socializing process. It exists in direct relationship to the audience it claims to serve. The decadence and inanity of the contemporary American theatre is an accurate reflection of the state of American society. Albee's *Who's Afraid of Virginia Woolf?* is very American: sick white lives in a homosexual hell hole. The theatre of white America is escapist, refusing to confront concrete reality. Into this cultural emptiness come the musicals, an up-tempo version of the same stale lives. And the use of Negroes in such plays as *Hello Dolly* and *Hallelujah Baby* does not alert their nature; it compounds the problem. These plays are simply hipper versions of the minstrel show. They present Negroes acting out the hang-ups of middle-class white America. Consequently, the American theatre is a palliative prescribed to bourgeois patients who refuse to see the world as it is. Or, more crucially, as the world sees them. It is no accident, therefore, that the most "important" plays come from Europe—Brecht, Weiss, and Ghelderode. And even these have begun to run dry.

The Black Arts theatre, the threatre of LeRoi Jones, is a radical alternative to the sterility of the American theatre. It is primarily a theatre of the Spirit, confronting the Black man in his interaction with his brothers and with the white thing. [33]

Our theatre will show victims so that their brothers in the audience will be better able to understand that they are the brothers of victims, and that they themselves are blood brothers. And what we show must cause the blood to rush, so that prerevolutionary temperaments will be bathed in this blood, and it will cause their deepest souls to move, and they will find themselves tensed and clenched, even ready to die, at what the soul has been taught. We will scream and cry, murder, run through the streets in agony, if it means some soul will be moved, moved to actual life understanding of what the world is, and what it ought to be. We are preaching virtue and feeling, and a natural sense of the self in the world. All men live in the world, and the world ought to be a place for them to live.

The victims in the world of Jones' early plays are Clay, murdered by the white bitch-goddess in *Dutchman,* and Walker Vessels, the revolutionary in *The Slave*. Both of these plays present Black men in transition. Clay, the middle-class Negro trying to get himself a little action from Lula, digs himself and his own truth only to get murdered after telling her like it really is:

Just let me bleed you, you loud whore, and one poem vanished. A whole people neurotics, struggling to keep from being sane. And the only thing that would cure the neurosis would be your murder. Simple as that. I mean if I murdered you, then other white people would understand me. You understand? No. I guess not. If Bessie Smith had killed some white people she wouldn't needed that music. She could have talked very straight and plain about the world. Just straight two and two are four. Money. Power. Luxury. Like that. All of them. Crazy niggers turning their back on sanity. When all it needs is that simple act. Just murder. Would make us all sane.

But Lula understands, and she kills Clay first. In a perverse way it is Clay's nascent knowledge of himself that threatens the existence of Lula's idea of the world. Symbolically, and in fact, the relationship between Clay (Black America) and Lula (white America) is rooted in the historical castration of black manhood. And in the twisted psyche of white America, the Black man is both an object of love and hate. Analogous attitudes exist in most Black Americans, but for decidedly different reasons. Clay is doomed when he allows himself to participate in Lula's "fantasy" in the first place. It is the fantasy to which Frantz Fanon alludes in *The Wretched Of The Earth* and *Black Skins, White Mask:* the native's belief that he can acquire the oppressor's power by acquiring his symbols, one of which is the white woman. When Clay finally digs himself it is too late.

Walker Vessels, in *The Slave,* is Clay reincarnated as the revolutionary confronting problems inherited from his contact with white culture. He returns to the home of his ex-wife, a white woman, and her husband, a literary critic. The play is essentially about Walker's attempt to destroy his white past. For it is the past, with all of its painful memories, that is really the enemy of the revolutionary. It is impossible to move until history is either recreated or comprehended. Unlike Todd, in Ralph Ellison's *Invisible Man,* Walker cannot fall outside history. Instead, Walker demands a confrontation with history, a final shattering of bullshit illusions. His only salvation lies in confronting the physical and psychological forces that have made him and his people powerless. Therefore, he comes to understand that the world must be restructured along spiritual imperatives. But in the interim it is basically a question of *who* has power:

EASLEY. You're so wrong about everything. So terribly, sickeningly wrong. What can you change? What do you hope to change? Do you think Negroes are [34] better people than whites . . . that they can govern a society *better* than whites? That they'll be more judicious or more tolerant? Do you think they'll make fewer mistakes? I mean really, if the Western white man has proved one thing . . . it's the futility of modern society. So the have-not peoples become the haves. Even so, will that change the essential functions of the world? Will there be more love or beauty in the world . . . . more knowledge . . . because of it?

WALKER. Probably. Probably there will be more . . . if more people have a chance to understand what it is. But that's not even the point. It comes down to baser human endeavor than any social-political thinking. What does it matter if there's more love or beauty? Who the fuck cares? Is that what the Western ofay thought while he was ruling . . . that his rule somehow brought more love and beauty into the world? Oh, he might have thought that concomitantly, while sipping a gin rickey and scratching his ass . . . but that was not ever the point. Not even on the Crusades. The point is that you had your chance, darling, now these other folks have theirs. *Quietly.* Now they have theirs.

EASLEY. God, what an ugly idea.

This confrontation between the black radical and the white liberal is symbolic of larger confrontations occurring between the Third World and Western society. It is a confrontation between the colonizer and the colonized, the slavemaster and the slave. Implicit in Easley's remarks is the belief that the white man is culturally and politically superior to the Black Man. Even though Western society has been traditionally violent in its relation with the Third World, it sanctimoniously deplores violence or self assertion on the part of the enslaved. And the Western mind, with clever rationalizations, equates the violence of the oppressed with the violence of the oppressor. So that when the native preaches self-determination, the Western white man cleverly misconstrues it to mean hate of *all* white men. When the Black political radical warns his people not to trust white politicians of the left and the right, but instead to organize separately on the basis of power, the white man cries: "racism in reverse." Or he will say, as many of them do today: "We deplore both white and black racism." As if the two could be equated.

There is a minor element in *The Slave* which assumes great importance in a later play entitled *Jello*. Here I refer to the emblem of Walker's army: a red-mouthed grinning field slave. The revolutionary army has taken one of the most hated symbols of the

Afro-American past and radically altered its meaning.* This is the supreme act of freedom, available only to those who have liberated themselves psychically. Jones amplifies this inversion of emblem and symbol in *Jello* by making Rochester (Ratfester) of the old Jack Benny (Penny) program into a revolutionary nationalist. Ratfester, ordinarily the supreme embodiment of the Uncle Tom Clown, surprises Jack Penny by turning on the other side of the nature of the Black man. He skillfully, and with an evasive black humor, robs Penny of all of his money. But Ratfester's actions are "moral." That is to say, Ratfester is getting his back pay; [35] payment of a long over-due debt to the Black man. Ratfester's sensibilities are different from Walker's. He is *blues people* smiling and shuffling while trying to figure out how to destroy the white thing. And like the blues man, he is the master of the understatement. Or in the Afro-American folk tradition, he is the Signifying Monkey, Shine, and Stagolee all rolled into one. There are no stereotypes any more. History has killed Uncle Tom. Because even Uncle Tom has a breaking point beyond which he will not be pushed. Cut deeply enough into the most docile Negro, and you will find a conscious murderer. Behind the lyrics of the blues and the shuffling porter loom visions of white throats being cut and cities burning.

Jones' particular power as a playwright does not rest solely on his revolutionary vision, but is instead derived from his deep lyricism and spiritual outlook. In many ways, he is fundamentally more a poet than a playwright. And it is his lyricism that gives body to his plays. Two important plays in this regard are *Black Mass* and *Slave Ship. Black Mass* is based on the Muslim myth of Yacub. According to this myth, Yacub, a Black scientist, developed the means of grafting different colors of the Original Black Nation until a White Devil was created. In *Black Mass,* Yacub's experiments produce a raving White Beast who is condemned to the coldest regions of the North. The other magicians implore Yacub to cease his experiments. But he insists on claiming the pri-

---

* In Jones' study of Afro-American music, *Blues People,* we find the following observation: ". . . Even the adjective *funky,* which once meant to many Negroes merely a stink (usually associated with sex), was used to qualify the music as meaningful (the word became fashionable and is now almost useless). The social implication, then, was that even the old stereotype of a distinctive Negro smell that white America subscribed to could be turned against white America. For this smell now, real or not, was made a valuable characteristic of 'Negro-ness.' And 'Negro-ness,' by the fifties, for many Negroes (and whites) was the only strength left to American culture."

macy of scientific knowledge over spiritual knowledge. The sensibility of the White Devil is alien, informed by lust and sensuality. The Beast is the consummate embodiment of evil, the beginning of the historical subjugation of the spiritual world.

Black Mass takes place in some pre-historical time. In fact, the concept of time, we learn, is the creation of an alien sensibility, that of the Beast. This is a deeply weighted play, a colloquy on the nature of man, and the relationship between legitimate spiritual knowledge and scientific knowledge. It is LeRoi Jones' most important play mainly because it is informed by a mythology that is wholly the creation of the Afro-American sensibility.

Further, Yacub's creation is not merely a scientific exercise. More fundamentally, it is the aesthetic impulse gone astray. The Beast is created merely for the sake of creation. Some artists assert a similar claim about the nature of art. They argue that art need not have a function. It is against this decadent attitude toward art—ramified throughout most of Western society—that the play militates. Yacub's real crime, therefore, is the introduction of a meaningless evil into a harmonious universe. The evil of the Beast is pervasive, corrupting everything and everyone it touches. What was beautiful is twisted into an ugly screaming thing. The play ends with destruction of the holy place of the Black Magicians. Now the Beast and his descendants roam the earth. An off-stage voice chants a call for the Jihad to begin. It is then that myth merges into legitimate history, and we, the audience, come to understand that all history is merely someone's version of mythology.

Slave Ship presents a more immediate confrontation with history. In a series of expressionistic tableaux it depicts the horrors and the madness of the Middle Passage. It then moves through the period of slavery, early attempts at revolt, tendencies toward Uncle Tom-like reconciliation and betrayal, and the final act of liberation. There is no definite plot (LeRoi calls it a pageant), just a continuous rush of sound, groans, screams, and souls wailing for freedom and relief from suffering. This [36] work has special affinities with the New Music of Sun Ra, John Coltrane, Albert Ayler, and Ornette Coleman. Events are blurred, rising and falling in a stream of sound. Almost cinematically, the images flicker and fade against a heavy back-drop of rhythm. The language is spare, stripped to the essential. It is a play which almost totally eliminates the need for a text. It functions on the basis of movement and energy—the dramatic equivalent of the New Music.

3

LeRoi Jones is the best known and the most advanced playwright of the movement, but he is not alone. There are other excellent playwrights who express the general mood of the Black Arts ideology. Among them are Ron Milner, Ed Bullins, Ben Caldwell, Jimmy Stewart, Joe White, Charles Patterson, Charles Fuller, Aisha Hughes, Carol Freeman, and Jimmy Garrett.

Ron Milner's *Who's Got His Own* is of particular importance. It strips bare the clashing attitudes of a contemporary Afro-American family. Milner's concern is with legitimate manhood and morality. The family in *Who's Got His Own* is in search of its conscience, or more precisely its own definition of life. On the day of his father's death, Tim and his family are forced to examine the inner fabric of their lives: the lies, self-deceits, and sense of powerlessness in a white world. The basic conflict, however, is internal. It is rooted in the historical search for black manhood. Tim's mother is representative of a generation of Christian Black women who have implicitly understood the brooding violence lurking in their men. And with this understanding, they have interposed themselves between their men and the object of that violence—the white man. Thus unable to direct his violence against the oppressor, the Black man becomes more frustrated and the sense of powerlessness deepens. Lacking the strength to be a man in the white world, he turns against his family. So the oppressed, as Fanon explains, constantly dreams violence against his oppressor, while killing his brother on fast weekends.

Tim's sister represents the Negro woman's attempt to acquire what Eldridge Cleaver calls "ultrafemininity." That is, the attributes of her white upper-class counterpart. Involved here is a rejection of the body-oriented life of the working class Black man, symbolized by the mother's traditional religion. The sister has an affair with a white upper-class liberal, ending in abortion. There are hints of lesbianism, i.e. a further rejection of the body. The sister's life is a pivotal factor in the play. Much of the stripping away of falsehood initiated by Tim is directed at her life, which they have carefully kept hidden from the mother.

Tim is the product of the new Afro-American sensibility, informed by the psychological revolution now operative within Black America. He is a combination ghetto soul brother and militant intellectual, very hip and slightly flawed himself. He would change the world, but without comprehending the particular history that produced his "tyrannical" father. And he cannot be the man his father was—not until he truly understands his father. He must understand why his father allowed himself to be insulted daily by the "honky" types on the job; why he took a demeaning job in the "shit-house"; and why he spent on his family the violence that he should have directed against the white man. In short, Tim must confront the [37] history of his family. And that is exactly what happens. Each character tells his story, exposing his falsehood to the other until a balance is reached.

Who's Got His Own is not the work of an alienated mind. Milner's main thrust is directed toward unifying the family around basic moral principles, toward bridging the "generation gap." Other Black playwrights, Jimmy Garrett for example, see the gap as unbridgeable.

Garrett's *We Own the Night* takes place during an armed insurrection. As the play opens we see the central characters defending a section of the city against attacks by white police. Johnny, the protagonist, is wounded. Some of his Brothers intermittently fire at attacking forces, while others look for medical help. A doctor arrives, forced at gun point. The wounded boy's mother also comes. She is a female Uncle Tom who berates the Brothers and their cause. She tries to get Johnny to leave. She is hysterical. The whole idea of Black people fighting white people is totally outside of her orientation. Johnny begins a vicious attack on his mother, accusing her of emasculating his father—a recurring theme in the sociology of the Black community. In Afro-American literature of previous decades the strong Black mother was the object of awe and respect. But in the new literature her status is ambivalent and laced with tension. Historically, Afro-American women have had to be the economic mainstays of the family. The oppressor allowed them to have jobs while at the same time limiting the economic mobility of the Black man. Very often, therefore, the woman's aspirations and values are closely tied to those of the white power structure and not to those of her man. Since he cannot provide for his family the way white men do, she despises his weakness, tearing into him at every opportunity until, very often, there is nothing left but a shell.

The only way out of this dilemma is through revolution. It either must be an actual blood revolution, or one that psychically redirects the energy of the oppressed. Milner is fundamentally concerned with the latter and Garrett with the former. Communication between Johnny and his mother breaks down. The revolution-

Larry Neal

ary imperative demands that men step outside the legal framework. It is a question of erecting *another* morality. The old constructs do not hold up, because adhering to them means consigning oneself to the oppressive reality. Johnny's mother is involved in the old constructs. Manliness is equated with white morality. And even though she claims to love her family (her men), the overall design of her ideas is against black manhood. In Garrett's play the mother's morality manifests itself in a deep-seated hatred of Black men; while in Milner's work the mother understands, but holds her men back.

The mothers that Garrett and Milner see represent the Old Spirituality—the Faith of the Fathers of which DuBois spoke. Johnny and Tim represent the New Spirituality. They appear to be a type produced by the upheavals of the colonial world of which Black America is a part. Johnny's assertion that he is a criminal is remarkably similar to the rebel's comments in Aimé Césaire's play, *Les Armes Miraculeuses* (*The Miraculous Weapons*). In that play the rebel, speaking to his mother, proclaims: "My name—an offense; my Christian name—humiliation; my status—a rebel; my age—the stone age." To which the mother replies: "My race—the [38] human race. My religion—brotherhood." The Old Spirituality is generalized. It seeks to recognize Universal Humanity. The New Spirituality is specific. It begins by seeing the world from the concise point-of-view of the colonialized. Where the Old Spirituality would live with oppression while ascribing to the oppressors an innate goodness, the New Spirituality demands a radical shift in point-of-view. The colonialized native, the oppressed must, of necessity, subscribe to a *separate* morality. One that will liberate him and his people.

The assault against the Old Spirituality can sometimes be humorous. In Ben Caldwell's play, *The Militant Preacher,* a burglar is seen slipping into the home of a wealthy minister. The preacher comes in and the burglar ducks behind a large chair. The preacher, acting out the role of the supplicant minister, begins to moan, praying to De Lawd for understanding.

In the context of today's politics, the minister is an Uncle Tom, mouthing platitudes against self-defense. The preacher drones in a self-pitying monologue about the folly of protecting oneself against brutal policemen. Then the burglar begins to speak. The preacher is startled, taking the burglar's voice for the voice of God. The burglar begins to play on the preacher's old time religion. He *becomes* the voice of God insulting and goading the preacher on until the preacher's attitudes about protective violence change. The next day the preacher emerges militant, gun in hand, sounding like Reverend Cleage in Detroit. He now preaches a new gospel—the gospel of the gun, an eye for an eye. The gospel is preached in the rhythmic cadences of the old Black church. But the content is radical. Just as Jones inverted the symbols in *Jello,* Caldwell twists the rhythms of the Uncle Tom preacher into the language of the new militancy.

These plays are directed at problems within Black America. They begin with the premise that there is a well defined Afro-American audience. An audience that must see itself and the world in terms of its own interests. These plays, along with many others, constitute the basis for a viable movement in the theatre—a movement which takes as its task a profound re-evaluation of the Black man's presence in America. The Black Arts Movement represents the flowering of a cultural nationalism that has been suppressed since the 1920's. I mean the "Harlem Renaissance"—which was essentially a failure. It did not address itself to the mythology and the life-styles of the Black community. It failed to take roots, to link itself concretely to the struggles of that community, to become its voice and spirit. Implicit in the Black Arts Movement is the idea that Black people, however dispersed, constitute a *nation* within the belly of white America. This is not a new idea. Garvey said it and the Honorable Elijah Muhammad says it now. And it is on this idea that the concept of Black Power is predicated.

Afro-American life and history is full of creative possibilities, and the movement is just beginning to perceive them. Just beginning to understand that the most meaningful statements about the nature of Western society must come from the Third World of which Black America is a part. The thematic material is broad, ranging from folk heroes like Shine and Stagolee to historical figures like Marcus Garvey and Malcolm X. And then there is the struggle for Black survival, the coming confrontation between white America and Black America. If art is the harbinger of future possibilities, what does the future of Black America portend? [39]

III: APPENDICES

BIOGRAPHICAL NOTES

JAMES BALDWIN (1924–   ), born and educated in New York, established his reputation as a novelist with *Go Tell It on the Mountain* (1953). He has also achieved success as an essayist and playwright. *Giovanni's Room* (1956) was written while Baldwin was in self-exile in Paris. Some of his more recent publications, *Another Country* (1961) and *Nobody Knows My Name* (1961), reflect upon the years of exile and his return to the United States.

JULIAN BOND (1940–   ) was born in Nashville, Tennessee, but moved to Atlanta, Georgia, where he attended Morehouse College and became a worker for SNCC. He received nationwide attention when he was elected to the Georgia State Legislature in 1966, where he was refused seating because of his stand on the Vietnam war, and when his name was placed in nomination for the presidency of the United States at the Democratic National Convention in 1968. He previously worked on the *Atlanta Inquirer*.

ARNA BONTEMPS (1902–   ), a teacher, editor, and writer whose work has been identified with the movement known as the Negro Renaissance, was born in Alexandria, Louisiana. He was educated in California and attended Columbia University and the University of Chicago. In 1965, Bontemps became Director of University Relations at Fisk University. His major works include *God Sends Sunday* (1931), which was later made into a musical, *Black Thunder* (1935), *Story of the Negro* (1958), and more recently, *One Hundred Years of Negro Freedom* (1961).

GWENDOLYN BROOKS (1917–   ) is a prize-winning poetess and novelist. Born in Topeka, Kansas, she moved as a youngster to Chicago. At the age of thirteen one of her poems, "Eventide," was accepted by a popular magazine, and by seventeen her poems were appearing frequently in the *Chicago Defender*. In 1950, Miss Brooks received the Pulitzer Prize for *Annie Allen* (1949). Among her works are *A Street*

Biographical Notes

in Bronzeville (1945) and *Maud Martha* (1953). In 1962 she partici-
pated in the National Poetry Festival, reading her poems at the Library of Congress. She has been teaching at Chicago Teachers College
since 1967.

CHARLES CHESNUTT (1858–1932), born in Cleveland, Ohio, was one
of the earliest Negro novelists. As a teacher in North Carolina, he
gathered material for his stories and novels. In 1928 he received the
Spingarn gold medal award for his "pioneer work as a literary artist
depicting the life and struggle of Americans of Negro descent." Chesnutt spent his last years as a reporter in Cleveland. His major works
include *The Conjure Woman* (1899), *The Horse Behind the Cedars*
(1900), and *The Colonel's Dream* (1905).

JOHN HENRIK CLARKE (1915–   ) was born in Union Springs, Alabama and moved to New York, where he studied writing at New
York and Columbia Universities. His *Rebellion in Rhyme* was published in 1948, and he is editor of *Harlem: A Community in Transition* (1964). Since 1962 Clarke has been associate editor of *Freedom-
ways* magazine.

ELDRIDGE CLEAVER (1935–   ), born in Little Rock, Arkansas,
received most of his education in California prisons. Mr. Cleaver disappeared in late 1968 while on parole; at the time of his disappear-
ance, he was Minister of Information for the Black Panther Party for
Self-Defense. He is also on the staff of *Ramparts* magazine. Among his
publications are *Soul on Ice* (1968) and *Post-Prison Writings and
Speeches* (1969).

JAMES DAVID CORROTHERS (1869–1917) was a clergyman and poet
born in Michigan. During his lifetime he held a variety of odd jobs—
lumberjack, sailor, coachman, bootblack, janitor, and so on. Corrothers, influenced by his friend Paul Dunbar, composed dialect verse. He
also wrote for various journals and published a number of works including *The Black Cat Club* (1902), *Selected Poems* (1907), *The
Dream and the Song* (1914), and an autobiography, *In Spite of the
Handicap* (1916).

COUNTEE CULLEN (1903–1946), associated with the Negro Awakening, was a native of Harlem. Educated at New York University and
Harvard, he had won poetry prizes as well as scholastic honors as a
high school student. His first volume of poetry, *Color* (1925), established him as a poet, and thereafter he won many awards, particularly
for poems on racial themes. For a short period of time he edited a
Negro magazine, *Opportunity*. Other works of his include *The Black
Christ and Other Poems* (1929), *One Way to Heaven* (1931), and *On
These I Stand* (1947).

344

W.E.B. DuBois (1868–1963), teacher, editor, lecturer, and author, was born in Great Barrington, Massachusetts. Educated at Fisk and Harvard Universities and the University of Berlin, DuBois was a Greek and Latin scholar as well as a trained sociologist. He founded and edited *Crisis* from 1919–1932 and was also instrumental in founding the NAACP. In 1949 he was vice-chairman of the Council of African Affairs. Before his death in Accra, Ghana, DuBois left behind a prodigious list of works in various categories, among them *The Souls of Black Folks* (1903) and the *Autobiography of W.E.B. DuBois* (1968).

PAUL LAURENCE DUNBAR (1872–1906), the son of ex-slaves who found freedom via the underground railroad, was born in Dayton, Ohio. His first book, *Oak and Ivory* (1893), was privately printed and the publishing costs paid for by Dunbar himself through the sale of copies while he worked as an elevator operator. He traveled to England in 1897 and upon his return was given a position in the Library of Congress. He is the author of *Lyrics of a Lowly Life* (1896), probably his best known collection, and the *Uncalled* (1896), a novel.

RAY DUREM has had his poems anthologized in various publications in Europe and the United States. Born in Seattle, Washington, he ran away from home at the age of fourteen to join the Navy. He then served with the International Brigade during the Spanish Civil War. Thereafter he lived in Mexico where he and his wife operated a guest house. Durem died in California in 1963.

RALPH ELLISON (1914–   ), born in Oklahoma City, studied music at Tuskegee Institute. He has written several short stories and articles, which have been widely read, and has lectured at New York, Columbia, and Fisk Universities. His reputation rests largely on *Invisible Man* (1952), which has been hailed as an outstanding novel on the Negro in America. In addition, he has written *Shadow and Act* (1964).

ERNEST J. GAINES (1933–   ) was born in Louisiana, but moved to California where he attended San Francisco State College and Stanford University. His most recent publication, *Bloodlines* (1968), is a collection of stories. He is also the author of *Of Love and Dust* (1967) and *Catherine Carmier* (1964).

JIMMY GARRETT, a young playwright, has lived in San Francisco where he attended San Francisco State College. While there, he was chairman of the Black Students' Union. He has also worked for SNCC.

DAVID HENDERSON, born in New York City, studied writing at the New School for Social Research. His work has been widely anthologized and has appeared in *Liberator, Negro Digest,* and *Kulchur.* He is a member of the Teachers and Writers Collaborative at Columbia University and is currently teaching at City College of the City University of New York. He is also editor of *Umbra* quarterly.

LANGSTON HUGHES (1902–1967) gained nationwide renown as a poet, involved in the Harlem Renaissance. Born in Joplin, Missouri, he graduated from Central High in Cleveland, Ohio, and entered Columbia University in 1921. His education was interrupted when he went to sea as a messboy. He visited Africa and Europe during his years at sea, an experience that was to influence his later poetry. After giving up the sea, Hughes entered Lincoln University and graduated in 1929. The future years were filled with a rewarding literary career. Among his numerous works are *Weary Blues* (1926), *Shakespeare in Harlem* (1942), and *The Big Sea* (1940).

DON JOHNSON (1942–   ), born in Chattanooga, Tennessee, attended Central State College in Wilberforce, Ohio, before dropping out to travel the country. He uses the pen name of Mustafa.

JAMES WELDON JOHNSON (1871–1938) pursued various careers during his lifetime—teacher, diplomat, song-writer, poet, and lawyer. He held the position of executive secretary of the NAACP and was the first Negro admitted to the Florida bar since Reconstruction. He translated various Spanish and French plays and published a number of novels and poems. Among his works are *The Autobiography of an Ex-Colored Man* (1912), *Fifty Years and Other Poems* (1917), *Black Manhattan* (1930), and *Along This Way* (1933).

LEROI JONES (1934–   ), one of the leaders of the Black Arts movement, was born in Newark, New Jersey, and studied at Howard University, Columbia University, and the New School for Social Research. As a member of the Air Force, he traveled abroad extensively. He has taught poetry and creative writing at the New School and lectured at Columbia. Jones has impressed the literary world with his poetry, plays, essays, and fiction. His works include *Dutchman and the Slave* (1964), *Blues People* (1963), and *The Systems of Dante's Hell* (1965). He has also edited and helped found several little magazines, among them, *Yungen.*

JOHN OLIVER KILLENS (1916–   ) has been highly successful with his works, *Youngblood* (1954) and *And Then We Heard the Thunder* (1963), which was based on his wartime experiences. Born in Macon, Georgia, Killens has taught at Fisk University. He is presently living in New York.

ARMAND LANUSSE (1812–1867) was born in New Orleans, Louisiana, where he was principal of the Catholic School for Indigent Orphans of Color. He collected the poetry of young poets writing in French and had them published in *Les Cenelles* (1845).

CLAUDE McKAY (1891–1948), a Jamaica born writer, studied agriculture at Tuskegee Institute and Kansas State University. Before coming to the United States in 1912, he published *Songs of Jamaica* (1911), written in native dialect. He published *Spring in New Hampshire* (1920) in London and edited the *Liberator,* working under Max Eastman. He is also author of *Harlem Shadows* (1922).

WILLARD MOTLEY (1912–1965), a native of Chicago, wandered across the United States working at odd jobs, before the publication of his first novel, *Knock on Any Door* (1947). His other works include *We Fished All Night* (1951) and *Let No Man Write My Epitaph* (1958).

CONRAD KENT RIVERS (1933–196?) was born in Atlantic City and attended Wilberforce University, Indiana University, and Chicago Teachers College. He then served in the armed forces. He is the author of *Perchance to Dream, Othello* (1959), *These Black Bodies and This Sunburnt Face* (1962), and *Still Voices of Harlem* (1968). He acknowledges the influence of Carl Sandburg and Langston Hughes on his work.

LUCY SMITH, a Wilmington, North Carolina, poetess moved to Philadelphia where she now works as a furrier. She is the author of *No Middle Ground* (1952).

MARGRET WALKER (1915–   ) was born in Birmingham, Alabama. She attended Northwestern University and Iowa State University. At present she is teaching at Jackson State College in Mississippi. Her works include *For My People* (1942) and *Jubilee* (1966).

JOSEPH WHITE is a Newark playwright whose plays have been staged by the Black Arts Theatre in New York City and by Spirit House. In 1964 he received the John Hay Whitney Fellowship for creative writing. In early 1969 he was appointed playwright-in-residence at the New York Urban Arts Corps.

JOHN A. WILLIAMS (1925–   ) was born in Mississippi and raised in Syracuse, New York. He attended Syracuse University, but dropped out before graduating. He has traveled widely throughout Europe and Africa and is now living in New York City. Among his works are *Night Song* (1961), *This is My Country Too* (1965), and *The Man Who Cried I Am* (1967).

BRUCE McM. WRIGHT was born in Princeton, New Jersey and attended Lincoln University and Fordham's School of Law. Mr. Wright is currently practicing law in New York City. His collection of poems,

From the Shaken Tower (1944), was published in Wales while he was in the Army during World War II. Plans are afoot to issue his verse in French.

RICHARD WRIGHT (1908–1960), one of the most eloquent spokesmen of the American Negro of his generation, was born in Mississippi. Largely self-educated, Wright achieved success as a novelist and social critic. During the 1930's, while employed and on relief, he joined the Communist Party and published poetry and prose in many radical journals. His greatest success, *Native Son* (1940), became a best seller and was made into a stage production and then into a film, in which Wright himself played the lead. In later years he became disillusioned with the Communist Party and moved to Paris, where he remained until his death. His works include *Black Boy* (1945) and *The Long Dream* (1958).

FRANK YERBY (1916–   ), born in Augusta, Georgia has taught English at various southern colleges. Mr. Yerby made the best seller list several times with his historical romances, such as *The Foxes of Harrow* (1946) and *Benton's Row* (1954). His story, "Health Card," printed in this casebook, received the O'Henry Award for 1944. Mr. Yerby lives in Madrid. His more recent works include *Goat Song* (1967) and *Judas, My Brother* (1968).

SELECTED BIBLIOGRAPHY

GENERAL

The American Negro Writer and His Roots: Selected Papers from the First Conference of Negro Writers. New York: American Society of African Culture, 1960.

Barton, Rebecca. *Race Consciousness and the American Negro: A Study of the Correlations between the Group Experience and the Fiction of 1900–1930.* Copenhagen: A. Busck, 1934.

Birnbaum, Henry. "The Poetry of Protest." *Poetry* XCIV (1959): 408–413.

Bond, Frederick W. *The Negro and the Drama.* Washington, D.C.: Associated Publishers, 1940.

Bone, Robert A. *The Negro Novel in America.* New Haven: Yale University Press, 1958. Rev. ed. 1966.

Bronz, Stephen H. *Roots of Negro Consciousness. The 1920's: Three Harlem Renaissance Authors.* New York: Libra Publishers, Inc., 1964. The authors included are James Weldon Johnson, Countee Cullen, and Claude McKay.

Brown, Sterling. *Negro Poetry and Drama.* Washington, D.C.: Associates in Negro Folk Education, 1937.

Butcher, Margaret Just. *The Negro in American Culture.* New York: Alfred A. Knopf, Inc., 1956. Based on materials left by Alain Locke.

Emanuel, J. A., and Gross, T. L., eds. *Dark Symphony: Negro Literature in America.* New York: Free Press, 1968.

Essien-Udom, Essien U. *Black Nationalism: A Search for an Identity in America.* Chicago: University of Chicago Press, 1962.

Gayle, Addison, Jr., ed. *Black Expression.* New York: Weybright and Talley, 1969.

Gérard, Albert. "Humanism and Negritude: Notes on the Contemporary Afro-American Novel." *Diogenes* XXXVII (1962): 115–133.

Glicksberg, Charles. "Bias, Fiction, and the Negro." *Phylon* XIII (Second Quarter, 1952): 127–135.

Gross, Seymour L., and Hardy, John E., eds. *Images of the Negro in America.* Toronto: University of Toronto Press, 1966.

Hughes, Carl Milton. *The Negro Novelist.* New York: Citadel, 1953.

Jackson, Blyden. "The Negro's Image of the Universe as Reflected in His Fiction." *CLA Journal* IV (1960): 290–295.

Jackson, Ester Merle. "The American Negro and the Image of the Absurd." *Phylon* XXIII (1962): 359–371.

Jurges, Oda., comp. "Selected Bibliography." *The Drama Review,* Vol. 12, No. 4 (Summer 1968).

Lehan, Richard. "Existentialism in Recent American Fiction: The Demonic Quest." *Texas Studies in Literature and Language* I (Summer 1959): 181–202.

Littlejohn, David. *Black on White: A Critical Survey of Writing by American Negroes.* New York: Grossman, 1966.

Locke, Alain. "Of Native Sons: Real or Otherwise." *Opportunity* XIX (1941): 4–9, 48–52.

Loggins, Vernon. *The Negro Author: His Development in America to 1900.* New York: Columbia University Press, 1931. Reprint. Port Washington, N.Y.: Kennikat Press, 1964.

Marcus, Steven. "The American Negro in Search of Identity." *Commentary* XVI (1953): 456–463.

Margolies, Edward. *Native Sons.* New York: J.P. Lippincott, 1968.

Myrdal, Gunnar. *An American Dilemma.* Rev. ed. New York: Harper and Row, 1962.

"Negro Minstrelsy—Ancient and Modern." *Putnam's Magazine* V (1855): 72–79.

Nichols, Charles H., Jr. "Slave Narratives and the Plantation Legend." *Phylon* X (1949): 201–210.

Redding, Saunders. "The Problems of the Negro Writer." *Massachusetts Review* VI (1964): 57–70.

Shapiro, Karl. "The Decolonization of American Literature." *Wilson Library Bulletin* XXIX (June 1965): 842–853.

Tanner, Tony. "Pigment and Ether: A Comment on the American Mind." *British Association for American Studies Bulletin* No. 7 (1963): 40–45.

Wagner, Jean. *Les Poètes nègres des États-Unis.* Paris: Libraire Istra, 1963.

AUTHORS

JAMES BALDWIN

Go Tell It on the Mountain. New York: Alfred A. Knopf, Inc., 1953.

Notes of a Native Son. Boston: Beacon Press, 1955.

Giovanni's Room. New York: Dial Press, 1956.

Nobody Knows My Name: More Notes of a Native Son. New York: Dial Press, 1961.

Another Country. New York: Dial Press, 1962.

The Fire Next Time. New York: Dial Press, 1963.

Blues for Mister Charlie. New York: Dial Press, 1964.

Going to Meet the Man. New York: Dial Press, 1965.

Tell Me How Long the Train's Been Gone. New York: Dial Press, 1968.

The Amen Corner. New York: Dial Press, 1968.

GWENDOLYN BROOKS

A Street in Bronzeville. New York: Harper and Bros., 1945.
Annie Allen. New York: Harper and Bros., 1949.
Maud Martha. New York: Harper and Bros., 1953.
The Bean Eaters. New York: Harper and Bros., 1960.
Selected Poems. New York: Harper and Bros., 1963.
In the Mecca. New York: Harper and Row, 1968.

RALPH ELLISON

"Slick Gonna Learn." *Direction* (September 1939), 10–16.
"Flying Home." *Cross Section.* Edited by Edwin Seaver. New York: L. B. Fischer, 1944, 469–485.
"King of the Bingo Game." *Tomorrow* IV (November 1944): 29–33.
"Afternoon." *Negro Story* (March–April 1945).
Invisible Man. New York: Random House, 1952.
"A Coupla Scalped Indians." *New World Writing* 9. New York: The New American Library of World Literature, Inc., 1965.
"And Hickman Arrives." *The Noble Savage* I, 1956.
Shadow and Act. New York: Random House, 1964.

ROBERT E. HAYDEN

Heart-Shape in the Dust. Detroit: Falcon Press, 1940.
A Ballad of Remembrance. London: Paul Breman, Ltd., 1962.
Selected Poems. New York: October House, Inc., 1966.

LANGSTON HUGHES

The Weary Blues. New York: Alfred A. Knopf, 1926.
The Ways of White Folks. New York: Alfred A. Knopf, 1934.
Shakespeare in Harlem. New York: Alfred A. Knopf, 1942.
Montage of a Dream Deferred. New York: Henry Holt, 1951.
The Langston Hughes Reader. New York: George Braziller, 1958.
Selected Poems of Langston Hughes. New York: Alfred A. Knopf, 1959.
Tambourines to Glory. New York: John Day, 1959.
The Best of Simple. New York: Hill and Wang, 1961.
The Big Sea. New York: Hill and Wang, 1963.
Five Plays by Langston Hughes. Edited by Webster Smalley. Bloomington: Indiana University Press, 1963.
I Wonder As I Wander. New York: Hill and Wang, 1964.
The Panther and the Lash. New York: Alfred A. Knopf, 1967.

JAMES WELDON JOHNSON

Fifty Years and Other Poems. Boston: The Cornhill Company, 1917.
God's Trombones, Seven Negro Sermons in Verse. New York: The Viking Press, 1927.

Black Manhattan. New York: Alfred A. Knopf, 1930.

The Autobiography of an Ex-Colored Man. (American Century Series.) New York: Hill and Wang, 1960.

LeRoi Jones

Preface to a Twenty Volume Suicide Note. New York: Totem Press, Corinth Books, 1961.

Blues People: Negro Music in White America. New York: William Morrow and Co., 1963.

System of Dante's Hell. New York: Grove Press, 1963.

The Dead Lecturer. New York: Grove Press, 1964.

Dutchman and the Slave. New York: Apollo Editions, Inc., 1964.

Home: Social Essays. New York: William Morrow and Co., 1966.

Baptism; Toilet. New York: Grove Press, 1966.

Tales. New York: Grove Press, 1967.

Black Music. New York: William Morrow and Co., 1967.

Jean Toomer

Cane. New York: Boni and Liveright, 1923.

John A. Williams

Night Song. New York: Farrar, Straus and Cudahy, 1961.

Sissie. New York: Farrar, Straus and Cudahy, 1963.

This Is My Country Too. New York: New American Library, 1965.

The Man Who Cried I Am. Boston: Little, Brown, and Co., 1967.

Richard Wright

Native Son. New York: Harper and Bros., 1940.

Uncle Tom's Children: Five Long Stories. New York: Harper and Bros., 1940.

Black Boy; a Record of Childhood and Youth. New York: Harper and Bros., 1945.

The Outsider. New York: Harper and Bros., 1953.

Savage Holiday. New York: Avon, 1954.

Black Power; a Record of Reaction in a Land of Pathos. New York: Harper and Bros., 1954.

White Man, Listen! Garden City, New York: Doubleday, 1957.

Pagan Spain. New York: Harper and Bros., 1957.

The Long Dream. Garden City, New York: Doubleday, 1958.

Eight Men. Cleveland and New York: Avon, 1961.

Lawd Today. New York: Walker and Company, 1963.

TOPICS FOR STUDENT PAPERS

The topics listed here are only broad suggestions and have been divided somewhat arbitrarily by the size of the papers that can be developed. Obviously, there are many variations for each of these topics and they can be expanded to yield longer, more extensive studies.

Short Papers

1 Characteristics of black essay, poetry, or drama.
2 African influence in black poetry.
3 Comedy in the literature (specifically, the drama).
4 Relationship between environment and literature.
5 Influence of jazz and/or blues.
6 Treatment of pain.
7 Treatment of theme of despair and disorientation, or flight and pursuit.
8 Portrayal of slavery, or family life.
9 Treatment of police.
10 Handling of religion.
11 Black literature as part of American literature—agree or disagree.

Medium Length Papers

1 The generation "gap" in black fiction.
2 Negro dialect, its treatment and function, as used by a specific author.
3 Defense of the case for black aestheticism.
4 The search for a usable past in black literature.
5 Violence in Richard Wright's fiction.
6 Study of LeRoi Jones as the angriest young black poet.
7 The use of folktales by Charles W. Chesnutt.
8 The development and shaping of the black hero in the fiction of John A. Williams.
9 Study of the black tragic hero.

10 Relationship between the essays and novels of James Baldwin or Richard Wright.
11 Modern black poetry as protest poetry—agree or disagree.
12 Discussion of what is specifically black in black drama (using a major playwright).
13 Discussion of the well-known literary themes in a black artist of your choice.
14 The quest for identity in the black novel.
15 James Baldwin as critic of white America.

Long Papers

1 Treatment of blacks by white authors.
2 Portrayal of white elements in the black novel.
3 Man versus Society in black fiction.
4 Comparison of the North and South.
5 Comparative study of the plays of Hughes, Baldwin, and Jones.
6 Comparative study of the essays of Baldwin, Jones, and Cleaver.
7 The Black Arts Movement and its relationship to black drama.
8 Discovery of the "Black is Beautiful" theme in either a genre or major author.
9 Study of the Harlem Renaissance—its characteristics, authors, and influence.
10 Major elements of post-World War II black literature.
11 Major aspects of early (pre-Harlem Renaissance) black poetry emphasizing one specific aspect—subject matter, style, use of dialect.
12 Critical analysis of the Free Southern Theatre.